Handbook of Research in Language Development Using CHILDES

Edited by

Jeffrey L. Sokolov
University of Nebraska at Omaha
Harvard Graduate School of Education

and

Catherine E. Snow
Harvard Graduate School of Education

  LAWRENCE ERLBAUM ASSOCIATES, PUBLISHERS
1994   Hillsdale, New Jersey   Hove, UK

Copyright © 1994 by Lawrence Erlbaum Associates, Inc.
All rights reserved. No part of this book may be reproduced in any form, by photostat, microfilm, retrieval system, or any other means, without the prior written permission of the publisher.

Lawrence Erlbaum Associates, Inc., Publishers
365 Broadway
Hillsdale, New Jersey 07642

Library of Congress Cataloging-in-Publication Data

Handbook of research in language development using CHILDES / edited by Jeffrey L. Sokolov and Catherine E. Snow.
    p. cm.
Includes bibliographical references and index.
ISBN 0-8058-1185-0. -- ISBN 0-8058-1186-9 (pbk.)
1. Language acquisition--Research--Data processing. 2. Children--Language--Data processing. I. Sokolov, Jeffrey L. II. Snow, Catherine E.
P118.H35 1994
401Çé.93'0285--dc20   93-47128
                                                      CIP

Books published by Lawrence Erlbaum Associates are printed on acid-free paper, and their bindings are chosen for strength and durability.

Printed in the United States of America
10 9 8 7 6 5 4 3 2 1

Handbook of Research in Language Development Using CHILDES

Table of Contents

Preface vi

Foreword: Forward: Welcome Mongol No. 2000
Roger Brown ix

List of Contributors xi

1. Transcript Analysis Using the Child Language Data Exchange System
Jeffrey L. Sokolov and Catherine E. Snow 1
1.1. From Anecdotes to Automatic Coding 1
1.2. The CHILDES System: An Overview 4
1.3. The Tradeoffs: Advantages and Disadvantages of CHILDES . 18
1.4. The Goals of This Handbook 19
1.5. Getting Started 20
1.6. A Final Word 22

2. Basic Measures of Child Language
Barbara Alexander Pan 26
2.1. Introduction 27
2.2. Method 35
2.3. Results and Discussion 43
2.4. Exercises 46
2.5. Suggested Projects 47

3. The Babytalk Register: Parents' Use of Diminutives
Jean Berko Gleason, Rivka Y. Perlmann, Richard Ely, and David W. Evans 50
3.1. Introduction 50
3.2. Method 53
3.3. Results and Discussion 68
3.4. Conclusion 73
3.5. Exercises 74
3.6. Suggested Projects 74

4. What Kind of a Birdie is This? Learning to Use Superordinates
Laura Bodin and Catherine E. Snow 77
4.1. Introduction 77
4.2. The Research Questions 80
4.3. Study 1: How Frequent are Superordinates? 80
4.4. Study 2: Are Superordinates Taught? 89
4.5. Study 3: Does Superordinate Use Relate to Other Developments? . . . 97
4.6. General Discussion 103
4.7. Exercises 103
4.8. Suggested Project 105
Appendix 106

5. A Study of Some Common Features of Mothers' Vocabularies
Qian Hu 110
5.1. Introduction 110
5.2. Using CLAN to Study the Maternal Core Lexicon 114
5.3. Discussion 123
5.4. Conclusion 126
5.5. Exercises 126
5.6. Suggested Projects 128

6. Negative Evidence in the Language Learning Environment of Laterborns in a Rural Florida Community
Kathryn Nolan Post 132
6.1. Introduction 132
6.2. Method 140
6.3. Results and Discussion 152
6.4. Conclusion 160
6.5. Exercises 162
6.6. Suggested Projects 162
Appendix 165

7. Individual Differences in Linguistic Imitativeness
Jeffrey L. Sokolov and Joy Moreton 174
7.1. Introduction 174
7.2. Method 184
7.3. Results and Discussion 192
7.4. Conclusion 199
7.5. Exercises 200
7.6. Suggested Project 201
Appendix A 205
Appendix B 207
Appendix C 208

8. Early Morphological Development: The Acquisition of Articles in Spanish
Beatrice Schnell de Acedo 210
8.1. Introduction 210
8.2. Background 211
8.3. Research Questions 226
8.4. Method 227
8.5. Results and Discussion 232
8.6. Exercises 244
8.7. Suggested Project 246
Appendix A 250
Appendix B 252

9. Young Children's Hypotheses about English Reflexives
Margaret Thomas 254
9.1. Introduction 254
9.2. Method 262
9.3. Results 271
9.4. Discussion 278
9.5. Exercises 280
9.6. Suggested Project 282

10. Children's Acquisition of Different Kinds of Narrative Discourse: Genres and Lines of Talk
Dennie Wolf, Joy Moreton, and Linda Camp 286
10.1. Overview 286
10.2. Introduction 287
10.3. Methods 296
10.4. Discussion 307
10.5. Conclusion 315
10.6. Exercises 315
10.7. Suggested Project 316
Appendix 320

11. Phonological Analysis of Child Speech
Nan Bernstein Ratner 324
11.1. Introduction 324
11.2. Preliminaries to Phonological Analysis in CLAN 328
11.3. Using CLAN to Examine Phonetic Characteristics of Infant and
     Child-Directed Speech 329
11.4. Does Adult Input Shape the Early Phonetic Inventory?
     Adapting PHONFREQ to Nonphonetically Transcribed Data 339
11.5. Results of Our PHONFREQ Analyses 344
11.6. Discussion 351
11.7. What are Beginning Talkers *Trying to Say*? An Introduction
     to MODREP 354
11.8. Conclusions 362
11.9. Exercises 363
11.10. Suggested Project 364
Appendix 368

12. Language Profiles of Children with Specific Language Impairment
Pamela Rosenthal Rollins 373
12.1. Introduction 373
12.2. Method 379
12.3. Results 393
12.6. Discussion 396
12.7. Exercises 398
12.8. Suggested Projects 400
Appendix 407

13. New Horizons for CHILDES Research
Brian MacWhinney 408
13.1. The Recent Past 411
13.2. The Immediate Future 431
13.3. The Distant Horizon 447

Appendix: Answers to the Exercises
Linda Beaudin and Jeffrey L. Sokolov 453

Author Index 471

Subject Index 485

Preface

The availability of computerized child language transcripts and of procedures for doing at least some automated analyses on those transcripts has expanded the possibilities for child language research enormously. Though when first proposed, this idea was considered to have potentially dangerous consequences – including such perils as the suppression of new data collection efforts, the promotion of sloppy research, the distancing of researchers from their data, the proliferation of uninteresting research reports, and so on – in fact the availability of the Child Language Data Exchange System has had effects directly opposite to these. By making clear what gaps exist in our collective access to transcripts, it has promoted the collection of new datasets. By enabling historically important corpora to be directly compared, it has raised consciousness about issues of transcript quality. By making large quantities of real data available even to junior and underfunded researchers, it has increased their access to empirical bases for their analyses. Finally, it has served as a proving ground for major hypotheses and theories, raising rather than lowering the level of discourse in the field.

Information about the Child Language Data Exchange System (or CHILDES) has been disseminated in a number of ways – through journal articles, chapters in books, many workshops and demonstrations held in various places, and most authoritatively through **the manual**, MacWhinney's (1991) book entitled *The CHILDES Project: Tools for analyzing talk*. The manual documents the transcription conventions recommended for use within the system, describes the programs available for analyzing transcripts, and catalogues the corpora available through the system. For most people, it serves as a reference volume, rather than as a pedagogical manual. If automated transcript analysis is to become maximally useful, so that even beginners in the field of child language can learn to conduct these analyses, then an explicitly pedagogical tool is necessary. We hope the current handbook serves this purpose.

The idea for this Handbook emerged in a conversation among Barbara Pan, Pamela Rollins, Catherine Snow and Jeff Sokolov, the group at the Harvard Graduate School of Education working on the project *Foundations for Language Assessment in Spontaneous Speech*. The project served as a field test for CHILDES – one of the places where child language data were transcribed and analyzed using the system, and where problems and lacunae were noted and reported. The Harvard team had also undertaken to design a number of two 3-day workshops, at which we taught the use of CHILDES to interested researchers. Jeff Sokolov also developed materials to use in teaching CHILDES to students in the Child Language course taught at Harvard by Allyssa McCabe. As a group, we had developed several sets of exercises for the workshops and class, some of which were based on our own use of CHILDES. The idea seemed, once put into words, quite obvious: why not develop a book in which each chapter was, in effect, a lesson in the use of CHILDES? Furthermore, if each chapter in the book also treated an interesting empirical problem in child language research, it could be used in an introductory child language course as a supplementary text – a sort of lab manual for child language. That conception guided our selection of topics for this handbook; each chapter is designed to cover some real problem in child language research, to present the problem in its historical and theoretical context, and to report a piece of research designed to solve the problem. At the same time, the procedures for actually doing the research are reported in greater than normal detail, so that the reader can actually replicate many of the automated analyses on their own. The reader who replicates all the analyses reported in the chapters will have developed an acquaintance with many aspects of the CHAT transcription system, almost all of the CLAN programs, and a wide variety of different child language corpora. In order to increase the value of the handbook for use in conjunction with courses on child language, we have asked the authors also to include exercises that relate to the analyses presented in the chapter, as well as suggestions for projects that go far beyond those analyses. The buyer of this handbook should also receive a set of transcript data,[1] so that some of the analyses presented in each chapter can be replicated and so new analyses can be developed.

To make replicating the analyses presented in each chapter even easier, the handbook includes specially-designed command boxes which list the exact CLAN command that should be issued outside the box and a brief explanation for each component of the command inside the box. In addition, the results for many of these analyses are presented in a `different font` so that they are easily distinguishable from the expository text. Finally, sprinkled throughout the handbook

---

[1] There are several means for receiving the transcript data that go along with the handbook. The data can either be purchased separately through Lawrence Erlbaum Associates, bundled together with the handbook, or obtained via INTERNET file transfer from Carnegie Mellon University. More information about the latter alternative is provided in the CHILDES manual (MacWhinney, 1991).

are a series of hints or tricks of the trade that experienced CHILDES users have found to be helpful. Each hint is preceded by a special icon as in the following example from Chapter 2:

 A little known fact about CLAN is that typing a program name on a command line by itself will result in a list of the options for that program. This is very helpful for planning analyses and minimizes the need to consult the manual repeatedly.

Though the plan for the handbook was simple, carrying it out has, of course, been possible only because of the collaboration of many individuals. Colleagues, such as John Gilbert, Lise Menn, and Ann Peters, who had previously used CHILDES with their child language classes, generously shared their insights and solutions to logistical problems. Several persons teaching child language volunteered to use draft versions of the chapters and to give us feedback; we thank Jean Berko Gleason, Allyssa McCabe, Lowry Hemphill, and Ann Peters for their help along these lines. We are especially grateful to Ann Peters for providing detailed comments concerning several of the chapters and to Mabel Rice for reviewing an early version of the manuscript. Brenda Kurland, Alison Imbens-Bailey, Jane Herman, Masahiko Minami, Kendra Winner, Linda Beaudin, Diane May Sadr, Melanie Felton, and other students and teaching fellows at Harvard and the University of Nebraska at Omaha were enormously helpful in testing and improving the exercises. We would also like to thank the following students in Catherine Snow's course on Child Language and Education in the fall of 1993, who identified many infelicities in draft versions of chapters they were assigned: Judy Boyle, Linda Caswell, Sook Whan Cho, Julia Fritze, Susan Haley, Fran Hurley, Daliang Jin, Jane Katz, Chris Kennedy, Sarah Mandarus, Susan Miller, Michino Ohara, Kevin Roach, Barry Roth, Martha Shiro, Noriko Sugimori, Yvonne Swann, Masao Tada, Mayumi Yonemoto, and Ming-Chung Yu. Jeff Sokolov would like to thank members of the Department of Psychology at the University of Nebraska at Omaha for their support during his year there. In addition, help in preparing this manuscript was given by Phyllis Goldberg and Francie Fries. Both Judi Amsel and Kathy Dolan at Lawrence Erlbaum Associates helped in numerous ways. Most importantly, though, the vision of Brian MacWhinney and the programming skills of Leonid Spektor deserve mention; they have made the CHILDES system an invaluable resource for child language researchers.

Foreword

Forward: Welcome
Mongol No. 2000

Roger Brown
Harvard University

As Ursula Bellugi tells it – I myself cannot remember it – two psycholinguists from Japan came to call one day in the 1960s and asked to see the laboratory equipment we used in recording the speech of Adam, Eve, and Sarah. Ursula swears – I think it's just a story – that we both held aloft our yellow Mongol No. 2 pencils. Whether or not this episode ever happened, it is true that we used Stone Age technology and took a perverse pride in it and in the contrast with the quality of the transcriptions themselves. Imagine, if you can, Ursula Bellugi, Courtney Cazden, Melissa Bowerman, Richard Cromer, and Colin Fraser spending thousands of hours playing and replaying tapes so as to make a scrupulous record. To make it worthwhile, we must have had a vision of something like CHILDES coming along some day to make these data available to researchers everywhere who, with the help of this powerful instrument, would conceive of and carry out analyses more complex and subtle than could be dreamt of with Mongol pencils in hand.

Each chapter in this book begins by describing one kind of research – the range is great, from phonology to narrative – showing how to attack it and doing so. My interest is as easily engaged as ever, but I am too undisciplined for the Exercises and Projects, probably because I know my livelihood does not depend on being Mr. State of the Art. Now, as always, child language data triggers a process of playful induction. When it says in chapter 3 that parents might say *that's a bunny* but are unlikely to point at an insect on the wall and say *look at the roachie*, I start wondering whether the hypocoristic suffix (great name) is always used affectionately and never just diminutively. Disney's seven dwarfs include Happy, Sleepy, Grumpy, Dopey, and Sneezy. To imagine a Sleazy is perhaps to violate not only Disney's world, but English.

Then it seems we can say *bunny rabbit* but not *doggie dog* or *horsie horse*. What's the principle? Can't tell for sure but it looks as if the diminutive must be different enough in form from the head noun to be read as if it were a modifier. All students of child language know the lure of this game.

When I read in chapter 4 that our own Adam, between the ages of 2;11 and 3;6, made very heavy use of *what kind?* constructions, including, for instance, *what kind camera dat?* and *what kind a blueberry?*, it came back to me like an old refrain. Ursula and I had noticed the upsurge but not the connection with Adam's period of interest in superordinates. We missed also the fact that Adam asked his *what kind?* questions not only of things that come in kinds – like cameras – but of things that do not come in kinds – like blueberries. Protocols of child speech are almost as inexhaustible as *Hamlet*, and I look forward with interest to all that will unfold as a consequence of this fine book.

List of Contributors

Beatrice Schnell de Acedo	Harvard Graduate School of Education
Linda Beaudin	University of Nebraska at Omaha
Laura Bodin	Harvard University
Roger Brown	Harvard University
Linda Camp	Harvard Graduate School of Education
Richard Ely	Boston University
David W. Evans	Boston University
Jean Berko Gleason	Boston University
Qian Hu	Boston University
Brian MacWhinney	Carnegie Mellon University
Joy Moreton	Harvard Graduate School of Education
Barbara Alexander Pan	Harvard Graduate School of Education
Rivka Y. Perlmann	Boston University
Kathryn Nolan Post	Harvard Graduate School of Education
Nan Bernstein Ratner	University of Maryland at College Park
Pamela Rosenthal Rollins	Harvard Graduate School of Education
Jeffrey L. Sokolov	University of Nebraska at Omaha
Catherine E. Snow	Harvard Graduate School of Education
Margaret Thomas	Boston College
Dennie Wolf	Harvard Graduate School of Education

1 Transcript Analysis Using the Child Language Data Exchange System

Jeffrey L. Sokolov
University of Nebraska at Omaha
Harvard Graduate School of Education

Catherine E. Snow
Harvard Graduate School of Education

1.1. From Anecdotes to Automatic Coding

Child language research as we know it emerged from two minor revolutions of the 20th century: (a) the revised notion of language and how it works introduced by Chomsky, and (b) the invention of portable tape recorders. Long before the 20th century revolution in linguistic theorizing had rekindled interest in studying language development, though, many linguists, psychologists, and biologists had been keeping records of the words and utterances of their own children (Deutsch, 1992). Johann Heinrich Campe (1785), a German writer and man of science, held a competition in the last decades of the 18th century for the best new diary study of child development, but the winners were evidently somewhat disappointing. Some diaries, though, such as those by Leopold (1939-1949) and by Clara and William Stern (Behrens & Deutsch, 1991), constitute exemplary records of certain aspects of child language.

But such diaries are, of course, limited in the information available from them. Diary records can be the source of fairly good data about lexical acquisition and emerging morphological and syntactic structures, and they have served as an endless source of the kind of anecdotes that make child language such an enjoyable field. However, on-the-spot notes cannot provide the kind of data one needs for careful phonological analysis, for analysis of conversation or interaction, or for computing frequencies of occurrence, estimating incidence of errors, or describing a child's entire linguistic system. For these latter enterprises, one needs tapes that can be played again and again, transcripts of conversations, and many hundreds of transcribed utterances from every period in a child's development. One needs, in short, a tape recorder. By the early 1960s, not only were high quality tape recorders available to researchers, but newly formulated theories about innate universals and creative hypothesis testing as central processes in language development motivated their use in new research efforts.

1.1.1. Electronic Recording

The period from 1963 to 1983 might be characterized as the era of replicated case studies for child language research. Many researchers, inspired by the new questions about universals, emergence of rules, and systematicity in developing language systems, undertook to study intensively and longitudinally one or two (or if they were very brave, three) children. Observing a few children on a regular basis was challenging; transcribing the tapes so as to keep up with the developing child was soon discovered to be impossible. Roger Brown in his 1973 book, *A First Language: The Early Stages* told the story of the seminar established to process the transcripts from Adam, then being observed. His description of the rapidity with which Adam outstripped the seminar, and the difficulty of getting transcripts produced – let alone analyzed and thought about – before Adam had completely outgrown the phenomenon of interest, rang true for all of us emulating his case study approach.

Precisely because transcribing child language data was so time-consuming, Roger Brown made copies of transcripts from his study available to other researchers, using the state-of-the-art technology of the times, mimeography. The transcripts were typed, not onto paper, but onto mimeo masters, and as many copies as possible were then run off. Some masters generated more copies than others, and Roger with characteristic generosity had given copies away so freely that by 1983, when we went to collect a full set for inclusion in CHILDES, several sessions were down to the last copy, that one often embellished with marginal notes on negation by Ursula Bellugi, on morphological markers by Courtney Cazden, or other checks, codes, and analyses in unrecognized hands.

The continuing value of even a single corpus of child language data is easy to see from a casual cataloguing of the ways in which the Adam, Eve, and Sarah transcripts collected by Brown were used. Harvard theses by Cromer, by Bellugi, by Cazden and by others were based on those transcripts, and many books and journal articles are based on one or more of the Brown corpora. Nor has their value been exhausted; one of the chapters in this handbook uses Adam's data (Bodin & Snow, this volume). But meanwhile many other corpora had been collected, all at great cost and representing the investment of a great deal of time and energy. Too many of these languished on shelves or in file drawers after the study for which they were collected had been completed.

1.1.2. Electronic Storage and Analysis

In 1983, Brian MacWhinney and Catherine Snow first discussed the possibility of creating a child language transcript library, offering to everyone in the field the opportunity to be as generous with their data as Roger Brown had been with his. By then, a second electronic revolution, the emergence of affordable personal computers, dictated that this new transcript library involve electronic rather than paper-based systems, thus simplifying storage, exchange, and, of course, analysis. But the move to electronic storage and the associated possibilities for automated analysis raised many new issues: Automated analysis required a standardized transcription format and a high level of quality control for stored transcripts. Without these, the automated analyses simply would not be trustworthy. For example, a typographical error in a typed transcript would normally be interpreted correctly by a reader or coder, thus causing no problem. The same error would cause a word to be missed or incorrectly included in an automated search. For human readers, it makes little difference if the transcriber alternates between *doggy* and *doggie*, or between *mommy* and *mummy*. For the automated search routine, these difference are as great as those between *dog* and *cat* or *mom* and *dad*.

In addition to dealing with the problems of transcription consistency, making available large quantities of data to the field required also providing tools appropriate for the analysis of large datasets. It was time-consuming, but possible, to read through Adam's transcripts to find all the instances of past tense or possessive; if one has available data from 40 or 50 children, then automated searches become crucial. If one is dealing with hundreds of observation sessions rather than just dozens, then calculation of basic measures like mean length of utterance (MLU) and type-token ratio (TTR) must be automatic. Thus, the transcript library we contemplated quickly developed into a larger system – one which provided access to transcript data but in addition developed and distributed some basic tools for automatic transcript analysis. We called the system the **Child Language Data Exchange System (CHILDES)**, and proceeded to the task of soliciting transcripts and developing transcription guidelines and analytic tools.

1.2. The CHILDES System: An Overview

In this section, we provide a brief overview of the three tools provided by CHILDES. A more complete description of the CHILDES system can be found in MacWhinney (1991). The three tools include a database of child language transcripts, a system of Codes for the Human Analysis of Transcripts of child speech (CHAT), and a collection of Child Language ANalysis programs (CLAN). Although these three tools form the basic components of CHILDES, each of the analyses reported in the following chapters uses them somewhat differently. CHILDES was designed to provide a *toolkit* from which researchers could choose freely whatever tool was most useful for their own purposes. In deciding on transcription format, on analytic strategies, or on datasets to be analyzed, the researcher retains considerable freedom. The chapters collected in this handbook display the variety of tools offered by CHILDES and give some indication of the variety of ways in which those tools can be used.

1.2.1. The Database

Given the historical significance of the Brown corpus, it was the first entry into CHILDES. In those days (as long ago as 1985), the entry of child language corpora into the CHILDES system was a laborious process which consisted of sending the typed pages to the Kurtzweil Institute for scanning followed by months of manual corrections of the scanning errors caused by faded or misaligned type. Scores of assistants (well at least three) worked day and night (well at least all day) for years (well at least one year) to produce a clean version of the Brown corpus for distribution to the hordes of hungry child language researchers eager to conduct detailed analyses of large longitudinal corpora.

Since those early days, CHILDES has grown continuously; Brown's three longitudinal corpora have been complemented by dozens of additional cross-sectional and longitudinal corpora in over a dozen different languages from both typically developing and atypically developing populations. Some of the languages represented are Afrikaans, Danish, Dutch, French, German, Hebrew, Hungarian, Italian, Polish, Spanish, Tamil, and Turkish, and more are being added regularly. The special populations component, which is the most rapidly growing segment of the database, currently includes children with the following disabilities: Down syndrome, autism, specific language impairment, and brain lesions.

As noted in MacWhinney (1991), the database of child language transcripts has made it possible for child language researchers to test research hypotheses on larger and more diverse samples than had previously been possible. For example, Sokolov (1992) recently compared the imitation of 47 children with Down syndrome from the Hooshyar (1985, 1987) and Rondal (1978) corpora to 58 children without retardation. Without the generosity of a large number of child researchers who have contributed their data, such analyses would not have been possible. Although detailed longitudinal studies of individual children will always be of central importance to the field of child language, additional options are now available to a larger group of child language researchers.

1.2.2. CHAT: Codes for the Human Analysis of Transcripts

In 1979, Elinor Ochs published an influential article documenting many examples of the ways in which theoretical biases may be incorporated unwittingly in a transcription format. Her central thesis was that different transcription formats embody theoretical implications for our view of parent-child interaction, the relative roles of verbal and nonverbal behaviors, and our view of the child as either a passive (adult-centered transcription) or an active (child-centered transcription) learner. One clear implication of the Ochs argument is that researchers should recognize the goals of their research program and choose a transcription format that best suits these goals. At the same time, of course, researchers should be aware of the theoretical biases introduced unavoidably by the transcription format they choose. Thus, in designing and evaluating various frameworks for the transcription of child language, we must provide child language researchers enough flexibility to be able to design a transcription framework which allows them to achieve their research goals, without sacrificing the uniformity that enables transcripts to be shared and used collaboratively.

With this in mind, users of the CHILDES system and this book will need to remember the goals of the CHAT system. These goals include the following:

- the provision of clear and readable symbols for accurate and detailed transcription of child speech.

- the provision of a well-defined framework for the insertion of codes relevant to the analysis of child language transcripts.

- the provision of a precise and consistent syntax and semantics which permit automated analyses.

As MacWhinney (1991) noted, the goal of a transcription system is to represent as faithfully as possible the content and the flow of the original interaction. Interestingly, this goal exerts simultaneous pressure towards both a readable and a comprehensive system, but readability and comprehensiveness sometimes conflict with one another. More comprehensive systems of transcription require the use of more symbols, but every additional symbol inserted into a transcript makes it more difficult to read.

A good system for the transcription and analysis of child speech must support both goals: readability and comprehensiveness. As you will see, CHAT provides human transcribers with many options for the detailed transcription of different aspects of child speech and interaction, and CLAN provides several computer programs which are intended to enhance readability, for example by suppressing the symbols when desired. Other CLAN programs provide for alternative formats of transcript presentation (e.g., a column for each speaker), so as not to impose the "playscript" format on all researchers.

Of course, not all researchers strive for the same degree of comprehensiveness in every domain. For example, a researcher who is interested in classifying speech at the level of communicative intent may find gestures and eye gaze crucial but have little need for phonetic detail, while researchers interested in phonological development need a detailed phonetic transcript but may include less non-verbal behavior in their transcripts than the investigator studying speech acts.

How much and what type of information to include in transcripts of child speech is really a decision that is made by individual researchers according to their research goals. The CHAT system provides child language researchers with an extremely large array of transcription symbols and options for including contextual information. No one researcher has ever (or probably will ever) use all of the tools provided by CHAT to transcribe a segment of child speech.

We think of CHAT as a toolkit of transcription symbols. As with any toolkit, there are basic tools and more specialized ones. The basic tools within the CHAT system are included in what we call minCHAT. MinCHAT prescribes the minimum amount of transcript coding that must be performed in order for a transcript to be analyzable by the CLAN programs. The following segment is a sample of a minCHAT transcript:

```
@Begin
@Participants: ROS Ross Child, BRI Brian Father
*ROS:   why isn't Mommy coming?
%com:   Mother usually picks Ross up around 4pm.
*BRI:   don't worry.
*BRI:   she'll be here soon.
*ROS:   good (be)cause I'm xxx hungry.
*BRI:   what would you like to eat?
@End
```

There are several components of this minCHAT transcript that are significant. These include the following:

1. All of the characters in the transcript must be from the ASCII set.

2. All lines must end with a <CR>.

3. There are three major file headers: **@Begin** and **@End** mark the beginning and end of the transcript while **@Participants** signals the line in which the conversational participants are identified. **@Begin** and **@Participants** should be the first and second lines of the transcript while **@End** should be the last.

4. Each speaker tier begins with an asterisk (*), followed by a three-letter identification code for the speaker (e.g., CHI), followed by a colon (:), and finally, followed by a <tab>.

5. Each speaker line must consist of only one utterance. Multi-utterance turns must be split up into separate speaker tiers.

6. Standard punctuation (. ? !) and several prosodic symbols (see MacWhinney, 1991, chapter 6) are permitted as utterance delimiters.

7. Comments may be indicated on a special line which is identified by a **%com:** symbol. Comments may be written in standard spelling.

8. Upper case is used only for proper nouns and the letter *I*. Commas are to be avoided.

9. MinCHAT includes several additional symbols for transcription. These include **xxx** for unintelligible segments, **&g** for false starts (the **&** marks the false start and is followed by whatever sounds are produced), and parenthetical word segments for non-pronounced elements (e.g., *(be)cause*).

There are many ways to extend minCHAT to describe more specific aspects of child language. Several of the chapters in this handbook and in MacWhinney (1991) document many extensions to minCHAT.

1.2.3. CLAN: Child Language Analysis Programs

An Overview of the Programs

After creating an archive of child language transcripts formatted consistently, the obvious next step was to develop some computational tools for analyzing these transcripts. The overall goal in doing so was to automate analyses that were widely used, time-consuming, and/or error-prone. Child language researchers typically had been coding their transcripts by placing pen and pencil marks in the margins and then counting the various codes by hand. Using this method, modifying coding systems was difficult, counting was error-prone, and filtering representative examples from the complete corpus of transcripts was time-consuming. With the advent of computational tools for performing these analyses, accuracy is enhanced and child language researchers are freer to spend their valuable time interpreting their data rather than counting and collating it.

As CHILDES has grown over the last five years, so has the variety of programs for the analysis of language transcripts. Programs now exist for counting items (FREQ), for searching for individual keywords in context (KWAL) and for searching for combinations of keywords in context (COMBO). In addition, programs have been created for the analysis of word and utterance lengths (MAXWD) and for the computation of the mean length of utterance (MLU) and turn (MLT). Furthermore, as a first step toward truly automated transcript analysis, two programs have been developed that introduce codes into the transcript (CHIP and MOR). A program even exists for verifying whether or not a transcript conforms to CHAT convention (CHECK)!

The increase in the number of analysis programs highlights the importance of the toolkit metaphor for the CLAN programs. With an increasing number of available programs, the child language researcher is now able to choose increasingly more appropriate tools for a wider range of research goals. As illustrated in Table 1.1, there exist so many tools that we have now taken to categorizing them according to their major functions.

Command Syntax

The following is a typical CLAN command:[2]

mlu +t*CHI jamie.cha

This command tells the MLU program to compute the mean length of utterance of all of the child's utterances (indicated by **+t*CHI**) in the **jamie.cha** transcript. As you can see quite clearly from this example, there are three elements to this CLAN command:

1. **mlu**   the name of the program you wish to execute

2. **+t*CHI**   a list of options you select for the program

3. **jamie.cha** the name of the child language transcripts or other files you wish to analyze

---

[2] Please note that this command and many of the subsequent commands listed in this chapter are replicable. In other words, if you sit in front of a computer while reading each chapter, you can execute many of the commands listed within the Method sections. In many cases, the actual results are also provided, so you can verify the accuracy of your analyses. We return to this topic in Section 1.6.

Table 1.1: The CLAN programs (developed by Leonid Spektor except where noted).

General CLAN:	
MAXWD:	Locates the longest strings
FREQ & STATFREQ:	Computes frequency counts
KWAL:	Searches for keyword and returns the KeyWord And Line
COMBO:	Performs a combinatorial search
Assessment Tools:	
MLU & MLT:	Computes Mean Length of Utterance and Turn
DSS:	Computes the developmental sentence score (Lee, 1974)
IPSYN:	Computes the index of productive syntax (Scarborough, 1990)
Discourse Analysis:	
GEM:	Searches for chunks of bracketed data
KEYMAP:	Performs a contingency analysis
CHAINS:	Provides a graphical display of sequences of codes and some descriptive statistics of these codes
CHIP:	Codes lexical overlap and lexical change in conversational interaction (developed by Sokolov; Sokolov & MacWhinney, 1990)
Phonological Analyses	
PHONFREQ:	Performs a phonological frequency analysis
MODREP:	Performs a model and replica phonological analysis

Table 1.1 (*continued*): The CLAN programs (developed by Leonid Spektor except where noted).

Utilities:

BIBFIND:	Finds selected entries in the CHILDES/BIB database (Higginson & MacWhinney, 1990)
CED:	Editing tool for coding transcripts
CHECK:	Verifies correct use of CHAT syntax
CHSTRING:	Changes strings in a transcript
DATES:	Given date of birth and date of transcription, computes child age
MOR:	Part-of-speech tagger
RECALL:	Command editing and history list
SALTIN:	Converts SALT files to CHAT format

Data Display:

COLUMNS:	Displays transcripts in multi-column format
FLO:	Displays transcripts with simplified main line
LINES:	Displays transcripts with line numbers
PAGE:	Displays transcripts one page at a time
SLIDE:	Displays transcripts sliding across the screen

Put in a more graphical form, the syntax of a typical CLAN command is as follows:

mlu	+t*CHI	jamie.cha
Command	Options	Filename

In a typical command, the program name comes first, followed by a list of zero, one, or more options (options can come in any order), and ending with an input file.

General and Program-Specific Options

Each CLAN program accepts several options which modify its performance. These options are very useful in limiting analyses to particular speakers and particular aspects of language. As we saw in the previous example, the +t option when used in conjunction with the speaker identification for the child (**CHI**) is helpful in focusing the MLU analysis on the child's speech only.

Thus, one of the most important steps in being able to use the CLAN programs is learning the different options that are available for individual programs and for the system as a whole. Of course, there are both program-general and program-specific options. For example, the +t option is one of the most general of all of the options. Nearly all of the CLAN programs accept this option. Another very general option is the +s option. This option tells the majority of programs to focus their analysis on particular strings. So, if you were interested in analyzing a Wh-word like *who*, then you would include the option +s"who" in your command string. If you were interested in counting the number of *who* strings in a child language transcript, you could type:

freq +s"who" jamie.cha

or if you were interested in collecting all the utterances in the **jamie.cha** transcript that contained the word *who*, you would type:

kwal +s"who" jamie.cha

If you wished to expand your analysis to all of the Wh-words in English, you could create a file that contained all of these words and then use this file as an **include file** in the following command:

kwal +s@whwords jamie.cha

Now recall that the **+t** option *includes* speaker tiers. In order to *exclude* speaker tiers, all you need to do is reverse the option from +t to –t. Supposing you were interested in analyzing all of the instances of Wh-words that were produced by all of the speakers in the transcript *except* the investigator, whose utterances you wish to *exclude*. If this was the case, you would type:

kwal –t*INV +s@whwords jamie.cha

Thus, not only can you *include* speech from particular speakers (+t), you may *exclude* speech from them as well (–t). This also works for the +s option. Recall that we used the +s option to include specific strings in our analysis. We may also use the –s option to exclude particular strings from our analysis. For example, suppose that you wished to exclude particular strings (e.g., *mm* or *oh* as suggested in Brown, 1973; p. 54) from your analysis of a child's mean length of utterance (MLU). To do this, you would type:

mlu +t*CHI –s"mm" –s"oh" jamie.cha

Of course, the +/–s option can be modified to include or exclude a list of strings from a file. If you had already created a file called **exmlu** (for **ex**clude from **MLU**), which contained a list of words you wished to exclude from your MLU analysis, then you would use the –s@ option as in the following command:

mlu +t*CHI –s@exmlu jamie.cha

There are additional program-general options which you will encounter in the chapters of this handbook. These include +w/–w for specifying the size of the window of context you wish to include in your analysis or the various versions of the +d option which control the amount and type of output that you receive from various CLAN programs. The +d option is an interesting case. It is an option that is available in a wide variety of CLAN programs, but its effects are not the same for each one. For example, in the FREQ program, the various levels of the +d option control the type of data that is output. However, in the KWAL program, the +d option determines whether or not the output will be in CHAT format. As you will see, this is a very important determination. For example, whether or not the output from a KWAL analysis is in CHAT format will determine whether or not you will be able to perform additional analyses, such as mean length of utterance, on it.

Continuing with our analysis of Wh-questions, suppose you were interested in analyzing the MLU of Jamie's attempts to produce questions. You could do this with one command by directing or **piping** the output of the search for Wh-questions to the MLU program:

kwal −t*INV +s@whwords +d jamie.cha | mlu +t*CHI −s@exmlu

The +d option causes the output from the KWAL program to be in CHAT format so that the MLU program can analyze it.

Wildcards

The ability to take advantage of wildcards is one of the more powerful features of CLAN. Suppose, like Bodin and Snow (this volume), you were interested in determining the frequency of the word *toy* in a child's speech. You could perform this analysis with the following command:

freq +t*CHI +s"toy" jamie.cha

Unfortunately, this command would fail to find any instances of *toy* in the **jamie.cha** file. If you stopped your analysis here, you would mistakenly conclude that no instances of this word were found in this file. However, if you went a step further and used a wildcard (*):

freq +t*CHI +s"toy*" jamie.cha

your efforts would be rewarded by the discovery of the word *toy-s*. This is because the "*" is a wildcard that can match any number of characters in a word. For example, the string *ch** would match *chair, change, chip, chuckle,* and so forth.

Wildcards can be placed anywhere in a word. For example, the string *J*f* would match *Jeff* and the string *C*e* would match *Catherine*. Thus the "*" wildcard helps you to find different instances of a word without having to individually specify each one. Not only is this an important shortcut, but it is extremely helpful when you are not sure which versions of a particular word are present in a particular transcript.

The "*" wildcard is not the only wildcard in the CLAN system: The "%" character can also be used as a wildcard. The difference is that the "%" wildcard removes the characters to which it matches. To see how this works, let us compare the results of the following two commands:

freq +t*CHI +s"*–s" jamie.cha
freq +t*CHI +s"%–s" jamie.cha

The first command with the "*" wildcard returns the following output:

```
    1 balloon-s
    1 bear-s
    2 bird-s
    1 chick-s
    1 dog-s
    1 pig-s
    2 thing-s
-------------------------------
    7   Total number of different word types used
    9   Total number of words (tokens)
0.778   Type/Token ratio
```

while the second command with the "%" wildcard returns the following output:

```
    9 -s
-------------------------------
    1   Total number of different word types used
    9   Total number of words (tokens)
0.111   Type/Token ratio
```

As you can see, the second command did, in fact, match all of fifteen of the plural nouns that the child produced. However, it removed the stems and then counted only the instances of the suffix *–s*. Thus, the "%" wildcard can be extremely helpful in searching for parts of words. For more discussion of the different wildcards in CLAN, see MacWhinney (1991).

Sending Program Output to a File

Many of the analyses that you will perform using CLAN will be either too big to fit on one screen or so important that you will want to save them for future use. As MacWhinney (1991) notes, "the advantages of sending the program's results to a file is that you can go over the [results of the] analysis more carefully" (p. 201). In the following discussion, we will describe three methods for sending program output to a file in CLAN. The simplest method is to use the **+f** option:

freq +f jamie.cha

This will send the output of this FREQ command to the file **jamie.frq**. A sure-fire way to tell that this is true is to check the output header:

```
FREQ.EXE (04-MAY-93) is conducting analyses on:
  ALL speaker tiers
****************************************
From file <jamie.cha> to file <jamie.frq>
Done with file <jamie.frq>
```

As you can see, the default file extension for the FREQ program is **.frq**. Each CLAN program has its own default extension. For example, the MLU program uses the **.mlu** extension and the KWAL program uses the **.kwa** extension.

The **+f** option in CLAN will not overwrite previously created files; for example, if you type the following command after already creating a **jamie.frq** file:

freq +s"you" +f jamie.cha

you would receive the following output header:

```
FREQ.EXE (04-MAY-93) is conducting analyses on:
  ALL speaker tiers
****************************************
From file <jamie.cha> to file <jamie.fr0>
Done with file <jamie.fr0>
```

In other words, rather than overwrite previously created files, CLAN numbers the different versions of the file. However, the **.frø** extension is not very mnemonic. Ideally, you would like to be able to specify file extensions that are more meaningful and easier to remember. The best way to do this is to use the **+f** option but specify a three-letter extension as in **.pro**:

freq +s"you" +fpro jamie.cha

This would result in the following output header:

```
FREQ.EXE (04-MAY-93) is conducting analyses on:
  ALL speaker tiers
*****************************************
From file <jamie.cha> to file <jamie.pro>
Done with file <jamie.pro>
```

The most popular means of saving program output to a file is by using the **+f** option. However, for some uses, this option can be somewhat limiting. One obvious limitation is that sometimes a three-letter file extension is not enough to distinguish the results of one analysis from another. A second, more important, limitation involves analyses that combine several files. For example, suppose you would like to search for all the instances of pronouns in a longitudinal corpus (e.g., the Adam corpus in Brown, 1973). To perform a combined analysis and save the results in a single file, you would type the following command:

freq +s@pronoun +u adam*.cha > profreq.ada

This command would result in the creation of the file **profreq.ada** (for *pronoun FREQ for Adam*). The " > " is a *redirect* symbol, which causes the program output to be *redirected* to the file that you specify.

This ends our overview of CLAN. This discussion is intended to provide readers with a basic knowledge of the three components of the CHILDES system. The individual chapters in this handbook provide you with a more detailed discussion of each of these topics.

1.3. The Tradeoffs: Advantages and Disadvantages of CHILDES

It should be obvious that CHILDES, despite its advantages over paper-and-pencil methods of transcription and analysis, does not solve all problems in child language. Some questions about language development require testing children for imitation, comprehension, or interpretation of utterances. Some require cueing or marking transcribed utterances so that one has simultaneous access to audio or video representations of the utterance event, a facility that CHILDES cannot yet offer (but see MacWhinney, this volume, for a discussion of ongoing work in this area). Some require having access to more information about the child, or the family, or the culture from which the child comes than is ever accessible from a transcript alone; though corpora stored in CHILDES come accompanied by "readme" files that give background information about the subjects, these are often less complete than one might wish.

The mere availability of CHILDES even gives rise to certain possible problems. Researchers can quickly grind out enormously complicated analyses on huge datasets, but large quantities of data never compensate for an absence of interesting questions. It takes only a few minutes, for instance, to find all the cases in the entire data archive where someone uses the word *chocolate*. The fact that one **can** does not necessarily mean that one **should**.

Furthermore, cross-corpus analyses must be undertaken with caution, to ensure that in each case the original corpus was collected and transcribed in a way consistent with the new research undertaking. Few of the corpora stored in CHILDES are appropriate for a study of phonological development, for example, or for careful analysis of conversational phenomena like interruptions, latching, overlaps, back-channels, or filled pauses; the original transcription was simply not detailed enough. Many transcriptions give too little phonetic detail for one to be sure if a child is saying *a* or *the*, distinguishing *wanna* from *want to*, or segmenting *you* in *could you* and *would you*. For many analyses these imprecisions do not matter; for some they matter enormously.

Like any toolkit, CHILDES solves no problems on its own. It can help thoughtful analysts try out hypotheses, and definitively disprove some. It can save time and trouble, and vastly improve the power of statistical analyses by increasing sample size. It can hardly substitute, though, for the experience of actually observing children talk or of recording and transcribing their conversations, an experience every serious child language researcher should have.

1.4. The Goals of This Handbook

As we have already noted, the ability to analyze transcripts of child language with the help of computers has provided researchers with a means for conducting analyses that were previously too difficult or time-consuming to undertake. Although previous publications by Brian MacWhinney and Catherine Snow (1985, 1990) have described the tools provided by the Child Language Data Exchange System (CHILDES), they have not provided examples of research in action or tutorials for the creative application of these tools by individual researchers. This edited volume fulfills this need by aspiring to achieve two goals: (a) to present original research across a variety of areas within child language and (b) to teach students and researchers to use the tools provided by CHILDES by providing annotated demonstrations.

Goal #1: *The presentation of original research across a wide variety of areas within child language*

Each of the 12 empirical chapters included in this volume presents original research in child language. The domains of language analysis represented include phonology (chapter 11), morphology (chapter 8), semantics (chapter 4), syntax (chapter 9), pragmatics (chapter 12), and discourse (chapter 10); major issues addressed include measuring typical and atypical growth (chapters 2 and 12), the role of imitation (chapter 7), parental input (chapters 3, 4, 5, 6, 11), universals (chapter 9), categorization (chapter 4), individual differences (chapter 7), and sociolinguistic variability (chapter 3).

These research topics are presented in a way accessible to both advanced undergraduate and graduate students. Each of the chapters maintains a slightly modified journal style of research reporting. All the chapters include the traditional introduction, method, results, and discussion sections. The modifications to the traditional journal style are designed to enhance the pedagogical value of the handbook. In several cases, these include a lengthened literature review and justification of the research area, as well as extra detail about the process of making methodological decisions.

Goal #2: Teach students and researchers to use the tools provided by CHILDES

This goal is achieved through several design features that highlight the pedagogical intent of the volume: (a) Each chapter begins with an outline of the CHILDES-related skills readers should expect to learn within the chapter; (b) computer commands are presented and explained in numbered command boxes; (c) special hints are peppered throughout the text to provide readers with additional information; (d) materials are provided so readers can replicate the analyses performed in each chapter (see footnote 1 in this chapter); and (e) each chapter includes a set of exercises and suggested projects. Thus, the handbook should also be of value to experienced child language researchers who seek a relatively painless hands-on tutorial in computer analyses of child language transcripts.

1.5. Getting Started

One of the first questions, readers of this handbook may ask is, *What do I need to know to get started?* In general, we assume that readers will be referring to the computational procedures presented in the handbook. However, some readers may be asking about the conceptual aspects of child language. Many experienced child language researchers still remember the experience of having to learn all of the terminology inherent in child language research. As editors of this handbook, we have endeavored to soften the blow of what is sometimes rather technical research. For those readers that still find certain terms or concepts difficult to understand, we recommend returning to an introductory child language textbook (e.g., Berko-Gleason, 1993) and reading the relevant materials.

As stated earlier, we expect that the majority of our readers will be more concerned with being able to perform the computational procedures presented in this handbook. As we mentioned in the previous section, we have designed several pedagogical features to make it easier for readers to learn the computational procedures presented in each of the research chapters. However, in doing so, we have assumed basic computer literacy among our readers. By this we mean a basic ability to work within one operating system (DOS, the MACINTOSH, or UNIX) and knowledge of one word processor (e.g,. WordPerfect or Microsoft Word). We consider a basic ability to work in an operating system to include the following capacities:

- to understand the concept of directories and subdirectories
- to be able to switch from one directory to another
- to be able to make and remove directories
- to understand how files are named (including their extensions)
- to be able to display, copy, move, delete, and print files
- to understand the difference between an ASCII and a non-ASCII file

If you do not have these basic abilities, then we recommend that you acquire some additional background knowledge concerning these topics. We have found, in the course of giving many tutorials and workshops, that people who have this knowledge find the information presented in this handbook to be more meaningful, easier to remember, and easier to implement.

1.5.2. Installation of the Programs and Transcript Data

The CLAN Programs

Detailed instructions for installing the programs are listed in the CHILDES manual (MacWhinney, 1991). Brief instructions for the two-step process are listed below:

1. Copy the programs and library files (using the install program if possible) to your hard-disk. Be sure to maintain the directory structure supported by CLAN: Programs go in the **bin** subdirectory under the **clan** directory while all other files go in the **lib** subdirectory. For example: For DOS, the correct directory for the programs would be: "\childes\clan\bin." For the MACINTOSH, the CLAN and CED applications would go under: "childes:clan." For UNIX, the correct directory would be: "/childes/clan/bin."

2. Modify your path variable (for DOS and UNIX) or set the working and library directories (for MACINTOSH). To do this, you must edit the file **autoexec.bat** for DOS by adding the string "\childes\clan\bin." For UNIX, you must edit the file **.cshrc** by adding the string "childes/clan/bin."

Users of DOS should be sure to place the line **recall -i** in your **autoexec.bat** file. This program permits users to edit previous commands by using the arrow keys on your keyboard (see the hint in chapter 6).

The Transcript Data

Each of the chapters in the handbook assume that you have created a subdirectory called **handbook** under the **childes** directory and placed all of the transcript data in that directory. It is important to maintain the directory structure of the data. For example, make sure you place the **hooshyar** data in the **hooshyar** subdirectory. For DOS, the correct directory would be: "\childes\handbook\hooshyar." For the MACINTOSH, the correct folder would be: "childes:handbook:hooshyar." For UNIX, the correct directory would be: "/childes/handbook/hooshyar."

1.5.3. Checking the Installation

If you have done everything right, then you should be able to type any CLAN command to your prompt and get a list of options and a short description as output. For example, if you type **mlu**, you should get the output listed in Table 1.2 as the result. Note that this is also an excellent means of obtaining reminders about the availability and meaning of options for particular programs without having to look them up in the CHILDES manual (MacWhinney, 1991). If you find that this procedure does not work, first check the path your system uses to find programs. You can do this in DOS, by typing the command "path" and in UNIX by typing the command "set." If this does not work, be sure you have installed the programs in the correct directories (as described in Section 1.5.2).

1.6. A Final Word

It is important to stress that whenever possible, we recommend that you attempt to replicate the commands highlighted by the various command boxes. This requires sitting in front of a computer while reading the Method section of each chapter. We firmly believe that doing so will not only quicken the learning curve but also lessen the inevitable memory decay. This we know from cognitive psychological research, which tells us that elaborative processing during learning results in better retention.

This book is meant as a companion volume to MacWhinney's (1991) manual, which documents CHILDES in a more traditional way. Like any computer-based

Transcript Analysis 23

system, CHILDES is subject to change, expansion, and improvement. The basic skills acquired by anyone who works through even a few chapters in this volume will be a solid basis for understanding any changes that might occur in later editions of the MacWhinney manual and the updated software. We urge you to join INFO-CHILDES, an electronic bulletin board that will provide regular updates on problems and improvements in CLAN if you become a regular user. To join INFO-CHILDES, send a request to be added to the distribution list to one of the following electronic mail addresses:

> info-childes-request@andrew.cmu.edu *(for INTERNET users)*
> info-childes-request@andrew.bitnet *(for BITNET users)*

You can also obtain the CLAN programs via anonymous FTP from poppy.psy.cmu.edu. Detailed instructions for doing so are provided in MacWhinney (1991).

Table 1.2: The output from typing **mlu** on a command line by itself.

```
Mean Length Utterance computes the number of utterances,
morphemes and their ratio.
Usage:    mlu [bS cS gF d fS k m pF rN sS tS u yN zN ]
             filename(s)
+bS:  make all S characters morpheme delimiters (default: &-#)
-bS:  do not consider all S characters to be morpheme delimiters
+cS:  look for unit marker S
+gF:  exclude utterance consisting solely of specified words
+d :  output in STATFREQ format. Must include speaker
      specifications
+fS:  send output to file (program will derive filename)
-f :  send output to the screen or pipe
+k :  treat upper and lower case as different
+m :  store output file(s) in the directories of input file(s)
+pF:  define punctuation set according to file F
+rN:  if N = 1 then "get(s)" goes to "gets", 2- "get(s)", 3-
      "get", 4- Remove Prosodic Symbols in Words, 5- do not do
      Text Replacement: [: *]
+sS:  either word S or words in file @S to search for in a given
      input file
-sS:  either word S or words in file @S to be exclude from a
      given input file
+tS:  include tier code S
-tS:  exclude tier code S
+u :  merge all specified files together.
+y :  work on non-CHAT format files one line at the time
+y1:  work on non-CHAT format files one utterance at the time
+zN:  compute statistics on a specified range of input data
```

References

Behrens, H., & Deutsch, W. (1991). Die Tagebücher von Clara und William Stern. In W. Deutsch (Ed.), *Über die verborgene Aktualität von William Stern*. Frankfurt: Lang.

Berko-Gleason, J. (1993). *The development of language*. Third Edition. Columbus, OH: Merrill Publishing Co.

Brown, R. (1973). *A First Language*. Cambridge, MA: Harvard University Press.

Campe, J. H., Editor. (1785). *Allgeneine Revision des gesamten Schul- und Erziehungswesens von einer Gesellschaft praktischer Erzieher*. Hamburg: Bohn.

Deutsch, W. (1992). Hoe oud is het onderzoek naar taalverwerving? [How old is language acquisition research?] In P. Jordens & A. Wijnands (Eds.), *Fourth NET-Symposium*. Amsterdam: Department of Applied Linguistics, Vrije Universiteit.

Higginson, R., & MacWhinney, B. (1990). *CHILDES/BIB: An annotated bibliography of child language and language disorders*. Hillsdale, NJ: Lawrence Erlbaum Associates.

Hooshyar, N. (1985). Language interaction between mothers and their non-handicapped children. *International Journal of Rehabilitation Research, 4*, 475-477.

Hooshyar, N. (1987). The relationship between maternal language parameters and the child's language constancy and developmental condition. *International Journal of Rehabilitation Research, 10*, 321-324.

Lee, L. (1974). *Developmental sentence analysis*. Evanston, IL: Northwestern University Press.

Leopold, W. (1939-1949). *Speech development of a bilingual child: A linguist's record. Volumes 1-4*. Evanston, IL: Northwestern University Press.

MacWhinney, B. (1991). *The CHILDES Project: Computational tools for analyzing talk*. Hillsdale, NJ: Lawrence Erlbaum Associates.

MacWhinney, B., & Snow, C.E., (1985). The child language data exchange system. *Journal of Child Language, 12*, 271-295.

MacWhinney, B., & Snow, C. (1989). The Child Language Data Exchange System: An update. *Journal of Child Language, 17*, 457-472.

Ochs, E. (1979). Transcription as theory. In E. Ochs & B. Schieffelin (Ed.), *Developmental pragmatics*. New York: Academic.

Rondal, J. A. (1978). Maternal speech to normal and Down's syndrome children matched for mean length of utterance. In C. E. Meyers (Ed.), *Quality of life in severely and profoundly mentally retarded people: Research foundations for improvement.* Washington, DC: American Association on Mental Deficiency.

Scarborough, H. S. (1990). Index of productive syntax. *Applied Psycholinguistics, 11*, 1-22.

Sokolov, J. L. (1992). Linguistic imitation in children with Down syndrome. *American Journal on Mental Retardation, 97, 2*, 209-221.

Sokolov, J. L., & MacWhinney, B. (1990). The CHIP framework: Automatic coding and analysis of parent-child conversational interaction. *Behavior Research Methods, Instruments, and Computers, 22, 2*, 151-161.

2 Basic Measures of Child Language

Barbara Alexander Pan
Harvard Graduate School of Education

In this chapter, you will learn the following skills:

- To compute Mean Length of Utterance using the CLAN program MLU.

- To limit CLAN analyses to a specified number of utterances using the +z option.

- To perform an analysis on a group of files at once using wildcards.

- To save the results of an analysis in a file.

- To identify the longest word or longest utterance in a file using the CLAN program MAXWD.

- To pipe the results of one CLAN analysis to another CLAN program for further analysis.

- To compute a Type-Token Ratio using the CLAN program FREQ.

- To compute the Mean Length of Turn for a given speaker using the CLAN program MLT.

To replicate the analysis and to do the exercises, you will need the data in the **20mos** and **30mos** subdirectories under the **NEngland** directory.

2.1. Introduction

Most children learn to use the language they hear around them with relative ease. Development in the early stages proceeds at what often seems breakneck speed: The average child beginning to produce her first words at twelve months, has by age three a vocabulary of as many as a few thousand words and a good grasp of at least the simpler grammatical constructions used in her language. Still, the wide variation in rate of language development and the different routes that children take to adult-like competence make it impossible to predict exactly what the speech of any given child will be like at a particular age. How then can child language researchers know that they are studying children of comparable levels of development? How also are clinicians, teachers, and parents to know whether a child is proceeding at a rate and in a fashion that fall within the range of normal variation? While the search for accurate, reliable, and efficient indices of language development continues, researchers and clinicians have relied to some degree on several measures that are discussed in this chapter. Some of these measures are intended to tap the length and complexity of children's utterances, while others have to do with the number and variety of words the child uses, and still others explore ways of indexing conversational skills. We consider first how we might deal with length and complexity issues, next turn to ways of characterizing children's vocabularies, and finally look at how the conversational load is shared by child and adult.

2.1.1. Grammatical Complexity: Mean Length of Utterance

As children begin to acquire grammar, they produce utterances that are made up of more than one word or that include grammatical elements such as plural markers or articles. The child who earlier answered the question "What's that?" with "cat," now answers "a cat"; the child who had simply commented "Daddy" as her dad pulled into the driveway now announces "Daddy's home." In the early stages, these more complex utterances also tend to be longer. Researchers have used utterance length as a measure of language development for many years (Brown, 1973; McCarthy, 1954). One obvious way to measure length is to count the number of words produced in a sample of speech and compute the average length. A slightly more refined measure, however, is **mean length of utterance** (or MLU) measured in **morphemes** rather than in words (Brown, 1973). In this way, we capture the added complexity of words such as *cats* and *looked*, which are composed of more than one morpheme (i.e., *cat+plural* and *look+past-tense*). Since Roger Brown's work in the early 1970s, MLU in morphemes has become the standard way of measuring children's average utterance length, both for research and for clinical purposes. For the remainder of this chapter, I will use the term MLU to refer to mean length of utterance in morphemes.

What Does MLU Measure?

Brown (1973) suggested MLU as a simple index of grammatical growth because each new morphological or syntactic structure the child uses (at least in the early stages of development) increases utterance length. For example, the addition of articles, such as *a* and *the*, noun and verb inflections, negatives, auxiliaries (*am, will*), modals (*would, could*), conjunctions, prepositions, and relative clauses all result in longer utterances. While all of these structures can contribute to increased utterance length, some tend to emerge earlier than others in young children's speech. Plural marking of nouns (e.g., *books*), for example, tends to be used by children well before they are routinely using modals or relative clauses (Miller, 1981).

In following the development of three children, Adam, Eve, and Sarah, Brown and his colleagues observed that similar grammatical structures tended to characterize the children's speech at similar MLU levels. They also found that, although MLU increased with age in all three children, the rate of increase was not the same: While Adam's and Sarah's speech gradually increased in length and complexity from MLU 2.00 to 4.00 over a period of approximately 14 months, the speech of Eve, the third (and younger) child, showed a similar increase over only 8 months (see Figure 2.1). In order to more easily compare the language of children of comparable grammatical levels, Brown proposed five MLU stages:

Stage I	MLU 1.0-2.0
Stage II	MLU 2.0-2.5
Stage III	MLU 2.5-3.0
Stage IV	MLU 3.0-3.5
Stage V	MLU 3.5-4.0

While syntactic development continues well beyond Stage V, Brown felt that MLU ceased to be a good index of complexity beyond this point, in part because increased

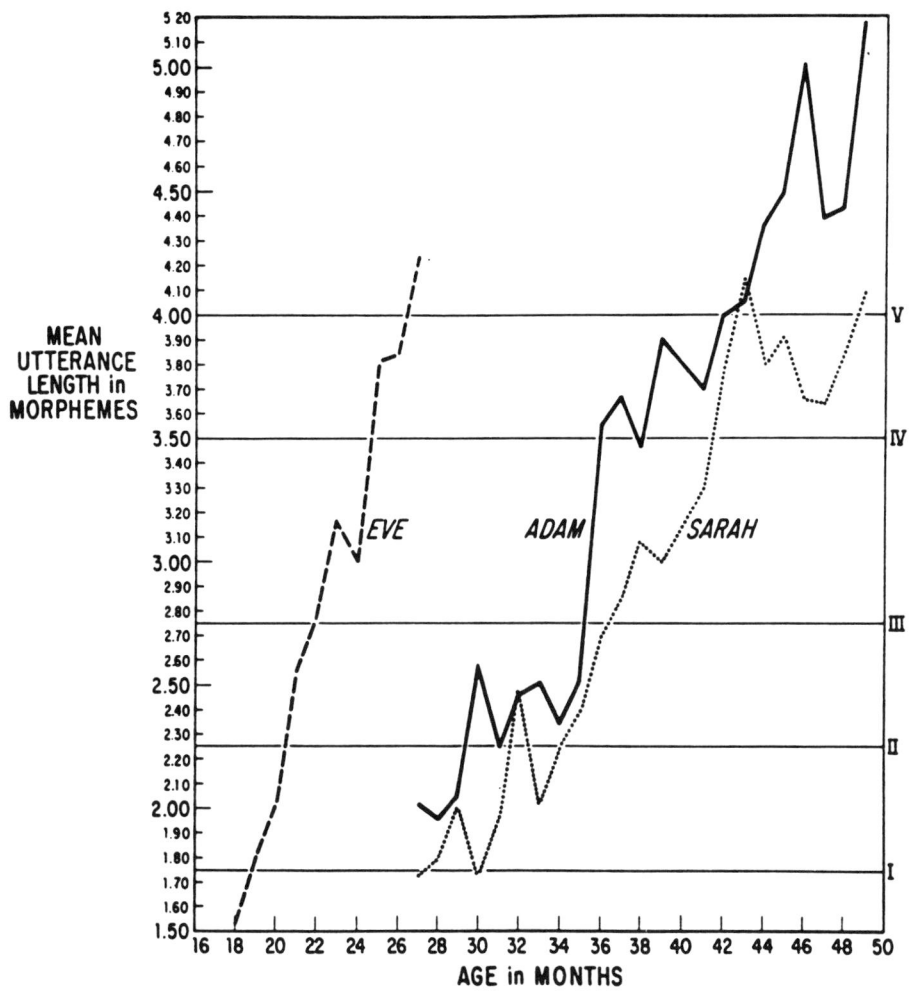

Figure 2.1: Mean Length of Utterance in morphemes and chronological age in months for three children (Reprinted by permission of the publishers from *A First Language* by Roger Brown, Cambridge, MA: Harvard University Press, Copyright © 1973 by the President and Fellows of Harvard College).

syntactic sophistication on the part of the child does not continue to reveal itself in longer utterances.

Since Brown's work, MLU or MLU Stage has been widely used as a basis for comparing groups of normally developing children, as well as for comparing the language development of delayed children to that of normally developing children. While MLU has proved useful as a general index of grammatical development, researchers continue to explore exactly what it is that MLU measures (e.g., Klee & Fitzgerald, 1985; Rondal, Ghiotto, Bredart, & Bachelet, 1987; Scarborough et al., 1991). As noted above, different structures emerge and begin to contribute to utterance length at different points in development. Growth in MLU, then, almost certainly reflects different things at different levels. Bates and her colleagues (Bates, Bretherton, & Snyder, 1988), for example, have suggested that MLU at 20 months reflects primarily the use of rote or unanalyzed strings, rather than true productive understanding of grammatical morphemes. In addition, growth in MLU may also reflect individual differences across children in terms of the elements they choose to elaborate. For example, young children can increase their utterance length by adding inflectional elements such as articles or plural markers (*ball* → *a ball*; *book* → *books*); by incorporating new semantic relations (*hit ball* → *Kati hit ball*); or by adding modifiers such as adjectives and adverbs (*bear* → *big brown bear*; *run* → *run really fast*). For some children, growth in MLU in the early stages may reflect primarily an increase in morphological sophistication, while for others it may reflect semantic elaboration (Pan & Elkins, 1989; Rollins, Pan, & Snow, 1991).

Limits of the Utility of MLU

There has been considerable discussion over the years about the general validity of MLU as a measure of morphosyntactic development, and about the developmental range for which it is most useful (see, for example, Crystal, 1974; Klee & Fitzgerald, 1985; Rondal, Ghiotto, Bredart, & Bachelet, 1987; Scarborough et al., 1991). Clearly, MLU is a composite measure, and as such cannot in itself provide information about either the emergence or the mastery of particular grammatical structures. Moreover, its utility decreases markedly above MLUs of about 3.00, when use of sophisticated devices, such as ellipsis, results in shorter, rather than longer, utterances. In addition, MLU computed in words and/or morphemes has been found to be sensitive to transcript length and to interactional factors, such as familiarity of interlocutor and type of activity engaged in (Cowan, Weber, Hoddinott, & Klein, 1967; Kramer, James, & Saxman, 1979). Of course, the criteria the researcher uses in counting morphemes also influences the outcome. Many researchers follow Brown's counting rules (see Table 2.1) for excluding certain types of utterances and for deciding how to deal with special words, such as fillers, compound words, and auxiliaries, and forms that the child may have learned

Table 2.1: Rules for calculating Mean Length of Utterance (Reprinted by permission of the publishers from *A First Language* by Roger Brown, Cambridge, MA: Harvard University Press, Copyright © 1973 by the President and Fellows of Harvard College).

1. Start with the second page of the transcription unless that page involves a recreation of some kind. In this latter case start with the first recitation-free stretch. Count 100 utterances satisfying the following rules.

2. Only fully transcribed utterances are used; none with blanks. Portions of utterances, entered in parentheses to indicate doubtful transcription, are used.

3. Include all exact utterance repetitions (marked with a plus sign in records). Stuttering is marked as repeated efforts at a single word; count the word once in the most complete form produced. In the few cases where a word is produced for emphasis or the like (*no, no, no*) count each occurrence.

4. Do not count such fillers as *mm* or *oh*, but do count *no*, *yeah*, and *hi*.

5. All compound words (two or more free morphemes), proper names, and ritualized reduplications count as single words. Examples: *birthday*, *rackety-boom*, *choo-choo*, *quack-quack*, *night-night*, *pocketbook*, *see saw*. Justification is that there is no evidence that the constituent morphemes function as such for these children.

6. Count as one morpheme all irregular pasts of the verb (*got, did, went, saw*). Justification is that there is no evidence that the child related these to present forms.

7. Count as one morpheme all diminutives (*doggie, mommie*) because these children at least do not seem to use the suffix productively. Diminutives are the standard forms used by the child.

8. Count as separate morphemes all auxiliaries (*is, have, will, can, must, would*). Also all catenatives: *gonna, wanna, hafta*. These latter counted as single morphemes rather than as *going to* or *want to* because evidence is that they function so for the children. Count as separate morphemes all inflections, for example, possessive $\{s\}$, plural $\{s\}$, third person singular $\{s\}$, regular past $\{d\}$, progressive $\{ing\}$.

9. The range count follows the above rules but is always calculated for the total transcription rather than for 100 utterances.

32   Chapter 2

as unanalyzed chunks. Other researchers and clinicians (e.g., Scarborough, Wyckoff, & Davidson, 1986; Wells, 1985) advocate excluding imitations, self-repetitions, and one-word answers to yes/no questions in order to generate a stricter measure of *syntactic* development. These issues can be particularly important for assessing MLU in children with delayed or deviant language development, whose language may include a disproportionately high incidence of echolalia or imitation (tending to inflate MLU) or of one-word yes/no responses (tending to deflate MLU).

In the years since Brown first suggested MLU as a measure of a child's grammatical development, a number of alternative measures or tools have been proposed. The more widely used ones include Lee's Developmental Sentence Score (DSS; Lee, 1974); the Language Assessment, Remediation and Screening Procedure (LARSP; Crystal, Fletcher, & Garman, 1976); Miller's Assigning Structural Stage (ASS; Miller, 1981); and Scarborough's Index of Productive Syntax (IPSYN; Scarborough, 1990). Like Brown's MLU, each of these takes as the basis for its analysis a sample of 50 or 100 spontaneous child utterances. Unlike MLU, each of these tools scores for the occurrence of particular grammatical structures (e.g., plurals, irregular past tense forms, copulas) and thus provides somewhat more specific information about a child's grammatical usage. This information can then be used to guide intervention therapies for children with language delays. Despite these more recently developed tools, however, MLU has continued to be a widely used index of children's linguistic development, and is nearly always one of the basic measures included in a child's language profile.

MLU of Five Longest Utterances

In addition to Mean Length of Utterance, researchers and clinicians sometimes also compute the length of the child's **longest**, or five longest, utterances. Unlike MLU, which is influenced equally by every utterance in the corpus, MLU of the five longest utterances provides an indication of the upper limits of the child's production at a given point in time. Wells (1985) has found that increases in MLU of the five longest utterances tend to parallel those in MLU, with both levelling off after about 42 months of age. Brown (1973) and, more recently, Bennett and his colleagues (Bennett, James, & Prosek, 1991) have suggested that MLU of the longest utterance tends, in children developing normally, to be approximately three times greater than MLU. It should be noted that MLU of either the longest or the five longest utterances may be particularly sensitive to context. For example, in a bookreading session, where parent and child are engaged primarily in labelling activities, the child may be less likely to produce multiword utterances than in a less structured free play setting.

2.1.2. Lexical Diversity: Type-Token Ratio

In the past, philosophers, linguists, and others interested in children's vocabularies kept handwritten records of the speech produced by children. Because of the time and labor involved, such records tended to concentrate on one child at a time and often recorded only the child's first use of a particular word, new applications of an old word, or incorrect uses of a word. While diary studies are still an important source of information about children's lexical development (see, for example, Dale, Reznick, & Morisset, 1989; Goldfield & Reznick, 1990), the advent of audiotape recording devices has permitted researchers to record entire stretches of speech for later transcription and analysis. Based on such transcripts, researchers are then able to catalogue the individual words a child produced in a particular speech sample and the number of times she produced each of those words. This information may be used to generate what is called a **Type-Token Ratio (TTR)** for the child's speech sample. Type-Token Ratio (Templin, 1957) is perhaps the most widely used measure of lexical diversity. It is computed by dividing the number of **different** words used by a speaker by the **total** number of words the speaker produced in the speech sample. For example, a child who produced 58 different words and a total of 109 words in a given sample, would have a type-token ratio of 58/109 or 0.532 for that speech sample. Recently, some researchers have begun using number of word types per 50 utterances (Miller, 1981) or per unit of time as an alternative to traditional Type-Token Ratios (see Richards, 1987, for a discussion of the sensitivity of TTR to sample size).

Issues in Computing Type-Token Ratios

In order for Type-Token Ratios computed by one researcher to be comparable to those computed by another, it is of course important that both use the same criteria for counting words. Some of the issues that must be decided include how to deal with inflected forms of stems, contractions, and hyphenated forms. For example, are *look* and *looked* to be counted as two different word **types** or as two

tokens of a single word type? How are contractions such as *I've* and *I'm* to be counted? Because Type-Token Ratios are intended to give some indication of the child's lexical diversity or vocabulary use, many researchers choose not to count inflected forms and contractions as different word types. Templin (1957, p. 15) outlines the criteria she used for counting such things as contractions, hyphenated and compound words, and expressions that function as a single form for the child.

2.1.3. Conversational Participation: Mean Length of Turn

Conversational skill is one area of language development for which there are few sensitive assessment tools. However, a number of researchers (e.g., Snow, 1977) have used **MLT** or **mean length of turn** as a rough measure of conversational participation. The idea is that, as children become more proficient conversational partners, they begin to shoulder more of the conversational load and take turns that are more comparable in length to those of their adult partners. The child's MLT (usually, expressed as mean number of words per turn) is interpreted relative to the MLT of her conversational partner. Factors which might be expected to influence MLT include the type of conversation being carried on and the child's familiarity with her adult partner.

2.1.4. Research Goals

In the sections that follow, I describe how CLAN was used to generate the four measures of spontaneous language production discussed above for a group of normally developing children at 20 months. The goals were (a) to use data from a sizeable sample of normally developing children to inform us as to the average (mean) performance and degree of variation (standard deviation) among children at this age on each measure; and (b) to explore whether individual children's performance relative to their peers was constant across domains. That is, were children whose MLU was low relative to their peers also low in terms of lexical diversity and conversational participation? Conversely, were children with relatively advanced syntactic skills as measured by MLU also relatively advanced in terms of lexical diversity and the share of the conversational load they assumed?

2.2. Method

2.2.1. Subjects

The speech samples analyzed here were taken from the New England corpus (Dale, Reznick, & Morisset, 1989; Snow, 1989) of the CHILDES database, which includes longitudinal data on 52 normally-developing children.[3] Spontaneous speech of the children in interaction with their mothers was collected in a play setting when the children were 14, 20, and 30 months of age. Transcripts were prepared according to the CHAT conventions of the Child Language Data Exchange System, including conventions for morphemicizing speech, such that MLU could be computed in terms of morphemes rather than words. Data were available for 48 of the 52 children at 20 months. The means and standard deviations for MLU5, TTR, and MLT reported below are based on these 48 children. Because only 33 of the 48 children produced 50 or more utterances during the observation session at 20 months, the mean and standard deviation for MLU50 is based on 33 subjects. For illustrative purposes here, I discuss 5 children: the child whose MLU was the highest for the group, the child whose MLU was the lowest, and one child each at the first, second, and third quartiles. Transcripts for these 5 children at 20 months can be found in the **20mos** subdirectory under the **NEngland** directory. The file names are of the form **kidxxxb.cha**, where xxx is the child's subject number, the letter **b** represents the second (i.e., 20-month) data point, and the file extension **.cha** indicates that the files are in CHAT format.

2.2.2. CLAN Procedure

Our goal was to compile the following basic measures for each of the five target children: MLU on 50 utterances, MLU of the five longest utterances, TTR, and MLT. We then compared these five children to their peers by generating z-scores based on the means and standard deviations for the available sample for each measure at 20 months. In this way, we were able to generate language profiles for each of our five target children.

---

[3] Transcripts in the New England corpus will continue to be enriched and updated after publication of this manual. Performing the analyses described here on updated files may result in slightly different results than those reported for illustrative purposes here.

MLU

The first CLAN analysis we performed was to calculate MLU for each child on a sample of 50 utterances. By default, the MLU program excludes the strings **xxx, yyy, www,** as well as any string immediately preceded by one of the following symbols: **0, &, +, –, #, $,** or **:** (see the CHILDES manual for a description of CHAT transcription conventions). The MLU program also excludes from all counts material in angle brackets followed by **[/], [//],** or **[% bch]** (see the CHILDES manual for list of symbols CLAN considers to be word, morpheme, or utterance delimiters). Remember that to perform any CLAN analysis, you need to be in the directory where your data is when you issue the appropriate CLAN command. The command string we used to compute MLU for all five children is listed in Command Box 2.1.

mlu +t*CHI +z50u +f *.cha

+t*CHI	Analyze the child speaker tier only
+z50u	Analyze the first 50 utterances only
+f	Save the results in a file
*.cha	Analyze all files ending with the extension **.cha**

Command Box 2.1

The only constraint on order of elements in a CLAN command is that the name of the program to be used (here, MLU) come first. Many users find it good practice to put the name of the file on which the analysis is to be performed last, so that they can tell at a glance both what program was used and what file(s) were analyzed. Other elements may come in any order.

Note that the string **+t*CHI** tells CLAN that we want only CHI speaker tiers considered in the analysis. Were we to omit this string, a composite MLU would be computed for all speakers in the file. The string **+z50u** tells CLAN to compute MLU on only the child's first 50 utterances. We could, of course, have specified the child's first 100 utterances (**+z100u**) or utterances from the 51st through the 100th (**+z51u-100u**). With no **+z** option specified, MLU is computed on the entire file. The string **+f** tells CLAN that we want the output recorded in output files, rather than simply displayed on-screen. CLAN will create a separate output file for each

.cha file on which it computes MLU. If we wish, we may specify a three-letter file extension for the output files immediately following the +f option in the command line (for example, to remind ourselves that the output files generated by this command line include information about the child's MLU, we might specify the extension +fchm). If a specific file extension is not specified, CLAN will assign one automatically. In the case of MLU, the default extension is .mlu. Finally, the string *.cha tells CLAN to perform the analysis specified on each file ending in the extension .cha found in the current directory. To perform the analysis on a single file, we would specify the entire filename (e.g., kid068b.cha). It was possible to use the wildcard * in this and following analyses, rather than specifying each file separately, because:

1. all the files to be analyzed (and *only* those files) ended with the same file extension (in this case, .cha) and were in the same directory; and

2. in each file, the target child was identified by the same speaker code (i.e., CHI), thus allowing us to specify the child's tier by means of +t*CHI.

Utilization of wildcards whenever possible is not only more efficient than repeatedly typing in similar commands, but also cuts down on typing errors.

By default, CLAN computes MLU in morphemes, rather than words, *if* the transcript is *morphemicized* (see chapter 5 in MacWhinney, 1991). The user may override this default and have CLAN ignore morphemicization symbols by using the –c option, followed by those symbols to be ignored. For example, –c# would instruct CLAN to ignore the prefix symbol in words such as *un#tie*; –c#– would result in both the # and – symbols in *un#tie–ed* being disregarded. Thus, the researcher can choose not to count morphemes she believes the child is not yet using productively. To have all morphemicization symbols ignored, one would use –c#&–.

A little known fact about CLAN is that typing a program name on a command line by itself will result in a list of the options for that program. This is very helpful for planning analyses and minimizes the need to consult the manual repeatedly.

For illustrative purposes, let us suppose that we ran the above analysis on only a single child (by specifying **kid068b.cha**), rather than for all five children at once (by specifying ***.cha**). We would use the following command:

mlu +t*CHI +z50u kid068b.cha

The output for this command would be as follows:

```
MLU.EXE +t*CHI +z50U kid068b.cha
MLU.EXE (04-MAY-93) is conducting analyses on:
  ONLY speaker main tiers matching: *CHI;
*****************************************
From file <kid068b.cha>
MLU for Speaker: *CHI:
  MLU (xxx and yyy are EXCLUDED from the utterance and
  morpheme counts):
    Number of: utterances = 50, morphemes = 132
      Ratio of morphemes over utterances = 2.640
      Standard deviation = 1.480
```

Note that the MLU program reports the number of utterances (in this case, the 50 utterances we specified); the number of morphemes that occurred in those 50 utterances; the ratio of morphemes over utterances (**MLU in morphemes**); and the standard deviation of utterance length in morphemes. The standard deviation statistic gives some indication of how variable the child's utterance length is. This child's average utterance is 2.64 morphemes long, with a standard deviation of 1.48 morphemes.

Check line 1 of the output for typing errors in entering the command string. Check lines 3 and possibly 4 of output to be sure the proper speaker tier and input file(s) were specified. Also check to be sure that the number of utterances or words reported is what was specified in the command line. If CLAN finds fewer utterances or words than the number specified with the +z option, it will still run the analysis but will report the actual number of utterances or words analyzed.

MLU of Five Longest Utterances

The next CLAN analysis we performed was to compute the mean length in morphemes of each child's five longest utterances. To do this, we directed the output of one program to a second program for further analysis. This process is called **piping**. Although we could have accomplished the same goal by running the first program on each file, sending the output to files and then performing the second analysis on the output files, piping is more efficient. The tradeoff is that the analysis must be done on one file at a time (by specifying the full filename), rather than by using the * wildcard. The CLAN command string we used was:

maxwd +t*CHI +g1 +c5 +d1 kid068b.cha | mlu > kid068b.ml5

+t*CHI	Analyze the child speaker tier only
+g1	Identify the longest utterances in terms of morphemes
+c5	Identify the five longest utterances
+d1	Output the data in CHAT format
kid068b.cha	The child language transcript to be analyzed
| mlu	Pipe the output to the MLU program
> kid068b.ml5	Redirect the output to a file named **kid068b.ml5**

Command Box 2.2

The string **+g1** tells MAXWD to identify longest utterances in terms of **morphemes** per utterance. If length is to be determined instead by the number of **words** per utterance, the string **+g2** would be used; if by number of **characters** per utterance, **+g3** would be used. The string **+c5** tells MAXWD to identify the **five** longest utterances. The string **+d1** tells MAXWD to send output to the output file in CHAT form, that is, in a form that can be analyzed by other CLAN programs. The piping symbol | (upright bar or vertical hyphens) separates the first CLAN command from the second, and indicates that the output of the first command is to be used as the input to the second. Finally, the redirect symbol > followed by the output filename and extension specifies where the final output file is to be directed (i.e., saved). Omission of the redirect symbol and filename will result in output being displayed on-screen rather than recorded in a file. Here we are specifying that the output from MLU be recorded in an output file called **kid068b.ml5**. The contents of this file are as follows:

```
MLU (xxx and yyy are EXCLUDED from the utterance and
morpheme counts):
    Number of: utterances = 5, morphemes = 31
        Ratio of morphemes over utterances = 6.200
        Standard deviation = 0.748
```

> The procedure for obtaining output files in CHAT format differs from program to program but it is always the **+d** option that performs this operation. You must check the **+d** options for each program to determine the exact level of the **+d** option that is required.

Type-Token Ratio

The third CLAN analysis we performed for each child was to compute Type-Token Ratio. For this we used the program FREQ. By default, FREQ ignores the strings **xxx** (unintelligible speech) and **www** (irrelevant speech researcher chose not to transcribe). It also ignores words beginning with the symbols **0**, **&**, +, –, or **#**. Here we were interested not in whether the child uses plurals or past tenses, but how many different vocabulary items she used. Therefore, we wanted to count **cats** and **cat** as two tokens (i.e., instances) of the word-type **cat**. Similarly, we wanted to count **play** and **played** as two tokens under the word-type **play**. When computation is done by hand, the researcher can exercise judgment "on line" to decide whether a particular string of letters should be counted as a word type. Automatic computation, however, is much more literal: Any unique string will be counted as a separate word type. In order to have inflected forms counted as tokens of the uninflected stem (rather than as different word types), we **morphemicized** inflected forms in transcribing (see chapter 5 in MacWhinney, 1991). That is, we transcribed **cats** as **cat–s** and **played** as **play–ed**. Using our morphemicized transcripts, we then instructed FREQ to ignore anything that followed a hyphen (–) within a word. The command string used was:

Basic Measures 41

freq +t*CHI +s"*-%%" +f *.cha

+t*CHI	Analyze the child speaker only
+s"*-%%"	Ignore the hyphen and subsequent characters
+f	Save output in a file
*.cha	Analyze all files ending with the extension .cha

Command Box 2.3

The only new element in this command is **+s"*-%%"**. The +s option tells FREQ to search for and count certain strings. Here we asked that in its search, FREQ ignore any hyphen that occurred within a word, as well as whatever followed the hyphen. In this way, FREQ produced output in which inflected forms of nouns and verbs were not counted as separate word types, but rather as tokens of the uninflected form. The TTR output generated from the **kid068b.cha** file for this analysis was as follows:

```
   85  Total number of different word types used
  233  Total number of words (tokens)
0.365  Type/Token ratio
```

Mean Length of Turn

The final analysis we performed for each child was to compute MLT (Mean Length of Turn) for both child and mother. Note that unlike the MLU program, the CLAN program MLT includes the symbols **xxx** and **yyy** in all counts. Thus, utterances that consist of only unintelligible vocal material still constitute turns, as do nonverbal turns indicated by the postcode **[+ trn]** as illustrated in the following example:

```
*CHI:    Ø. [+ trn]
%gpx:    CHI points to picture in book
```

Using the CLAN program MLT, we computed MLT first for the child and then for the mother:

mlt +t*CHI kid068b.cha
mlt +t*MOT kid068b.cha

+t*CHI	Analyze the child speaker tier only
+t*MOT	Analyze the mother speaker tier only
kid068b.cha	The child language transcript to be analyzed

Command Box 2.4

The output generated by the second command above was:

```
MLT.EXE +t*MOT kid068b.cha
MLT.EXE (04-MAY-93) is conducting analyses on:
   ONLY speaker main tiers matching: *MOT;
****************************************
From file <kid068b.cha>
MLT (xxx and yyy are INCLUDED in the utterance and morpheme
counts):
    Number of: utterances = 330, turns = 228, words = 1398
        Ratio of words over turns = 6.132
        Ratio of utterances over turns = 1.447
        Ratio of words over utterances = 4.236
```

Note that the output allows us to consider Mean Length of Turn either in terms of words per turn or utterances per turn. We chose to use words per turn in calculating the ratio of child MLT to mother MLT, reasoning that words per turn is likely to be sensitive for a somewhat longer developmental period. MLT ratio, then, was calculated as the ratio of child MLT to mother MLT:

$$\text{MLT ratio} = \text{CHI MLT} \div \text{MOT MLT}$$

As the child begins to assume a more equal share of the conversational load, the MLT ratio should approach 1.00. For this example, the MLT ratio would be:

$$2.243 \div 6.132 = 0.366$$

Generating Language Profiles

Once we had computed these basic measures of utterance length, lexical diversity, and conversational participation for our five target children, we wanted to see how each child compared to his or her peers in each of these domains. To do this, we used the means and standard deviations for each measure for the whole New England sample at 20 months (see Table 2.2) to generate z-scores for each of our five target children. Z-scores, or standard scores, are computed by subtracting each child's score on a particular measure from the group mean and then dividing the result by the overall standard deviation:

$$(\text{child's score} - \text{group mean}) \div \text{standard deviation}$$

The resulting z-scores for each target child are shown in Table 2.3. We then plotted the scores for each subject to generate the language profiles shown in Figure 2.2.

2.3. Results and Discussion

The means, standard deviations, and ranges given in Table 2.2 allowed us to begin to address our first research goal, which was to index the syntactic, lexical, and conversational abilities of normally developing 20-month-olds. In addition to the figures given in the table, however, we need also to consider the shape of the distribution of scores for these measures. For example, while the sample mean for MLU50 was 1.41, univariate analysis indicated that the distribution of MLU50 scores was quite skewed, with the majority of children who produced at least 50 utterances falling in the MLU range of 1.00-1.20. As noted earlier, 15 of the 48 children failed to produce even 50 utterances. At this age, then, the majority of children in

Table 2.2: Means, standard deviations, and ranges for the basic measures for the New England sample at 20 months.

Measure	Mean	SD	Range
MLU50	1.400	0.400	1.02-2.64
MLU5 longest	2.848	1.310	1.00-6.20
TTR	0.433	0.102	0.266-0.621
MLT Ratio	0.246	0.075	0.126-0.453

44   Chapter 2

Table 2.3:   Z-scores for the five target children at 20 months.

Subject	MLU50	MLU5	TTR	MLT Ratio
kid098b	-0.95	-1.11	-0.55	0.31
kid055b	-0.70	-0.65	-0.15	-0.94
kid066b	-0.25	-0.19	-0.68	-1.14
kid014b	0.10	0.12	1.84	-0.90
kid068b	3.10	2.56	-0.67	1.60

the sample are essentially still at the one-word stage, producing few utterances of more than one word or morpheme. Like MLU50, the shape of the distributions for MLU5 and for MLT ratio were also somewhat skewed toward the lower end, though not as severely as was MLU50.

Turning now to our second research question, let us examine the language profiles generated for each of our 5 target children at 20 months (Figure 2.2). These profiles will give us a rough snapshot of how each child's skills in each domain compare with those of his or her peers at the same age. Because all 5 of the target children, as well as the larger group of 48, were chosen in part based on the fact that they were developing language normally, We would not expect to see radical departures from the group means on any of the measures. For the most part, this expectation is borne out: we do not see departures greater than 2 standard deviations from the mean on any measure for any of the 5 children, except for the particularly high MLU50 and MLU5 observed for Subject 068.

It is not the case, however, that all five of our target children have "flat" profiles. As is immediately obvious from Figure 2.2, some children show marked strengths or weaknesses relative to their peers in particular domains. For example, Subject 014, while very close to the mean in terms of utterance length (MLU50 and MLU5), shows marked strength in lexical diversity (TTR), even though she shoulders relatively little of the conversational burden (as measured by MLT ratio). The strengths of Subject 068, on the other hand, appear to be primarily in the area of syntax (at least as measured by MLU50 and MLU5); her performance on both the lexical and conversational measures (i.e., TTR and MLT ratio) is only mediocre. The subjects at the second and third quartile in terms of MLU (Subject 055 and Subject 066) do have profiles that are relatively flat: Their z-scores on each measure fall

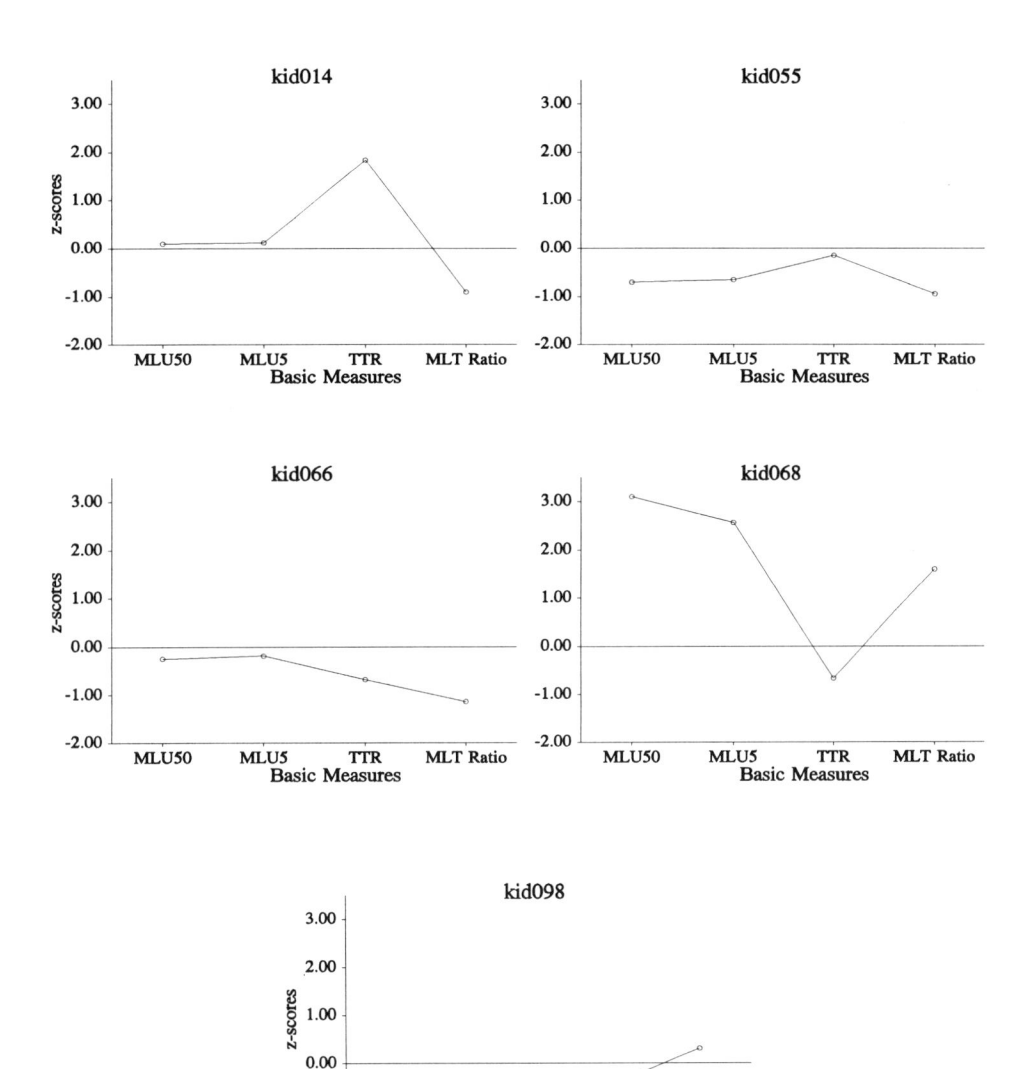

Figure 2.2: Cross-domain profiles for 5 children from the New England sample at 20 months. Plotted scores are z-scores based on means and standard deviations for the entire sample.

between −1 and 0. However, the child with the lowest MLU50 (Subject 098) again shows an uneven profile. Despite her limited production, she manages to bear her portion of the conversational load. You will recall that unintelligible vocalizations transcribed as **xxx** or **yyy**, as well as nonverbal turns indicated by the postcode **[+ trn]**, are all counted in computing MLT. Therefore, it is possible that many of this child's turns consisted of unintelligible vocalizations or nonverbal gestures.

What we have seen in examining the profiles for these five children is that even among normally developing children, different children may have strengths in different domains, relative to their age mates. For illustrative purposes here I have considered only three domains, as measured by four indices. In order to get a more detailed picture of a child's language production, we might choose to include other indices, or to further refine the measures we use. For example, we might compute TTR based on a particular number of words, or we might time-sample by examining the number of word types and word tokens the child produced in a given number of minutes of mother-child interaction. We might also consider other measures of conversational competence, such as number of child initiations and responses; fluency measures, such as number of retraces or hesitations; or pragmatic measures, such as variety of speech acts produced. Computation of some of these measures would require that codes be entered into the transcript prior to analysis; however, the CLAN analyses themselves would, for the most part, simply be variations on the techniques I have discussed in this chapter. In the exercises that follow, you will have an opportunity to use these techniques to perform analyses on these five children at both 20 months and 30 months.

2.4. Exercises

The files needed for the following exercises are in two directories: transcripts for the five target children at 20 months are in the **20mos** subdirectory under the **NEngland** directory; transcripts for four of the five target children at 30 months are in the **30mos** directory (Note: No data are available for kid014 at 30 months).

2.4.1. Compute the length in morphemes of each target child's **single** longest utterance at 20 months. Compare with the MLU of the five longest utterances. Consider why a researcher might want to use MLU of the five longest rather than MLU of the single longest utterance.

2.4.2. Use the +z option to compute TTR on each child's first 50 **words** at 30 months. Then do the same for each successive 50-word band up to 300. (note: Check the output each time to be sure that 50 words were in fact found. If you specify a range of 50 words where there are fewer than 50 words available in the file, FREQ still performs the analysis, but the output will show the actual number of tokens found.) What do you observe about the stability of TTR across different samples of 50 words?

2.4.3. Use the MLU and FREQ programs to examine the mother's language to her child at 20 months and at 30 months. (note: The mother's speaker code is ***MOT**.) What do you observe about the length/complexity and lexical diversity of the mother's speech to her child? Do they remain generally the same across time or change as the child's language develops? If you observe change, how can it be characterized?

2.5. Suggested Projects

2.5.1. Perform the same analyses for the four target children for whom data are available at age 30 months. Use the data in Table 2.4 to compute z-scores for each target child on each measure (MLU 50 utterances, MLU of five longest utterances, TTR, MLT ratio). Then plot profiles for each of the target children at 30 months. What consistencies and inconsistencies do you see from 20 to 30 months? Which children, if any, have similar profiles at both ages? Which children's profiles change markedly from 20 to 30 months?

2.5.2. Conduct a case study of a child you know to explore whether type of activity and/or interlocutor affect Mean Length of Turn. Videotape the child and mother

Table 2.4: Means, standard deviations, and ranges for the basic measures for the New England sample at 30 months.

Measure	Mean	SD	Range
MLU50	2.317	0.664	1.40-3.94
MLU5 longest	7.850	3.539	3.40-23.00
TTR	0.355	0.062	0.231-0.476
MLT Ratio	0.488	0.200	0.171-1.183

engaged in two different activities (e.g., bookreading, having a snack together, playing with a favorite toy). On another occasion, videotape the child engaged in the same activities with an unfamiliar adult. If it is not possible to videotape, you may audiotape and supplement with contextual notes. Transcribe the interactions in CHAT format. You may wish to put each activity in a separate file (or see CHILDES manual for how to use CLAN program GEM). Compare the MLT ratio for each activity and adult-child pair. Describe any differences you observe.

References

Bates, E., Bretherton, I., & Snyder, I. (1988). *From first words to grammar: Individual differences and dissociable mechanisms*. New York: Cambridge University Press.

Bennett, C.W., James, C.C., & Prosek, R.A. (1991). *Relationship between mean length of utterance and upper morpheme boundary*. Paper presented at the annual meeting of the American Speech-Language-Hearing Association in Atlanta, GA.

Brown, R. (1973). *A first language: The early stages*. Cambridge, MA: Harvard University Press.

Cowan, P.A., Weber, J., Hoddinott, & Klein, J. (1967). Mean length of spoken response as a function of stimulus, experimenter, and subject. *Child Development, 38*, 191-203.

Crystal, D. (1974). Review of Brown, R., *A first language*. *Journal of Child Language, 1*, 289-306.

Crystal, D., Fletcher, P., & Garman, M. (1976). *The grammatical analysis of language disability: A procedure for assessment and remediation*. New York: Elsevier-North Holland Publishing Co.

Dale, P., Bates, E., Reznick, S., & Morisset, C. (1989). The validity of a parent report instrument. *Journal of Child Language, 16*, 239-249.

Goldfield, B. A., & Reznick, J.S. (1990). Early lexical acquisition: Rate, content, and the vocabulary spurt. *Journal of Child Language, 17*, 171-183.

Klee, T., & Fitzgerald, M. (1985). The relation between grammatical development and MLU in morphemes. *Journal of Child Language, 12*, 251-269.

Kramer, C.A., James, S. L., & Saxman, J. H. (1979). A comparison of language samples elicited at home and in the clinic. *Journal of Speech and Hearing Disorders, 44*, 321-330.

Lee, L. (1974). *Developmental sentence analysis.* Evanston, IL: Northwestern University Press.

McCarthy, D. (1954). Language development in children. In L. Carmichael (Ed.), *Manual of child psychology* (2nd ed.). New York: Wiley & Sons.

Miller, J. (1981). *Assessing language production in children: Experimental procedures.* Baltimore: University Park Press.

Pan, B.A., & Elkins, K. (1989). *An alternative measure of morphological development in young children's spontaneous speech.* Paper presented to the New England Child Language Association, Boston, MA.

Richards, B. (1987). Type/token ratios: What do they really tell us? *Journal of Child Language, 14,* 201-209.

Rollins, P.R., Pan, B.A., & Snow, C.E. (1991). *Phrase saturation as a measure of morphological skills.* Paper presented at the annual meeting of the American Speech-Language-Hearing Association in Atlanta, GA.

Rondal, J.A., Ghiotto, M., Bredart, S., & Bachelet, J. (1987). Age-relation, reliability and grammatical validity of measures of utterance length. *Journal of Child Language, 14,* 433-446.

Scarborough, H. (1990). Index of Productive Syntax. *Applied Psycholinguistics, 11,* 1-22.

Scarborough, H., Rescorla, L., Tager-Flusberg, H., Fowler, A., & Sudhalter, V. (1991). The relation of utterance length to grammatical complexity in normal and language-disordered groups. *Applied Psycholinguistics, 12,* 23-46.

Scarborough, H., Wyckoff, J., & Davidson, R. (1986). A reconsideration of the relation between age and mean utterance length. *Journal of Speech and Hearing Research, 29,* 394-399.

Snow, C.E. (1977). The development of conversation between mothers and babies. *Journal of Child Language, 4,* 1-22.

Snow, C.E. (1989). Imitativeness: Trait or skill? In G. Speidel & K.E. Nelson (Eds.), *The many faces of imitation in language learning.* New York: Springer-Verlag.

Templin, M.C. (1957). *Certain language skills in children.* Minneapolis: University of Minnesota Press.

Wells, G. (1985). *Language development in the pre-school years.* Cambridge: Cambridge University Press.

3 The Babytalk Register: Parents' Use of Diminutives

*Jean Berko Gleason, Rivka Y. Perlmann,
Richard Ely, and David W. Evans*
Boston University

In this chapter you will learn the following skills:

- To use the CLAN programs FREQ, MLU, and COMBO to answer questions about the use of diminutives.

- To create include files to generate data on diminutives in parents' speech.

- To utilize file management techniques (file renaming and the use of wild cards) to help organize the data by gender of parent and child.

To replicate the analyses and to do the exercises, you will need the files called **kid010b.cha**, **kid025b.cha**, and **suffix.dim** in the **gleason** directory.

3.1. Introduction

This chapter focuses on some of the lexical features of input language to children that characterize the speech register known as *babytalk*. Our goal in this chapter is to illuminate the use of computerized methods in the study of a particular characteristic of the babytalk register, the use of diminutives. Our study of diminutives in parents' speech to children was guided by an interactive view of the language acquisition process, as well as by the larger theoretical framework of sociolinguistics.

The chapter is organized as follows: First, we place our study of diminutives in context by briefly describing our theoretical framework. We then introduce our own study of diminutives in the speech of mothers and fathers, laying out a set of research questions that draw on our theoretical framework. Our Method and Results sections introduce readers to those computer programs in CLAN specially suited to addressing these research questions. Finally, we present a series of exercises and suggested projects for readers wishing to try their hand at performing these analyses.

3.1.1. Background

Sociolinguistic studies have demonstrated that communicatively competent speakers vary their speech according to the participants' roles, the situation, the topic, and the medium of communication (Ervin-Tripp, 1969; Hymes, 1974; Ure & Ellis, 1972). These systematic variations in speech are termed *registers*.

Ferguson (1977) described the babytalk register as one of a set of simplified registers available for use in addressing babies as well as others, such as foreigners or nursing home residents, who are perceived as less linguistically competent. Ferguson described three characteristics of the babytalk register: simplification (e.g., omitting inflections or replacing pronouns with proper names); clarification (e.g., speaking slowly, with clear pronunciation and many repetitions); and the expression of positive affect through the use of intonation and hypocoristic, or diminutive, affixes, which convey endearment.

Diminutives are termed *hypocoristics* (from the Greek words *koros* 'boy', *kore* 'girl', and the verb *korizesthai* 'to caress'). Use of the hypocoristic carries with it the parent's own world view: The ending implies both approval and affection. For example, parents say *that's a bunny*, but are unlikely to point at an insect on the wall and say *look at the roachie*.

Diminutives are a commonly noted feature of babytalk. Their derivation from standard words reflects structural linguistic, as well as social and affective, processes. Ferguson (1964) and others (Bynon, 1968; Casagrande, 1948; Crawford, 1970; Dil, 1975; Gleason & Réger, 1985; Goldman, 1987; Kelkar, 1964; Ruķe-Dravina, 1977; Stoel-Gammon, 1976) have provided rich data on babytalk in cross-cultural perspective. Whereas some languages (e.g., Latvian) have a rich repertoire of diminutives in both adult speech and babytalk, English relies heavily on the hypocoristic ending *–y/ie*, as in *dog → doggy*, *foot → footie*, and to a slight extent on suffixes such as *–kin*, as in *babykin*, *–ette* as in *kitchenette*, and *–ling* as in *duckling*. Ferguson speculates that the characteristic babytalk suffix may play a role in the acquisition of grammar, since it may be the first morphological marker noted and manipulated by the child.

52 Chapter 3

The study of the social and affective meanings conveyed by the use of diminutives is particularly relevant to a sociolinguistic perspective. The process of socialization itself may be marked by variation in the use of diminutives depending, for example, on the age and gender of the child and the gender of the caretaker.

3.1.2. Research Questions

This study explores these sociolinguistic dimensions in the use of diminutives by examining parents' use of diminutives with their daughters and sons during spontaneous conversation in playtime situations. The targets of our investigation were conventional babytalk words, such as *doggy*, *kitty*, *bitty*, *duckie*, *bunny*, *lovey*, and *tummy*, as well as innovations, such as *ballie* or *shirtie*, which are inspired by ongoing activities. In particular, we address the following set of questions:

1. Is parents' use of diminutives when speaking with infants and small children pervasive? Perhaps our belief that diminutives abound in parents' speech is based upon a stereotypic view.

2. Is there a greater tendency for mothers or for fathers to use diminutives? Other work, both psychological and linguistic in nature (Gilligan, 1982; Lakoff, 1975), might lead us to hypothesize that women would use more diminutives in their speech. Diminutives might, for instance, be a lexical feature of the female register, or they might reflect greater psychological willingness to express warmth or affection on the part of mothers.

3. Do little girls hear more diminutives than little boys? If they do, this would support the view that girls and boys are not only treated differently, but that speech to girls contains more positive affect, and is kinder and gentler. In a previous study (Perlmann & Gleason, 1990), we found, for instance, that mothers were more likely to say *no* to their infant sons and to use more indirect ways of deflecting their daughters from prohibited activities. Dunn, Bretherton, and Munn (1987) found that mothers use more words referring to feelings when conversing with their infant daughters than with sons.

4. What kinds of patterns of diminutive use can we describe over time? At what ages does the use of diminutives begin to decrease, and what kinds of terms

tend to remain? Further, are there gender differences over time in the kinds of words used by fathers and mothers to girls and boys?

5. What is the ratio of use of a standardized form of a particular word (e.g., *rabbit*) versus its diminutive form (*bunny*)? How does this ratio change over time?

3.2. Method

3.2.1. Subjects

Subjects were 88 parents in two subject groups. The first group consisted of 40 middle-class mothers who were recorded in a laboratory play and book reading situation with their infants at two points in time: When the infants were 14 months and when they were 20 months old. A subset of 22 of these mothers were recorded with their children at 30 months.

The second group of subjects consisted of middle-class parents of a somewhat older sample of 24 children between the ages of 2 and 5 who were also recorded in a book reading and play situation. There were two sessions for each child, one with the father and one with the mother. For both groups of subjects, interactions took place in a laboratory playroom and were audio- and video-recorded.

The data for both groups of subjects were drawn from CHILDES (Child Language Data Exchange System; see MacWhinney & Snow, 1990), where they are referred to as the New England corpus (Dale, Bates, Resznick, & Morisset, 1989; Snow, 1989), and the Gleason corpus (Gleason, 1980), respectively.

3.2.2. CLAN Tools

In the following sections we proceed by first providing a general description of three CLAN programs: FREQ, MLU, and COMBO. Within each program, those features most relevant for our analyses will be highlighted. We then demonstrate how these programs were used to address each of the research questions in our study. In our general sketch of the CLAN programs, we also include a description of several techniques we used in managing our data files. A sample file of a 20-

month-old girl from the New England corpus is used to illustrate each of the CLAN programs. This file is referred to as our **replication file** and its name is **kid010b.cha**. By following the instructions provided in the following sections, you will able to replicate the commands that use the **kid010b.cha** file. The Results section describes the results obtained from analyses performed on the whole data base.

FREQ

The FREQ program counts, or derives the frequencies, of words or strings of characters. In its simplest mode, it generates a list of all the words in a transcript along with the frequency with which they occur. We can also ask FREQ to find the frequency of a particular word (e.g., the pronoun *you*), or set of words (e.g., color terms or pronouns) or character strings (e.g., speech act codes like $IMIT, referring to utterances coded as imitations, or $YN, referring to utterances coded as responses to Yes/No questions). This is done by using what is called an **include file** (described in more detail later). Finally, we can limit the analysis to a particular speaker or tier. Command 3.1 will cause the FREQ program to generate a list of all the words and their respective frequencies from the mother's tier (**+t*MOT**) from our replication file, which we named **kid010b.cha**.

freq +t*MOT kid010b.cha

+t*MOT	Analyze the mother speaker tier only
kid010b.cha	The child language transcript to be analyzed

Command Box 3.1

A portion of the outcome of this command looks like this:

```
    23 a
     2 about
     2 ahead
     4 all
    12 all+right
     1 already
     1 and
     4 are
```

The wordlist is printed in alphabetical order and some summary statistics are provided at the end. Thus, the end of this file looks like this:

```
    27  yeah
    36  you
     1  you-'re
     5  your
     1  zoo
-------------------------------
   198  Total number of different word types used
   773  Total number of words (tokens)
 0.256  Type/Token ratio
```

To avoid having the results or output flash across the screen at an unreadable rate, we can add the **+f** option. This tells the computer to save the results in a file, which it will automatically name **kid010b.frq**. A second possibility is to use the option **+fmot**, which would give the file the **mot** extension (e.g., **kid010b.mot**). Or a third possibility would be to direct the output to a file that you yourself name by using the **>** symbol. The following command would send the same results or output to a file named **rep.frq**.

freq +t*MOT kid010b.cha > rep.frq

+t*MOT	Analyze the mother speaker tier only
kid010b.cha	The child language transcript to be analyzed
> rep.frq	Redirect the output to the file **rep.frq**

Command Box 3.2

MLU

The MLU program is used primarily to determine the mean length of utterance of a specified speaker. However, it also provides additional information, including the total number of utterances, as well as the total number of morphemes in a file. The following command would perform an MLU analysis on the mother's tier (**+t*MOT**) from the file **kid010b.cha**.

56   Chapter 3

mlu +t*MOT kid010b.cha

+t*MOT	Analyze the mother speaker tier only
kid010b.cha	The child language transcript to be analyzed

Command Box 3.3

The output from this command looks like this:

```
MLU.EXE +t*MOT kid010b.cha
MLU.EXE (04-MAY-93) is conducting analyses on:
  ONLY speaker main tiers matching: *MOT;
*****************************************
From file <kid010b.cha>
MLU for Speaker: *MOT:
MLU (xxx and yyy are EXCLUDED from the utterance and
morpheme counts):
   Number of: utterances = 273, morphemes = 873
      Ratio of morphemes over utterances = 3.198
      Standard deviation = 2.208
```

Thus, we have the mother's MLU or ratio of morphemes over utterances (3.292) and her total number of utterances (264).

COMBO

COMBO is a powerful program that searches the data for specified combinations of words or character strings. For example, COMBO will find instances where a speaker says both *bunny* and *rabbit* within a single utterance. The following command would search the mother's tiers (**+t*MOT**) of the specified file (**kid010b.cha**) for utterances that contained the word *bunny* immediately followed by the word *rabbit*.

combo +t*MOT +s"bunny^rabbit" kid010b.cha

+t*MOT	Analyze the mother speaker tier only
+s"bunny^rabbit"	Search for strings beginning with *bunny* immediately followed by *rabbit*
kid010b.cha	The child language transcript to be analyzed

Command Box 3.4

Note that when searching for a particular combination of words with COMBO it is necessary to precede the combination with **+s** (e.g., **+s"bunny^rabbit"**) in the command line. The symbol ^ specifies that the word *rabbit* immediately follows the word *bunny*. A portion of the output of this use of COMBO (there are many other uses) would look like this:

```
COMBO.EXE  +t*MOT  +s"bunny^rabbit"  kid010b.cha
COMBO.EXE (04-MAY-93) is conducting analyses on:
  ONLY speaker main tiers matching: *MOT;
****************************************************

Strings matched 0 times
```

What this means is that when searching our replication file for the combination *bunny rabbit*, the CLAN program COMBO found none. A hypothetical file containing *bunny rabbit* would look like this:

```
****** line 190; file x
*MOT:   is the bunny rabbit jumping?
                     1

Strings matched 1 times
```

See the CHILDES manual (MacWhinney, 1991) for other uses of COMBO.

File Management

While many aspects of file management depend on the type of computer system you are using (PC compatible, Macintosh, UNIX), other aspects are found across most systems. Here, we will briefly describe two approaches to managing files: renaming and the use of wildcards.

58   Chapter 3

Renaming Files. Assuming that you are working with more than one transcript or file, you will need to be able to identify which transcripts or files you want any particular program to operate on. Let us say you have received the following files and placed them in your directory:

kid001b.cha	kid005b.cha
kid002b.cha	kid006b.cha
kid003b.cha	kid007b.cha
kid004b.cha	kid008b.cha

Note that there is no way of knowing the gender of the subject from the file identification number. If you are interested in analyses based on the child's gender (as we were), it would be useful to be able to identify files by gender of child. This would allow you to run a CLAN program on files with girls, then files with boys, and compare the respective outcomes.

If you do not already know the child's gender, it may be necessary to read the beginning lines, or header tiers, of each file. The fourth line of our replication file introduces information about the child's gender as follows: **@Sex of CHI**. Assume for now that we already know that subjects 1, 3, 4, and 8 (we have dropped the double 0s) are boys, and 2, 5, 6, and 7 are girls. Using the technique appropriate to your computer system, rename the files. Your directory would then look like this:

kid001b.boy	kid005b.grl
kid002b.grl	kid006b.grl
kid003b.boy	kid007b.grl
kid004b.boy	kid008b.boy

Another way of doing this is to change the prefixes from **kidxxxb** to **kidxxxbb** for boy and **kidxxxbg** for girl. With this file-naming convention, the string **kid*bb.cha** would only match the files for the boys.

Use of Wildcards. With files now identified by child gender, you can run CLAN programs on boys, girls, or both. To do this, you use what is called a *wildcard*. A wildcard uses the asterisk (*) as a symbol that stands for or takes the place of something else.[4] For example, if you used the following command while in the directory above, it would generate word frequency lists from the child's tier (+t*CHI, in this case just boys) from the 4 files, **kid001b.boy**, **kid003b.boy**, **kid004b.boy**, and **kid008b.boy**.

freq +t*CHI +ffrb *.boy

+t*CHI	Analyze the child speaker tier only
+ffrb	Save the results in a file with the extension **.frb**
*.boy	Analyze all files ending in **.boy**

Command Box 3.5

Because you used the +**ffrb** option, the output of this command would appear in the directory as four files named **kid001b.frb**, **kid003b.frb**, **kid004b.frb**, and **kid008b.frb**. In the case of the first file, the asterisk (*) took the place of the letters **kid**, the numbers **001** (e.g., **kid001**), and the letter **b** indicating a 20-month-old, that preceded the three-letter ending **.boy**, or *extension*, as it is more commonly called. Command 3.6 would perform a similar analysis on the four files with the extension **.grl**, the four female subjects, and generate four comparable output files with **.frg** extension. Using explicit extensions of the +**f** option helps to preserve the gender information in the **.frb** and **.frg** files.

freq +t*CHI +ffrg *.grl

+t*CHI	Analyze the child speaker tier only
+ffrg	Save the results in a file with the extension **.frg**
*.grl	Analyze all files ending in **.grl**

Command Box 3.6

Even though we have divided files by gender, we can still perform analyses on all subjects at the same time. Let us say we wanted to be able to report the total number of child utterances produced by all the children in our corpus. Recall that

---

[4] The asterisk is also used to mark speaker tiers, as in *CHI and *MOT, but this is a CHAT convention and has nothing to do with wild cards.

60   Chapter 3

MLU will generate information regarding number of utterances. To get the information we want we would enter the following command, which illustrates the use of a wildcard and demonstrates the function of the +u option:

mlu   +t*CHI   +u   kid*.boy   kid*.grl

+t*CHI	Analyze the child speaker tier only
+u	Merge all input files into a combined analysis
kid*.boy kid*.grl	Analyze all files beginning with **kid** and ending with either **.boy** or **.grl**

Command Box 3.7

Here we are asking the program MLU to do an analysis on the child tier (+t*CHI). The +u option directs the program to treat all the files on which it will perform analyses as if they were *one large file*. Thus the output will represent the total number of utterances from all the (pooled) files in our directory. The strings **kid*.boy** and **kid*.grl** direct the MLU program to find and analyze all files that begin with **kid** and end in either the **boy** or **grl** extension.[5] In our directory, that would mean the following 8 files:

kid001b.boy   kid005b.grl
kid002b.grl   kid006b.grl
kid003b.boy   kid007b.grl
kid004b.boy   kid008b.boy

However, if you had been running a series of analyses using the +f option, which automatically names output files based on their original name, your directory might contain, in addition to the eight data files above, files like **kid001b.frq** or **kid002b.frq**. If this were the case, and you entered the MLU command above using the string **kid*.***, you would get an error message that would announce that a particular file or files (e.g., **kid001b.frq**) was not in proper CHAT format. This is

---

[5] When working with PC compatible computers, which use DOS as the operating system, the format of file names and extensions is strictly regulated. This is less true for the Macintosh. Nevertheless, we would recommend that Macintosh users follow the DOS format, in order to expedite exchange of data files with users of PC compatible computers.

because this file contains output from a FREQ analysis and not text from a transcript. Use any of the strings **kid*.cha**, **kid*.boy**, or **kid*.grl** to avoid this.

Rather than overwrite files with the same extension (e.g., **.frq**), CLAN updates the version number of the file extension with each new analysis (e.g., **.fr0**, **.fr1**, ..., **.fr9**). For example, if a file name **kid010b.frq** already exists and you issue the command **freq +f kid010b.cha** then CLAN would save the results in a file called **kid010b.fr0**.

3.2.3. CLAN Procedures

Question 1: How pervasive is the use of diminutives?

To answer this question we had to determine a way of finding diminutives in parents' speech. We could perform a FREQ on the mothers' tier, for example, and read through the word frequency list that such a command would generate. However, in a study of 40 mother-infant dyads in a brief laboratory session, the frequency list totaled over 1,300 different words (Gleason et al., 1990). As an alternative, we elected to use our knowledge of the morphology of diminutives, specifically, the presence of the *–ie* and *–y* endings, to create what is called an **include file**. An include file is simply a list of words or characters (e.g., dashes, dots, or other symbols). As with all data on which CLAN runs, the list must be in a text (ASCII) format. This means that if you use a word processing program, you would have to save the file as unformatted text. In the include file, the list should begin on the first line, have only one word or string of characters per line, and each line should end with a carriage return. The contents of our include file, which we called **suffix.dim**, looked like this:

```
*ie
*ie-s
*ie-'s
*y
*y-s
*y-'s
*ie@*
*y@*
```

Note the use of the wildcard as well as the hyphens. The data that formed our corpus were morphemized – that is, each morpheme was individually transcribed – as illustrated below:

*MOT: see the birdie–'s egg–s?
*MOT: that–'is where a birdie live–es.

The morpheme that marks the possessive in *birdie's* is noted separately, as –'s, as is the plural –s of *eggs*. The @ symbol following a word is a CHAT transcription convention which marks the word, or the word ending, as a special form. Once created, the include file should be placed in the same directory as the data to be analyzed. The following command generated a list of all words from the mother (+t*MOT) that ended in –*ie* or –*y* (+s@suffix.dim) from all the data files (kid*.cha) in our directory.

freq   +t*MOT   +s@suffix.dim   +u   kid*.cha   >   firstry.frq

+t*MOT	Analyze the mother speaker tier only
+s@suffix.dim	Include the words from the file **suffix.dim**
+u	Merge all input files into a combined analysis
kid*.cha	Analyze all files beginning with **kid** and ending with the extension **.cha**
> firstry.frq	Redirect the output to the file **firstry.frq**

Command Box 3.8

The +s@ option directs the FREQ program to find all instances of those words whose endings correspond to those contained in our include file **suffix.dim**.[6] Again, the +u option directs the program to treat all files as if they were a single pooled file. The output of this command was directed to a file we named

---

[6] Note here that the @ symbol for CLAN programs is different from the @ symbol used in transcription in CHAT format. In CLAN, the @ symbol, used in conjunction with the +s option, tells the computer to find items contained in a specified include file. In CHAT, the @ symbol introduces tiers (e.g., *@Comment*) and is placed at the end of specialized word forms (e.g., for child specific forms like *guggie@c*).

firstry.frq. Of course, it included many words that were not diminutives, words like *every*, *lie*, and *say*. We then edited this list by removing all nondiminutives and renamed the file **real.dim**.[7] We then used the following commands (note the absence of the +u option):

```
freq  +t*MOT  +s@real.dim  kid*.boy  >  boydim.frq
freq  +t*MOT  +s@real.dim  kid*.grl  >  grldim.frq
```

+t*MOT	Analyze the mother speaker tier only
+s@real.dim	Include the words from the file **real.dim**
+u	Merge all input files into a combined analysis
kid*.boy	Analyze all files beginning with **kid** and ending with the extension **.boy**
kid*.grl	Analyze all files beginning with **kid** and ending with the extension **.grl**
> boydim.frq	Redirect the output to the file **boydim.frq**
> grldim.frq	Redirect the output to the file **grldim.frq**

Command Box 3.9

This generated *individualized* frequency lists of the diminutives contained in the **real.dim** include file for the subjects of both genders, respectively. By individualized, we mean that each subject's frequencies are noted separately, as can be seen in a portion of this output file below:

```
     1  birdie
     2  blankie
     3  bunny
     8  doggie
    10  kitty
     1  piggy
    -------------------------
     6  Total number of different word types used
    25  Total number of words (tokens)
 0.240  Type/Token ratio
```

---

[7] We also had to remove the numbers that preceded each word. Alternatively, we could have used the +d1 option in running the FREQ program. This would have generated a list of words only, omitting frequency counts.

64   Chapter 3

```
1   doggie
6   kitty
-----------------------------
2       Total number of different word types used
7       Total number of words (tokens)
0.286   Type/Token ratio
```

Thus, the first subject used the diminutive word *birdie* once, the word *blankie* twice; the second subject used *kitty* six times, and so on. If we had used the +u option in the commands above, the four male subject files would have been pooled and treated as one large file; the same would be true of the four female subject files. While the output totals produced by using the +u option would have been useful, we can get the same information by totaling our individualized data. Additionally, we need individual data to perform our statistical analyses.

Now let us run the same set of procedures on our replication file **kid010b.cha**. The following command will generate a list of all words ending with *–ie* or *–y* (as well as all other endings included in the **suffix.dim** include file) from the mother in our replication file. (A copy of the **suffix.dim** file can be found in the **gleason** directory.)

freq +t*MOT +s@suffix.dim kid010b.cha > firstry.frq

+t*MOT	Analyze the mother speaker tier only
+s@suffix.dim	Include the words from the file **suffix.dim**
kid010b.cha	The transcript to be analyzed
> firstry.frq	Redirect the output to the file **firstry.frq**

Command Box 3.10

A portion of the output file will look like this:

```
1   already
4   baby
1   blankie@
2   bunny
1   daddy
1   doggie
1   donkey
1   hey
```

By editing the list (to exclude all words ending in *–y* or *–ie* that are *not* diminutives: *already*, *baby*, *hey*, etc.), we get a list that contains all the diminutives used by the mother while playing and interacting with her 20-month-old girl in the laboratory. Here is the list you should end up with:

```
 1 blankie@
 2 bunny
 1 daddy
 1 doggie
 1 horsie@
 1 kitty
 1 kitty@f
11 mommy
 2 mommy-'s
```

With only one subject (our replication file **kid010b.cha**), there is no reason to make this list into an include file. However, with many subjects, you would want to proceed as we did earlier, by first generating a list of all diminutives used by all parents (using the **+u** option). This list could then be used as an include file (**real.dim** in our example) to determine the frequency of diminutives by *any* individual subject, or subgroup of subjects, in the corpus.

In sum, to address the first question we posed – how pervasive is the use of diminutives? – we needed to employ the various tools demonstrated in the preceding pages. These techniques enabled us to retrieve the diminutives parents used in speaking with their children, setting the stage for further analysis of diminutive use as posed by the next questions.

Questions 2 and 3: Is there a greater tendency for mothers or for fathers to use diminutives? Do girls hear more diminutives than boys?

To answer these questions we used our second set of data (the Gleason corpus), which included both fathers and mothers interacting with their children. These data were divided into two separate directories, one with mother-child dyads and the other with father-child dyads. Again, we renamed individual files, identifying them by gender of child. We used the following commands in the mother-child directory:

```
freq +t*MOT +s@real.dim kid*.boy > motboy.dim
freq +t*MOT +s@real.dim kid*.grl > motgrl.dim
```

and these commands in the father-child directory:

> freq +t*FAT +s@real.dim kid*.boy > fatboy.dim
> freq +t*FAT +s@real.dim kid*.grl > fatgrl.dim

Note that we did not have to worry about identifying the gender of the parent in the file name, as mother and father tiers are generally noted, by CHAT convention, as *MOT and *FAT. Also, we had already placed mother and father files in separate directories. The output of these files gave us individualized data, the raw frequencies of diminutives used by mothers to boys and girls, and fathers to boys and girls, respectively.

In order to account for differences in amount of speech across parents, we needed to determine how many utterances each parent produced. As we noted earlier, the MLU program generates this information. The following set of commands entered in the appropriate directories produced individualized data on numbers of parents' utterances:

> mlu +t*MOT kid*.boy > motboy.mlu
> mlu +t*MOT kid*.grl > motgrl.mlu
> mlu +t*FAT kid*.boy > fatboy.mlu
> mlu +t*FAT kid*.grl > fatgrl.mlu

Using a statistics program, we computed standardized frequencies for the number of diminutives per 100 utterances. We were then able to make comparisons by gender of parent and gender of child.

Question 4: What is the pattern of diminutive production in parents' speech over time, and does it vary according to child gender? What words are used and do they change over time?

The first portion of this question was answered using the New England corpus sample and the procedures outlined above in three separate directories, for mothers of 14-, 20-, and 30-month-old children. The second portion of the question was addressed by comparing frequency lists generated by the FREQ program with the +u option.

Question 5: What is the rate of diminutized reference? Does this rate change over time?

This question sought to determine how often, when parents referred to a specific entity, they used a diminutized form. In other words, when referring to the species *Lepus cuniculus*, how often do parents use *rabbit* versus *bunny*? We selected six animal terms (*bird*, *cat*, *dog*, *duck*, *pig*, and *rabbit*), whose diminutized forms had appeared relatively frequently in our data. Using our first data set (mother-infant dyads only), we generated frequency lists of all words used by all mothers using the following command:

freq +t*MOT +u kid*.cha > mototal.frq

Again, note the **+u** option that pools all the files, creating, in essence, an automatically alphabetized "master list" of all mothers' words. From this frequency list, we were able to create an include file that contained the non-diminutized forms of our six animal terms. For *duckie*, for example, we found these morphemized variants, *duck*, *duck–'is* and *duck–s*. We entered all these non-diminutized forms into an include file and called it **notdim.fil**. We then used the following command:

freq +t*MOT +s@notdim.fil +u kid*.cha > notdim.frq

The output of this command (the file **notdim.frq**) represented the total number of occurrences of our six nondiminutized animal terms.

Before proceeding to compute the rate of diminutized reference, we needed to make one adjustment in our figures. Note that while *bunny* is the diminutized form of *rabbit*, it may appear in combination with *rabbit* as in *bunny rabbit*. In order to determine if this in fact occurred, we used the following command:

combo +t*MOT +s"bunny^rabbit*" kid*.cha > bunrab.cmb

This use of the COMBO program asks the computer to search the mothers' tiers (**+t*MOT**) to find all instances where *bunny* is immediately followed by *rabbit* (**+s"bunny^rabbit*"**). Additionally, the wildcard (*) at the end of *rabbit* will find alternate forms (e.g., *rabbit–s* or *rabbit–'s*). The output was directed to a file we named **bunrab.cmb** that gave the specified combination in context, an example of which was illustrated earlier. We counted the number of instances where *bunny* and

68   Chapter 3

rabbit co-occurred and adjusted our figures by treating co-occurrence as a single diminutized term, like *kitty cat*. We then proceeded to make the following computation over the three data points corresponding to each age group:

$$\frac{\text{number of diminutized terms}}{(\text{number of diminutized forms} + \text{number of non-diminutized forms})}$$

3.3. Results and Discussion

3.3.1. How Pervasive is the Use of Diminutives?

In our studies the use of diminutives was pervasive but not universal. In the first sample (New England corpus), more than 90% of mothers used them. In the second sample (Gleason corpus), where both mothers and fathers were present and where the children ranged in age all the way up to 5 years, three quarters of the mothers and more than two thirds of the fathers used them. Parents who did not use diminutives appeared to be exhibiting their own stylistic tendency – they were not exclusively the parents of either boys or girls.

3.3.2. Is there a Greater Tendency for Mothers or for Fathers to Use Diminutives?

Here we concentrated on the Gleason corpus, in which both mothers and fathers came to the laboratory. Mothers used a total of 248 diminutives, whereas fathers used only 185, across approximately equal utterance totals. Thus, mothers produced 1.9 diminutives for every 100 utterances and fathers used 1.3, a difference that is just short of significance ($p < .09$).

3.3.3. Do Little Girls Hear More Diminutives than Little Boys?

Here we were able to use both samples. In the mother-only sample, mothers produced approximately as many diminutives to boys and girls at 14 months. However, by 30 months they were producing twice as many diminutives to girls (1.4 per 100 utterances) as to boys (0.7 per 100 utterances). In the second sample, where we saw both fathers and mothers, parents used more diminutives to girls, especially to the youngest girls, those who were aged 2 to 3½. Girls did indeed hear more diminutives than boys at all ages studied.

3.3.4. What is the Time Course of Diminutive Production in Parents' Speech, and How Does it Vary to Boys and to Girls? What Kinds of Words are Used?

Our results show, as we might expect, that use of diminutives by parents declines as children grow older. What is perhaps surprising was that the decline was evident by the time children were less than 3 years old. In the New England corpus (mothers only), boys at 14 months heard three times as many diminutives as they did at 30 months. In the Gleason corpus, girls at 2½ heard three times as many diminutives as girls in the 4 to 5 year range. The children who heard the most diminutives were the youngest girls in either of our samples (Figure 3.1). Figure 3.2 illustrates the finding that the youngest group of girls in the Gleason corpus heard the most diminutives.

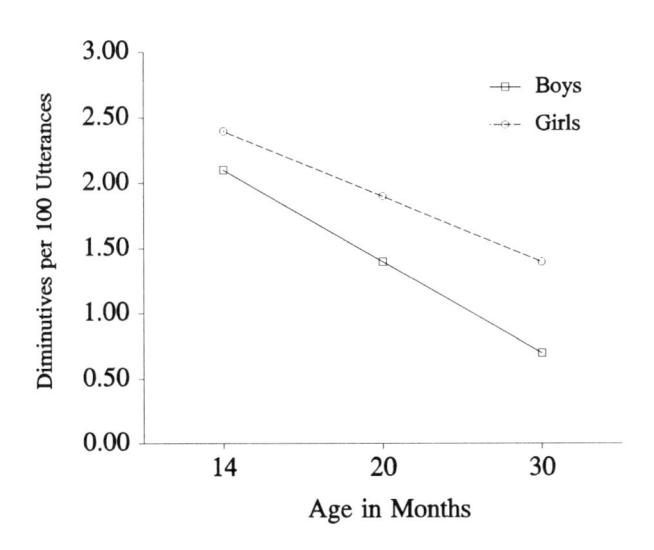

Figure 3.1: Mothers' diminutives to children at 14, 20, and 30 months.

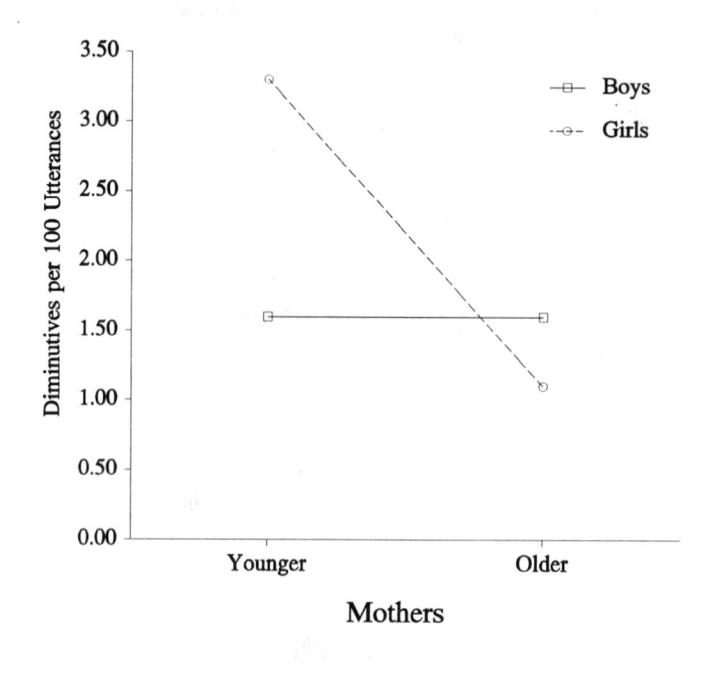

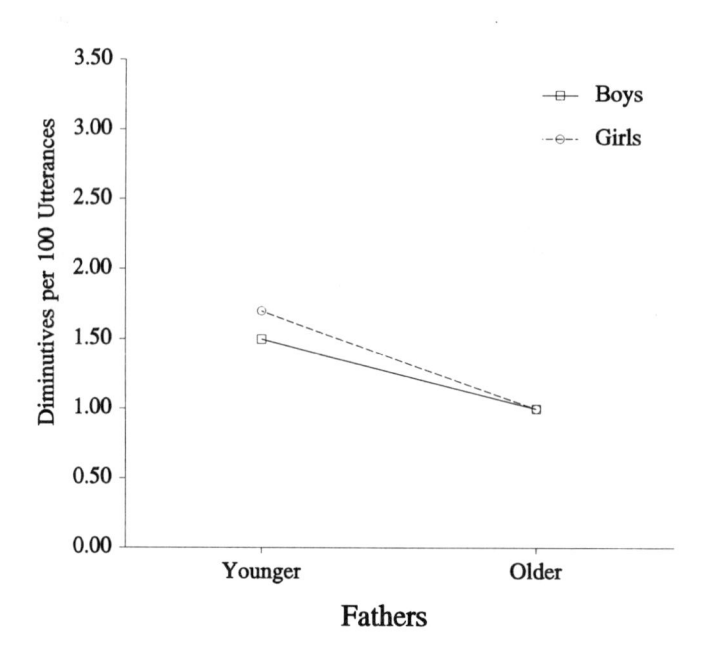

Figure 3.2: Mothers' and fathers' diminutives to younger (M = 35 months) and older (M = 50 months) boys and girls for the Gleason corpus.

There was also a decline in the number of types used as the children's ages increased, and there tended to be a wider variety of terms (types) used with girls. This can be seen in Table 3.1, which shows diminutives used at each age to boys and to girls. At each age the number of diminutive types (i.e., different words) directed to girls was greater than that directed to boys. Additionally, parents appeared to "diminutivize" a wider range of lexical types to girls as compared to boys, for example, objects such as *ballie*, *dolly*, *kiddie*; adjectives such as *teensie* and *bitsy*; prepositions such as *upie*; and other expressive kinds of words such as *hoppity*. Boys heard a more conventional or frozen set: words such as *doggy*, *duckie*, and *kitty*.

A qualitative comment on diminutization may be in order here. Obviously, all diminutives are not necessarily babytalk words; there are other lexical ways of marking speech intended for young children with the dimension of smallness. We found, for instance, that mothers' uses of the word *little*, which also means "diminutive," also carried an affective, babytalk-like component. Mothers tended to describe objects to their children as *little*, regardless of the actual sizes of the objects. For example, one mother while putting her child in a chair, said, "Oh, look, it has *little* straps to hold you in." Another mother said, "See the *little* camera taking your picture?" In both cases, the actual objects being referred to were not necessarily any smaller than their prototypes, but when they were called *little*, they took on a more sympathetic and less threatening aspect. By contrast, the word *big* was used in some instances to convey negative feelings; for instance, one mother referred in a negative way to a *big frog*.

3.3.5. What is the Ratio of Use of a Standard (*duck*) versus a Diminutive (*duckie*) Form?

For mothers addressing both girls and boys, nearly 60% of their use of six animal terms was diminutized at 14 months (Figure 3.3). At 20 months, this number dropped slightly for girls (to 48%) and more so for boys (to 33%). At 30 months, the ratio peaked for girls (74%). For boys, the rise was less dramatic. This gender-specific divergence in ratio of standard versus diminutized reference is congruent with other data presented here. Girls were more frequently exposed to diminutives, heard a wider range of diminutized terms, and were also more likely to hear the diminutized variant of any particular term.

Table 3.1: Mothers' diminutives to children at 14, 20, and 30 months.

	Boys only	Girls only	Boys and Girls
14 months	blankie	ballie bitsy dolly gaggy guggy hoppity kiddie teensie tummy uppie	birdie bunny chickie doggie ducky froggie horsie kitty kittycat piggie puppy
20 months	boogie bookie chickie eggie reddy	allrightie fishy froggie jacky lookie puppy poopy	birdie blankie bunny ducky horsie kitty lambie piggie
30 months	cowie duckie eggie	allrightie beddy blankie doggy dolly froggie googly huggie kitty orangy puppy yummy	buggie bunny

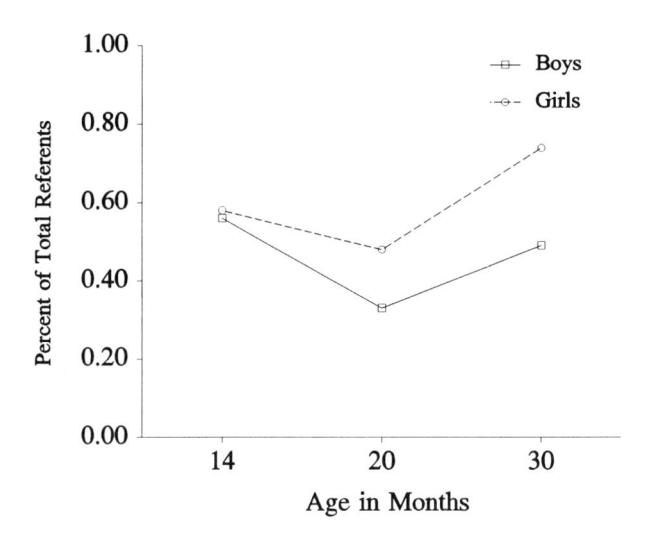

Figure 3.3: Percent of total referents for six animal terms diminutized by mothers of children at 14, 20, and 30 months.

3.4. Conclusion

Our results indicate that parents use diminutives pervasively, although not in great numbers. In general, diminutives are used with only a fairly restricted class of the already small lexeme pool in child-directed speech (with, for instance, proper nouns, some body parts, kinship terms, games, and with objects of immediate relevance to the child). Moreover, there is a steady decline in the number of types used as children's ages increase. In general mothers, rather than fathers, use the highest number and the largest variety of diminutives in their speech, especially to their young daughters. Thus they provide a differential linguistic role model and they treat girls and boys differently. Previous work has shown that mothers address a larger number and a wider range of feeling state words to young girls than to boys (Dunn, Bretherton, & Munn, 1987; Schell & Gleason, 1989), and we have found more direct prohibitives to young boys (Perlmann & Gleason, 1990). Differential use of babytalk words thus adds to a growing picture of differential linguistic socialization in our society.

3.5. Exercises

3.5.1. How might you use the FREQ program to search for occurrences of *bunny rabbit*? What is the advantage in using COMBO to search for occurrences of *bunny rabbit*?

3.5.2. We have argued that diminutives are affectively marked elements of the babytalk register. We found the word *little* was used in a similar manner. The co-occurrence of *little* plus a diminutive, as in that *little bunny*, might represent one extreme of this register. How would you go about determining how frequently the word *little* accompanied diminutives in parents' speech to their infants? Use both transcript files (**kid010b.cha** and **kid025b.cha**) provided in the **gleason** directory to answer this question.

3.5.3. How would you go about determining whether there was any relationship between parents' use of diminutives and the syntactic complexity of utterances that contain diminutives? In other words, do diminutives tend to appear in abbreviated and simple sentence structures? Are parents, when using diminutives, keeping their utterances short and sweet?

3.6. Suggested Projects

3.6.1. Using a data set with subjects of different socioeconomic status (e.g., New England corpus), determine whether parents' use of diminutives differs by SES. Then determine if there is an interaction between SES and child gender.

3.6.2. We commented that parents are unlikely to refer to a cockroach as *roachie*. In general, parents affectively mark a variety of entities (objects, people, behaviors) in the child's environment. Using a corpus of parent-child speech, generate a frequency list of words used by parents and *select* a sample of words that express affect, both positively (e.g., *good*, *nice*, the verb *like*) and negatively (e.g., *bad*, *yucky*, *no*, and the negative use of the verb *like*). Enter your selection of words into an include file and, using the KWAL program with a wide "window," analyze parents' use of these terms.

3.6.3. Determine whether the use of diminutives or the use of other affectively marked words are indicative of a particular parental interactional style. From a suitable corpus, select several parents who use affectively marked words frequently and those who use them rarely. Choose a small set of discourse structures (e.g., imperatives, expansions) that may differentiate the degree to which parents seek to control behavior and conversation versus encourage interaction and conversation. Is there any association between the use of affectively marked terms and parental interactional style?

Acknowledgments

This research was supported in part by grant number HD23388 from the National Institute of Child Health and Human Development. A portion of this research was presented at the Annual Linguistic Society of America Meeting, January 4, 1991.

References

Bynon, J. (1968). Berber nursery language. *Transactions of the Philological Society*, 107-161.

Casagrande, J.B. (1948). Comanche baby language. *International Journal of American Linguistics*, *14*, 11-14.

Crawford, J.M. (1970). Cocopa babytalk. *International Journal of American Linguistics*, *36*, 9-13.

Dale, P., Bates, E., Reznick, S., & Morisset, C. (1989). The validity of a parent report instrument. *Journal of Child Language*, *16*, 239-249.

Dil, A. (1975). Bengali babytalk. *Word*, *27*, 11-27.

Dunn, J., Bretherton, I., & Munn, P. (1987). Conversations about feeling states between mothers and their young children. *Developmental Psychology*, *23*, 132-139.

Ervin-Tripp, S. (1969). Sociolinguistics. In L. Berkowitz (Ed.), *Advances in experimental social psychology* (Vol. 4), New York: Academic Press.

Ferguson, C.A. (1964). Babytalk in six languages. *American Anthropologist*, *66*, 103-114.

Ferguson, C.A. (1977). Babytalk as a simplified register. In C. Snow & C. Ferguson (Eds.), *Talking to children*. New York: Cambridge University Press.

Gilligan, C. (1982). *In a different voice: Psychological theory and women's development*. Cambridge, MA: Harvard University Press.

Gleason, J. B., & Réger, Z. (1985). Aspects of language acquisition by Hungarian Gypsy children. In J. Grumet (Ed.), *Papers from the Fourth and Fifth Annual Meetings, Gypsy Lore Society, North American Chapter* (pp. 76-83). New York: Gypsy Lore Society.

Gleason, J. B. (1980). The acquisition of social speech and politeness formulae. In H. Giles, W.P. Robinson, & P. M. Smith (Eds.), *Language: Social psychological perspective*. Oxford: Pergamon.

Goldman, L.R. (1987). Ethnographic interpretations of parent- child discourse in Huli. *Journal of Child Language, 14,* 447-466.

Hymes, D. (1974). *Foundations in sociolinguistics: An ethnographic approach.* Philadelphia.

Kelkar, A. (1964). Marathi babytalk. *Word, 20,* 40-54.

Lakoff, R. (1975). Language and woman's place. *Language in Society, 2,* 45-80.

MacWhinney, B. (1991). *The CHILDES Project: Tools for analyzing talk.* Hillsdale, NJ: Lawrence Erlbaum Associates.

Menn, L., & Gleason, J. B. (1986). Babytalk as a stereotype and register: Adult reports of children's speech patterns. In J. A. Fishman et al. (Eds.), *The Fergusonian impact* (Vol. 1, pp. 111-125). Berlin: Mouton de Gruyter.

Perlmann, R. Y., & Gleason, J. B. (July, 1990). *Patterns of prohibition in mothers' speech to children.* Paper presented at the Fifth International Congress for the Study of Child Language, Budapest, Hungary.

Rūķe-Drāviņa, V. (1977). Modifications of speech addressed to young children in Latvian. In C. Snow & C. Ferguson (Eds.), *Talking to children*. New York: Cambridge University Press.

Snow, C.E. (1989). Imitativeness: Trait or skill? In G. Speidel & K. E. Nelson (Eds.), *The many faces of imitation in language learning*. New York: Springer-Verlag.

Stoel-Gammon, C. (1976). Babytalk in Brazilian Portuguese. *Papers and Reports on Child Language Development, 11.* Stanford, CA: Stanford University.

Ure, E., & Ellis, J. (1972). Register in descriptive linguistics and linguistic sociology. In O. Uribe Villegas (Ed.), *Las problemas y concepciones actuales de la sociolinguistica*. Mexico City: University of Mexico Press.

4

What Kind of a Birdie is This?
Learning to Use Superordinates

Laura Bodin and Catherine E. Snow
Harvard Graduate School of Education

In this chapter, you will learn the following skills:

- To derive the frequency of superordinates in the speech of children and their mothers using the FREQ program.

- To retrieve CHAT-formatted samples of maternal responses to children's production of superordinates using the KWAL program.

- To code the sample of maternal responses using the CED program.

- To use the FREQ program to count investigator-generated codes.

- To use the FREQ and KWAL programs to test hypotheses about children's conceptual development of hierarchical classifications.

To replicate the analyses and do the exercises, you will need the files in the **Adam** directory as well as those in the **Hooshyar** and the **Sarah** directories.

4.1. Introduction

The first words that children learn are typically words useful for communicating about what is most important to toddlers: words for greeting and leave-taking; names for important people and pets; words to express one's desire to be carried, tickled, hugged, read to, given food, or played with; and words to name the objects that one puts on, takes off, eats, plays with, or sleeps with (Dale, Bates, Reznick, & Morisset, 1989). It is quite simple to see how children learn words like these – they hear them often, can recognize what they mean quite easily, and have many chances to use them.

Most of the words that adults use, however, do not fall in the category of being easily mappable onto social meanings or objects in the world. Words like *memory, communicate, radiant*, and *however* cannot be learned simply by noticing what people are doing when they use them, as is the case for *hi, bye-bye*, or *thank you*; they certainly cannot be learned through procedures of ostensive definition (holding up the referent or pointing to it), like *sock, daddy*, or *book*. How early do children learn to use these more complicated, more abstract words? And how do they learn to use them – do their parents help them in any way to figure out the meanings of such words? These questions are addressed in this chapter.

We have narrowed the scope of this question to manageable proportions by choosing just one kind of more difficult lexical item – one that children might have some relatively early need to learn and that parents might well use with fairly young children. The words we focus on are called **superordinates**; a superordinate is a word that refers to a class of similar items. *Animal* is a superordinate term, which can be used to refer to any of a number of specific animals (e.g., to a dog, a bat, a cow, or an elephant). As Roger Brown pointed out in 1958, each of the types of animals that the word *animal* can be used to refer to also has another, more specific name, which is called its **basic object level** term. Children might easily learn basic object level terms like *dog* ostensively – their mothers can point to real dogs or to pictures of dogs and say *Dog!*. But any time a mother might point to a picture and say *dog* or *cat* or *elephant*, she might just as correctly say *animal*. So how does a young child learn that *animal* can mean any of the different kinds of animals, and that every animal has, in effect, two names, its basic object level name and its superordinate class name?

A considerable amount of research has been carried out on children's acquisition of superordinate terms. It is quite clear that superordinates are learned later and produced less willingly than basic object level terms (Rosch, Mervis, Gray, Johnson & Boyes-Braem, 1976; Waxman & Hatch, 1992); not surprisingly, mothers also use superordinates less frequently (Anglin, 1977; Macnamara, 1982) than basic object level terms. Experimental studies have shown that 5- and 6-year-olds can be taught superordinate terms relatively easily, much more easily than younger children (Horton & Markman, 1980). But we still do not understand much about how such terms are acquired in everyday life by very young children.

Most of the information available about children's acquisition of superordinates comes from experimental or laboratory studies, rather than from naturalistically collected records of spontaneous speech (e.g., Anglin, 1977; Keil, 1979). The reasons for this are obvious – if one was starting out to study superordinates, it would take many hours of observation and transcription to collect enough relevant examples in a natural conversation for a reasonable analysis. It is much more efficient to do what Jeremy Anglin did, for example, and engage children in conversation about dogs and cats and animals, about knives and forks and silverware, and so on, in order to collect a sufficiently rich dataset in a reasonable time. Alternately, it is very sensible to attempt to chart out children's comprehension of superordinates in carefully controlled studies, rather than just waiting for children to demonstrate comprehension in real world contexts.

There are disadvantages to the laboratory method, however. Children often perform at a higher level of sophistication at home with familiar conversational partners than they do in strange places with strange adults. For this reason, the laboratory approach may underestimate children's age of acquisition of superordinates. Furthermore, the laboratory approach gives us no information about children's access to situations in which they can learn about superordinates; we cannot know from contrived conversations in laboratories whether naturally occurring conversations provide information about the meaning of these terms. In order to have this sort of information, we must turn to transcripts of mother-child conversation occurring in the home, in everyday settings. Fortunately, the transcript archive provided by the Child Language Data Exchange System contains many longitudinal corpora of mother-child interaction sessions, collected originally for purposes quite different from the study of superordinates. We will use one of these corpora – that collected by Brown (1973) on the child Adam – in the study to be presented here.

4.1.1. The Corpus

Fifty-five samples of spontaneous speech were collected from Adam from the time he was 2;3 until he was 5;2. Approximately 1 hour of conversation between Adam and his mother and/or the observers (Ursula Bellugi and Richard Cromer) was recorded every 2 weeks. Adam was the firstborn child of college-educated parents living in Cambridge, Massachusetts. The transcripts were created by the observers, and context notes taken during the observation were added. The transcriptions are orthographic, that is to say, regularized to normal spellings of words no matter how they were pronounced, with only moderately systematic indications of Adam's phonological system. The transcripts have not been morphemicized – that is to say, MLU calculated through CLAN reflects MLU in words, not in morphemes. Thus, the Adam corpus is much better suited to analyses at the lexical than at the morphological level.

4.2. The Research Questions

The specific questions of interest were the following:

1. How frequently do superordinate terms occur in natural conversation between Adam and his mother? Does the frequency increase as Adam gets older? Does Adam use superordinates more often than his mother, or is she mostly modelling their use? These questions are answered in Study 1.

2. What kind of explicit or implicit information is available to Adam from the interactions with his mother about the meanings of superordinate terms? In other words, does she say things that would help him learn superordinates? Does she ever define superordinates explicitly? Does she use superordinates in conjunction with basic object level terms? These questions are addressed in Study 2.

3. Can Adam's use of superordinates be related to any more general change in his cognitive development, for example, the development of general classification abilities? This question motivated Study 3.

4.3. Study 1: How Frequent are Superordinates?

In looking for relatively rare items in large corpora, the first task is to decide how to divide the corpus into reasonable sections, each of which is large enough to support the analysis of interest. In the analysis of Adam, we are interested in age effects, but we do not expect very subtle effects of age. Accordingly, we have taken the entire corpus and divided it into seven epochs, each of which covers several months. In the beginning, when the data were collected more frequently, we used intervals of 3 months, but by the end we used an interval of 7 months (see Table 4.1).

Table 4.1: Ages and files included in each of the seven age periods analyzed for Adam.

Epoch	Age Range	Files
1	2;3 – 2;6	1 – 8
2	2;7 – 2;10	9 – 16
3	2;11 – 3;2	17 – 24
4	3;3 – 3;7	25 – 33
5	4;0 – 4;5	34 – 41
6	4;0 – 4;5	42 – 48
7	4;7 – 5;2	49 – 55

The second task was to decide what superordinate terms were likely to occur in the conversations with sufficient frequency to be worth counting. After some exploratory analyses of representative samples, and relying on the literature on children's comprehension of superordinates, we decided to focus on the following terms: animal(s), toy(s), bird(ie)(s), food, and furniture. Obviously, we were interested in finding these words in any of the various alternative forms they might take, indicated by the material in parentheses. We created an **include file**, called **super**, containing the five words whose occurrences we were interested in counting. This file was then placed in the data directory called **snow**. The contents of the file are as follows:

```
toy%
bird%
animal%
food
furniture
```

82   Chapter 4

> The % symbol indicates that any material whatsoever can occur in place of the %. Thus, CLAN programs will search for forms of the target words that include plural, possessive, or diminutive markings, such as *birdie*, *birds*, *birdies*, *birdy*, *bird's*, and so on. In addition, because the % wildcard was used instead of the * wildcard, all of the above instances of *bird* will be counted as different tokens of the same type.

Searching for the frequency with which Adam used the terms specified by **super** in any file simply requires using the following CLAN command:

freq   +t*ADA   +s@super   +fsa   *.cha

+t*ADA	Analyze Adam's speaker tier only
+s@super	Include the words from the file **super**
+fsa	Save the results in a file with the extension **.sa**
*.cha	Analyze all files ending in **.cha**

Command Box 4.1

This command string has directed that the output files from this command have the extension **.sa** – to remind us that they are FREQ files that tell us about Adam's superordinate use (we will later make **.sm** files for Adam's mother). The first part of each file name will be the same as that of the input file – **adam01.cha** will generate the output file **adam01.sa**, **adam02.sa**, and so on. An example of a single output file from this analysis applied to **adam24.cha** follows:

```
FREQ.EXE +t*ADA +s@super +fsa adam24.cha
FREQ.EXE (04-MAY-93) is conducting analyses on:
  ONLY speaker main tiers matching: *ADA;
*****************************************
From file <adam24.cha> to file <adam24.sa>
   4   animal
   6   bird
   2   food
   2   toy
  -----------------------------
       4   Total number of different word types used
      14   Total number of words (tokens)
    0.286  Type/Token ratio
```

Learning to Use Superordinates   83

To display this file, we used the CLAN command **page adam24.sa**.

We do not, however, want a single frequency output file for every one of the 55 files in the Adam corpus. Instead, we would like to direct FREQ to help us produce frequencies for a series of files grouped together. The command for including the eight files from the first epoch in a single analysis is:

>   freq +t*ADA +s@super +fsa +u adam01.cha adam02.cha
>   adam03.cha adam04.cha adam05.cha adam06.cha adam07.cha adam08.cha

+t*ADA	Analyze Adam's speaker tier only
+s@super	Include the words from the file **super**
+fsa	Save the results in a file with the extension **.sa**
+u	Merge all input files into a combined analysis
adam01.cha – adam08.cha	Analyze the files **adam01.cha** through **adam08.cha**

Command Box 4.2

Here, the output file will have the extension **.sa** and will take the first part of its name from the first file in the list of files to be analyzed (i.e., it will be called **adam01.sa** but will include the results of the merged analysis of the files **adam01.cha** through **adam08.cha**). The +u option indicates that the results of analyzing each of the separate files should be unified into a single output file. Without the +u option, we would get eight separate frequency lists as output. One can modify this command to analyze other time periods simply by changing the file names to be analyzed. The data directory for this chapter (which we have called **snow**) includes the files from Adam at ages 3;7 to 3;11 (**adam34.cha** through **adam41.cha**), the fifth epoch indicated in Table 4.1. If you analyze those files for the frequency of Adam's superordinates, you will get output from the **adam34.sa** file that looks like this:

```
FREQ.EXE +t*ADA +s@super +fsa +u ADAM34.CHA
ADAM35.CHA ADAM36.CHA ADAM37.CHA ADAM38.CHA
ADAM39.CHA ADAM40.CHA ADAM41.CHA
FREQ.EXE (04-MAY-93) is conducting analyses on:
  ONLY speaker main tiers matching: *ADA;
*******************************************
From file <ADAM34.CHA> to file <ADAM34.SA>
From file <ADAM35.CHA> to file <ADAM34.SA>
From file <ADAM36.CHA> to file <ADAM34.SA>
From file <ADAM37.CHA> to file <ADAM34.SA>
From file <ADAM38.CHA> to file <ADAM34.SA>
From file <ADAM39.CHA> to file <ADAM34.SA>
From file <ADAM40.CHA> to file <ADAM34.SA>
From file <ADAM41.CHA> to file <ADAM34.SA>
 38 animal
 33 bird
  9 food
 21 toy
-------------------------------
    4  Total number of different word types used
  101  Total number of words (tokens)
 0.040 Type/Token ratio
```

Table 4.2 summarizes the output from all seven age periods for Adam's use of these superordinates.

To determine Adam's mother's use of superordinates for the first epoch, we simply modify the command given above slightly:

freq   +t*MOT   +s@super   +fsm   +u   adam01.cha adam02.cha adam03.cha adam04.cha adam05.cha adam06.cha adam07.cha adam08.cha

+t*MOT	Analyze the mother's speaker tier only
+s@super	Include the words from the file **super**
+fsm	Save the results in a file with the extension **.sm**
+u	Merge all input files into a combined analysis
adam01.cha – adam08.cha	Analyze the files **adam01.cha** through **adam08.cha**

Command Box 4.3

Table 4.2: Frequencies for superordinate terms and total words per epoch for Adam.

	1	2	3	4	5	6	7
animal	0	2	4	4	38	24	22
bird	41	4	30	20	33	25	28
food	6	2	8	7	9	19	3
furniture	0	0	0	4	0	0	1
toy	94	6	13	23	21	15	33
Total Super	141	14	55	58	101	83	87
Total Words	16,754	15,111	25,065	30,207	24,243	25,997	26,911
% Super	0.84	0.09	0.22	0.19	0.42	0.32	0.32

The output from the file **adam01.sm** for this analysis looks like this:

```
FREQ.EXE +t*MOT +u +fsm +s@super adam01.cha
adam02.cha adam03.cha adam04.cha adam05.cha
adam06.cha adam07.cha adam08.cha
FREQ.EXE (04-MAY-93) is conducting analyses on:
  ONLY speaker main tiers matching: *MOT;
*****************************************
From file <adam01.cha> to file <adam01.sm>
From file <adam02.cha> to file <adam01.sm>
From file <adam03.cha> to file <adam01.sm>
From file <adam04.cha> to file <adam01.sm>
From file <adam05.cha> to file <adam01.sm>
From file <adam06.cha> to file <adam01.sm>
From file <adam07.cha> to file <adam01.sm>
From file <adam08.cha> to file <adam01.sm>
    7 bird
    2 food
   21 toy
-------------------------------
      3  Total number of different word types used
     30  Total number of words (tokens)
  0.100  Type/Token ratio
```

Table 4.3: Frequencies for superordinate terms and total words per epoch for Adam's mother.

	1	2	3	4	5	6	7
animal	0	1	3	0	28	10	5
bird	7	3	6	12	18	5	3
food	2	1	4	8	1	8	0
furniture	0	0	0	1	1	0	0
toy	21	4	12	14	16	9	8
Total Super	30	9	25	35	64	32	16
Total Words	14,096	12,234	15,132	17,440	16,947	9,992	7,074
% Super	0.21	0.07	0.17	0.20	0.38	0.32	0.23

If you conduct these analyses on the data in files **adam34.cha** through **adam41.cha**, you should obtain results that match those presented in Table 4.2 (for Adam) and Table 4.3 (for Adam's mother).

The results in Table 4.2 show, not surprisingly, that the superordinate Adam uses most often is *toy*%, whereas *furniture* is very rare. Second, comparing Tables 4.2 and 4.3 reveals that for every word, and for every age period as well, Adam uses these superordinate terms more often than his mother. Even at the youngest age that he produced a particular superordinate, Adam used it more frequently than his mother did, and overall he used superordinate terms 539 times, whereas his mother used them only 211 times in these transcripts.

Age effects are not easy to see during this period. The terms *furniture* and *animal* only started to be used at older ages, indicating that they may be harder than the earlier used ones. Clearly the word *toy* dominates the early period; in fact, during Session 1 Adam participated in the following, somewhat obsessive discussion of toys, which displays very little interest in issues of classification or category membership:

Learning to Use Superordinates 87

*ADA: put toy in (th)ere.
*MOT: you going to put your toys in there?
*ADA: put toy.
*ADA: goo(d) night # toy.
*ADA: goo(d) night # train.
*ADA: where train go?
*ADA: play toy.
*ADA: play toy.
*ADA: play toy.
*MOT: play toy?
*MOT: what about your play toy?
*ADA: play toy.
*ADA: play toy.
*ADA: play toy.
*ADA: play toy.
*ADA: where play toy?
*MOT: <play toy> ["]?
*ADA: play toys.
*ADA: put fin(ger) (i)n (th)ere.
*MOT: <put finger in (th)ere> ["]?
*ADA: play toy play toy.
*MOT: what happened to the play toy?
*ADA: happen drop play toy.
*MOT: you dropped the play toy?
*ADA: yeah.
*ADA: goo(d) night.
*ADA: where choo+choo train go?
*ADA: play toy.
*ADA: come play toy.
*ADA: play toy play toy play toy play toy.
*MOT: how many play toys do you have?
*ADA: play toy.
*ADA: play toy.
*ADA: play toy.
*ADA: play toy.
*ADA: Adam play toy.
*ADA: what happen # Mommy?
*ADA: what happen # Mommy?
*MOT: Adam fell down.

Except for the decline of his interest in the word *toy*, there is neither a clear increase nor a steady decrease with age in the frequency of superordinate terms in Adam's speech.

It is possible, of course, that these results have been influenced by the total amount of talk by Adam and his mother at each of the age periods. Perhaps Adam's mother simply talked less overall than Adam, but used superordinates in the same proportion as he did. And perhaps if we look at superordinates as a proportion of total words, we will see age effects emerge. To do these analyses, we need to use the FREQ program again, to count total words by each speaker. To do this for the first age period, we would use the following basic commands. The command for Adam would be:

freq +t*ADA +d4 +fta +u adam01.cha adam02.cha adam03.cha adam04.cha adam05.cha adam06.cha adam07.cha adam08.cha

while the command for Adam's mother would be:

freq +t*MOT +d4 +ftm +u adam01.cha adam02.cha adam03.cha adam04.cha adam05.cha adam06.cha adam07.cha adam08.cha

These FREQ commands are just like the ones we used to find the frequency of superordinate terms, except that we have deleted the +s option. We did this because we are interested in the total frequency of all the words in these files rather than the frequency of particular words. Since we are only interested in total frequencies, we used the +d4 option to restrict the output to the type and token frequencies. The output for Adam during the first epoch looks like this:

```
-------------------------------
  1093   Total number of different word types used
 16754   Total number of words (tokens)
 0.065   Type/Token ratio
```

You can perform these analyses for the fifth epoch using the data provided in the **snow** directory. These data concerning the total number of words used during each epoch and the proportion of those that are superordinates are presented in the bottom lines of Tables 4.2 and 4.3. It can be seen that Adam produces only slightly more words than his mother during the first five epochs, but then starts seriously to out-talk her at about age 2;11. His use of superordinates is generally higher than hers when we look at proportions, just as for frequencies, though, especially at the higher ages, the disparity is not great.

The proportional analysis also suggests an intriguing increase of interest in superordinates at around the fifth epoch, when Adam is 3;7 to 3;11. His use almost doubles from the previous period, and stays relatively high thereafter. (Of course, during the first period he used many superordinates as well, but almost all of them were *toy* or *toys*, which some have argued is not a true superordinate; it is a term used to refer to collections of category members, as in *Pick up your toys*, rather than to classify the members.) This rise of interest in superordinates might identify their emergence as a "problem space" or a domain in which Adam is trying to work things out (see Karmiloff-Smith, 1979, for a discussion of problem spaces in child language). We could use KWAL to go look at the specific uses of superordinates to see whether this speculation is correct. Additionally, we might consider alternate indicators of interest in the problem space of classification, as we do in Study 3.

4.4. Study 2: Are Superordinates Taught?

We have seen in Study 1 that Adam learned superordinates without being exposed to them with very great frequency. Perhaps, though, the relatively few times his mother used superordinate terms to him, she also gave him information about what they meant – information that helped him acquire the terms quickly and efficiently. We know that mothers often introduce subordinate level terms (like *collie*) together with basic object level terms (*dog*) (Callanan, 1985, 1989); perhaps they do the same thing with superordinates (*a dog is an animal*). In order to find out if Adam's mother did anything like this, we need to look at specific examples of interactions between Adam and his mother when superordinate terms were used, and classify them as being helpful and informative or not. Consider the following examples:

```
*ADA:  what is dis one?
*MOT:  that's a lizard.
*ADA:  what's a lizard?
*MOT:  he's a little animal who lives outside.
       [age 3;8, file 36, line 424]
```

In this example, MOT explicitly tells ADA that lizards and animals have a particular hierarchical relation. Interactions like these can be coded as *explicitly informative*. Consider in contrast the following example:

>*MOT: and let the birds eat it?
>*ADA: yeah.
>*MOT: remember when you fed the pigeons?
>[age 3;0, file 19, line 533]

In this interaction, there is information available that pigeons are a kind of bird, but it is much less explicit than in the previous case. This interaction might be classified as *implicitly informative*. Other examples of implicitly informative interactions included discussions of features common to all members of a superordinate class (*birds fly* or *furniture is not for jumping on*).

Finally, many cases in which Adam's mother used superordinate terms included neither implicit nor explicit reference to relevant basic object level items, to features or functions of the superordinate class, or to other useful information. These were coded as *uninformative*, as in the following example, which gives no information about examples or features of clothes:

>*MOT: no no Adam.
>*MOT: don't write on your clothes.
>*MOT: don't write on you either.
>*ADA: what is dat on me?
>[age 3;3, file 26, line 1288]

In order to code Adam's mother's uses of superordinates, it was necessary to locate their use in the transcripts, and to have enough information about the context of their use to be able to code the entire interaction. In order to do this, we used the CLAN program KWAL, which is designed to provide occurrences of *key words* in the context in which they occur. A KWAL command for the first epoch looks like this:

kwal   +s@super   +w5 −w5   +d1   +u   +fkw   adam01.cha adam02.cha
adam03.cha adam04.cha adam05.cha adam06.cha adam07.cha adam08.cha

+s@super	Search for the superordinates in the include file **super**
+w5	Output a window of 5 utterances after the target
−w5	Output a window of 5 utterances before the target
+d1	Output the data in CHAT format
+u	Merge all input files into a combined analysis
+fkw	Save the results in a file with the extension **.kw**
adam01.cha – adam08.cha	Analyze the files **adam01.cha** through **adam08.cha**

Command Box 4.4

The +w and −w options give an indication of how many lines of text should be included before and after the search words – a so-called *window of text*. We include a +d option in this command because we want the files that are produced to be analyzable after they are coded; for the KWAL command, +d1 gives us output that is in legal CHAT format. The +u option gives us unified output. We do not specify MOT (i.e., the mother) as the speaker in the +t option because we are interested in all the conversations about superordinates, though we are only coding the informativeness of her responses (i.e., her use of superordinate or basic object level terms). Sometimes her utterance is a response that does not contain a superordinate to an utterance of Adam's that does.

The first and second examples from the file **adam01.kw** look like the following (the target line is always the sixth one, displayed with a window of five lines before and five after):

```
@Comment:       ---------------------------------------
@Comment:       *** File adam01.cha. Line 111. Keyword: toy
*ADA:   horse go # Mommy.
*ADA:   horse.
*ADA:   Mott apple juice.
*ADA:   Mott apple juice.
*ADA:   Mott apple juice.
*MOT:   why don't you look at some of the toys in the basket.
*MOT:   want to?
*ADA:   no.
*ADA:   water # Mommy.
*ADA:   Mott apple juice.
*MOT:   do you want to see what I have?
@Comment:       ---------------------------------------
@Comment:       *** File adam01.cha. Line 340. Keyword: toy
*ADA:   night+night.
*ADA:   ok kitty xxx.
*MOT:   ok kitty what?
*ADA:   ok kitto@w.
*ADA:   oh Adam fall.
*ADA:   toy.
*ADA:   Adam fall toy.
*MOT:   Adam fall toy.
*MOT:   you didn't fall that time.
*MOT:   you just sat down.
*ADA:   Adam fall # toy.
```

To see the combined KWAL output for the fifth epoch, perform this analysis on the files available to you in the **snow** directory. Use the PAGE command to view the output file named **adam34.kw**. Remember, use the **+f** option if you want to create an output file; do not use it if you just want to see the results scroll across the screen.

> If you want to analyze all the files in the data directory for this chapter, you do not need to list all the file names in the command string. Instead, you can just use a wildcard (e.g., ***.cha**), and all of the files in your current directory ending in **.cha** will automatically be included in the analysis. Be sure to check the directory first, though, to be sure there are no **.cha** files in there that you wish to exclude from the analysis.

Learning to Use Superordinates   93

Of course, one way to proceed after we have the KWAL output files would be to print them out and code them by hand. However, it is more efficient and more error-free to code them in CHAT, so that we can eventually use CLAN to count the codes for us automatically. To code the output files in CHAT, we can use CED (Coder's Editor) to add a coding tier to each interaction involving the use of a superordinate; we will call the coding tier **%sup** (for *superordinates*). Coding with Coder's Editor requires first making a file called **codes.lst**, in which the possible codes are listed. Our codes.lst file looks like the following (<tab> = tab, <sp> = space):

```
\ +l1 +s1 +b100
%sup:<tab>
<sp>"<sp>$EXP
<sp><sp>:toy
<sp><sp>:ani
<sp><sp>:fod
<sp><sp>:fur
<sp><sp>:bir
<sp>"<sp>$IMP
<sp>"<sp>$UNI
```

The first line in this file sets a number of basic options that are available within CED (see MacWhinney, this volume, for more discussion of the CED program).

\	Indicates to CED that this line contains a list of options
+l1	Reorder the codes based on the frequency of their use within coding episodes
+b100	Set the automatic backup interval to 100 keystrokes
+s1	The codes listed directly under each other can all be nested similarly; i.e., **toy, ani, fod, fur,** and **bir** can all be coded after IMP and UNI as well as EXP in our case.

Command Box 4.5

The entries in the **codes.lst** file represent a three-step coding process. First, the second line in the **codes.lst** file directs CED to insert a coding tier called **%sup** at the beginning of each coding cycle; second, to let the coder choose among the codes EXP (explicit), IMP (implicit), and UNI (uninformative); and third, to let the coder

94   Chapter 4

add an indicator of which superordinate category is being discussed: toys, animals, food, furniture, or birds. Obviously, some **codes.lst** files would be much longer and more complicated. This **codes.lst** file should be stored in your working directory, in our case **snow**. To start coding a single file, one simply types CED and the filename to be analyzed. Since we want to analyze our combined KWAL files, we will use the following command:

ced adam01.kw

If your filename does not include a standard file extension (e.g., **.cha** or **.kwa**) then CED will start-up in non-CHAT mode. In order to change to CHAT-mode, you must type **<ESC>-m** to CED. To check whether you are in non-CHAT mode, examine the box in the mode line at the bottom of the screen. If the box contains either a [C-] or a [E-], then you are in non-CHAT mode and must change to CHAT-mode in order for CED to work correctly. If the box contains either a [C] or a [E], then you are in CHAT-mode. You can exit CED by pressing the **F7** function key.

A portion of the coded **adam01.kw** file, containing the KWAL segments from the first eight Adam CHAT files, follows:

```
    @Comment:    *** File adam02.cha. Line 1487. Keyword: toy
    *ADA:   Adam fell down.
    *URS:   when did Adam fall down?
    *ADA:   put hot [?].
    *ADA:   beep beep.
    *MOT:   you beep beep # Adam.
    *MOT:   you move some of your toys?
    *ADA:   move bike?
    *MOT:   yes # move your bike.
    %sup:   $EXP:toy
    *ADA:   right dere.
    *ADA:   beep beep beep beep.
    *ADA:   drive.
    @Comment:   -----------------------------------------
```

Learning to Use Superordinates 95

```
@Comment:     *** File adam03.cha. Line 473. Keyword: toy
*ADA: be careful.
*URS: what is that # Adam?
*ADA: trash.
*ADA: trash (i)n (th)ere.
*ADA: put.
*MOT: you're going to put all of your toys away.
%sup: $UNI:toy
*ADA: dere pencil # Mommy.
*ADA: put pencil in (th)ere.
*ADA: put (i)n (th)ere # on?
*ADA: put ball in.
*ADA: goo(d) night # ball.
@Comment:     ----------------------------------------
@Comment:     *** File adam03.cha. Line 487. Keyword: toy
*ADA: have a box.
*ADA: what dat?
*ADA: sand (i)n (th)ere?
*ADA: sand?
*MOT: yes it does sound like sand # but it doesn't have any
      sand in it.
*ADA: put toy in (th)ere.
*MOT: you going to put your toys in there?
%sup: $UNI:toy
*ADA: put toy.
   *ADA: goo(d) night # toy.
   *ADA: goo(d) night # train.
   *ADA: where train go?
   @Comment:     ----------------------------------------
```

Of course, with a window as large as five lines on either side of the target, we must be careful not to code any particular instance more than once, since adjacent kwal segments often overlap.

Note that the first line (labeled **@Comment**) of every segment in a KWAL output file specifies the name of the file from which that segment was drawn (e.g., **adam02.cha**). Of course, the entire KWAL output file must get one filename; if no name was specified in the KWAL command (using the **+f** option or a redirection command), CLAN calls the output file by the name of the first input file. So the merged analysis results in the creation of a single file, **adam01.kw**, which contains all of the relevant segments for the first eight files in the Adam corpus, with each segment containing a header noting the original source file. Applying CED to the file containing the KWAL output does not change its name.

96   Chapter 4

You can code the files from the fifth epoch by following the coding rules in the Appendix. To see whether you agree with our coding, check the results given in Table 4.4 for all the age periods. After all the files are coded (and a portion are coded by a second researcher, to establish reliability; see Bakeman & Gottman, 1986, for reliability guidelines), we want to count the co-occurrence of each of the codes with each of the search words. To do this, we simply use the FREQ program on the coding tier:

freq   +t%sup   +s$*   adam*.kw

+t%sup	Include the coding tier (**%sup**) for maternal responses to Adam's superordinate use
+s$*	Include any and all strings beginning with **$**
adam*.kw	Analyze all files beginning with **adam** and ending with the extension **.kw**

Command Box 4.6

It can be seen from Table 4.5 that, while uninformative interactions are the most frequent type, almost half the interactions for every word, except *food*, were either

Table 4.4:   Adam's access to informative interactions across the seven epochs.

Age period	# of interactions	% explicit	% implicit	% uninformative
1	29	17.2	24.1	58.7
2	9	33.3	11.1	55.6
3	32	18.8	21.9	59.3
4	39	30.8	17.9	51.3
5	54	27.8	13.0	59.2
6	36	27.8	22.2	50.0
7	24	37.5	12.5	50.0
TOTAL	223	26.9	17.9	55.2

Table 4.5: Adam's access to informative interactions regarding five superordinate terms.

	# of interactions	% explicit	% implicit	% uninformative
animal	44	25.0	20.5	54.5
bird	58	39.7	5.2	55.1
food	27	14.8	14.8	70.4
furniture	4	25.0	25.0	50.0
toy	90	23.3	25.6	51.1
TOTAL	223	26.9	17.9	55.2

explicitly or implicitly informative. Thus, it seems that Adam has considerable access to useful information about the meaning of words like *animal* or *bird*, that might help explain how he learned them so effectively.

4.5. Study 3: Does Superordinate Use Relate to Other Developments?

The essence of the ability required to use superordinates is the ability to classify items that are not identical into the same category. Understanding that two things as different from each other as a dog and a lizard should nonetheless be grouped together because both are animals represents a real cognitive achievement. We have seen some evidence from Study 1 and Study 2 that Adam at age 3;7 to 3;11 showed the beginning of a sustained high level of interest in certain difficult superordinates; in this age period he also enjoyed a relative wealth of informative interactions about superordinates with his mother. Perhaps this period was a time when he was worried about classification in general. If so, that interest might be reflected in aspects of his language use beyond superordinates – he might be using words that explicitly ask or tell about classification, like *kind of* or *sort of*. A quick look at some FREQ analyses searching for the word *kind* revealed that this word did, indeed, occur rather often – suggesting that Adam or his mother might be talking a lot about issues of classification: what *kind of* thing something was. To explore this, we performed a more targeted search, using KWAL, for cases in which either Adam or his mother used the words *kind* or *kind of*. We used the following CLAN command to perform this analysis for Adam's first age period:

kwal +t*ADA +s"kind" +d1 +u +fka adam01.cha adam02.cha
adam03.cha adam04.cha adam05.cha adam06.cha adam07.cha adam08.cha

+t*ADA	Analyze Adam's speaker tier only
+s"kind"	Search for the word *kind*
+d1	Output the data in CHAT format
+u	Merge all input files into a combined analysis
+fka	Save the results in a file with the extension **.ka**
adam01.cha – adam08.cha	Analyze the files **adam01.cha** through **adam08.cha**

Command Box 4.7

We included the +d1 option so we could submit the output files to further CLAN analyses. In this case we did not use the +w or –w option because we did not want a large window of text – we really just want to know how many times Adam or his mother includes statements or questions about *kind of*. Fortunately, we did look through the files before doing further analyses; it turned out that a few instances of the word *kind* were in sentences like *be kind to him*. We used CED in editor mode and deleted these from the **.ka** files, and subsequently from the **.km** files that included identical information for Adam's mother.

After finding all the instances of *kind of* produced by Adam and by his mother (using the same command and changing only the +t option), we submitted the output files to the MLU program. Using the following CLAN command, MLU automatically counted the number of utterances in each file containing these terms:

mlu +fmla *.ka

+fmla	Save the results in a file with the extension **.mla**
adam*.ka	Analyze all files beginning with **adam** and ending in **.ka**

Command Box 4.8

This analysis is possible because the term *kind of* never occurred more than once in any utterance. The previous command gives us seven separate MLU output files, one for each of the age periods, with number of utterances by Adam. There is no need to specify +t*ADA because only Adam's utterances were included in the .ka files. We changed the command only slightly to do the same analysis for Adam's mother's utterances:

mlu +fmlm *.km

The following is the output of this MLU analysis for Adam's mother for the first file:

```
MLU.EXE +fmlm ADAM01.KM
MLU.EXE (04-MAY-93) is conducting analyses on:
  ALL speaker tiers
*****************************************
From file <ADAM01.KM> to file <ADAM01.MLM>
MLU (xxx and yyy are EXCLUDED from the utterance and
morpheme counts):
    Number of: utterances = 31, morphemes = 176
       Ratio of morphemes over utterances = 5.677
       Standard deviation = 1.730
```

All we need to look at in this output, of course, is the **number of utterances**. We are not interested in the number of morphemes (words, in the Adam files) or the mean length of utterance. By asking KWAL to output only a single line, we were able to equate number of utterances to number of instances of the phenomenon we were interested in counting.

It is also interesting to know, though, whether Adam and his mother were mostly asking questions like *what kind of an animal is this?* or mostly making statements like *a penguin is a kind of bird*. In order to find this out, we could code every utterance in the KWAL output files. Alternately, if we trust the transcribers to have used question marks correctly, we can simply use the FREQ program to find the number of question marks in each of the KWAL output files:

100   Chapter 4

> freq +s"?" +fqa *.ka
> freq +s"?" +fqm *.km

+s"?"	Search for the string "?"
+fqa	Save the results in a file with the extension .qa
+fqm	Save the results in a file with the extension .qm

Command Box 4.9

We do not use the +u option here because we want each of the coded KWAL files to be analyzed separately, so we can compare the number of questions to the number of utterances produced by the MLU analysis. See Tables 4.6 and 4.7 for the frequencies of utterances with *kind of* by Adam and by his mother, and for the proportion of those that were questions. Since these frequencies might be influenced by the total size of the corpus, we thought it would be valuable to characterize each age period in terms of the total number of utterances produced by Adam and by his mother, as well. Once again we used MLU because number of utterances is included in its output. The command for Adam would be:

> mlu +t*ADA +u +fmta adam01.cha adam02.cha adam03.cha
> adam04.cha adam05.cha adam06.cha adam07.cha adam08.cha

Table 4.6: Adam's use of classificatory statements and questions for each of the seven age periods.

Age	# *kind*	% Question	# utterances	% utterances with *kind*
1	0	–	7,417	0.00
2	1	0	6,034	0.02
3	41	87.8	7,640	0.54
4	44	88.6	7,919	0.56
5	5	80.0	6,023	0.08
6	32	34.4	5,630	0.57
7	38	55.3	5,830	0.65

Table 4.7: Adam's mother's use of classificatory statements and questions for each of the seven age periods.

Age	# *kind*	% question	# utterances	% utterances with *kind*
1	31	96.8	3,255	0.95
2	21	95.2	2,900	0.72
3	47	78.7	3,344	1.41
4	36	91.7	3,681	0.98
5	40	82.5	3,560	1.12
6	13	92.3	2,046	0.64
7	12	83.3	1,384	0.87

The command for Adam's mother would be:

mlu +t*MOT +u +fmtm adam01.cha adam02.cha adam03.cha adam04.cha adam05.cha adam06.cha adam07.cha adam08.cha

The following is an example of output that lists the number of utterances:

```
MLU.EXE +t*MOT +u +fmtm ADAM17.CHA ADAM18.CHA
ADAM19.CHA ADAM20.CHA ADAM21.CHA ADAM22.CHA
ADAM23.CHA ADAM24.CHA
MLU.EXE (04-MAY-93) is conducting analyses on:
  ONLY speaker main tiers matching: *MOT;
****************************************
From file <ADAM17.CHA> to file <ADAM17.MLM>
From file <ADAM18.CHA> to file <ADAM17.MLM>
From file <ADAM19.CHA> to file <ADAM17.MLM>
From file <ADAM20.CHA> to file <ADAM17.MLM>
From file <ADAM21.CHA> to file <ADAM17.MLM>
From file <ADAM22.CHA> to file <ADAM17.MLM>
From file <ADAM23.CHA> to file <ADAM17.MLM>
From file <ADAM24.CHA> to file <ADAM17.MLM>
MLU (xxx and yyy are EXCLUDED from the utterance and
morpheme counts):
   Number of: utterances = 3344, morphemes = 15169
      Ratio of morphemes over utterances = 4.536
      Standard deviation = 2.852
```

Using the output of these analyses, Tables 4.6 and 4.7 also present the data on *kind of* utterances as proportions. It is clear that there is a peak of use of these forms by Adam starting at 2;11 and continuing until 3;6 – the period just before he showed his most intense interest in superordinates. This might seem paradoxical, until we look at the actual utterances Adam produced using *kind of*. Here are some excerpts from the KWAL output file from the third epoch:

*ADA:	what kind letter?	(adam17.cha; line 1774)
*ADA:	what kind feather dat?	(adam18.cha; line 852)
*ADA:	yeah # what kind church dat?	(adam18.cha; line 1019)
*ADA:	what kind feather dat?	(adam18.cha; line 1126)
*ADA:	what kind tractor dat?	(adam18.cha; line 1193)
*ADA:	what kind wagon dat # hmm?	(adam18.cha; line 1209)
*ADA:	what kind fire truck dat?	(adam19.cha; line 649)
*ADA:	what kind block dat?	(adam19.cha; line 1162)
*ADA:	what kind bag is it?	(adam19.cha; line 1344)
*ADA:	what kind space scanner dat?	(adam19.cha; line 1760)
*ADA:	what kind pilot dat?	(adam19.cha; line 1849)
*ADA:	some kind of bug # dat a [?	(adam20.cha; line 359)
*ADA:	what kind car dat?	(adam20.cha; line 483)
*ADA:	what kind statue xxx are dose?	(adam20.cha; line 515)
*ADA:	what kind # fire truck # is dat?	(adam20.cha; line 621)
*ADA:	I don't know what kind of bed dat.	(adam20.cha; line 704)
*ADA:	what kind guns are dose?	(adam20.cha; line 771)
*ADA:	what kind o(f) rope is dat?	(adam20.cha; line 1666)
*ADA:	what kind house up dere?	(adam20.cha; line 1866)
*ADA:	what kind camera dat?	(adam21.cha; line 168)
*ADA:	what kind a blueberry?	(adam23.cha; line 138)
*ADA:	dis another kind o(f) watch.	(adam23.cha; line 228)
*ADA:	what kind pencil?	(adam23.cha; line 779)
*ADA:	what kind o(f) game?	(adam23.cha; line 1381)
*ADA:	what kind o(f) children?	(adam23.cha; line 1643)
*ADA:	what kind book is dose?	(adam24.cha; line 36)

Like these examples, most of Adam's questions during this period refer to basic object level items – he has discovered the possibility of creating taxonomies, but has perhaps not yet fully figured out what categories need further subcategorization. This would explain his asking questions like, for example, *what kind of fire truck?* and *what kind of blueberry is that?*; it is hard to think of any relevant subcategorization for blueberries. In addition, it is worth pointing out that Adam shifts from an almost exclusive use of classificatory questions before 3;6 to a relatively more frequent production of classificatory statements after 4;0, when he starts to say things like *Dis is a different kind of airplane.*

One way of interpreting these findings is to suggest that Adam's acquisition of superordinate terms was facilitated by two complementary sorts of events: changes in his cognitive development, such that he showed increasing interest in classificatory relationships starting around age 2;11; and responsiveness by his mother to his changing interest, such that she provided both explicit and implicit information about everyday taxonomies.

4.6. General Discussion

We have seen that examining the frequency and context of use of a relatively small and infrequently produced set of words by one child and his mother gives us a very rich picture of development in a particular domain. This domain was an interesting one to choose precisely because it is hard to understand how children come to know the meanings of superordinate terms; the acquisition of such terms may provide a model for how children learn even more abstract terms acquired during the later preschool and early school period. We have seen that a good proportion of the conversations involving superordinate terms between Adam and his mother provided him with some information about the meanings of those terms. However, we must acknowledge that Adam's prior interest in issues of classification generated the opportunities for those informative interactions; we cannot conceive of his acquisition of superordinates as the simple product of his mother's teaching. Rather, it represents the result of his own earlier cognitive and linguistic achievements, his mother's sensitivity to his interests, and her willingness and ability to provide the specific lexical items needed to express the relations about which he was curious.

4.7. Exercises

4.7.1. We selected five frequently occurring superordinates for our analyses, but many others could have been included. Does one get a different picture of the frequency of Adam's or his mother's superordinate use if one analyzes the following superordinates: tree(s), dinosaur(s), building(s), dish(es), or meat(s)? Use the files for Adam in the **snow** directory to answer this question.

4.7.2. Kinship terms (e.g., *brother, uncle, grandfather, cousin*) are complex for children to learn in a way that is rather similar to superordinates; it is easy to point to examples of *cousin*, at least in large families, but it is hard to explain what all the cousins have in common that causes them to qualify as cousins. Another subject in Brown's original study, Sarah, was a working-class girl who had a large extended family, many of whom lived close to her. Her mother also placed considerable importance on Sarah's learning who was who in the family. Using KWAL and at least the kinship terms *brother, aunt, uncle, cousin*, and *grandmother (nana)*, classify the interactions Sarah engaged in with her mother in session 33 (file sarah33.cha, in the **snow** directory) around matters of kinship as *explicitly informative, implicitly informative*, and *uninformative*. Were there certain kinship categories for which Sarah's mother used more explicit teaching? Try doing a FREQ first to see if other important kinship terms occur in the file that should be included in the analysis. (See Goldfield & Snow, 1992, for more information about Sarah's kinship system.)

4.7.3. Some analyses suggest that children with developmental delays show slower progress in language development in part because adults interact with them in ways that are less challenging or demanding than they would use with normally developing children. Six files in the **Hooshyar** directory contain transcripts of play sessions between children with Down syndrome and their mothers at home. Find the frequency of use of the common superordinates already analyzed for Adam in those files, and compare to see if the children with Down syndrome or their mothers use superordinates more or less frequently than Adam and his mother. If you find differences, be sure to consider in your conclusions comparisons between Adam and the children with Down syndrome on MLU or other measures of language sophistication. If you find few or no examples of superordinate use in these children for these samples, then consider constructing your own include file based on a concordance of all the samples.

4.8. Suggested Project

Superordinates are only one of the categories of lexical items that children must acquire by inferring their meaning from use, without the help of ostensive definitions. Another such category is *internal state terms* – e.g., adjectives that refer to emotions or feelings, like *hungry, sleepy, happy, angry, sad*, and *surprised*, and verbs that refer to mental activities, like *think, worry, wonder, doubt*, and *consider*. Using the files in the **snow** directory (Adam 34 to Adam 41) that you have already analyzed for superordinates, and identify those mental state terms that Adam uses, as well as any used by his mother that he has not yet acquired. Carry out the same analysis for Adam55 (the file **adam55.cha** in the **thomas** directory) to see if his use of these terms became more sophisticated as he grew older. Discuss and demonstrate ways in which his mother may help him learn how to use these words and what they mean. Present your findings about Adam's use in the context of what has been reported in the literature by Bretherton and Beeghley-Smith (1982) and by Dunn, Bretherton, and Munn (1987).

Acknowledgments

This chapter is based on Laura Bodin's honors thesis, submitted to Harvard College for honors in linguistics. The authors would like to express their appreciation to Brenda Kurland Dernis, who helped enormously in the transformation of the thesis into this chapter. Preparation of the chapter was supported by NIH grant HD23388. The second author's address is Harvard Graduate School of Education, Larsen 3, Cambridge, MA 02138.

References

Anglin, J. M. (1977). *Word, object, and conceptual development*. New York: W. W. Norton & Co., Inc.

Bakeman, R., & Gottman, J. M. (1986). *Observing interaction: An introduction to sequential analysis*. New York: Cambridge University Press.

Bretherton, I., & Beeghley-Smith, M. (1982). Talking about internal states: The acquisition of an explicit theory of mind. *Developmental Psychology, 18*, 906-921.

Brown, R. (1958). *Words and things: An introduction to language.* New York: The Free Press.

Brown, R. (1973). *A First language: The early stages.* Cambridge: Harvard University Press.

Callanan, M. A. (1985). How parents label objects for young children: The role of input in the acquisition of category hierarchies. *Child Development, 56,* 508-523.

Callanan, M. A. (1989). Maternal speech strategies and children's acquisition of hierarchical category labels. *Genetic Epistemologist, 17,* 3-12.

Dale, P., Bates, E., Reznick, J., & Morisset, C. (1989). The validity of a parent report instrument of child language at twenty months. *Journal of Child Language, 16,* 239-250.

Dunn, J., Bretherton, I., & Munn, P. (1987). Conversations about feeling states between mothers and their young children. *Developmental Psychology, 23,* 132-139.

Goldfield, B., & Snow, C. E. (1992). "What's your cousin Arthur's mommy's name?" Features of family talk about kin and kin terms. *First Language, 12,* 187-205.

Horton, M. S., & Markman, E. (1980). Developmental differences in the acquisition of basic and superordinate categories. *Child Development, 51,* 708-719.

Karmiloff-Smith, A. (1979). *A functional approach to child language: A study of determiners and reference.* New York: Cambridge University Press.

Keil, F. (1979). *Semantic and conceptual development.* Cambridge, MA: Harvard University Press.

Macnamara, J. (1977). *Names for things.* Cambridge, MA: The MIT Press.

Rosch, E., Mervis, C., Gray, W., Johnson, D., & Boyes-Braem, P. (1976). Basic objects in natural categories. *Cognitive Psychology, 8,* 382-439.

Waxman, S., & Hatch, T. (1992). Beyond the basics: Preschool children label objects flexibly at multiple hierarchical levels. *Journal of Child Language, 19,* 153-166.

Appendix: The Coding of Interactions Involving Superordinates

An "interaction" can be defined as the window (target utterance plus and minus five utterances) in which the keyword occurs. Because the focus of the interaction sometimes shifted, more than one interaction within a window was occasionally coded.

Since we were interested in the value of the interactions as a source of information to the child, only utterances by Adam's mother or the experimenters were coded. Even Adam's use of superordinates that were explicit about hierarchical relations ("What kind of birdie dat?") were not coded. However, if Adam's mother answered these questions explicitly, her response would be coded as explicit.

Explicit: Members of the superordinate category are explicitly identified as category members, or explicit information about the distinguishing features of category members is given, for example:

```
1.   @Comment:     *** File adam19.cha. Line 942. Keyword: toy
     *ADA: d(o) you wan(t) me hit Perro ?
     *MOT: no .
     *ADA: why not ?
     *MOT: because he's one of your toys .
     %sup: $EXP:toy
```

Adam's mother here places Perro in the category of "toy" and, furthermore, states that anything that falls into the category of "your toy" should be handled with care.

Implicit: The superordinate term is used in close association with identification of members of the category, without explicit statement of category membership:

```
2.   @Comment:     *** File adam19.cha. Line 1162. Keyword: animal
     *MOT: what d(o) you think the lion is doing ?
     *ADA: what he doing ?
     *MOT: yes .
     *ADA: what he standing on ?
     *MOT: well # that's a special kind of block they have for
           animals that perform .
     %sup: $IMP:ani
```

Here, the lion is being discussed, yet the mother describes the block in terms of its use for "animals." Implicitly, then, the lion is an animal.

```
3.   @Comment:     *** File adam21.cha. Line 518. Keyword: toy
     *ADA: I put dose toys in (th)ere .
     *MOT: you put what in there ?
     %sup: $IMP:toy
     *ADA: toys .
     *ADA: take dose toys out of here .
```

Here, the mother's response could have elicited names of individual toys from Adam, so the interaction is coded as implicit.

Uninformative: The superordinate term is used but no information is given about members of the category or about features of the category, for example:

```
4.   @Comment:    *** File adam22.cha. Line 1388. Keyword: food
     *ADA: dat's funny .
     *ADA: dat's funny .
     *MOT: careful # you'll drop all your food out .
     %sup: $UNI:fod
```

There is no information available from this conversation about what "food" is or that "food" includes different types of edibles.

```
5.   @Comment:    *** File adam21.cha. Line 782. Keyword: toy
     *ADA: xxx choose some toys .
     *MOT: oh good .
     *ADA: Mommy # hold dem .
     *MOT: no # put them back in or we won't play with them
           again.
     %sup: $UNI:toy
     *ADA: let me play with dem again .
```

Since *them* refers to the toys, the mother's response clearly includes a response to Adam's use of the word *toys*. However, the response is uninformative.

```
6.   @Comment:    *** File adam23.cha Line 809. Keyword: food
     *ADA: you going to the grocery store to get some food ?
     *ADA: what you want ?
     *MOT: what do I want ?
     *ADA: yep .
     *MOT: I'd like a can opener .
     %sup: $UNI:fod
```

Here, Adam makes the link between grocery store and food. However, his mother's response to his request, "What do you want?" is a non-food item, so the response is coded as uninformative. "I'd like some orange juice" would have been coded as implicit ($IMP).

Learning to Use Superordinates 109

Uncoded: Conversations in which Adam used a superordinate but was talking for several utterances in a row by himself, or in which the adult response was not relevant to the topic of the superordinate, were not coded, for example:

7. @Comment: *** File adam20.cha. Line 415. Keyword: bird
   *ADA: it goes down steps # on Paul .
   *MOT: oh # on Paul .
   *ADA: yeah .
   *MOT: it might frighten Paul .
   *ADA: dat's a fly # in here .
   *ADA: dat not a fly # dat a bird .
   *ADA: we not going make a bird .
   *ADA: we going make a duck .
   *ADA: Mommy # make a road .
   *MOT: no # we already have a road .
   *ADA: make a street light wif dat .

Here, Adam mentions birds but his mother does not respond to those utterances, so no interaction is coded.

5   A Study of Some Common Features of Mothers' Vocabularies

Qian Hu
Boston University

In this chapter, you will learn the following skills:

- To derive the shared vocabulary across six mothers using FREQ.

- To analyze the content and function of the shared vocabulary using KWAL.

To replicate the analyses and do the exercises, you will need the transcripts of the six mother-child dyads from the files in the **hu** directory.

5.1. Introduction

Language input from mothers is a very important source of information for early childhood language acquisition. Vocabulary in maternal speech is the primary pool from which young children select words to constitute their own lexicon. Thus, investigations into the content, frequency, and function of mothers' vocabulary will reveal a great deal about common features of maternal lexical input. These common features, in turn, may later predict some characteristics of children's lexical development. Modern techniques using computer programs make it possible to determine the shared vocabularies of a large number of subjects. The goal of this chapter is to demonstrate how we analyzed the shared vocabularies of six mothers and to invite you to use these techniques to perform similar analyses on the vocabularies of the children. In this section, we will first discuss some general issues regarding motherese and lexical simplification, including type-token ratios and object-naming levels. Then we will raise a set of questions about the characteristics of mothers' vocabulary in child-directed speech and define the notion of a maternal core lexicon.

5.1.1. Motherese

Mothers addressing their language-learning children modify their speech in important ways. For instance, they use shorter utterances with simpler syntactic constructions and with higher frequency lexical items (Garnica, 1977; Phillips, 1973; Remick, 1976; Snow, 1972). There seem to be general tendencies among the mothers to engage in child-appropriate language (Nelson, 1973). It is commonly believed that maternal speech to young children in middle-class English-speaking families contains many shared features. This tendency to favor child appropriate language is believed to facilitate children's language acquisition. Maternal speech containing some of the above mentioned features is often referred to as *motherese* or *babytalk* (Snow & Ferguson, 1977).

Realizing the importance of motherese in assisting early childhood language acquisition, many child language researchers have conducted analyses on mothers' speech to children (Barnes, Gutfreund, Satterly, & Wells, 1983; De Villiers, 1985; Phillips, 1973; Snow, 1972). However, most of these studies focus on the syntactic and phonological features of motherese (Kavanaugh & Jen, 1981; Lipscomb & Coon, 1983; Low & Moely, 1988), while relatively few focus on the lexical features (Hayes & Ahrens, 1988; Mervis & Mervis, 1982).

5.1.2. Do Mothers Use the Same Vocabulary to Children as to Adults?

Several studies have been devoted to exploring whether there is a difference in vocabulary choice between mothers' speech to children and to adults. Phillips (1973) found that adults do not speak to children as they speak to other adults; not only do they produce simpler syntax, but the sentences they do produce contain less lexical diversity. This result was obtained by comparing the type-token ratio (see Pan, this volume) of mother-child speech to that of mother-adult speech. The type-token ratio for mothers was found to be smaller in child-directed speech than in adult-directed speech. This suggests that mothers use more diverse vocabulary in speaking to adults than to children. In other words, mothers use a somewhat restricted, or repetitious, vocabulary when speaking to children (Phillips, 1973). In addition, Hayes and Ahrens (1988) reported that adult word usage in speech to children is skewed toward more frequent words as compared with their speech to adults. This finding further confirms the presence of maternal modification in lexical input to children. However, it is still not known exactly what lexical items all mothers use when addressing their language-learning children.

5.1.3. Object Naming in Maternal Input

One explanation for how mothers modify their lexical input to children is derived from the notion of the basic object level. According to this notion, the basic object level is defined as "the level at which the most basic category cuts are made" (Rosch, Mervis, Gray, Johnson, & Boyes-Braem, 1976, p. 382). The relevance of basic object theory to child lexical acquisition is revealed in the following quote:

> Basic objects are shown to be the most inclusive categories for which a concrete image of the category as a whole can be formed, to be the first categorizations made during perception of the environment, to be the earliest categories sorted and named by children... (p. 382)

This study, though not directly concerned with maternal lexical modification, had a great impact on later studies of maternal lexical input. For example, under the assumption that basic object categories are easier for the child to acquire, Mervis and Mervis (1982) conducted a study testing which object level mothers would use when naming an object for their children. They found that mothers tended to choose names for objects at their children's object-naming level rather than at the adult's. Thus, even at the risk of mislabeling, mothers tend to call a *leopard* a *kitty-cat* to suit their children's object categories. In this way, maternal lexical modification is illustrated by the mother's fine-tuning of her lexical input to the child's object-naming level (see chapter 4 for an analysis of maternal input at the superordinate level).

All this suggests that mothers not only simplify their speech by using syntactically shorter and simpler sentences, but they also restrict their vocabulary choice. However, there has been little research on shared features of mothers' vocabulary in addressing young children; we know little about how uniform such vocabularies may be. We know even less about the specific content of the maternal lexicon and the differential frequency and function of mothers' most commonly used words.

5.1.4. Current Goals

This study addresses some of the questions that have been raised concerning shared words in the vocabularies of mothers when speaking to 2-year-old children. A major goal of the study is to extract the common words used by all mothers. If middle-class English-speaking mothers restrict their vocabulary choice by adjusting their speech to the child's object-naming level, then we hypothesized that all mothers would produce very similar speech, in the form of a core lexicon, when addressing children of the same age in the same situation.

To test this hypothesis, I will explore the following research questions:

1. *Is there a core vocabulary used by mothers when speaking to 2-year-olds in a given situation?* (In this chapter, we define this core vocabulary as the lexical items used by all of the mothers in the study.)
2. *To what extent do mothers share one another's vocabulary?*
3. *Which words are shared by a majority of the mothers and why?*
4. *What percentage of maternal input is composed of the core vocabulary?*
5. *What is the composition and function of the core vocabulary?*

The answers to these questions will reveal the characteristics of mothers' core vocabulary and throw some light on the nature and function of maternal lexical input to children. The answers may also provide evidence concerning whether or not mothers simplify their vocabulary and whether or not mothers all use the same object-naming level when speaking to their children. This, in turn, will help to establish some estimate of the common words that all children should hear in order to have a typical lexical development.

In the sections that follow, I demonstrate how answers to these questions were obtained with the help of two CLAN programs (MacWhinney, 1991). I also illustrate the exact CLAN procedures utilized to answer each of the five questions listed above. As these procedures are cumulative (i.e., one analysis is based on the result from another analysis), I present the results along with the presentation of each procedural step. Finally, I interpret the results and explore their implications in the concluding section.

5.2. Using CLAN to Study the Maternal Core Lexicon

5.2.1. The Transcript Data

The transcript data for the study were drawn from the Gleason corpus (Masur & Gleason, 1980) in CHILDES (MacWhinney, 1991). We analyzed mothers' speech from transcripts of mother-child interactions that took place in a laboratory playroom situation. The subjects were six mothers of 2-year-old children (3 boys and 3 girls with a mean age of 2;5 ranging from 2;1 to 2;11). All of the mother-child dyads were from middle-class American families.

In each half-hour laboratory playroom session, the same kinds of toys and instructions were provided. The mothers were told to interact with their children while engaged in three different activities: reading a wordless picture book, assembling a toy car, and playing store. The data were standardized by extracting from the original 30-minute interaction only the portion during which the mother-child dyads were engaged in the play-store activity. For this situation, all subjects were provided with a toy cash register, some play money, and some miniature goods usually found in a grocery store such as baby cereal, milk, napkins, cups, soup, and so on. See Table 5.1 for individual mothers' MLUs, type-token ratios, total number of different words, and total number of words produced. The following are the names of the six files for each of the mothers we used for the study: laurel.sto, martin.sto, nanette.sto, patricia.sto, victor.sto, william.sto.

5.2.2. The Step-by-Step CLAN Procedure with Results

Question 1: Is there a core vocabulary used by these mothers when speaking to their 2-year-olds in a given situation?

The FREQ program lists all the words in the sample along with their frequencies. In addition, it calculates the total number of different word types, the total number of word tokens, and the type-token ratio of the entire transcript.

As our first goal was to search for the core vocabulary among the six mothers, we were not initially interested in word frequencies, but in the word-list that the FREQ program generates. By taking advantage of the **+d1** option, we could first

Table 5.1: Basic measures for each of the mothers in the study.

Subjects	MLU	Word Types	Word Tokens	TTR
Laurel's Mom	4.303	148	466	0.318
Martin's Mom	5.306	193	1,117	0.173
Nanette's Mom	6.427	245	1,334	0.184
Patricia's Mom	4.444	254	1,359	0.187
Victor's Mom	4.215	165	554	0.298
William's Mom	4.728	158	623	0.254
MEAN	4.979	193	909	0.236

use FREQ to obtain a word inventory for every mother without the frequency and type-token summary. This analysis would be performed with the following command:

freq +t*MOT +d1 +s"*-%%" +fmot *.sto

+t*MOT	Analyze the mother speaker tier only
+d1	Output in CHAT format without frequency or TTR information
+s"*-%%"	Include all strings ignoring everything after the hyphen
+fmot	Save the results in a file with the extension **.mot**
*.sto	Analyze all files ending in **.sto**

Command Box 5.1

In addition, by using the +s"*-%%" option, we indicated that variations of a word with different suffixes were to be counted as a single word-type. For example, this FREQ analysis would consider *toy* and *toy-s* to be one word-type instead of two. It is important to note that +s"*-%%" is only an option when the transcripts are morphemicized (i.e., when *toys* is transcribed as *toy-s*). As a result of this command, six output files with the extension **.mot** would be generated. Each of these files would contain the word inventory for each mother. However, this analysis would only take us half of the distance to our ultimate goal. We would still need to determine the subset of words that were used by all the mothers. It would still be very time consuming and cumbersome to read and compare the six wordlists to derive the maternal core lexicon. So we used the six word inventories as input to another FREQ analysis to derive the mothers' core vocabulary:

freq +y +u +o *.mot > motcore

+y	Work on files not in CHAT format (e.g., the results from FREQ)
+u	Merge all input files into a combined analysis
+o	Output words in descending order of frequency
*.mot	Analyze all files ending in **.mot**
> motcore	Redirect the output to the file **motcore**

Command Box 5.2

Note that this time we did not omit the frequency information in the analysis. Recall also that the input to this FREQ analysis was not the original transcripts but the six word-lists obtained from the mothers. Therefore, the frequency in the output does not represent the actual frequency in the original transcripts, but the number of mothers who used the word. Therefore, *all words whose frequency was 6 were shared by all six mothers*. These words constitute the core vocabulary in the speech of our six mothers when addressing their children.

With this important point in mind, I will now show you a shortcut for performing this analysis. Within CLAN, it is possible to combine two related analyses with the piping option. We took advantage of this option by combining the first two FREQ analyses into one command using the pipe symbol ('|'). The following CLAN command demonstrates this combination:

freq +t*MOT +d1 +s"*-%%" *.sto | freq +y +u +o > motcore

+t*MOT	Analyze the mother speaker tier only
+d1	Output in CHAT format without frequency and TTR information
+s"*-%%"	Include all strings ignoring everything after the hyphen
*.sto	Analyze all files ending in **.sto**
| freq	Pipe the output to FREQ

+y	Work on files not in CHAT format
+u	Merge all input files into a combined analysis
+o	Sort output in descending order of frequency
*.mot	Analyze all files ending in **.mot**

> motcore	Redirect the output to the file **motcore**

Command Box 5.3

The first FREQ analysis in Command Box 5.1 generated six output files, each consisting of a word-list for one mother. In the combined analysis, we do not need to save each of the output files (note the absence of +**f** option). Instead of saving the output in six separate files, the output from the first FREQ command is sent or *piped* directly to the second FREQ analysis, which follows the pipe symbol ('|'). Thus, the six word-lists from the first FREQ analysis would neither appear on the screen nor be saved in files. This results in more efficient file management.

As a result of using the +**u** option, the input to the second FREQ analysis (after the pipe) consisted of the six word-lists combined into one unified input. The +**u** option has the effect of merging the individual files into one larger analysis. Table 5.2 lists the words with a frequency of 6 from the **motcore** file along with the complete type-token summary information.

The file **motcore** not only lists all the different word-types used by the six mothers, but more importantly, how many mothers used a particular word. The number on the left of each word in the output file is the word's frequency which, in this case, represents the number of speakers who used the word. Therefore, all words preceded by a 6 are words that were used by all the mothers in our sample.

118   Chapter 5

Table 5.2: The first part of the FREQ output from Command Box 5.3. showing the words shared by all six mothers in speech to their children together with the summary statistics.

6	a	6	just	6	some
6	and	6	know	6	thank
6	at	6	let	6	that
6	be	6	like	6	the
6	can	6	look	6	there
6	do	6	me	6	thing
6	for	6	milk	6	think
6	go	6	money	6	this
6	gonna	6	my	6	to
6	have	6	of	6	wanna
6	here	6	oh	6	we
6	how	6	okay	6	what
6	i	6	one	6	would
6	in	6	open	6	yeah
6	is	6	put	6	you
6	it	6	see	.	

494 Total number of different word types used
1163 Total number of words (tokens)
0.425 Type/Token ratio

These 47 words constitute the core vocabulary for this group of mothers. This core lexicon represents the complete list of words shared by all six mothers when addressing their 2-year-old children in the play store situation.

Question 2: To what extent do mothers share one another's vocabulary?

From the results of the first procedure, we now know that there is a core vocabulary among the mothers in our study. Next we would like to determine the proportion of shared word-types in relation to the total number of word-types for all the mothers. This will tell us the amount of the mothers' vocabulary that is shared. To accomplish this task, we divided the number of word-types in the core vocabulary (47) by the total number of different word-types spoken by all six of the mothers (494). These numbers were taken from Table 5.2. Out of a total of 494 different lexical items produced by the six mothers, only 47 different words were shared. This means that the core lexicon consists of only 9.5% of all the words used by all the mothers.

Question 3: Which words are shared by a majority of the mothers and why?

Besides listing the core vocabulary, the **motcore** file also indicates which words were shared by a portion of the mothers. Recall that the frequencies listed in the **motcore** file indicate the number of speakers who produced the word rather than the actual frequency of the word. This means that words with a higher frequency in the **motcore** file were shared by more mothers than words with a lower frequency number. This is all we need to know to answer this question.

Apart from the maternal core lexicon, we found that some words were shared more than others. Those that were salient to the activity such as *buy* (5), *cash* (5), *pay* (4), *play* (5), *push* (5) *register* (5), *shop* (5), and the like were shared by four or five of the six mothers. In addition, superordinate terms were found to be more shared than subordinate terms. For instance, superordinate terms, such as *food* (5) and *store* (5), were shared more than their respective subordinate terms: *cereal* (2), *bread* (1), and *supermarket* (2). On the other hand, words that were not salient to the activity or not pertinent to the child's daily life were found to be less shared. For instance, one mother used the word *inflation*, which, according to Carroll's (1971) word frequency book, does not appear in children's readers until Grade 6 and has an estimated frequency of 0.6862 per million tokens. This word seems quite difficult for a child of 2 to understand, and not unexpectedly, was not used by the other mothers.

Question 4: What percentage of maternal input is composed of the core vocabulary?

One way of investigating the nature of mothers' core vocabulary is to examine the frequency with which the core items are produced in maternal speech. To do this, we must shift our focus from the number of different word-types to the number of word-tokens in the core vocabulary. In order to discover what proportion of the entire speech sample was made up of the core vocabulary, we first obtained the total number of word-tokens produced by the six speakers and the total frequency of the core lexicon (in tokens). Then we divided the total number of tokens in the maternal core lexicon by the total number of tokens in the entire speech sample. The result of this calculation was the percentage of the core vocabulary in the total speech sample. In order to perform the first operation, we used the following CLAN command to obtain the total number of tokens produced by the six mothers during the entire play store activity:

freq +t*MOT +d4 +u *.sto

+t*MOT	Analyze the mother speaker tier only
+d4	Output type-token summary only
+u	Merge all input files into a combined analysis
*.sto	Analyze all files ending in .sto

Command Box 5.4

Note that we dropped the +s"*-%%" option, as we are now interested in the number of word-tokens and not word-types. The following is the type-token summary taken from this command:

```
  599 Total number of different word types used
 5454 Total number of words (tokens)
0.110 Type/Token ratio
```

As you may have realized, the information provided by the first line of the summary, the total number of different word types produced by all mothers, is different from the earlier result in Table 5.2. This is due to the omission of the +s"*-%%" option. However, in this summary, we are interested in the result listed in the second line, that the total number of words or tokens produced by all six mothers is 5454.

The goal of the second operation is to compute the total number of tokens in the mothers' lexical core. To obtain this goal, we first need to create an include file containing the core vocabulary. If we did not use an include file, we would have to repeat the FREQ procedure many times: once for each core word until all 47 core words were searched and counted. With the include file, however, all we need to do is list the entire core vocabulary in a file and include it in a single FREQ analysis. As the **motcore** file contains the core vocabulary, though with non-shared vocabulary as well, it was easier to modify the **motcore** file than to create a new file. We did this in three steps: (a) we extracted those words with a frequency of six from the **motcore** file; (b) we deleted the frequency number associated with each entry; and (c) we added "–%%" to the end of all nouns, verbs, and pronouns. For example, we changed toy to *toy–%%* to insure that both *toy* and *toy-s* would be counted. As with all include files, this editing can be performed with any word processor, with the constraints that there can only be a single word per line and that the file must be saved as ASCII text. We named the edited file **motcore.inc** and used the following CLAN command to obtain the total number of core tokens in maternal input:

freq +t*MOT +u +o +s@motcore.inc +d4 *.sto

+t*MOT	Analyze the mother speaker tier only
+u	Merge all input files into a combined analysis
+o	Output the words in descending order of frequency
+s@motcore.inc	Search for the words in the include file **motcore.inc**
+d4	Output type-token summary only
*.sto	Analyze all files ending in **.sto**

Command Box 5.5

The following is the type-token summary taken from this command (see Table 5.3 for the complete file):

```
   47 Total number of different word types used
 3288 Total number of words (tokens)
0.014 Type/Token ratio
```

This summary indicates that the 47 different words in the core lexicon accounted for 3,288 of the word-tokens produced in the speech of all six mothers.

The next step was to divide the frequency (3,288) of all maternal core words by the total number of words produced by the mothers (5,454) to obtain the percentage of the core vocabulary in the entire corpus of maternal speech. Thus, in terms of word-tokens, the core lexicon made up a total of 60.3% (3,288 ÷ 5,454) of the mothers' actual speech.

Table 5.3 The frequency of the words in the mothers' core vocabulary.

342 you	170 it	170 what	160 the
150 that	147 do	142 i	140 okay
130 a	125 is	123 this	79 to
74 here	70 we	64 and	63 oh
62 one	59 see	58 can	58 in
57 there	53 some	52 for	52 know
50 have	50 like	47 gonna	47 money
45 wanna	44 how	42 me	41 put
35 let	35 of	35 think	34 look
29 go	29 milk	25 just	20 thank
20 would	20 yeah	18 open	17 be
16 at	13 my	11 thing	

Question 5: What is the composition and function of the core vocabulary?

The goal of this analysis was to determine the relative percentages of content and function words in the core lexicon. The class of content words consists of nouns, verbs, adjectives, and adverbs. The class of function words consists of everything else (e.g., articles, conjunctions, deictic terms, pronominals, prepositions, modals, auxiliary and copular verbs, interjections, filler words, etc). In order to perform the analysis, we coded each item in the core vocabulary by part-of-speech and by its membership in one of the two major categories: content or function words. Then we calculated the percentage of content and function words in the maternal core lexicon. Finally, we examined the function of the content words in the core vocabulary.

Of course, the part-of-speech of some lexical items may be ambiguous. In other words, some lexical items can have different meanings depending on the context in which they appear. For instance, *do* may function as a main verb in *You can do it* or as an auxiliary verb in *Do you know what it is?* We identified three such ambiguous lexical items in the core lexicon: *do, like,* and *some*. The only way to solve the problem of ambiguity is to analyze the part-of-speech of each of these items in the context in which they occur. We used KWAL to aid us in this analysis. The KWAL program can be used to search for a keyword within a transcript and then to return the whole utterance in which the word appears. We can then use the complete utterance to disambiguate the word's part-of-speech. For example, if we are not sure whether *do* is used as an auxiliary or main verb, we can use the following CLAN command to extract all of the utterances in our sample containing the word *do*:

kwal +t*MOT +s"do–%%" +u *.sto > do.mot

+t*MOT	Analyze the mother speaker tier only
+s"do–%%"	Include all types of the word *do* in the analysis
+u	Merge all input files into a combined analysis
*.sto	Analyze all files ending in **.sto**
> do.mot	Redirect the output to the file **do.mot**

Command Box 5.6

The CLAN commands for analyzing the context of *like* and *some* are as follows:

kwal +t*MOT +s"like–%%" +u *.sto > like.mot
kwal +t*MOT +s"some-%%" +u *.sto > some.mot

The resulting files from these three KWAL procedures contain the utterances in which the target words appear. By examining these files, we can determine the most frequent part-of-speech for each of these words. *Do* was used primarily as an auxiliary verb in yes/no questions and negations, so we coded it as a function word. *Like* was used about half of the time as a preposition or conjunction and half of the time as a verb, so it was divided into two classes. Since *some* was predominantly used as an adjective, we coded it as a content word.

The results of this analysis indicated that the maternal core lexicon was composed of 65% function words and 35% content words. The content words were 13 verbs: *go, gonna, have, know, let, like, look, open, put, see, thank, think,* and *wanna*; 3 nouns: *money, milk,* and *thing*; and 1 adjective: *some*.

5.3. Discussion

In this section, I will discuss the results in the following manner. First, I will discuss the maternal core lexicon in terms of its size, frequency, and possible relationship to children's lexical acquisition. Second, I will discuss the composition and function of the core vocabulary. Finally, I will discuss whether mothers restrict their vocabulary choice when addressing young children.

5.3.1. Uniformity and Variability in Maternal Lexical Input

Our results indicate that mothers' lexical input to young children is both uniform and variable. Uniformity is primarily revealed by the existence of a core lexicon that comprises 9.5% of the word-types produced by the six mothers. Although small, the presence of any core vocabulary at all suggests that mothers do share some of the same words. More importantly, the small number (47) of core vocabulary items produced by the six mothers accounts for a considerable portion (60.3%) of their entire speech. Not surprisingly, this implies that core items are very frequent in child-directed speech. From this perspective, maternal lexical input to 2-year-olds appears quite homogeneous: 60.3% of all the words that these children hear in their mothers' speech was taken from a pool of only 47 lexical items. The high frequency of the maternal core lexicon may be influential in children's lexical acquisition. Although other factors, such as the word's meaning and saliency, play a role in lexical acquisition, frequent items are more likely to be acquired by children (Schwartz, 1983).

The small number of different word-types in the maternal core lexicon suggests variability more than uniformity. About 90% of the word-types produced by the mothers in our sample were not shared. In other words, while 47 words were shared, a much larger number (447 words) were not universally shared, of which 239 word types were used by only one mother. Despite the larger number of non-shared words, they comprised only 39.7% of the mothers' speech.

Our research and past work conducted by Hayes and Ahrens (1988) suggest that uniformity in use is more likely to be found among the function words, while variability is more likely to be found among the content words (especially for nominals). The variability in mothers' choice of content words does not automatically lead to the conclusion that mothers do not modify their lexical input to accommodate their children's limited range of linguistic and world knowledge. The content of mothers' vocabulary might still be a good predictor of their children's lexicon. For example, De Villiers (1985) discovered that children used the same verb-argument structures that they heard their mothers use. She suggested that maternal use of verbs and their predicate arguments were a highly significant predictor of the children's use of the same verbs.

5.3.2. The Content and Function of the Maternal Core Lexicon

The maternal core lexicon consisted mostly of high-frequency function words and relatively fewer content words. The former is determined by the nature of language in general; the latter, by the nature of child-directed speech. There are three reasons why the function words are more likely to be shared: (a) they are the building blocks with which utterances are constructed; (b) they are finite in number; and (c) they are often non-substitutable. As a result, function words are more likely to be shared among speakers than content words. This is true not only for child-directed speech, but also for speech in general. The fact that mothers use these function words frequently when addressing their 2-year-old children indicates that young children are exposed not only to object names, but also to function words, which ultimately help them to expand their utterances.

The content words in the maternal core lexicon are mostly verbs. These verbs play a special role in child-directed speech. Some function to engage children in activities. These include *let, see, put, have, like, gonna*, and *wanna*. Some probe children's knowledge of objects and activities (e.g., *know* and *think*). The use of these verbs in child-directed speech may also help to orient and direct children's attention to the activity. Since Tomasello and Todd's (1983) research suggests that mothers who maintain sustained bouts of joint attentional focus have children with larger vocabularies, this function may have a profound impact on language development. The finding that all of the mothers use these verbs supports the theoretical notion that these verbs have instructive and directive value in sustaining children's attention and in assisting lexical acquisition.

5.3.3. Do Mothers Restrict Their Vocabularies?

The general tendency of mothers to share words suggests that they may restrict their choice of lexical items to a small pool of highly frequent words when addressing 2-year-old children. In our study, mothers selected words that were salient to the activity and familiar to the children in their daily lives. Though many words were not shared, the total number of different words used by the six mothers was quite small. Mothers also tended to select lexical items they thought were at their child's level of knowledge. Since children's levels of knowledge differ from one another, these mothers' terms for the same object may also vary. This would explain the counterintuitive result that not all six mothers used the word *store* or *cash register* despite the fact that they were all performing the playstore activity. Although mothers all tended to select words at their child's knowledge level, with the exception of the major function words and some verbs that provide instruction or sustain attention, they did not use the same set of vocabulary items. We believe this is due to the following factors: (a) a variation in children's knowledge levels; as a result, there is more variability among mothers in regard to the use of content words, especially the nominals; (b) mothers' individual preferences for some words as opposed to others in referring to the same object; and (c) the availability of various terms for the same object. For instance, we found that mothers used such varied terms as *storeman*, *storekeeper*, *grocer man*, *lady*, and *supermarket lady* to refer to a cashier.

5.4. Conclusion

In conclusion, this study uncovered a small core lexicon shared by all the mothers. This information could aid in the creation of assessment measures of lexical input. With greater knowledge of the typical maternal core lexicon, it would be possible to diagnose potential contributors to delayed lexical development. Delayed lexical, or even cognitive, development could be due, in part, to lack of exposure to a basic vocabulary that supports joint attention (Tomasello & Farrar, 1986). In addition, the study of variability in maternal lexical input may prove useful in the study of individual differences in language development (Lieven, 1978; Hampsen & Nelson, 1990).

5.5. Exercises

5.5.1. Use the procedures described in this chapter to collect the core vocabulary among the children in our sample. Perform the analyses that will allow you to answer the following questions:

A. Is there a core vocabulary among the six children?
B. To what extent do children share one another's vocabulary?
C. Which words are shared by a majority of the children?

D. What percentage of the children's speech is composed of their core vocabulary?
E. What is the composition and function of the children's core vocabulary?

Compare the maternal core lexicon (from Table 5.2) with that of the children to see if there is any overlap between these two core lexicons. Which lexical items are the same? Which are different? Why do you think this is so? What are the implications for lexical development?

5.5.2. In this exercise, you are asked to derive the core vocabulary for each of the individual mother-child pairs. To do this, you will need to perform the CLAN analyses listed in Section 5.2.2. for each of the six mother-child pairs separately. You should end up with a frequency list in which all words with a frequency of 2 are shared by both the mother and her child, and all words with a frequency of 1 are used either by the mother, or her child, but are not shared. Include the results to the following questions in this table:

A. How many words are there in each of the six core lexicons?

B. To what extent do individual mother-child pairs share each other's vocabulary? In other words, what percentage of the total number of word types is accounted for by the core vocabulary for each mother-child dyad? **Hint**: This exercise is similar to Question 2 in Section 5.2.2.

C. Calculate the mean for the percentages of the six core vocabularies derived in 5.5.2.B. This number will be the average for all six of the mother-child dyads.

What are the implications of your results for lexical development? Do they provide evidence for individual differences in maternal input? If so, how? How can you use these results to compare and contrast different populations of parent-child dyads?

5.5.3. In this exercise, you are asked to analyze the use of basic level terms in both mother and child speech. To do this, you will first need to create a list of basic level terms. What is a basic level term? How did you create your list? Second, you will need to determine the frequency of these items in both mother and child speech. In whose speech are they more frequent? Why do you think this is so? Do all children use all the basic level terms that their mothers use? Third, you will want to analyze the context in which the mother uses these basic level terms. Does the mother tend to use basic level terms following the child's mention of a specific instance of the basic category? What are the implications for lexical development?

5.6. Suggested Projects

5.6.1. It is not hard to imagine that some children may share a high percentage of their mothers' vocabulary while others may not. This is an interesting question because these individual tendencies may have important implications for the assessment of lexical development. For example, the percentage of total lexical types accounted for by the core vocabulary between mothers and their children may prove useful in assessing children's lexical development. Scores for this measure that are different than those for other children of similar age or linguistic ability may place a child at a particular lexical level of development. The goal of this project is to test this hypothesis. To do so, you will need to duplicate the analyses in Question 5.5.2 for six mother-child dyads in which the child has Down syndrome and then compare these new results with those obtained in the previous exercise.

In order for you to perform this exercise, transcripts of mother-child interaction between six mothers and their children with Down syndrome have been provided for you. The names of the files correspond to the children's pseudonyms and are stored in the **hooshyar** directory. This sample of six mother-child dyads was selected from a larger sample within the Hooshyar corpus (1985, 1987). The three boys and three girls with the highest MLUs were selected (see Table 5.4 for a description of the subjects and MacWhinney, 1991, for a short description of the corpus). The mental ability of these children was measured by the Vineland Adaptive Behavior Scale. Only the play time setting was included in this sample.

5.6.2. Derive the core vocabulary used by a mother and her child, and that used by the father and the same child. Compare these two shared vocabularies. Are there any differences between the mother-child core and that of the father-child? Does the child share more maternal or paternal words? What are the implications of this for lexical development? For a review of the role of the father in early language development, see Barton and Tomasello (1993).

Table 5.4: Descriptions of the six children with Down syndrome.

Subject ID	Age (months)	Gender	Vineland	MLU
67	105	male	67	2.668
66	119	female	79	2.423
68	112	female	75	2.580
71	84	female	58	2.369
70	95	male	29	2.214
65	113	male	48	1.993

Acknowledgments

I would like to thank J. Berko Gleason for her guidance, insights, and support throughout the research, and R. Y. Perlmann for many valuable discussions and suggestions. I would also like to thank C. E. Snow, B. A. Pan, J. L. Sokolov, M. Mentis, and B. Schwartz for reading and commenting on the various versions of this paper. This research was supported in part by grant number HD23388 from the National Institute of Child Health and Human Development. A portion of this research was presented at the Fifteenth Annual Boston University Conference on Language Development, October 10, 1989.

References

Barnes, S., Gutfreund, M., Satterly, D., & Wells, G. (1983). Characteristics of adult speech which predict children's language development. *Journal of Child Language*, *10*, 65-84.

Barton, M. E., & Tomasello, M. (1993). The rest of the family: The role of fathers and siblings in early language development. In C. Gallaway & B. Richards (Eds.), *Input and interaction in language acquisition*. New York: Cambridge University Press.

Carroll, J. B., Davies, P., & Richman, B. (1971). *The American Heritage word frequency book*. Boston, MA: Houghton Mifflin Company.

de Villiers, J. G. (1985). Learning how to use verbs: Lexical coding and the influence of the input. *Journal of Child Language, 12*, 587-595.

Garnica, O. (1977). Some prosodic and paralinguistic features of speech to young children. In C. E. Snow & C.A. Ferguson (Eds.), *Talking to children: Language input and acquisition*. New York: Cambridge University Press.

Hampsen, J., & Nelson, K. (1990). Early relations between mother talk and language development: Masked and unmasked. *Papers and Reports in Child Language Development, 29*, 78-85.

Hayes, D. P., & Ahrens, M. G. (1988). Vocabulary simplification for children: A special case of 'motherese'? *Journal of Child Language, 15*, 395-410.

Hooshyar, N. (1985). Language interaction between mothers and their non-handicapped children. *International Journal of Rehabilitation Research, 4*, 475-477.

Hooshyar, N. (1987). The relationship between maternal language parameters and the child's language constancy and developmental condition. *International Journal of Rehabilitation Research, 10*, 321-324.

Kavanaugh, R. D., & Jen, M. (1981). Some relationships between parental speech and children's object language development. *First Language, 2*, 103-115.

Lieven, E. (1978). Conversations between mothers and young children: Individual differences and their possible implications for the study of language learning. In N. Waterson & C. Snow (Eds.), *The development of communication*. New York: Wiley.

Lipscomb, T. J., & Coon, R. C. (1983). Parental speech modification to young children. *Journal of Genetic Psychology, 143*, 181-187.

Low, J. M., & Moely, B. E. (1988). Early word acquisition: Relationships to syntactic and semantic aspects of maternal speech. *Child Study Journal, 18 (1)*, 47-59.

MacWhinney, B. (1991). *The CHILDES Project: Computational tools for analyzing talk*. Hillsdale, NJ: Lawrence Erlbaum Associates.

Masur, E., & Gleason, J. B. (1980). Parent-child interaction and the acquisition of lexical information during play. *Developmental Psychology, 16*, 404-409.

Mervis, C. B., & Mervis, C. A. (1982). Leopards are kitty-cats: Object labeling by mothers for their thirteen-month-olds. *Child Development, 53*, 267-273.

Nelson, K. (1973). Structure and strategy in learning to talk. *Monographs of the Society for Research in Child Development, 38* (Vol. 1-2, No. 149).

Phillips, J. R. (1973). Syntax and vocabulary in mothers' speech to young children: Age and sex comparisons. *Child Development, 44*, 182-185.

Remick, H. (1976). Maternal speech to children during language acquisition. In W. von Raffler & E. Y. Lebrun (Eds.), *Baby talk and infant speech*. Amsterdam: Swets and Zeitlinger.

Rosch, E., Mervis, C. B., Gray, W. D., Johnson, D. M., & Boyes-Braem, P. (1976). Basic objects in natural categories. *Cognitive Psychology, 8*, 382-439.

Schwartz, R. G. (1983). The role of input frequency in lexical acquisition. *Journal of Child Language, 10*, 67-64.

Snow, C. (1972). Mothers' speech to children learning language. *Child Development, 43*, 549-565.

Snow, C. E. (1977). Mothers' speech research: From input to interaction. In C. E. Snow & C. A. Ferguson (Eds.), *Talking to children: Language input and acquisition*. New York: Cambridge University Press.

Tomasello, M., & Farrar, M. (1986). Joint attention and early language. *Child Development, 57*, 1454-1463.

Tomasello, M., & Todd, J. (1983). Joint attention and lexical acquisition style. *First Language, 4*, 197-212.

6   Negative Evidence in the Language Learning Environment of Laterborns in a Rural Florida Community

Kathryn Nolan Post
Harvard Graduate School of Education

In this chapter, you will learn the following skills:

- To compute mean length of utterance using the CLAN program MLU.

- To tag crucial passages of data for further analyses using the GEM program.

- To count the frequency of codes in dependent tiers using the FREQ program.

To replicate the analysis and to do the exercises, you will need the data in the **Post** directory.

6.1. Introduction

The research question guiding this set of analyses is: Are the social interaction patterns seen in families living in a rural, White, working-class southern community different from those described for urban, White, middle-class families? The following literature review gives a brief overview of the interaction patterns found for firstborns of White, middle-class families.

Since 1970, a major focus of research in language development has concerned the interaction of the mother-and-child dyad. Prelinguistic infants and their mothers have been studied by many different researchers (e.g., Bates, 1979; Bruner, 1977; Gleason, 1977; Phillips, 1973; Ratner & Bruner, 1978; Schaffer, 1977; Snow, 1972, 1977a). This research has described elements of mother-infant interaction that they believe are important to the normal development of language. Among these elements are the necessity of shared reference or attention, games and routines, the mother's acceptance of the preverbal child as a conversational partner, and the mother's adjustment of her speech to the child's level of comprehension. In a review article, Snow (1977b) stated that "... language acquisition is the result of a process of interaction between mother and child which begins early in infancy, to which the child makes as important a contribution as the mother, and which is crucial to cognitive and emotional development as well as to language acquisition" (p. 31). The social interaction framework, with its greater sensitivity to the ecological validity of the environment in which language acquisition is studied and the importance placed on the actions of both members of the dyad, was a great improvement over earlier methodology in which only the mother's input or the child's utterances were studied.

Most of the subjects described in these early studies were White, middle-class, college-educated women and their firstborn children (e.g., Bloom, 1973; Clarke-Stewart, 1973; Phillips, 1973). These studies resulted in excellent descriptions of how a firstborn child from the described culture learns language. One of the leading descriptions of the acquisition process was that of a conversational paradigm (Schaffer, 1977; Snow, 1977b; and others). Gleason (1977) stated that " ... language acquisition is to a great extent the learning of how to make conversations" (p. 203).

In general, White, middle-class, firstborn children learning language have mothers who are very responsive to them. Such a mother is very likely to acknowledge any attempt by the infant to communicate as a valuable contribution to the ongoing interaction and to respond to that communicative attempt with a contingent response. The mother modifies her speech to the infant so that it is shorter, simpler, and more redundant. The mother also asks the child many questions and gives prompts to facilitate the child's understanding and learning of language. The mother tends to match her level of linguistic input to the child's level of understanding as the child grows and becomes more linguistically mature. The child, however, is not just a passive recipient of the mother's language instruction. The child produces verbalizations and vocalizations that are accepted by the mother as the child's turn in the conversation. The mother assumes the child is trying to converse with her and facilitates that conversation in any way she can. These descriptions were derived from observations of firstborn children and their mothers from White, middle-class, mostly urban settings.

According to this view of mother-child interaction, maternal input should play a significant role in the development of language. Of the ways in which maternal input could be beneficial to the first-language learner, the most controversial is the possibility that somehow mothers may provide their children with feedback concerning their errors. Child language researchers who have studied this problem have called this form of input *negative feedback*. The possibility that mothers provide their children with information concerning the grammaticality of their utterances is very important to explanations of language learnability. Without negative feedback, it is logically possible that children would continue to make the same errors over and over again, never realizing that they are producing ungrammatical speech.

6.1.1. The Presence of Negative Evidence

Brown and Hanlon (1970), in their landmark study of language development in children, determined that parents did not provide explicit feedback to children based on the grammaticality of their utterances. They reported that "approval and disapproval are not primarily linked with the grammatical form of the utterance. They are rather linked to the truth value of the proposition, which the adult fits to the child's generally incomplete and often deformed sentence" (p. 47). This finding has been widely held as truth for the past 20 years and has had a great deal of influence on language acquisition research. Learnability theorists (e.g., Gold, 1967; Pinker, 1984; Wexler & Culicover, 1980) have incorporated the notion that children do not receive information on well-formedness from their environment into their language-learning theories. Because of this reported dearth of parental feedback, nativists propose that children cannot learn language without a great deal of inborn knowledge of the nature of language. In other words, in the absence of negative feedback, children must be innately predisposed to entertain only those grammatical hypotheses for which negative feedback is not necessary.

Recently the results of Brown and Hanlon (1970) have been challenged by other child language researchers. Hirsh-Pasek, Treiman, and Schneiderman (1984) replicated Brown and Hanlon's (1970) study and then extended the notion of negative evidence. They were motivated by two considerations. First, the small sample size used by Brown and Hanlon (three children at two levels of MLU), and second, Brown and Hanlon's decision to only consider explicit approval and disapproval. Hirsh-Pasek et al. hypothesized that parents may express their awareness of the grammaticality of the child's utterance in less explicit ways, such as by different forms of repetition, depending on the well-formedness of the child's utterance. They confirmed Brown and Hanlon's finding that explicit approval and disapproval were not contingent on the well-formedness of the child's utterance. However, they did find that mothers of 2-year-olds repeated significantly more ill-formed than well-formed child utterances and that almost all of the repetitions of the ill-formed utterances contained a correction of the child's error. They concluded that mothers are aware of the grammaticality of their child's utterance, but that the feedback they provide is more subtle than had been previously thought.

In another study, Demetras, Post, and Snow (1986) examined the feedback given to first-language learners. They, as well as Hirsh-Pasek et al., questioned Brown and Hanlon's (1970) findings on the grounds that only explicit approval and disapproval were considered and that only the mothers' responses that immediately followed the child's utterance were scrutinized. Demetras et al. proposed that subsequent, but nonadjacent, maternal responses may have contained valuable feedback for the child and would have been overlooked by Brown and Hanlon's analysis. Demetras et al. expanded Hirsh-Pasek et al.'s notion of more subtle forms of feedback to include two types of feedback: explicit and implicit. *Implicit feedback* included repetitions, clarification questions, and move-ons. According to Demetras et al., both explicit and implicit feedback provide children with negative evidence. With *explicit feedback*, the mother gives the child a very clear indication of the well-formedness of the child's utterance by responding with *yes, that's right* or *no, that's not right*. With implicit feedback, which was found to be much more common, the mother is thought to give the child more subtle indications as to the well-formedness of the child's utterance by asking a clarification question, indicating the utterance was not completely understood, or by repeating the utterance and expanding it to add missing elements or to correct some error. In addition, all maternal responses subsequent to the child utterance were analyzed, not just the response adjacent to the child's utterance. It was hypothesized that if only adjacent maternal utterances were analyzed, many of the instances of negative evidence the child might receive from the mother would be overlooked. Demetras et al. found that explicit feedback was infrequent and not related to the grammatical correctness or incorrectness of the child's utterance. Implicit feedback, however, was found to be produced differentially to well-formed and ill-formed child utterances. They offer their findings as evidence that "... a high proportion of maternal responses qualify as negative feedback" (p. 286) and that children could use this feedback to help confirm or change their linguistic rules.

In a third study, Penner (1987) studied parental responses to child utterances from children at two different MLU levels. She found that parent responses that would be described as implicit responses were produced differentially to grammatically correct and incorrect utterances by the child. This trend was more robust for the lower MLU level than the higher one. Penner also confirmed that explicit approval and disapproval were not related to the grammaticality of the child's utterance.

In a fourth study, Bohannon and Stanowicz (1988) examined adult (both parents and nonparents) responses to four types of errors in child utterances. They determined that "... all adults tended to use exact repetition after a well-formed utterance and recasts and elaborated repetition after ill-formed utterances" (p. 686). Again, these responses would be classified as implicit rather than explicit feedback. Interestingly, Bohannon and Stanowicz also found that parents provided specific information to the child significantly more than nonparents and that all the adults provided feedback to utterances containing a single error more often than to one containing multiple errors. They reasoned that if a child's utterance contained several errors, the adult might not be able to understand what the child was trying to say, and therefore a recast would not be possible.

To summarize, several recent studies have challenged the long-held notion that children do not receive negative evidence from their environment concerning the well-formedness of their utterances. These studies support the assertion that explicit approval and disapproval from parents is not contingent on the grammaticality of the child's utterance. However, all of these studies (and others) have shown that parents do provide subtle forms of negative evidence to children regarding their errors. As will be discussed in more detail in the coding section, Demetras et al. have called this implicit feedback. The results, described above, suggest that children do have access to negative evidence on the correctness or incorrectness of their speech from adult sources in their learning environment. Whether or not children use this negative evidence in honing their linguistic rules is quite another issue.

6.1.2. Negative Evidence and Learnability Theory

The presence of negative evidence is of fundamental importance to the theory of language development that deals with *language learnability*. Recall that many nativist theories of language acquisition (Hyams, 1987; Pinker, 1984, 1989; Roeper

& Williams, 1987; Wexler & Culicover, 1980) begin with the assumption that children do not receive consistent, correct feedback from the adult concerning their grammatical errors. Thus, these theorists propose that, in order to explain how each and every normally developing child eventually learns language, it is necessary to hypothesize special innate mechanisms designed specifically for learning language.

Therefore, if negative evidence is available to the language-learning child, it may not be necessary to resort to innate mechanisms to explain language learnability. In other words, to the degree that the child can learn the grammar of the language he or she is acquiring from the environment, then language learning would be similar to other types of learning, and no special innate mechanism would be required. As Bohannon and Stanowicz state, "... if children's conversational partners provide some form of corrective feedback (i.e., negative evidence), then many of the innate linguistic constraints recently proposed would become unnecessary" (p. 684). They go on to argue that when, in learning language, the child makes errors in decoding the input and then in producing speech, an adult's recast containing a correction of the child's error may be encoded by the child as a better way to express that meaning. Alternatively, an exact repetition by the adult may be taken by the child to be an affirmation that the prior utterance was correct.

There is still disagreement on the importance or the validity of the findings that negative evidence is available to the child from the learning environment. Morgan and Travis (1989) studied certain parent responses to errors in Brown's (1973) Adam, Eve, and Sarah data. Even though they found results consistent with Hirsh-Pasek et al. and Demetras et al. for two of the three children, they concluded that "although we would not deny that some parental responses may sometimes supply the perspicacious child with correction, we fail to see sufficient evidence to warrant the conclusion that language input generally incorporates negative information" (p. 551).

Furthermore, Gordon (1990) argued that even if negative evidence exists, it has no relevance to learnability theory. He stated that "the point here is simply that this has no bearing on the issue of learnability and, in particular, on whether innate knowledge is required for language acquisition" (p. 219). He challenged Bohannon and Stanowicz to prove that natural languages can be learned without innate knowledge when only "partial and inconsistent feedback is available" (p. 219). In their reply to Gordon, Bohannon, MacWhinney, and Snow (1990) disagreed with his assertion that negative evidence has no bearing on the question of learnability.

They argued that because the problem of negative evidence is regularly cited by learnability theorists, it has been made a critical issue for theories relying on innate knowledge.

In addition, Bohannon et al. (1990) countered Gordon's criticism that only 34% of children's errors were given negative evidence in the Bohannon and Stanowicz study by citing concept learning studies that have shown that concepts can be learned and hypotheses can be confirmed when less than 25% of the trials contain feedback. They emphasized that what is important is that the evidence clearly supports the correct choice over time, not that every trial receive some type of reinforcement. Bohannon et al. also discounted Gordon's anecdotal evidence that all cultures do not use negative feedback. They concluded by stating that "... parents do correct their children's language mistakes and it is probably important that they do so" (p. 225).

6.1.3. Current Goals

The major research question for this chapter is: Do parents provide negative evidence to children by responding differentially to their well-formed and ill-formed utterances? This study is an extension of the Demetras et al. study in that the subjects are children who are not firstborns and whose parents are not college-educated. This population was chosen to supplement the literature that is disproportionately weighted with studies of firstborn children of college-educated parents. Because laterborn children were studied, we also shifted from the normally studied dyadic interaction to a triadic one involving the child, the mother, and the child's closely spaced older sibling. There is a paucity of information in the language acquisition literature concerning triadic interaction, which is a very commonly occurring scenario in real life. Though not reported in this chapter, this methodology also allows a look at the interaction patterns between closely spaced siblings.

It seems reasonable to conjecture that the presence of another child changes the interaction pattern between the mother and the target child. The evidence that does exist suggests that, in the presence of an older sibling, the younger child receives less responsive and more directive feedback from the older sibling (Wellen & Broen, 1982), receives fewer questions from the mother that might help the child (Wellen, 1985), and receives less "language-focused" feedback from the mother (Jones &

Adamson, 1987). This study presents an attempt to look at how the presence of an older sibling influences the interaction between the mother and the child. At the same time, the mothers studied here differ from those most often studied in that they are members of a rural working-class community; differences in interaction might well emerge because of social class or cultural differences between these mothers and groups previously studied. The current study gives us no basis for separating the effect of culture or social class from the effect of interaction with a laterborn child or in a triadic situation.

The focus of this chapter concerns the presence of negative evidence in the maternal input provided to these children. For the purposes of the present study, negative evidence may be taken to mean feedback from the parent (or other adult) has the potential to give the child information about the grammaticality of his or her utterance. We are interested in discovering if parents respond differentially to well-formed and ill-formed utterances by the child, thus providing negative evidence that the child might use in learning his or her native grammar.

We accomplish this goal by using several of the tools provided by the Child Language Data Exchange System (MacWhinney, 1990; CHILDES): Both the Computerized Language ANalysis (CLAN) programs and the transcription guidelines in Codes for the Human Analysis of Transcripts (CHAT; MacWhinney, 1991) are utilized. The coding system used is described in Demetras et al. (1986), modified somewhat to accommodate the three-way interaction (see the Appendix). This coding scheme classifies the child's utterances as well-formed, ill-formed, or other, based on criteria that include the areas of morphology, phonology, semantics, and syntax. The category "other" includes singing, counting, laughing, and vocalizations that were not considered to be interactive communication. The mother's responses to the child's utterances are categorized into four main types: repetitions, clarification questions, move-ons, and no response. Repetitions are further broken down into exact, contracted, expanded, and extended repetitions. Here is an example of an expanded repetition from Kalie's data:

    *CHI: brush pony hair.
    *MOT: brush the pony–'s hair.

Here the mother expands the child's utterance by adding the article and the possessive, but does not add any new information to the child's utterance. Clarification questions are also broken down into Wh-questions, occasional or embedded questions, yes/no questions, and repetition questions. Here is an example of a Wh-question from Kalie's data:

    *CHI: Bert.
    *MOT: what–'is he do–ing?

Move-ons are taken as confirmation by the mother that the child's utterance was understood, and they often precede a change in topic. Here is an example of a move-on from Kalie's data:

    *CHI: duckie.
    *MOT: there–'is the duckie.

Here, the mother understands what the child has said and is confirming it.

Because the data come from triadic interactions among the mother (MOT), the target child (CHI), and the closely spaced older sibling (SIB), it was necessary to include an addressee tier to clarify to whom the mother's response was directed. Also the categories of *no response* and *shared response* by the mother were added to address the situation in which the mother could not respond immediately to the child's utterance or her response was intended to be shared by the target child and the sibling.

The question we are asking is, given the child's utterance which was coded as well-formed, ill-formed, or other, what is the mother's response (repetition, clarification, move-on, or no response)? (See the Appendix for definitions and more examples of the classifications.) Do the mothers give exact repetitions to well-formed utterances more frequently than ill-formed utterances as was reported in the literature? Do mothers recast ill-formed utterances and correct the error within the recast?

6.2. Method

In the following sections, our methodology for investigating the occurrence of negative evidence in the maternal responses to children's utterances will be presented. First, the subjects in our study will be described. Then, the CLAN programs used to analyze the data collected from these children will be detailed. The programs used are MLU, GEM, and FREQ. KEYMAP could have been used in the context of the present study if I had only been interested in the mother's response that occurred immediately after the child's utterance. Since this is not the case, it was determined that KEYMAP was not the best way to look for the answers to our research questions. This is because all maternal responses (both adjacent and nonadjacent) to each child utterance should be analyzed so that possible incidences of negative feedback will not be overlooked.

6.2.1. Subjects

The subjects were three White females, their mothers, and their closely spaced older siblings from a rural area with a predominantly working-class population in Suwannee County, Florida. The subjects were recruited from the immunization records of the Suwannee County Health Department. They were all the products of normal pregnancies and deliveries and were within normal limits for hearing and developmental milestones as reported by the mother or screening tests. The subjects were enrolled in the study between the ages of 19-22 months and were followed for 9 months. At the beginning of the taping sessions, two of the girls were 19 months and the third was 22 months of age. Ten tapes were made for each family, approximately 1 month apart. Each taping session lasted approximately 1 hour. I videotaped the subjects in their homes and transcribed all tapes. I provided a toy bag containing appropriate toys, books, puzzles, and a Fisher-Price playset, and the family was allowed to play with whatever interested them. The tapes consist of conversations among the Mother (MOT), the Target Child (CHI), and the Older Sibling (SIB). Occasionally, conversations included the Experimenter (EXP), but none of these were included in the analyses. The results from all 30 taping sessions (10 from each family) are presented here when applicable.

6.2.2. Procedure – CLAN Tools

Three CLAN programs were used to analyze the speech of the participants and any associated codes: MLU, GEM, and FREQ. The MLU program was used to calculate the mean length of utterance for each speaker. These MLU scores were then used to match the children according to language level. The GEM program was used to divide the transcripts according to the different types of child utterances (e.g., well-formed, ill-formed, or other). By dividing the transcripts in this manner, separate analyses could be conducted on each utterance type. Each

142   Chapter 6

collection of child utterance type was then submitted to the FREQ program, which counted the different kinds of responses the mother made to each particular child utterance type. As stated earlier, the KEYMAP program was not used because it performs a contingency analysis on adjacent utterances only. Thus, I had to use the less efficient method of first dividing the data into the different types of child utterances using GEM and then obtaining frequency counts of the different types of maternal responses using FREQ.

6.2.3. Procedure – CHAT Coding

The methodology for coding the children's utterances and their mothers' responses will be described here. Because this study examined triadic interaction, it was first necessary to include an addressee tier (**%add**) after each speaker's utterance in order to clarify to whom the utterance was directed. Addressee codes included the following:

aim:	infant to mother
ais:	infant to sibling
ami:	mother to infant
ams:	mother to sibling
amb:	mother to both
asi:	sibling to infant
asm:	sibling to mother
aie:	infant to experimenter
aei:	experimenter to infant

The second step involved coding the well-formedness of the target child's utterances. A modified version of the coding scheme used by Demetras et al. (1986) was employed to accomplish this goal. This information was included in a **%cod** tier after each of the target child's utterances. The child's utterances were classified as well-formed, ill-formed, or other, and as either a single-word or multi-word utterance. The exact codes are as follows:

$W:MW	well-formed, multi-word utterances
$W:SW	well-formed, single-word utterances
$I:MW	ill-formed, multi-word utterances
$I:SW	ill-formed, single-word utterances
$O:MW	other, multi-word utterances
$O:SW	other, single-word utterances

The criteria for judging the child's utterances can be found in the Appendix. As with the development of any coding system, I had the flexibility to determine how many categories I wished to use in analyzing the data. Developing a coding system always represents a compromise between exhaustiveness of coding and feasibility. Fortunately, the availability of Coder's Editor within CLAN makes it relatively easy to apply even complex hierarchical coding schemes (see Bodin & Snow, this volume; MacWhinney, this volume).

The third coding step involved classifying the mother's response to the child's utterance. Each maternal response that was addressed to the target child was classified as providing either explicit ($EX) or implicit ($IM) feedback. This information was included in a %res tier after each maternal response. Explicit feedback states clearly that the child's utterance was correct or not correct. Implicit feedback gives the child information about the utterance without explicitly stating whether it was correct or was not. Within each of these categories, a second level of coding was performed, which further identified the type of explicit or implicit feedback. These are described in the Appendix (and summarized in Table 6.8). Finally, if the maternal response was a *no response* ($NRS) or a *shared response* from the mother to both of the siblings ($SRS), this was also noted.

The mother's response was also coded for adjacency to the child's utterance. This constituted a third level of coding. Thus, an adjacent expanded repetition would be coded as $IM:EPR:ADJ. Nonadjacent maternal responses (NAD) were coded as well as adjacent ones (ADJ). Maternal responses were coded as nonadjacent if they did not immediately follow the child's utterance. For example, the sibling may have spoken to the mother or the target child between the target child's utterance and the mother's response to it, or the mother may have produced several utterances to the target child with no intervening child utterance.

144   Chapter 6

An excerpt from Melissa's transcripts is provided to sum up what has been described so far:

```
*CHI:      what this Mama?
%add:      aim
%cod:      $I:MW
*MOT:      oh let'–us look at Lowly Worm–'s school bag.
%add:      ami
%res:      $IM:MVO:ADJ
*MOT:      oh look, little book–s.
%add:      ami
%res:      $IM:MVO:NAD
*MOT:      see the little book–s?
%add:      ami
%res:      $IM:YNQ:NAD
```

In this interaction, the mother responds to the child's ill-formed utterance first with a move-on, which is scored as adjacent (ADJ). The next response from the mother is another move-on, which is scored as nonadjacent (NAD) and the last response in this turn is a yes/no question, which is also scored as nonadjacent (NAD).

There is a fourth and final coding step to describe before we can go on to discuss the analysis. Remember that our ultimate goal is to determine how mothers respond to children's well-formed and ill-formed utterances. In order to accomplish this goal, we need to consider maternal responses in the context of the preceding (but not necessarily adjacent) child utterance. Thus, we need to find a way in which we can group child utterances and all subsequent maternal responses.

In order to do this, we need to find a way to mark each child utterance as the beginning of a sequence of utterances and the last maternal response (before the next child utterance) as the end of the sequence. Specifically, we use codes recognized by the GEM program to mark the beginning and the end of each sequence of child-parent interaction. For example, to code a sequence of interaction beginning with a child's well-formed, multi-word utterance, the following code would be inserted just prior to the child's utterance:

```
@bg:    $W:MW
*CHI:   help me Mama.
```

The symbol **@bg** marks the **b**eginning of a **g**em (as we like to call these passages). Then a different code would be placed after the last maternal response to indicate the end of the sequence:

@bg:	$W:MW
*CHI:	help me Mama.
%add:	aim
%cod:	$W:MW
*MOT:	what do you want me to do?
%add:	ami
%res:	$IM:WHQ:ADJ
@eg:	$W:MW

This last code, **@eg**, marks the **e**nd of the **g**em and indicates that the coded sequence is complete. Note that this coding system will permit us to include nonadjacent maternal responses in each interactional sequence.

Since this type of GEM coding must be performed for the entire transcript, it can be a tedious and time-consuming task. Fortunately, GEM coding can be performed automatically with the help of a word-processing macro. One way of doing this would be to search for the appropriate child utterance code (e.g., $W:MW) and then type in the GEM marker **@bg:<tab>$W:MW** before the child speaker tier. Next, to find the end of the interactional sequence, simply search for the next child utterance and insert the end-of-sequence marker (**@eg:<tab>$W:MW**) before it. The capability for creating macros is available with most word-processing programs.

Before moving on to the analysis, two more reminders are in order. First, prior to working with the CHAT-formatted transcripts, remember that these files must be saved as ASCII text in order for the CLAN analyses to work. Our files were named with the **.cha** suffix. Second, I recommend creating a test file small enough to allow a hand tally of the desired analyses to compare to the analyses obtained from CLAN. This is strongly recommended for all new analyses of speech and codes performed on your data. This is the only way to insure that the analyses being performed are the analyses you intend.

146   Chapter 6

6.2.4. Procedure – CLAN Analysis

Computing MLU

Our first goal was to determine the MLU for each of the children in our sample. The following is an example of how this was done for Kalie. If we were analyzing the MLU of Kalie's seventh transcript (when she was 25 months old), we would type the following CLAN command:

mlu +t*CHI kal7.cha

+t*CHI	Analyze the child speaker tier only
kal7.cha	The child language transcript to be analyzed

Command Box 6.1

MLU would then produce the following output:

```
MLU.EXE +t*CHI kal7.cha
MLU.EXE (04-MAY-93) is conducting analyses on:
  ONLY speaker main tiers matching: *CHI;
*****************************************
From file <kal7.cha>
MLU for Speaker: *CHI:
   MLU (xxx and yyy are EXCLUDED from the utterance
   and morpheme counts):
       Number of: utterances = 282, morphemes = 771
          Ratio of morphemes over utterances = 2.734
          Standard deviation = 1.359
```

We would use the *ratio of morphemes over utterances* as the measure for MLU. The MLU for Kalie during her seventh sample is 2.734. However, as can be seen above, the output from the MLU program gives information in addition to the mean length of utterance. This includes the number of utterances for the specified speaker, the number of morphemes (which are used in calculating MLU), and the standard deviation. The standard deviation gives you an idea of how similar the utterances in your data are. If most of the utterances are close to the same number in length, the standard deviation would be a small number. If the length of utterances in the data is quite variable, the standard deviation will be a larger number.

Always check the first line of the output to make sure the desired analysis is being performed. Be sure to check that the program is conducting analyses on the appropriate main tiers and files.

> If the +**f** option is added to the command line, a file will be created by the computer in which the results of this MLU analysis would be stored. By default, this file would be named **kal7.mlu**. If a second MLU analysis is run on these data, the MLU program would create a second file called **kal7.ml0**. A third run would create another file called **kal7.ml1**, and so on. It is very easy to be confused if you do not keep track of what is stored in each output file, so be sure to make a list of what is in each file.

Retrieving Different Types of Child Utterances

Recall that our ultimate goal is to see if the mothers in our sample respond differently to well-formed child utterances than to ill-formed child utterances. In order to achieve this goal, we must be able to separate well-formed child utterances from ill-formed ones. Thus, the next step in our analysis is to separate the different types of child utterances so that we will be able to analyze the maternal responses to each type separately.

In the previous section, I described the use of specific markers to code the beginning and end of each sequence involving a child utterance and subsequent maternal responses. Once the beginning and end of these crucial sequences have been marked, we can use the GEM program to retrieve them. The following CLAN command was used to retrieve Kalie's well-formed multi-word utterances ($W:MW):

Chapter 6

gem +s$W:MW +t%res +d +f kal7.cha

+s$W:MW	Search for all GEM sequences coded as $W:MW
+t%res	Include the mother's response tier (**%res**) in the search
+d	Output the data in CHAT format
+f	Save the results in a file with the default extension **.gem**
kal7.cha	The child language transcript to be analyzed

Command Box 6.2

This command results in the creation of a file called **kal7.gem**. The first five sequences of well-formed multi-word child utterances and maternal responses from this file are as follows:

```
@bg:    $W:MW
*CHI:   what-'is that ?
*MOT:   Ø .
%res:   $NRS
@eg:    $W:MW
@bg:    $W:MW
*CHI:   what-'is that Mama ?
*MOT:   Ø .
%res:   $NRS
@eg:    $W:MW
@bg:    $W:MW
*CHI:   oh I need money .
*MOT:   Ø .
%res:   $NRS
@eg:    $W:MW
@bg:    $W:MW
*CHI:   give me money .
*MOT:   Ø .
%res:   $NRS
@eg:    $W:MW
```

```
@bg:     $W:MW
*CHI:    I need money .
*MOT:    you need some money ?
%res:    $IM:PRQ:ADJ
*MOT:    ok hold your hand down there ready ?
%res:    $IM:YNQ:NAD
@eg:     $W:MW
```

Counting the Frequency of Maternal Responses

After retrieving this subsample of child utterances, we are now in a position to determine the frequency of the different kinds of maternal responses to this type of child utterance. In this example, we are only considering the child's well-formed, multi-word utterances; therefore, the following analysis will only be able to determine the frequency of various maternal responses to this type of child utterance. The CLAN command for such an analysis would be as follows (the results are listed in Table 6.1):

freq +t%res +s$* kal7.gem

+t%res	Include the mother's response tier (**%res**) in the search
+s$*	Include any and all strings beginning with **$**
kal7.gem	The file containing the results from the previous GEM analysis

Command Box 6.3

The Type-Token ratio is not useful for our current purposes. These results show us that Kalie's mother responded with 21 different types of responses, the most common being move-ons, 28 of which were adjacent to the child's utterance and 28 of which were nonadjacent to the child's utterance. Note that there is often more than one type of maternal response in an utterance, such as in the second maternal response listed, the mother gives explicit approval and then an extended repetition of the child's utterance.

150   Chapter 6

Table 6.1: The results of the FREQ analysis from Command Box 6.2.

```
FREQ.EXE +t%res +s$* kal7.gem
FREQ.EXE (04-MAY-93) is conducting analyses on:
  ALL speaker tiers
    and those speakers' ONLY dependent tiers matching: %RES;
*****************************************
From file <kal7.gem>
   3 $ex:app:adj
   1 $ex:cor:adj
   3 $im:cnr:adj
   1 $im:epr:adj
   2 $im:etr:adj
   1 $im:exr:adj
   1 $im:exr:nad
  28 $im:mvo:adj
  28 $im:mvo:nad
   1 $im:ocq:adj
   5 $im:ocq:nad
   1 $im:prq:adj
   1 $im:trq:adj
  11 $im:whq:adj
  13 $im:whq:nad
   5 $im:ynq:adj
   8 $im:ynq:nad
  17 $nrs
   6 $srs
-------------------------------
   19    Total number of different word types used
  136    Total number of words (tokens)
 0.140   Type/Token ratio
```

A more efficient way of performing this analysis would be to "pipe" the results of the GEM analysis directly to the FREQ program. This alternative is more efficient because the investigator does not need to save the results of the GEM analysis in an intermediate file. The CLAN command for the analysis would be:

gem +s$W:MW +t%res +d kal7.cha | freq +t%res +s$* > kal7.wmw

+s$W:MW	Search for all GEM sequences coded as $W:MW
+t%res	Include the mother's response tier (%res) in the search
+d	Output the data in CHAT format
kal7.cha	The child language transcript to be analyzed
| freq	Pipe the output to FREQ
+t%res	Include the %res tier in the search
+s$*	Include any and all strings beginning with $
> kal7.wmw	Redirect the output to the file **kal7.wmw**

Command Box 6.4

This analysis provides us with the frequency of the different kinds of maternal responses to Kalie's well-formed multi-word utterances. Note that the results of this analysis are stored in a file with the extension **.wmw**. This extension signifies that this file contains the results for well-formed multi-word utterances. In order to complete our analysis, we must perform the same procedure for the other five types of child utterances. To do this, we must run five slightly modified versions of the command listed in Command Box 6.4. For each version of this command, two changes must be made: First, the **+s** option must be changed to reflect the changing child utterance type (e.g., from **+s$W:MW** to **+s$W:SW**); second, the name of the output file must be changed according to the type of child utterance under consideration (e.g., from **wmw** to **wsw**). The file extensions for each of the six child utterance types are as follows:

wmw	well-formed multi-word child utterances ($W:MW)
wsw	well-formed single-word child utterances ($W:SW)
imw	ill-formed multi-word child utterances ($I:MW)
isw	ill-formed multi-word child utterances ($I:SW)
omw	multi-word child utterances coded as other ($O:MW)
osw	single-word child utterances coded as other ($O:SW)

152   Chapter 6

For DOS users, CLAN includes a utility, called RECALL, that can eliminate the necessity for typing the same command numerous times. The program can be installed in memory by typing **recall –i**. Once installed, RECALL allows users to edit previous command strings by pressing the up (↑) and down (↓) arrow keys. The investigator may then simply type only the change in the command rather than re-typing the entire command again. On some of the more complicated commands, this really saves time and lessens the chances of a typographical error. This feature is a default for MACINTOSH users and part of the UNIX operating system.

6.3. Results and Discussion

Let us now return to the questions raised in Section 6.1.4. The first question we are interested in answering concerns maternal responses to the different types of child utterances: well-formed, ill-formed, or other? In order to answer this question, we must examine both explicit feedback and implicit feedback.

6.3.1. Explicit Feedback

With respect to explicit feedback, the mothers of these three girls exhibited the trend reported by other researchers (Brown & Hanlon, 1970; Demetras et al., 1986; Hirsh-Pasek et al., 1984; Penner, 1987) in that the explicit feedback was apparently not based on the grammaticality of the child's utterance. The mothers seem to be responding to the truth value or semantic content of the child's utterance rather than to its well-formedness:

```
*MOT:     where is your baby?
*MOT:     your–'s had the close-ed eye-s.
*CHI:     <that mine> [/] that mine Mama.
*MOT:     no it-'is not.
```

However, a difference was found in that these mothers gave their laterborn children more explicit corrections/disapprovals than the mothers in the Demetras et al. study gave their children. As illustrated in Table 6.2, the Demetras et al. mothers produced a greater proportion of explicit approvals and almost twice the percentage of explicit feedback as these mothers. It may be that the added communicative

Table 6.2: Percentage of total maternal utterances judged to be explicit feedback for Sally, Melissa, and Kalie and the Demetras et al. (1986) subjects at equivalent MLUs (MLU = 3.4).

Child	% Approvals	% Corrections/ Disapprovals
Sally	4.0	3.0
Melissa	3.9	3.1
Kalie	8.6	3.4
Alex	8.0	0.0
Amy	4.1	0.8
Ben	6.0	2.0
Jim	5.0	1.0

pressure caused by the older sibling made it more efficient for these mothers to use explicit corrections with their laterborn children. Telling a child that something is wrong may seem to be a faster and easier way to correct incorrect verbal behavior than waiting until the child has produced the correct form and then confirming the child's correct productions.

Table 6.3 shows the mean percentages of each type of child utterance receiving various sorts of explicit maternal feedback. Each child appears to receive a different pattern of explicit feedback from her mother. The only common finding for these three girls is that ill-formed utterances were more likely to receive both approvals and corrections/disapprovals than either well-formed or other utterances. In many cases, the mother is approving the semantic content of the child's utterance, not the grammaticality, which is consistent with the findings of other researchers. The following are examples of explicit feedback from the mother to ill-formed utterances. From Sally's data:

    *CHI: oh there he have some food.
    *MOT: yeah he do–es.

Table 6.3: Mean percentages of well-formed (WF), ill-formed (IF), and other (O) child utterances receiving explicit maternal feedback across all 10 sessions.

Child	Approvals WF	Approvals IF	Approvals O	Corrections/Disapprovals WF	Corrections/Disapprovals IF	Corrections/Disapprovals O
Sally	2.7	5.4	2.2	1.4	2.0	2.2
Melissa	2.0	5.0	0.6	4.0	5.0	3.7
Kalie	4.8	5.7	2.8	3.7	4.4	3.5

Here, Sally's mother is clearly approving what Sally has said, not the way she has said it. Kalie's example is different:

    *CHI: both of them.
    *MOT: no all of them.

In this example, Kalie's mother is correcting her child's incorrect use of language.

6.3.2. Implicit Feedback

Repetitions

In our examination of implicit feedback, we asked if mothers are more likely to provide exact repetitions to well-formed utterances than to ill-formed utterances. As Table 6.4 demonstrates, the answer here is clearly yes. For example, 45% of Sally's own utterances were well-formed. If her mother was producing exact repetitions without regard to Sally's utterances, we would expect that about 45% would follow well-formed child utterances. In fact, 60% do, suggesting that exact repetitions might serve as a signal that the child utterance was correct. Similarly, we would expect 45% of the amended repetitions to follow WF utterances, but only 27% do, indicating that these signal something wrong with the child utterance. Kalie's mother shows the same pattern. Melissa's mother, on the other hand, produces amended repetitions differentially to IF utterances, but is not more likely to use exact repetitions after WF child utterances. In general, over half of the exact repetitions followed well-formed utterances, while contracted, expanded, and extended repetitions, which are thought to provide negative evidence for the child, followed ill-formed utterances an average of 65% of the time.

Table 6.4: Exact and amended repetitions (contracted, expanded, and extended) by the mother to the child's well-formed (WF), ill-formed (IF), and other (O) utterances across all 10 sessions.

Child	Child Utterance Type	% of total utterances	# and % of exact repetitions	# and % of amended repetitions
Sally	WF	45%	35 (60%)	22 (27%)
	IF	47%	18 (31%)	60 (72%)
	O	8%	5 (9%)	1 (1%)
	Total	100%	(100%)	(100%)
Melissa	WF	40%	77 (37%)	32 (24%)
	IF	42%	74 (35%)	97 (72%)
	O	18%	59 (28%)	6 (4%)
	Total	100%	(100%)	(100%)
Kalie	WF	52%	47 (65%)	33 (39%)
	IF	41%	15 (21%)	45 (53%)
	O	7%	10 (14%)	7 (8%)
	Total	100%	(100%)	(100%)

These results are in agreement with those of Hirsh-Pasek et al., who found that the upper middle-class mothers of 2-year-olds were more likely to repeat the child's IF utterances, and that almost all of these repetitions contained a correction of the child's error. They only found this pattern for 2-year-old children, however. Also, Bohannon and Stanowicz's findings are supported in that they found more exact repetitions to WF utterances and "elaborated" repetitions (which we have termed *expanded* or *extended*) to IF utterances. Repetitions of all types were found to be adjacent to the child's utterance almost all of the time (90% for exact repetitions and over 80% for other repetitions), which is in agreement with the findings of the other studies.

These findings seem to be strong evidence that mothers are sensitive to the grammaticality of their children's speech. Since mothers repeat exactly more of the child's WF utterances, this could be taken as confirmation by the child that the utterance is acceptable. Similarly, since mothers repeat with correction more of the child's IF utterances, the child could take this as a signal that the utterance is not acceptable and must be altered.

The next question asked was whether maternal recasts of ill-formed utterances contained implicit corrections of the child's error. Here again, the answer is yes. Almost all (over 90%) of the repetitions of ill-formed utterances were expanded or extended repetitions, which means that the utterances were rephrased to correct grammatical errors or to add information. Once again, this replicates the findings of Hirsh-Pasek et al. (1984).

Clarification Questions and Move-Ons

Child language researchers have considered maternal clarification questions to provide implicit feedback because they probably signal to children that their utterance was not understood. Thus, it is hypothesized that they act as negative evidence by causing the child to change his or her utterance so that it can be understood by the mother. Recall that there are four kinds of clarification questions in the current coding scheme: Wh-questions, occasional (also known as embedded) questions, yes/no questions, and repetition questions. The number of clarification questions was much greater than the number of repetitions. Sally was asked a total of 847 clarification questions during all ten sessions, Melissa was asked 1,560, and Kalie was asked 1,017. Note that this total means that the children heard between 80 and 160 clarification questions per hour – an ample source of feedback if they are, indeed, produced differentially to IF child utterances. In fact, in comparison to the Demetras et al. mothers, these mothers produced a higher proportion of clarification questions (31.8%) than did the mothers in Demetras et al. (26.3%).

Negative Evidence 157

The next question to address is whether the clarification questions provided the children with any differential evidence concerning the well-formedness of their utterances. As Table 6.5 illustrates, the clearest evidence of differential usage of clarification questions in response to well-formed versus ill-formed child utterances is in repetition questions. The mothers of all three children were more likely to produce repetition questions following ill-formed child utterances than well-formed ones. None of the other question types showed a consistent pattern of differential usage.

Turning next to move-ons, Demetras et al. (1986) suggest that move-ons provide a signal of the mother's acceptance of the child's utterance. They infer that "the mother understands what the child said, accepts it, and moves on with the conversation" (p. 292). This is shown in an excerpt from Kalie's data:

```
*CHI:     Mama I wanna put my ponies up here.
*MOT:     ok.
```

As can be seen in Table 6.6, the Florida mothers produced more move-ons (60.9% of their own utterances) than did the mothers studied by Demetras et al. (50.7%). However, Demetras et al. found that move-ons were more likely to follow WF than IF utterances; this finding was replicated with the Florida mothers only in Sally's case. Sally produced more IF than WF utterances (47% vs. 45%), but her mother was more likely to produce move-ons after WF than after IF (50% vs. 41%). Kalie's and Melissa's mothers' move-ons occurred in much the same distribution as the children's utterances, except that Melissa's mother produced many move-ons following the rather infrequent "other" category of child utterance.

Differing proportions of implicit feedback and the higher proportion of move-ons for the laterborns may be a result of the presence of the older sibling. The mother has less time to negotiate for meaning with the younger child and may choose clarification questions as a faster, more efficient way to try to understand the younger sibling than repetitions.

Adjacent Versus Nonadjacent Feedback

In the Demetras et al. study, a consistent pattern was observed in which the mother's adjacent response (usually a repetition or clarification question) was followed by a single move-on or a series of move-ons. Thus, the children heard

Table 6.5: Mean percentage of maternal clarification questions to the child's well-formed (WF), ill-formed (IF), and other (O) utterances across all 10 sessions.

Child	Child Utterance Type	% of total utterances	Maternal Responses WH	OCC	Y/N	REP
Sally	WF	45	43	51	52	34
	IF	47	50	43	42	65
	O	8	7	6	6	1
	Total	100	100	100	100	100
Melissa	WF	40	37	35	40	28
	IF	42	42	51	39	68
	O	8	21	14	21	4
	Total	100	100	100	100	100
Kalie	WF	52	47	54	54	46
	IF	41	39	39	36	51
	O	7	14	7	10	3
	Total	100	100	100	100	100

many nonadjacent move-ons. For the laterborns, no such pattern was observed for the group or for individuals. Often the laterborns would have the same pattern as the firstborns, but it was also common to have a move-on for the adjacent response followed by a clarification question or repetition. Thus it seems that the mothers of the firstborns were more likely to make any corrections to the child's utterance in their adjacent response and then continue on in the same topic with a move-on. The mothers of the laterborns were about as likely to make the correction in a nonadjacent utterance as they were in the adjacent utterance. Again, part of this difference may be attributed to the presence of a third party or it may be a difference in style. A move-on can be interpreted in at least two different ways. First, it may be that the mother understands the child's utterance and does not need

Table 6.6: Mean percentage of maternal move-ons to the child's well-formed (WF), ill-formed (IF), and other (O) utterances across all 10 sessions.

	Child Utterance Type	% of Total Child Utterances	% of Maternal Move-ons
Sally	WF	45	50
	IF	47	41
	O	8	9
Melissa	WF	40	38
	IF	42	40
	O	8	22
Kalie	WF	52	53
	IF	41	38
	O	7	9

to negotiate its meaning, so the utterance is accepted and the pair moves on to a new topic. Second, it may be that the child's utterance contains so many errors that the mother has no idea how to correct or recast the error, so she moves on to a different topic. It seems reasonable that the mothers are using both types of move-ons within the same conversation, depending on the type of utterance the child produces.

Most Common Maternal Response

There appears to be a difference in the most common maternal response to the different types of child utterances (see Table 6.7). For these three laterborns and one of the Demetras et al. subjects, the most common response to an IF utterance was a move-on. For the remaining three Demetras et al. subjects, the most common response to an IF utterance was a clarification question. Thus, the majority of the mothers of firstborns are negotiating for meaning of the IF utterance more often than are the mothers of the laterborns. Mothers of the laterborns seem more willing to

160   Chapter 6

Table 6.7: Summary of predominant maternal responses to well-formed (WF) and ill-formed (IF) child utterances for both the Post and the Demetras et al. (1986) subjects.

Child	Explicit		Implicit	
	to WF	to IF	to WF	to IF
Sally	A	C	MO	MO
Melissa	A	C	MO	MO
Kalie	A	C	MO	MO
Alex	A	A	MO	CQ
Amy	A	A	MO	CQ
Ben	A	A	MO	CQ
Jim	A	A	MO	MO

accept the IF utterance and continue on in the interaction. Again, this may be a result of the increased demands on the mother in the triadic interaction.

6.4. Conclusion

There are many similarities between the interaction patterns of these laterborns from a rural working-class environment and those of firstborns from an urban, middle-class environment. For example, these mothers like those studied previously responded differentially to well-formed versus ill-formed child utterances: It is very clear from these data that mothers were more likely to respond to well-formed child utterances with exact repetitions than to ill-formed child utterances. Exact repetitions seem to work as confirmation for both the mother and the child that the idea being conveyed by the child has been successfully understood by the mother. In contrast, mothers tended to respond to ill-formed child utterances with other kinds of repetitions, the majority of which included a correction or addition of information to the ill-formed child utterance.

Mothers asked different kinds of clarification questions in response to well-formed versus ill-formed child utterances. Mother tended to ask more yes/no questions to well-formed utterances and more repetition questions to ill-formed utterances. Here again, the repetition questions generally contained a correction of the child's utterance in the mother's response. Move-ons to well-formed and ill-formed utterances did not look very different, but it is plausible that they were given for very different reasons.

However, there were also differences between the feedback received by the children in this study and that reported in the literature. The most notable difference is that these children receive many more explicit corrections and disapprovals from their mothers than has been reported, as well as more clarification questions and move-ons. Whether these differences can be attributed to the triadic nature of the interaction studied here, or to the cultural and social differences between these families and the highly educated, urban, middle-class mothers usually studied, can only be discovered by expanding our analyses to include interactions with urban middle-class laterborns, and with rural working-class firstborns.

The data presented in this chapter suggest that rural mothers without a college education are as sensitive to the grammaticality of their children's utterances as are middle-class, college-educated mothers. This finding suggests we should re-examine theories of language acquisition that are based on the assumption that children do not receive negative evidence from their environment. Of course, the next step in trying to understand the role of negative evidence in language development is to determine whether or not children use this information to advance their linguistic abilities and if they do, how they do so.

While the question "Do children use negative feedback?" is still open to debate, a study by Farrar (1992) offers some positive information. Farrar found that children were more likely to imitate a morpheme that was in a recast by an adult than the same morpheme that was in an adult utterance that was not a recast. In addition, Bohannon and Symons (1988) found that children were selective in their imitations of adult repetitions. The children imitated adult recasts and expansions eight times more often than adult exact repetitions. These results suggest that children may be sensitive to the differing responses adults make to their language errors. In addition, there is also evidence from numerous training studies that enriched input does facilitate language development (Nelson, Denninger, Bonvillian, Kaplan, & Baker, 1984; Roth, 1984; Shatz, Hoff-Ginsburg, & Maciver, 1989). Thus, not only do children receive rich and informative input, they also appear to attend to this input and use it to advance their linguistic skills.

6.5. Exercises

These exercises will be performed on the file named **kal7.cha** in the **Post** directory.

6.5.1. Find the frequency counts of the mothers' responses to the remaining five types of child utterances (i.e., $W:SW, $I:MW, $I:SW, $O:MW, and $O:SW). Use the techniques described in Section 6.2.4.

6.5.2. Code the first 100 of the siblings' (SIB) utterances for grammaticality and the maternal responses to those utterances, using the instructions in the Appendix. Determine each sibling's MLU and find the percentage of the sibling's utterances that are well-formed, ill-formed, or other. Then, taking advantage of the addressee tier (**%add**), analyze the maternal responses that are addressed to the sibling (ams). **Hint:** You may have to modify the gem markers used for the sibling's utterances to differentiate them from the target child's utterances. For example, you might change the code for well-formed utterances to $WS for *well-formed sibling*.

6.5.3. We have looked at maternal responses to the child's preceding utterances. How would you examine the child's response to the preceding maternal utterance? This is an attempt to determine if children use maternal feedback to correct their speech. Explain what steps you would take to design this study. How could you tell if children were learning from their mothers' feedback? Would you only examine immediate effects or would you also consider long-term effects? How could you tell if the mother's feedback caused the child's linguistic advances?

6.6. Suggested Projects

6.6.1. Carry out the study you designed to answer Exercise 6.5.3. concerning the effects of maternal feedback on children's speech. Either collect your own data or utilize the longitudinal data provided by CHILDES.

6.6.2. Using the methods described in this chapter, videotape three children at a similar MLU level interacting with their fathers and a closely spaced older sibling. Then, perform the analyses described here and compare them to the results obtained for mother-child-sibling triads. Are there differences between the triadic interaction with the father as the parent rather than the mother? What inferences can be made about triadic interaction in general?

Acknowledgments

I would like to express my gratitude to Jeffrey Sokolov for his help and patience in the preparation of this chapter. His editorial expertise greatly improved the quality of this work. Thanks, also, to Marty Demetras for her contributions to my understanding of the coding strategies in our earlier study. In addition, I want to thank Catherine Snow for her support in this work.

References

Bates, E. (1979). The emergence of symbols: Ontogeny and phylogeny. In W. A. Collins (Ed.), *Minnesota Symposia on Child Psychology: Vol. 12: Children's language and communication.* Hillsdale, NJ: Lawrence Erlbaum Associates.

Bloom, L. (1973). *One word at a time: The use of single word utterances.* The Hague: Mouton.

Bohannon, J., MacWhinney, B., & Snow, C. (1990). No negative evidence revisited: Beyond learnability or who has to prove what to whom. *Developmental Psychology, 26,* 221-226.

Bohannon, J. & Stanowicz, L. (1988). The issue of negative evidence: Adult responses to children's language errors. *Developmental Psychology, 24,* 684-689.

Bohannon, J. & Symons, V. (1988). *Conversational conditions of children's imitation.* Paper presented at the biennial Conference on Human Development, Charleston, SC.

Brown, R. & Hanlon, C. (1970). Derivational complexity and order of acquisition in child speech. In J.R. Hayes (Ed.), *Cognition and the development of language.* New York: Wiley.

Bruner, J. (1977). Early social interaction and language acquisition. In H. R. Schaffer (Ed.), *Studies in mother-infant interaction.* London: Academic Press.

Clark, E. (1987). The principle of contrast: A constraint on language acquisition. In B. MacWhinney (Ed.), *Mechanisms of language acquisition.* Hillsdale, NJ: Lawrence Erlbaum Associates.

Clarke-Stewart, A. (1973). Interactions between mothers and their young children: Characteristics and consequences. *Monographs of the Society for Research in Child Development, 38*, (6-7, No. 153).

Demetras, M., Post, K. & Snow, C. (1986). Feedback to first language learners: The role of repetitions and clarification questions. *Journal of Child Language*, 275-292.

Farrar, M. (1992). Negative evidence and grammatical morpheme acquisition. *Developmental Psychology, 28*, 91-99.

Gleason, J. (1977). Talking to children: Some notes on feedback. In C. Snow & C. Ferguson (Eds.), *Talking to children: Language input and acquisition*. Cambridge: Cambridge University Press.

Gold, E. (1967). Language identification in the limit. *Information and Control, 10*, 447-474.

Gordon, P. (1990). Learnability and feedback. *Developmental Psychology, 26*, 217-220.

Hirsh-Pasek, K., Treiman, R., & Schneiderman, M. (1984). Brown & Hanlon revisited: Mothers' sensitivity to ungrammatical forms. *Journal of Child Language, 11*, 81-88.

Hyams, N. (1987). *The acquisition of parameterized grammars*. Springer-Verlag.

Jones, C., & Adamson, L. (1987). Language use in mother-child and mother-child-sibling interactions. *Child Development, 58*, 356-366.

MacWhinney, B. (1991). *The CHILDES project: Computational tools for analyzing talk*. Hillsdale, NJ: Lawrence Erlbaum Associates.

Morgan, J., & Travis, L. (1989). Limits on negative information in language input. *Journal of Child Language, 16*, 531-552.

Nelson, K. E., Denninger, M. S., Bonvillian, J. D., Kaplan, B. J., & Baker, N. D. (1984). Maternal input adjustments and non-adjustments as related to children's linguistic advances and to language acquisition theories. In A. D. Pellegrini & T. D. Yawkey (Eds.), *The development of oral and written language in social contexts*. Norwood, NJ: Ablex.

Penner, S. (1987). Parental responses to grammatical and ungrammatical child utterances. *Child Development, 58*, 376-384.

Phillips, J. (1973). Syntax and vocabulary of mothers' speech to young children: Age and sex comparisons. *Child Development, 44*, 182-185

Pinker, S. (1984). *Language learnability and language development*. Cambridge, MA: Harvard University Press.

Pinker, S. (1989). *Learnability and cognition: The acquisition of argument structure.* MIT Press.

Ratner, N., & Bruner, J. (1978). Games, social exchange, and the acquisition of language. *Journal of Child Language, 5,* 391-401.

Roeper, T., & Williams, E. (1987). *Parameter setting.* Norwell, MA: Reidel Publishing.

Roth, F. (1984). Accelerating language learning in young children. *Journal of Child Language, 11,* 89-107.

Schaffer, R. (1977). Mothering. In J. Bruner, M. Cole, & B. Lloyd (Series Eds.), *The developing child.* Cambridge, MA: Harvard University Press.

Shatz, M., Hoff-Ginsburg, E., & Maciver, D. (1989). Induction and the acquisition of English auxiliaries: The effects of differentially enriched input. *Journal of Child Language, 16,* 121-140.

Snow, C. E. (1972). Mothers' speech to children learning language. *Child Development, 43,* 549-565.

Snow, C. E. (1977a). The development of conversation between mothers and babies. *Journal of Child Language, 4,* 1-22.

Snow, C. (1977b). Mothers' speech research: From input to interaction. In C. Snow & C. Ferguson (Eds.), *Talking to children: Language input and acquisition.* Cambridge: Cambridge University Press.

Snow, C. E. (1989). Understanding social interaction and language acquisition: Sentences are not enough. In M. Bornstein & J. Bruner (Eds.), *Interaction in human development* (pp. 83-104). Hillsdale, NJ: Lawrence Erlbaum Associates.

Wellen, C. (1985). Effects of older siblings on the language young children hear and produce. *Journal of Speech and Hearing Disorders, 50,* 84-99.

Wellen, C., & Broen, P. (1982). The interruption of young children's responses by older siblings. *Journal of Speech and Hearing Disorders, 47,* 204-210.

Wexler, K., & Culicover, P. (1980). *Formal principles of language acquisition.* Cambridge, MA: MIT Press.

Appendix: Instructions for Coding of Transcripts

Child Utterances

Child utterances may be well-formed (WF), ill-formed (IF), or other (O). Within the WF and IF categories, the utterances may be either a single word (SW) or a multi-word (MW) utterance. The specific guidelines for coding an utterance as one of the above are as follows:

Well-Formed (WF)

1. Must be semantically, syntactically, and phonologically appropriate for the context in which it is spoken.

    a. Diminutive endings are allowed: kitty, horsey

    b. Directives are allowed:

        *CHI: stop.
        *CHI: let go.

    c. Single words that call attention to an object, person, or location are allowed: cat, mama, here

2. Prosodic variables (e.g., stress) were not analyzed.

3. Interjections and normal disfluencies (e.g., repetitions of initial words and slight prolongations of vowels) are ignored.

Ill-Formed (IF)

1. Morphological errors:

    a. Lack of an obligatory grammatical marker:

        *CHI: what that?

    b. Lack of an article in response to a question:

        *MOT: what-'is that?
        *CHI: horsie.

c. Inaccurate or incomplete verb forms:

   *CHI: he bite.
   *CHI: she talk.

Note: Exceptions are made for local standard; for example,

   *CHI: he done it before

2. Syntactical errors:

   a. Incorrect order to morphemes or words:

      *CHI: what he–'is doing?

3. Lexical errors:

   a. Substitution of a nonword for a real word: bail for fail

   b. Combination of vocalizations and meaningful words in a single utterance if vocalizations do not have a known referent to the listener:

      *CHI: eh geh baby.

   c. Combination of unintelligible speech and ill-formed speech:

      *CHI: xxx dat bird–s

   d. Violation of semantic selection restrictions:

      *CHI: big money.

4. Phonological errors: evelator for elevator

5. Pragmatic errors:

   a. The beginning of an incomplete thought:

      *CHI: that is +...

   b. The initial portion of a self-corrected utterance:

      *CHI: <I need> [//] I lost my shoe-s.

Other (O)

1. Vocalizations with no meaningful words.

2. Laughter – must be clear from context; otherwise scored as a vocalization.

3. Counting, singing, rhyming, or saying the alphabet.

If an utterance contains words or a sequence of words that are clearly ill-formed, then the utterance is coded as IF and not O.

Adult Responses

If not coded as a no response, adult responses are coded as explicit feedback and/or implicit feedback (repetitions, clarification questions, or a move-on). The codes for each of these categories are summarized in Table 6.8.

No Response (NRS)

The family member does not respond to the child's utterance, usually because the sibling has interrupted. The parent responds to the sibling rather than to the other child, but often returns to the child within the same conversational turn.

        *CHI: horsey.
        *SIB: look what I draw-ed.
        %add: asm
        *MOT: Yeah # I see that.

Table 6.8: The codes for maternal responses.

For explicit feedback:

    Approval ($EX:APP)
    Correction ($EX:COR)

For implicit feedback:

    Move-Ons ($IM:MVO)

    Repetitions:

        Exact Repetitions ($IM:EXR)
        Contracted Repetitions ($IM:CNR)
        Expanded Repetitions ($IM:EPR)
        Extended Repetitions ($IM:ETR)

    Clarification Questions:

        Wh-Questions ($IM:WHQ)
        Occasional Questions ($IM:OCQ)
        Repetition Questions ($IM:XRQ, $IM:CRQ, $IM:PRQ, $IM:TRQ)
        Y/N Questions ($IM:YNQ)

    Tags ($IM:MVO:ADJ:TAG)

For shared responses: $SRS
For no responses: $NRS

Note: Each maternal response was also coded as either adjacent (ADJ) or nonadjacent (NAD).

Shared Response (SRS)

A response by the mother that is directed to both the INF and the SIB. This often occurs during reading.

Note: Unintelligible utterances by the mother to the infant were not scored since it was impossible to correctly classify them.

Explicit Responses (EX)

Approval/Correction (APP/COR)

These utterances are explicit responses to the child's preceding utterance that either approve or give negative feedback to the child. Words and phrases such as *yes*, *no*, or *that's right*, signal explicit feedback.

1. The APP/CORs refer only to the child's speech, not to his or her behavior.

    *CHI: egg.
    *MOT: egg # that–'is right.

This response is scored as an approval.

2. A response of *yes* or *no* to a child's question is not scored as explicit feedback.

    *CHI: climb up?
    *MOT: yes # you can climb up.

This response is not scored as explicit feedback. The context is used to judge whether the response is explicit APP/COR or an implicit move-on.

3. All words signifying affirmation are scored as an APP if the phrase, *that's right*, can be inserted afterward. Words, such as *yeah*, that are judged to be conversation fillers, are not scored as explicit approval.

4. Correction (COR), similar to approval, must be explicit:

    *CHI: ball.
    *MOT: No # that–'is not a ball.

5. Direct contradiction of a child's preceding utterance is scored as a COR.

    *CHI: that dog.
    *MOT: that–'is a cow.

6. The mother's repetition of *yes* or *yeah* is scored as a repetition not an approval.

Implicit Responses (IM)

For implicit feedback, the intent is to separate those utterances that continue the topic or initiate new topics (move-ons) from those utterances that restate what the child said or asks for additional information (repetitions and clarification questions).

Move-ons (MVO)

In these utterances, the mother uses the same topic or starts a new topic, but does not "negotiate" with the child for meaning. We infer that the mother understands what the child said, accepts it, and moves on with the conversation.

*CHI: mama.
*MOT: sweet girl.

*CHI: here.
*MOT: that–'is the right baby.

Repetitions

Four types of repetitions are coded: Exact, contracted, expanded, and extended. The use of deictic forms (e.g., substitution of *you* or *me*, *come* for *go*) are accepted as repetitions.

Exact (EXR):   Exact repetition of what the child said.

*CHI: nose.
*MOT: nose.

Contracted (CNR):   Shortening of the child's utterance in any way.

*CHI: that is a monster.
*MOT: that's a monster.

Expanded (EPR): Correction of the child's utterance with appropriate syntax or morphology.

    *CHI: he at work.
    *MOT: he–'is at work.

    *CHI: baby sleep–ing.
    *MOT: baby is sleep–ing.

Extended (ETR): Repetition of the child's utterance with new information added.

    *CHI: ball.
    *MOT: that–'is a blue ball.

Clarification Questions

These responses refer directly to the child's preceding utterance. The different types of questions are as follows:

WH (WHQ): Must start with a Wh-word and clarify, otherwise scored as a move-on.

    *MOT: where–'did you get that kitty?

Occasional (OCQ): Questions that have a Wh-word embedded in them:

    *MOT: the cat done what now?

Repetition Questions (exact XRQ, contracted CRQ, expanded PRQ, extended TRQ): These are repetitions (as described above) that have a rising intonation contour at the end of the sentence.

    *CHI: cookie–s.
    *MOT: cookie–s?
    %res: $IM:XRQ

```
*CHI:     want clothes on.
*MOT:     you want your clothes on?
%res:     $IM:PRQ
```

Yes/No (YNQ): Scored only if no other choice. Usually a repetition question can be scored as both a repetition and a yes/no question. In these cases, the response is scored as a repetition.

```
*CHI:     hold deh.
*MOT:     you want me to hold this?
```

Tags (TAG)

If the question is a tag, this is coded in addition to the code for the appropriate repetition question.

```
*CHI:     de bail.
*MOT:     yeah # he–'is get–ing his tail, is–'nt he?
```

If the child's utterance is a question, and the response is a repetition of that question, the response is scored as a repetition, and not a repetition question.

```
*CHI:     what–'is that?
*MOT:     what–'is that?
```

7

Individual Differences in Linguistic Imitativeness

Jeffrey L. Sokolov
University of Nebraska at Omaha
Harvard Graduate School of Education

Joy Moreton
Harvard Graduate School of Education

In this chapter, you will learn the following skills:

- To match children according to language ability using MLU.

- To analyze the linguistic imitation of children using CHIP.

- To identify and collect imitative utterances from a coded transcript using KWAL.

- To uncover both quantitative and qualitative aspects of individual differences in children's linguistic imitation.

To replicate the analyses, you will need the file **eve15a.cha** in the **sokolov** directory. To perform the exercises, you will need the files in the **conti** and **NEngland** directories.

7.1. Introduction

Since imitation is one of the earliest communicative strategies used by children, individual differences in imitativeness should have a broad impact on language development. The establishment of CHILDES (MacWhinney & Snow, 1990) has made it possible to explore individual differences in imitativeness for large samples of children more quickly and easily than was previously possible. This is true for two reasons: (a) the database component of CHILDES provides access to a large collection of child language transcripts; and (b) the Child Language ANalysis programs (CLAN) provide computational tools for the analysis of imitation. The goal of this chapter is to explain how this may be done and to invite readers to perform the analyses on their own. The chapter proceeds in the following manner: First, we provide an introduction to the study of individual differences in language development and the study of linguistic imitativeness; second, we develop a methodology for exploring individual differences in imitativeness in conversational interaction between parents and their children. Third, we implement the methodology on a sample of 58 children at three different levels of mean length of utterance (MLU; Brown, 1973; see also Pan, this volume). We establish a comparison range of linguistic imitativeness and then identify the characteristics of individuals that fall outside this range. Finally, we invite readers to conduct these analyses by performing several exercises provided at the end of the chapter.

7.1.1. Individual Differences

It is possible to view the earliest modern studies of language development as explorations in individual differences (cf. chapters in Bellugi & Brown, 1967). At that time, many researchers viewed children as little linguists and attempted to list the grammatical rules underlying the speech of individual children. Although the goal at that time was to discover universal grammatical rules in children's language, these researchers found that not all children utilized the same grammatical rules at the earliest stages of learning. In the early 1960s, Chomsky (1959, 1965) proposed a distinction between abstract linguistic knowledge, which he called *language competence*, and actual *language performance*. At that time, Chomsky argued quite strongly that differences in the way that language was used by individual children were uninteresting epiphenomena of language performance and that child language researchers should focus instead on finding models for the child's abstract knowledge of linguistic rules. This led to a decade of research that tended to ignore individual differences in favor of models of universal language competence.

As researchers began to discover variability among children, not just in the rate of language development, but also in the style of development, the focus began to shift once again (Bates et al., 1979; Bloom et al., 1974, 1975; Nelson, 1973; and many others). Hardy-Brown (1983) argued:

individual differences in language development are no longer dismissed as trivial deviations from an otherwise universal developmental pattern. To the contrary, while behavioral universals and individual differences may be of equal theoretical interest, the societally important questions about development (with implications for education, remediation, and child rearing) most often involve individual differences. (pp. 610-611)

In the 1970s and 1980s, several influential studies of individual differences were performed. The studies tended to focus on particular aspects of language development. In this review, we briefly discuss three areas: lexical, grammatical, and pragmatic development. However, before doing so, we introduce a framework for exploring individual differences in children's acquisition of language skills.

A Framework for Individual Differences

In thinking about the issues surrounding individual difference, we began to realize that this term has been used to refer to many kinds of difference. We thought it would help to organize our presentation of the literature on individual differences by situating our discussion within a general framework. Most commonly, the term *individual difference* is associated with variation in language behavior between individual children. For instance, some children have a propensity to repeat their parents' speech more than others. We might refer to this phenomenon as "individual differences in imitativeness." But beyond variation in the *amount* of imitation might lie other kinds of differences. Imitativeness changes with age for all children, but the *pattern of change* might differ across individuals. Some children may change faster or slower than others. Moreover, even within children who imitate a lot, we may see variability in imitative *profiles* – some children may tend to repeat whole utterances, while others have a tendency to repeat only parts of utterances. As we briefly demonstrate in the following sections, these three types of differences between individual children may be evident for any area of language development.

Individual Differences in Lexical Development

The most frequently documented individual difference finding is variation in noun use. From longitudinal research with 18 children (7 boys and 11 girls), Nelson (1973) discovered that children's early vocabularies differ in their composition. The vocabulary of one group of children, which she called *referential* children, tended to include a high proportion of common object names (e.g., chair, cup, etc.). In contrast, the vocabulary of another group of children, called *expressive*, tended to include more pronouns, modifiers, and function words, to focus on the social aspects of language, and to include more unanalyzed phrases (e.g., *Stop it* or *I love you*). Nelson argued that these differences reflected differing hypotheses about how language is used. The referential children were learning language to discuss and categorize objects in their environment; the expressive children were more socially oriented and used language to talk about themselves and those around them. Perhaps the most important (and later controversial) argument was that referential children were more advanced than expressive children. This argument was supported by Nelson's (1973) report that referential style was correlated with rate of development in children. These results were replicated and extended by Snyder, Bates, and Bretherton (1981) in a study of 32 children at 13 months of age: (a) They discovered evidence for the expressive/referential distinction when children's vocabularies included only 10-12 words; (b) the distinction was also evident in children's comprehension of language and not only their production; and (c) the referential children did appear to be more advanced in their language development.

Nelson (1973) also discovered a positive relationship between linguistic style and rate of imitation in an elicited imitation task. When asked to imitate linguistic stimuli, children with expressive language styles imitated more than children with referential styles. Bloom and her colleagues (1974, 1975) also replicated this finding. However, several other studies have reported conflicting results. For example, Leonard, Schwartz, Folger, Newhoff, and Wilcox (1979) discovered that referential children imitated the use of novel object names more often than did expressive children. We return to this issue in Section 7.1.2, when we discuss imitation in greater depth. At this stage in our exposition, the most important point to remember is that *imitation may serve more than one function*; this may help to explain the conflicting results.

Individual Differences in Grammatical Development

Within grammatical development, two styles of learning have also been identified. In a very influential monograph, Bloom, Lightbown, and Hood (1975) introduced a distinction between a *nominal* style and a *pronominal* style. Children with a nominal style tended to produce multiword constructions composed primarily of nouns and other content words (e.g., *Kathryn sock* or *Sweater chair*), while children with a pronominal style tended to produce multiword constructions, with heavy use of pronouns (e.g., *I finish* or *My truck*).

Interestingly, these two styles within grammatical development overlap with the two styles reported for lexical development. In other words, the children with an expressive style in lexical development also tended to have a pronominal style in grammatical development, and those children with a referential style also tended to have a nominal style. Not surprisingly, the pronominal/expressive children tended to be more imitative than their counterparts.

Individual Differences in Pragmatic Development

In her original study, Nelson (1973) noted that the speech of referential children functioned most often in the labelling of objects. In contrast, the speech of the expressive children was most often involved in the social functions of language (e.g., prohibitions, expressions of possession, etc.). Furthermore, expressive children tended to produce a greater variety of different communicative functions (Dore, 1974). In other words, the communicative intents expressed by the language of these children were more varied. However, in their review of this research, Bates, Bretherton, and Snyder (1988) argued that there are alternative explanations for the diversity in communicative functions in the speech of the expressive children. For example, since the expressive children are more imitative, certain forms may enter into their pragmatic repertoire prematurely, leading researchers to falsely believe they are more sophisticated in this realm. So, the question of who is more advanced has not yet been resolved.

Potential Explanations for Individual Differences

From our brief review of the individual differences literature, it is clear that variations in styles of language acquisition do exist. The great diversity in the range of individual differences makes it difficult to provide one simple explanation for why different children acquire language in different ways. Many researchers have sought to determine the sources of individual differences. We will briefly discuss three of these considerations: gender differences, social-environmental factors, and cognitive contributors.

One of the first sources suggested by researchers was gender differences. From a superficial analysis of the data, little boys appeared to be more expressive than little girls. However, correlational analyses between the sex of the child and acquisitional style demonstrated a less than complete correlation (Kempler, 1980). In other words, not all boys were expressive and not all girls were referential. This suggested that there were other contributing factors. One possibility may be that male and female children might be encouraged to use language differently, and it might be this difference, rather than a biological one, that leads to correlations between linguistic style and gender.

In fact, social-environmental factors have been suggested as contributors to differences in linguistic style. Nelson (1973) reported that the interactions of working-class parents with their children tended to include a large number of prohibitive directives, while the interactions of middle-class parents tended to include different cognitive activities. She suggested that this could contribute to a more analytic and referential style in children's language acquisition. Second, Lieven (1980) noted a greater tendency of the parents of expressive children to imitate their child's own statements. Thus, it is possible that expressive children imitate more because they learned to do so from their parents. Third, referential children tend to use showing or offering objects as a way to make social contact, and this tendency may provide these children with more opportunity to hear names for objects (Goldfield, 1987). In contrast, the expressive children were not less interested in objects but were more likely to interrupt their play sessions to seek attention without using a toy to mediate. It is likely that particular activities, such as book-reading, may contribute to the acquisition of object labels (Ninio, 1980; Ninio & Bruner, 1978). Other situations, such as play with siblings, may contribute to other aspects of language development. Fourth, temperament may play a role in individual differences. Kagan (1981) reported a distinction between reflective and impulsive children. He noted that impulsive children seize new means without careful analysis. These children may, in fact, be the ones with an expressive style of language acquisition.

However, the area that has been the subject of the most study regarding the sources of individual differences in language development is underlying cognitive abilities. Many different cognitive explanations have been proposed to account for individual differences in language development. One general theme has been to characterize one group of children as analyzers and the other as imitators: analytic versus gestalt (Peters, 1977); analytic versus holistic processing (Bretherton,

NcNew, Snyder, & Bates, 1983); analytic versus imitative learning (Kempler, 1980); and tool users versus imitators (Bates et al., 1979). Goldfield and Snow (1989) used the term *analysis for reproduction* to describe the strategy of making use of larger chunks of the input, and the term *analysis for understanding* to describe those children who instead looked for smaller linguistic units to use in combination. A slightly different proposal based on differences in symbolic play has been proposed by Wolf and Gardner (1979). They argued that in play, there are *patterners*, who break down patterns, permute their possibilities, and set up symmetries, and *dramatists*, who are concerned with approximations to reality, developing dramatic themes along social lines, and preserving the proper details in drawing. The dramatists are more oriented toward preserving whole patterns through imitation. These are the children who would most likely adopt an expressive style of language learning.

More recently, Bates et al. (1988) suggested a detailed proposal based on a large collection of longitudinal studies. They argued for the existence of related clusters of language abilities that emerge at different developmental stages. Based on their results, they suggested that the earliest phases of language development rely largely on rote or imitative processes, while later stages rely more heavily on analytic processes. Furthermore, individual differences may be accounted for by differential emphasis on one strategy or another during different phases of learning.

The presence of individual differences has broad implications for theories of language development. Perhaps the most important implication is that by studying how language development breaks down into individual components, we are opening the door to exploring diverse situations, populations of children, and cultures. As already quoted, Hardy-Brown argued that "the societally important questions about development ... involve individual differences" (see Section 7.1.1). For any theory of language development to be complete, it must incorporate this aspect of development. In the next section, we discuss how imitation plays a role in language development.

7.1.2. Imitation

As our earlier discussion indicates, imitation is a potentially rich area for the study of individual differences (Kempler, 1980). There are several competing theories of the role of imitation in language learning. Some theories of imitation have claimed that it is merely a means for learning new words (Rodgon & Kurdek, 1977). Others have claimed that imitation may constitute an intermediary stage in language development just after comprehension and just prior to production (Whitehurst & Vasta, 1975). Ruth Clark (1974, 1977) argued that imitation is a central process in language development. She argues that children use the whole of a previous parental utterance to be retained as a constituent of, or framework for, a subsequent utterance. According to Clark, this reflects a limited processing capacity on the part of the child, since it is more difficult to build a whole new plan than to copy portions of existing plans. By repeating portions of previous utterances, the child is also able to keep the linguistic context in short-term memory longer. This aids communication (in the short term) and learning (in the long term). The child need not immediately modify or analyze the internal structure of the imitated speech. Thus, imitation is used to build up larger structures than children could produce by themselves. Clark supported her argument with examples of progressive imitation. The examples included unanalyzed chunks of parental speech combined with the child's own words as in *That's not the right thing I wanted to do*.

On the other hand, imitation may also be a mechanism for maintaining conversational coherence (Keenan, 1977) or for other pragmatic purposes (Folger & Chapman, 1978). In addition, imitation by a child may signal comprehension, or lack thereof, to a point-sharing parent. One thing that is clear from Keenan (1977) is that imitation may serve many different communicative functions. She provides the following as an example:

(1) *MOT: It fits in the puzzle someplace.
    *CHI: Puzzle?
    *CHI: Puzzle someplace?
    *MOT: Turn it around.
    *CHI: Turn it around?
    *MOT: No, the other way.
    *CHI: Other way?
    *MOT: I guess you have to turn it around.
    *CHI: Guess turn it round.
    *CHI: Turn round.

From this example, she argues that "all repetitions are not imitations and all imitations are not repetitions" (p. 128). Some of the functions of imitation listed in her article are exclamation, agreement, self-informing, querying, imitation (mocking), matching claims, counter-claims, and commenting.

One of the most hotly debated subjects in child language is whether or not imitation is progressive. In other words, do children use imitation to acquire new grammatical devices? Researchers hypothesized that if children do use imitation to advance their language skills, then imitative utterances should be more progressive (i.e., longer or more complex) than their nonimitative counterparts. Studies by Ervin (1964) and Slobin and Welsh (1973) argued instead that children only imitate forms (both lexical and grammatical) that they already understand. Slobin and Welsh argued that all imitation is filtered through the child's current language abilities and therefore is not progressive. As in the next example from Snow (1981), what children imitate may reveal their understanding of grammar and their ability to process language.

(2) *MOT: Want some granola and yogurt for breakfast?
    *CHI: Yogurt granola.

In this example, the child's imitation reveals an inability to produce coordinate conjunctions. More recently, analyses of normal and language-impaired children by Tager-Flusberg and Calkins (1990) also indicated that imitated speech is not progressive. However, these analyses focused on exact imitations and reduced imitations but excluded expanded imitations. Exact imitations are exact reproductions of the parent's utterance, while reduced and expanded utterances, respectively, delete and add material.

With respect to the individual differences literature, Bates et al. (1988) citing evidence provided by Bloom et al. (1975), suggest that these findings are true for nominal/referential children. It appears that the imitations of these children are filtered through their current rule system. In contrast, for the pronominal/expressive children, imitative utterances are sometimes progressive. Since imitation is such a central aspect of communication and language development, and especially because it functions in so many diverse ways, we would expect that individual differences in language development could be either the consequence or cause of imitative behaviors or both. Let us now explore how we might discover these differences.

7.1.3. Goals of the Chapter

In this chapter, we define *imitation* as any attempt by the child to repeat partially or completely previous parental speech.[8] We are interested in discovering both the average rate of imitation for the children in our sample and differences in individual children's tendencies to imitate. Since Snow (1981) and Seitz and Stewart (1975) discovered that rate of imitation decreases with age, we will examine children at three different levels of mean length of utterance (1.5, 2.5, and 3.5). As discussed above, individual differences in linguistic imitativeness will have implications for the methods by which particular children acquire language and communicate with their parents. Not only is it our goal to identify *high* versus *low* imitators but we also want to characterize different imitative profiles. For example, do high imitators produce more exact or more reduced imitations than low imitators? We would like to determine what kind of imitation is most prevalent in high imitators and whether or not all high imitators perform in similar ways. For example, do some high imitators focus on object words more than others? If so, then perhaps these children can be characterized as being more referential than other children.

We plan to accomplish these goals with the help of a computer program called CHIP (Sokolov & MacWhinney, 1990). CHIP analyzes transcripts of conversational interaction by comparing the utterances of one speaker to the preceding utterances of another speaker. In comparing each utterance to the one that came before, CHIP codes the amount and content of lexical overlap and lexical change. One of the results of a CHIP analysis is a count of the frequency of several different measures of imitation. For our purposes, we will focus on six different measures of imitation. The first three measures provide information about the *general* linguistic imitativeness of a child. These include (a) the proportion of the child's utterances that overlap with a previous parental utterance, (b) the average proportion of overlapping words between the child utterance and a previous maternal utterance, and (c) the proportion of imitative child utterances. The next three measures

---

[8] Researchers have typically distinguished immediate from delayed imitation. Only immediate imitation will be considered for the present purposes. The reason for this is a practical one: It is sometimes very difficult to identify delayed imitation, since it is temporally discontinuous from its source.

provide more *specific* information about the way in which children might imitate their parents. These include the proportion of (d) exact imitations, (e) expanded imitations, and (f) reduced imitations. These six categories will enable us to characterize differences in children's performance with respect to linguistic imitation. In line with the literature described above, we predict the following results:

- Rate of imitation along all six measures will depend on level of MLU. As children's MLU increases, their rate of imitation will decrease.

- Within each MLU level, it will be possible to identify children who imitate at an extreme level (either high or low) for specific measures of imitation.

- Individual children who are high or low imitators will differ in terms of their imitative profiles.

7.2. Method

In the following sections, we present our methodology for exploring individual differences in imitativeness. We do this by first describing the sources of data in our study. Second, we describe the computer programs we used to analyze the data collected from these children. The two programs are MLU and CHIP (Sokolov & MacWhinney, 1990). The MLU program calculates the mean length of utterance for each child and is a standard measure employed by child language researchers to measure language development (Brown, 1973; Pan, this volume); CHIP codes parent-child conversational interaction. MLU is described first because we used it to group children into different developmental stages according to Brown (1973). These groups are used to determine the typical imitativeness of children at different MLU stages. Finally, we describe in detail the exact procedure we used to analyze the children's imitativeness.

7.2.1. Subjects and Subject Selection

Subjects included a cross-sectional sample of 58 children at three different levels of mean length of utterance (MLU). Transcripts were obtained from several different corpora within the CHILDES system: 24 children from the New England sample (Dale, Bates, Reznick, & Morisset, 1989; Snow, 1989), 20 children from the Ford Foundation sample (Snow & Dickinson, 1991), 4 from Rondal (1978), three from Howe (1981), 3 from Tager-Flusberg (Tager-Flusberg & Calkins, 1990), 2 from Brown (1973), 1 from Conti-Ramsden and Dykins (1989), and 1 from Higginson (1985). Child language data were taken from different corpora in order to achieve a larger sample size. In two cases (Rondal and Tager-Flusberg & Calkins), data were taken from nonhandicapped subjects from within a larger sample including a handicapped population. Subject samples from the different cross-sectional corpora were selected to fill the cells for each of the three MLU levels. Only one sample was selected from each of the longitudinal corpora. The sample that was selected depended on which of the three MLU levels needed entries the most. For example, as you will see in the next paragraphs, a portion of Eve's 15th sample was selected because the third MLU level was the hardest to fill. All the transcript data consisted of spontaneous mother-child conversational interaction during play and had been transcribed according to the CHAT format (MacWhinney, 1991).

Since MLU has been shown to be a good indicator of developmental level (Brown, 1973; Pan, this volume), we first used MLU to divide the children into groups. After calculating the MLU of the first 100 utterances for all the children separately, each child was designated as being at one of three MLU levels. The three levels were 1.5 ($N=20$, boys=10 and girls =10, range=1.05-1.77), 2.5 ($N=20$, boys=12 and girls=8, range=2.12-2.83), and 3.5 ($N=18$, boys=10 and girls=8, range=3.06-3.93).

The following is an example of how this was done. If we were analyzing the MLU of Eve (Brown, 1973) in her 15th sample (filename is **eve15a.cha**), then we would have used the following CLAN command:

mlu +t*CHI +z100u eve15a.cha

+t*CHI	Analyze the child speaker tier only
+z100u	Analyze the first 100 utterances only
eve15a.cha	The child language transcript to be analyzed

Command Box 7.1

MLU would produce the following output (from the file **eve15a.mlu**):

```
MLU.EXE +t*CHI +z100U eve15a.cha +f
MLU.EXE (04-MAY-93) is conducting analyses on:
  ONLY speaker main tiers matching: *CHI;
*****************************************
From file <eve15a.cha> to file <eve15a.mlu>
MLU for Speaker: *CHI:
  MLU (xxx and yyy are EXCLUDED from the utterance and
   morpheme counts):
   Number of: utterances = 100, morphemes = 382
   Ratio of morphemes over utterances = 3.820
   Standard deviation = 2.496
```

We would use the *ratio of morphemes over utterances* as the measure for MLU. The MLU for Eve during her 15th sample is 3.780. Thus, we would put Eve into the third MLU level (which has an average MLU of 3.5). This procedure was used for all 58 children in the subject sample. As we already mentioned, the groups were defined such that the average MLU of the groups was 1.5, 2.5, and 3.5.

7.2.2. Measuring and Analyzing Imitation

CHIP was used to calculate six different measures of linguistic imitativeness for each of the 58 children in the overall sample. These measures are briefly described below. The name of each measure, as listed in the CHIP output, is provided in parentheses. A more complete description of CHIP can be found in Appendix A. Three general measures of imitation were computed:

1. *Proportion of Overlapping Utterances* (%_Overlap): the number of child utterances with an overlap of at least one word with a previous maternal utterance divided by the total number of child utterances. This definition is represented in the following equation:

    (# Overlapping Child Utterances) ÷ (# Total Child Utterances)

2. *Repetition Index* (Rep_Index): the average proportion of overlapping words between the child utterance and a previous maternal utterance. An example is provided below in which there are two overlapping words

(*where* and *go*) in the child's utterance (ADA for Adam) out of a total of three words for a repetition index of 0.67.

    *MOT: where did it go?
    *ADA: where ball go?

3. *Proportion of Imitative Utterances* (%_IMITAT): the proportion of exact, expanded, and reduced child imitations divided by the total number of child utterances.

Three different types of imitative utterances were tabulated according to the definitions provided by CHIP (Sokolov & MacWhinney, 1990). These definitions and some examples are provided below:

4. *Proportion of Exact Imitations* (%_EXACT): The words in the source and response utterances match exactly:

    *MOT: ok here ya go.
    %com: "shoots" at CHI
    *MOT: stick um up.
    *CHI: stick um up.
    %com: laughing

5. *Proportion of Expanded Imitations* (%_EXPAN): The response utterance contains partial repetition with additions but no deletions:

    *CHI: gimme jelly.
    *MOT: peanut butter.
    *CHI: gimme peanut butter.

6. *Proportion of Reduced Imitations* (%_REDUC): The response utterance contains partial repetition with deletions but no additions:

    *CHI: coat.
    %com: coat = goat
    *MOT: it's not a goat.
    *MOT: it's a sheep.
    *CHI: sheep.

Whenever proportions of an imitative type are used, they refer to the number of imitations divided by the total number of child utterances.

CHIP was utilized to analyze the imitativeness of each of the child language transcripts. We used the **–h** option to instruct CHIP to ignore the interactional words listed in the file **exchip** (Appendix B). Thus, if the mother said *oh look* and then the child said *look*, the child's response would still be coded as an exact imitation. The following CLAN command was used to analyze the imitativeness of Eve:

chip +bMOT +cCHI +d1 –hexchip +f eve15a.cha

+bMOT	The adult speaker is MOT
+cCHI	The child speaker is CHI
+d1	Output summary statistics only
–hexchip	Exclude all the words from the file **exchip**
+f	Save the results in a file with the default extension **.chp**
eve15a.cha	The child language transcript to be analyzed

Command Box 7.2

The output for this CHIP analysis is listed in Table 7.1. These measures are called the *summary statistics* because they provide a quantitative summary of all the distinctions coded by CHIP. The crucial measures for the analysis of child imitation come from the CHI (Child responses to adult) column. The six measures of interest for the present analyses are set in bold font. They are %_Overlap, Rep_Index, %_IMITAT, %_EXACT, %_EXPAN, and %_REDUC.

One last analysis that we are interested in performing is a more qualitative one. This analysis has the goal of determining if there are differences among children in the content of their imitative utterances. To do this, we must be able to collect the imitative utterances that are of particular interest. For example, suppose we were interested in examining all the reduced imitations produced by Eve. To perform this analysis, we would need to combine the functions of two CLAN programs: CHIP and KWAL. CHIP will be used to identify the reduced imitations, while KWAL will be used to extract them from the transcript for later analysis. In order to combine the analyses performed by the two programs, we need to use the pipe symbol ("|").

Differences in Imitativeness 189

We also use the redirect symbol (" > ") to indicate the filename to which we wish the output to be directed. This is illustrated in Command Box 7.3.

chip +bMOT +cCHI +d –hexchip eve15a.cha |
   kwal +t*CHI +t%chi +s$REDUC –w3 +d1 > eve15a.red

+bMOT	The adult speaker is MOT
+cCHI	The child speaker is CHI
+d	Output the transcript with coding tiers only
–hexchip	Exclude all the words from the file **exchip**
eve15a.cha	The child language transcript to be analyzed
| kwal	Pipe the output to KWAL

+t*CHI	Analyze the child speaker tier only
+t%chi	Include the %chi tier in the search
+s$REDUC	Search for the keyword $REDUC
–w3	Output window of 3 utterances before target
+d1	Output the data in CHAT format

> eve15a.red	Redirect the output to the file **eve15a.red**

Command Box 7.3

This command results in the storage of all the reduced imitations produced by Eve in the file **eve15a.red**. The contents of this file are provided in Appendix C. We plan to analyze the reductions in the hopes of finding differences in their content among individual children. In particular, we are interested in analyzing the type and frequency of function words used by children in their reduced imitations.

7.2.3. Performing the Analyses on the Complete Corpus

The analyses for all 58 children are accomplished in virtually the same way as the ones for Eve. Instead of listing **eve15a.cha** as the file to be analyzed, we used a wildcard (***.cha**) to specify all the files in the directory with the extension **.cha**. Thus, the following command would compute the MLU for all 58 children:

mlu +t*CHI +z100u +f *.cha

Table 7.1: The CHIP output from Command Box 7.2 for the file **eve15a.cha**.

eve15a.cha	Measure	ADU	CHI	ASR	CSR
eve15a.cha	Utterances	354	312	354	312
eve15a.cha	Responses	348	277	335	297
eve15a.cha	Overlap	170	80	142	133
eve15a.cha	No_Overlap	178	197	193	164
eve15a.cha	**%_Overlap**	**0.480**	**0.256**	**0.401**	**0.426**
eve15a.cha	Avg_Dist	1.59	1.59	1.80	2.11
eve15a.cha	**Rep_Index**	**0.49**	**0.52**	**0.45**	**0.60**
eve15a.cha	ADD_OPS	222	87	189	139
eve15a.cha	DEL_OPS	202	114	195	140
eve15a.cha	EXA_OPS	223	97	167	163
eve15a.cha	%_ADD_OPS	0.34	0.29	0.34	0.31
eve15a.cha	%_DEL_OPS	0.31	0.38	0.35	0.32
eve15a.cha	%_EXA_OPS	0.34	0.33	0.30	0.37
eve15a.cha	ADD_WORD	498	211	515	300
eve15a.cha	DEL_WORD	406	268	493	301
eve15a.cha	EXA_WORD	370	161	276	282
eve15a.cha	%_ADD_WORDS	0.39	0.33	0.40	0.34
eve15a.cha	%_DEL_WORDS	0.32	0.42	0.38	0.34
eve15a.cha	%_EXA_WORDS	0.29	0.25	0.21	0.32
eve15a.cha	MORPH_ADD	25	8	20	9
eve15a.cha	MORPH_DEL	14	13	21	6
eve15a.cha	MORPH_EXA	27	17	33	20
eve15a.cha	MORPH_SUB	2	0	0	0
eve15a.cha	%_MORPH_ADD	0.07	0.05	0.07	0.03
eve15a.cha	%_MORPH_DEL	0.04	0.08	0.08	0.02
eve15a.cha	%_MORPH_EXA	0.07	0.11	0.12	0.07
eve15a.cha	%_MORPH_SUB	0.01	0.00	0.00	0.00
eve15a.cha	AV_WORD_ADD	2.24	2.43	2.72	2.16
eve15a.cha	AV_WORD_DEL	2.01	2.35	2.53	2.15
eve15a.cha	AV_WORD_EXA	1.66	1.66	1.65	1.73
eve15a.cha	IMITAT	34	13	26	44
eve15a.cha	**%_IMITAT**	**0.096**	**0.042**	**0.073**	**0.141**
eve15a.cha	EXACT	9	1	6	20
eve15a.cha	EXPAN	21	3	8	12
eve15a.cha	REDUC	4	9	12	12
eve15a.cha	**%_EXACT**	**0.025**	**0.003**	**0.017**	**0.064**
eve15a.cha	**%_EXPAN**	**0.059**	**0.010**	**0.023**	**0.038**
eve15a.cha	**%_REDUC**	**0.011**	**0.029**	**0.034**	**0.038**

Note that a second difference from Command Box 7.1 is the addition of the +f option. This option results in 58 MLU files being stored in your current working directory – one for each subject in the corpus. Since we are analyzing the MLU of so many children, this would result in the creation of 58 new files.

The next step is to sort the 58 children into the three MLU groups according to the criteria listed in Section 7.2.1. Then we recommend creating subdirectories for each MLU level (e.g., **level1**, **level2**, and **level3**) and placing the transcripts in the appropriate subdirectory (according to the MLU level of the child). Since all further data analyses depend on MLU level, this expedites matters and also leads to greater organization and less confusion.

In order to analyze the imitativeness of each of the 58 children, we would run the following command in each of the three MLU subdirectories. This command results in the creation of files with the default extension **.chp** containing summary statistics concerning the imitativeness of all the children:

chip +bMOT +cCHI +d1 –hexchip +f *.cha

For the present analysis, this would result in 20 new files in the **level1** subdirectory, 20 in the **level2** subdirectory, and 18 in the **level3** subdirectory. The final step in data collection is to create a data analysis file with 58 rows, each representing the data for a single subject. For example, the row for Eve would be as follows (the header row would not be included in the final data analysis file):

Subject	MLU Level	Overlap	RPI	IMIT	EXACT	EXPAN	REDUC
eve	3	0.256	0.52	0.042	0.003	0.010	0.029

Since these analyses result in the creation of so many data files, it is important to clean up your directories and subdirectories after each large analysis. Clean-ups can safely be performed after the comprehensive data analysis file is created, since all data is summarized in this file. To perform a clean-up, you should use whatever deletion method is appropriate to your system.

7.3. Results and Discussion

7.3.1. Does Rate of Imitation Depend on Level of MLU?

In order to test whether or not rate of imitation depends on the level of the child's MLU, one-way analyses of variance were conducted for each measure of imitation, with MLU as the independent variable. The means and standard deviations for each of the measures of imitation at each level of MLU are listed in Table 7.2. Four of the six measures of imitation declined with MLU, while two stayed about the same.

These results indicate that children with higher MLUs tend to imitate less than children with lower MLUs. This is true for both the general and the specific measures of imitation. With respect to the general measures of imitation, only the proportion of overlapping utterances does not significantly change as a function of MLU level. Since this measure taps into a general notion of conversational contingency, this suggests that children and their mothers are equally contingent across all the levels of child language abilities studied. In contrast, the repetition index decreases as children's abilities increase. This is more easily understood if we compare the young child with an MLU of 1.5 to an older child with an MLU of 3.5. If there is repetition of one word for both children, the repetition index will be much higher for the younger child ($1 \div 1.5$) than for the older child ($1 \div 3.5$). Similarly, the decrease in the proportion of imitative utterances is indicative of an increase in the variety of lexical items produced by the children. As children's linguistic skills increase, they are less likely to rely on lexical items produced by their parents to build contingent responses and are more likely to modify their speech according to their communicative intent. This explanation would also account for the decrease in specific imitations (exact and reduced). Finally, the lack of change in expanded imitations is unexpected. We might assume that as children's language abilities increase, they would produce more expanded imitations of their parent's speech. Nevertheless, the results do not support this assumption. The simplest explanation for this may be that these children are not advanced enough to be able to build upon adult utterances.

Differences in Imitativeness 193

Table 7.2: Means and standard deviations for the six measures of imitation across the three levels of MLU. The asterisks represent probabilities that the MLU groups differ from one another by chance.

	Mean Length of Utterance		
Measure	1.5	2.5	3.5
Overlap	0.18 (0.10)[a]	0.21 (0.07)	0.21 (0.07)
Repetition Index	0.79 (0.16)	0.57 (0.12)	0.48 (0.07)***[b]
Imitations	0.12 (0.09)	0.06 (0.04)	0.04 (0.02)***
Exact Imitations	0.03 (0.03)	0.01 (0.01)	0.01 (0.01)**
Expanded Imitations	0.09 (0.07)	0.04 (0.03)	0.02 (0.01)
Reduced Imitations	0.09 (0.07)	0.04 (0.03)	0.02 (0.01)***

[a] Scores are rounded to two decimal points.
[b] $* p < 0.05$, $** p < 0.01$, $*** p < 0.001$

7.3.2. How Can We Determine Whether a Child's Score is High or Low on a Single Measure of Imitation?

We can determine whether a child's score is high or low on a given measure of imitation with the aid of a *comparison range* (see Figure 7.1). We define the comparison range as the range of values within one standard deviation above and below the group mean for each level of MLU. In other words, this is the range within which most of the scores are expected to fall. This definition will remain the same for each of the six measures of imitation provided by CHIP.

With this definition, we can determine whether or not a child's score on a given measure of imitation is high or low by checking to see if the child's score falls above or below the comparison range for the child's MLU group. If the child's score is above the comparison range, then we can conclude that the child is more imitative than most of the children in his or her MLU group for that measure.

This method is easily illustrated by example. Suppose we were to focus on the proportion of reductions produced by Carl in our sample. The first piece of information we need to know about Carl is his MLU, which is 2.12. This places

194   Chapter 7

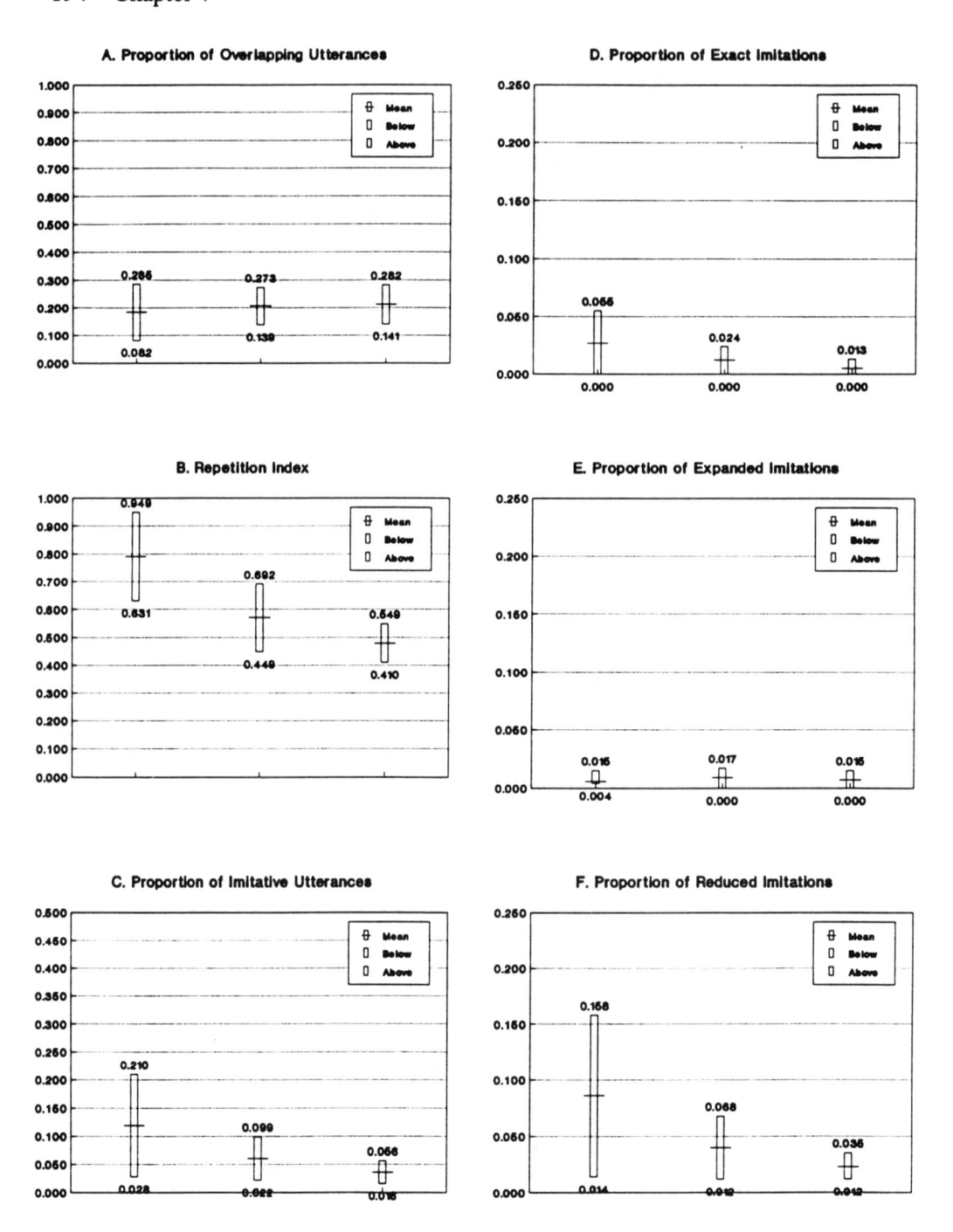

Figure 7.1: The comparison ranges for six CHIP measures as a function of mean length of utterance. Each box represents the range within a standard deviation above and below the mean.

him in the second MLU group. The second piece of information we need to learn about Carl is the proportion of reductions that he produced, which is 0.099. Translated into percentages, this means that 9.9% of all of Carl's utterances were reductions. To determine whether this number is high or low compared to other children with similar MLUs, we would examine the graph in Figure 7.1F. The comparison range of children with an MLU of 2.5 is 0.012-0.068. This suggests that Carl produces a very high proportion of reductions compared to MLU-matched children. In fact, if we use the information concerning the means and standard deviations provided in Table 7.2, we can see that Carl's production of reductions is nearly two standard deviations ($SD = 0.03$) above the mean (0.04) listed in Table 7.2.

7.3.3. Do Children Differ in Their Imitative Strategies?

In this section, we begin to explore the last research question listed earlier. In particular, we hypothesize that (a) individual children can be characterized as either high or low imitators for several measures of imitation, and (b) that the measures of imitation for which this is true will differ for individual children. Within our framework, children who are highly imitative will be consistently performing above the comparison range; while children who are less imitative will perform below the comparison range.

In order to test this hypothesis, we have selected six children who are extreme in their production of reduced imitations: the three with the highest proportion and the three with the lowest. The performance of each of these children goes beyond the comparison range with respect to reduced imitations. We have chosen reduced imitations because they are the most frequent type of imitation for all the children in the sample. Our goal is to compare their rate of imitation for all six measures of imitation to test whether or not they are consistently high or low on all of them. However, we cannot directly compare the scores for each measure. This is because a score of 0.85 at the first MLU level for the repetition index means something very different than a similar score for proportion of imitated utterances. In order to solve this problem, we must convert the regular scores into standardized ones. These are called *z-scores*. This is done by subtracting each child's score on a particular measure from the group mean and then dividing the result by the overall standard deviation:

$$(\text{child's score} - \text{group mean}) \div \text{standard deviation}$$

Let us perform this computation for Carl:

$$(0.099 - 0.040) \div 0.028 = 2.11$$

This computation was performed for all six measures of imitation for all six children with extreme performance on reduced imitations (see Figure 7.2). Each of the individual graphs in Figure 7.2 represent imitation profiles for each of the six subjects. By examining each subject profile, we can determine whether children who are high or low in reduced imitations are also high or low in all the other measures of imitation. The graphs in Figure 7.2 reveal that children who are extreme in their production of reduced imitations are also extreme in their scores for general imitativeness (with the exception of Renee). However, these subjects differ with respect to their tendencies on the other specific measures of imitation (exact and expanded). For example, only one subject among those who score high on reductions (Norman) also scores high on exact imitations.

The subject profiles in Figure 7.2 also reveal another interesting finding. Of the three children who score high in the production of reduced imitations, two are in the first MLU group and one is in the second. Of the children who score low, two are in the highest MLU group and one is in the middle group. Thus, even when standardizing scores within MLU groups, high scores in the production of reduced imitations tend to be associated with low MLUs, while low scores are associated with higher MLUs. More generally, this suggests that individual differences are more likely to be pronounced during developmental periods with a high incidence of the behavior being studied.

7.3.4. Do Children Differ in the Content of Their Imitations?

A major advantage of performing the quantitative analyses described so far is that they are useful in guiding further qualitative analyses. In other words, we can use the quantitative measures to identify particular children with interesting imitation profiles so that their imitative language may be explored in more qualitative detail. To illustrate this, let us examine more closely the reduced imitations produced by the three highly imitative children profiled in Figure 7.2. The goal of this section will be to determine if there are differences in the structure and content of the reduced imitations produced by these children.

Differences in Imitativeness 197

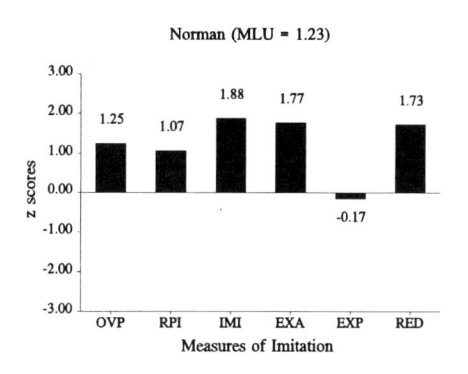

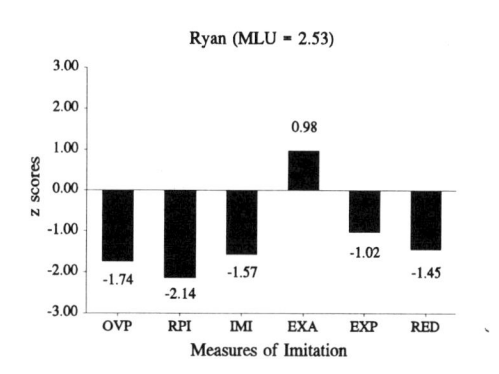

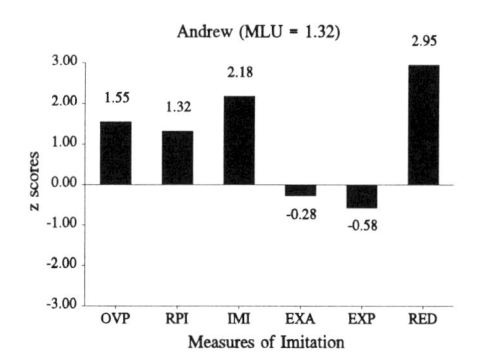

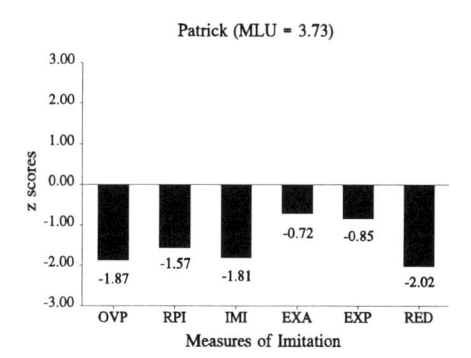

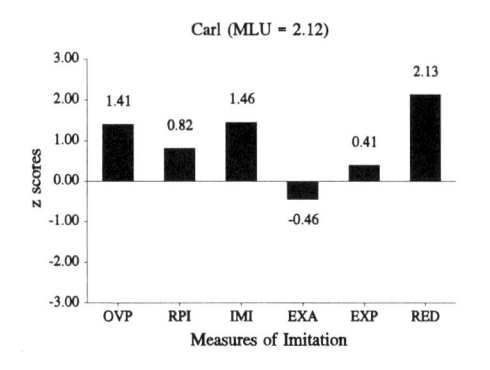

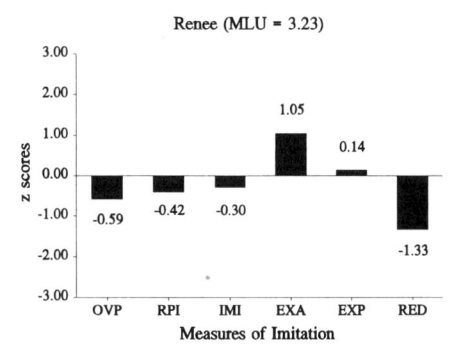

Figure 7.2: Imitation profiles for the three subjects who have the highest proportion of reduced imitations (on the left) and for three subjects with the lowest (on the right).

To perform this analysis, we must first collect all of the reduced imitations produced by each of the three children. The CLAN procedure described in Command Box 7.3 was utilized to accomplish this feat. For the purpose of this analysis, we focus on multiword reduced imitations only. A typical example for Norman is provided below:

(3)   Example from Norman.

    *MOT: and bounce the ball xxx.
    *CHI: bounce ball.

As we see from the example, Norman tends to imitate content words. In contrast, Andrew tends to include function words in his imitations:

(4)   Example from Andrew.

    *MOT: you wanna [: want to] go in our car and go home?
    *CHI: our car.

Finally, let us examine an example from Carl, whose MLU is longer than either Norman's or Andrew's. Carl also includes function words in his imitations:

(5)   Example from Carl.

    *MOT: you work on your truck huh?
    *MOT   are you gonna [: go-ing to] load up that truck?
    *CHI: that truck.

Table 7.3 provides a summary of some characteristics of the reduced imitations for these children. Several interesting results are reflected in this table. First, as we would expect given Carl's more advanced linguistic abilities, he produced the greatest number of multiword reductions. Second, despite the similarity in the overall MLU and proportion of reduced imitations for Norman and Andrew, Norman produced more than twice as many multiword reductions as did Andrew. However, 60% of Andrew's multiword reductions included function words (either *it* or *our*). Third, Carl had a strong tendency to use multiword reductions to express deictic functions (nearly exclusively with respect to a toy truck).

Table 7.3: Some additional features of the reduced imitations produced by the children with the highest frequency of reduced imitations (controlling for MLU group).

	Norman	Andrew	Carl
Overall MLU	1.23	1.32	2.12
Number	52	32	34
Proportion	0.211	0.299	0.099
Multiword	11	5	15
Contains Functors	2	3	14
List of Functors	a, it	it, our	more, that, the this

7.4. Conclusion

The study of imitation, in general, and linguistic imitation, in particular, is an extremely active area of research for developmental psychologists. In examining individual differences in linguistic imitativeness, we have only explored one aspect of this phenomenon. The results indicate that it is important to consider developmental level when examining linguistic imitation in children. Incorporating this finding into subsequent analyses, we discovered not only that children differ in their rate of imitation but also in terms of their overall imitative profiles. Individual children can be distinguished both by their overall tendency to imitate and by the specific ways in which they do so.

The procedures described in this chapter have great utility for comparing different populations of children. One particularly promising line of research is the analysis of linguistic imitation in children with language disorders (Sokolov, 1992). Sokolov found that children with Down syndrome imitate less than children without handicaps but only for levels of MLU lower than 2.0. These procedures provide a means for determining whether children from diverse populations imitate more or less than children with no language disorders and whether their imitations are of a different nature. In fact, we invite you to test this possibility in one of the exercises provided below.

7.5. Exercises

7.5.1. In this exercise, you are asked to analyze the imitativeness of children with specific language impairment (SLI) from the **Conti-Ramsden** corpus (Conti-Ramsden & Dykins, 1989). The Conti-Ramsden corpus consists of five British specific language-impaired children (SLI) matched for MLU with their younger siblings who were developing language normally. The children with SLI are: Abe, Clay, Kate, Rick, and Sid. The other five children are their MLU-matched siblings. Each child was videotaped at home interacting individually with his or her mother in a free play situation. Each transcript represents 10 minutes of continuous mother-child interaction. The three-letter speaker code for children in the Conti-Ramsden corpus is ***CHI** and for their mother's is ***MOT**. To perform these exercises, you will need the data stored in the following directory: **conti**.

- A. Which child with SLI produces the highest percentage of imitative utterances? Is this proportion above the comparison range for the appropriate group of MLU-matched nonhandicapped children? **Hint:** Use the +**d1** option to output summary statistics only.

- B. For this child, which is the most frequent type of imitative utterance? Do any other measures of imitation fall beyond the MLU-matched comparison ranges?

- C. Now perform an analysis combining the data from all of the children with SLI. Are children with SLI as a group more imitative than nonhandicapped children? **Hint:** CLAN programs may take a list of files as input. Use the +**u** option to merge the data from each of the input files.

- D. Does the difference in (C) hold for each measure of imitation?

7.5.2. Compare the rate and content of child self-repeated imitations with child imitations of mother in the five nonhandicapped children in the Conti-Ramsden corpus. You will find information about child self-repeated imitations in the column labelled CSR in the CHIP table of summary statistics. Do children produce more self-repeated imitations or imitations of mother? Why? Based on your answer to the first question, would you predict this to be true for all six measures of imitation? If not, why not?

7.5.3. Perform these same analyses for the adult imitations of children. Use the data in the **20mos** and **30mos** subdirectories under the **NEngland** directory. Are the adults more imitative of the children than the children are of the adults? **Hint**: The information about adult imitations of children is in the column labeled ADU.

7.5.4. Use KWAL to collect separate samples of exact, expanded, and reduced imitations for the child in the file **carl.cha** in the **sokolov** directory. Examine them carefully. Based on your examination of the CHIP-coded imitations and observations of the complete transcript, what do you think is the difference between automatically coded and manually coded imitations? If you were to code children's imitation manually, how would you do so?

7.6. Suggested Project

7.6.1. An important question concerning the role of imitation in language development is whether or not it is grammatically progressive. MLU has often been used as a measure of grammatical progress. In this exercise, you will be asked to answer the question: Do imitative utterances have a greater MLU than nonimitative utterances? Does this depend on the type of imitative utterance? Use the data in the **20mos** and **30mos** subdirectories in the **NEngland** directory for this project. You might also wish to consider developmental differences between the 20-month-old and 30-month-old children.

Hint: For the first question, you will need to include all three types of imitative utterances together in the same test; in the second, you will need to perform each test separately. Since you will be running MLU on the CHIP-coded output, you will need to use the **+d** option for each CHIP analysis.

Additional Questions:

A. Does your finding depend on the age or MLU level of the child?
B. For which 20-month-old child is the difference between imitative and nonimitative utterances the greatest? For which is it the least?
C. Do some children use imitation progressively and others not?
D. What aspects of language are children most likely to imitate in their exact imitations and reductions? What is likely to be added in expansions?

Answer these questions for the 20-month-old children and then test the relationship between imitation at 20 months and non-imitative use at 30 months.

References

Bates, E., Benigni, L., Bretherton, I., Camaioni, L., & Volterra, V. (1979). *The emergence of symbols: Cognition and communication in infancy.* New York: Academic Press.

Bates, E., Bretherton, I., & Snyder, I. (1988). *From first words to grammar: Individual differences and dissociable mechanisms.* New York: Cambridge University Press.

Bellugi, U., & Brown, R. (1964). The acquisition of language. *Monographs for the Society for Research in Child Development, 29*.

Bloom, L., Hood, L., & Lightbown, L. (1974). Imitation in language development: If, when, and why? *Cognitive Psychology, 6*, 380-420.

Bloom L., Lightbown, L., & Hood, L. (1975). Structure and variation in child language. *Monographs for the Society for Research in Child Development, 40*.

Bretherton, I., McNew, S., Snyder, L., & Bates, E. (1983). Individual differences at 20 months: Analytic and holistic strategies in language acquisition. *Journal of Child Language, 10*, 293-320.

Brown, R. (1973). *A first language: The early stages.* Cambridge, MA: Harvard University Press.

Chomksy, N. (1957). *Syntactic structures.* The Hague: Mouton.

Chomsky, N. (1965). *Aspects of a theory of syntax.* Cambridge, MA: MIT Press.

Clark, R. (1974). Performing without competence. *Journal of Child Language, 1*, 1-10.

Clark, R. (1977). What's the use of imitation? *Journal of Child Language, 4*, 341-358.

Conti-Ramsden, G., & Dykins, J. (1989). *Mother-child interaction with language-impaired children and their siblings.* Unpublished manuscript, University of Manchester.

Dale, P., Bates, E., Reznick, S., & Morisset, C. (1989). The validity of a parent report instrument. *Journal of Child Language, 16*, 239-249.

Dore, J. (1974). A pragmatic description of early language development. *Journal of Psycholinguistic Research, 4*, 343-351.

Ervin, S. (1964). Imitation and structural change in children's language. In E. H. Lenneberg (Ed.), *New directions in the study of language*. Cambridge, MA: MIT Press.

Folger, J. P., & Chapman, R. (1979). A pragmatic analysis of spontaneous imitation. *Journal of Child Language, 5*, 25-38.

Goldfield, B. (1987). The contributions of child and caregiver to referential and expressive language. *Applied Psycholinguistics, 8*, 267-280.

Goldfield, B., & Snow, C. (1985). Individual differences in language acquisition. In J. Gleason (Ed.), *Language development*. Columbus: Merrill.

Goldfield, B., & Snow, C. (1989). Individual differences in language acquisition. In J. B. Gleason (Ed.), *The development of language* (pp. 303-325). Columbus, OH: Merrill.

Hardy-Brown, K. (1983). Universals and individual differences: Disentangling two approaches to the study of language acquisition. *Developmental Psychology, 19*, 610-624.

Higginson, R. P. (1985). *Fixing-assimilation in language acquisition*. Unpublished doctoral dissertation, Washington State University.

Howe, C. (1981). *Acquiring language in a conversational context*. New York: Academic Press.

Kagan, J. (1981). *The second year: The emergence of self-awareness*. Cambridge, MA: Harvard University Press.

Keenan, E. O. (1977). Making it last: Uses of repetition in children's discourse. In S. Ervin-Tripp & C. Mitchell-Kernan (Eds.), *Child discourse*. New York: Springer.

Kempler, D. (1980). Variation in language acquisition. *UCLA Working Papers in Cognitive Linguistics*. Los Angeles: UCLA Linguistics Department.

Leonard, L., Schwartz, R., Folger, M., Newhoff, M., & Wilcox, M. (1979). Children's imitations of lexical items. *Child Development, 59*, 19-27.

Lieven, E. (1978). Conversations between mothers and young children: Individual differences and their possible implications for the study of language learning. In N. Waterson & C. Snow (Eds.), *The development of communication*. New York: Wiley.

Lieven, E. (1980). *Language development in young children*. Unpublished doctoral dissertation, Cambridge University.

Nelson, K. (1973). Structure and strategy in learning to talk. *Monographs of the Society for Research in Child Development, 38*.

Ninio, A. (1980). Picture book reading in mother-infant dyads belonging to two subgroups in Israel. *Child Development, 51*, 587-590.

Ninio, A., & Bruner, J. (1978). The achievements and antecedents of labelling. *Journal of Child Language, 5,* 1-15.

Peters, A. (1977). Language learning strategies: Does the whole equal the sum of the parts? *Language, 53,* 560-573.

Rodgon, M., & Kurdek, L. (1977). Vocal and gestural imitation in children under two years old. *Journal of Genetic Psychology, 131,* 115-123.

Rondal, J. A. (1978). Maternal speech to normal and Down's syndrome children matched for mean length of utterance. In C. E. Meyers (Ed.), *Quality of life in severely and profoundly mentally retarded people: Research foundations for improvement.* Washington, DC: American Association on Mental Deficiency.

Seitz, S., & Stewart, C. (1975). Imitations and expansions: Some developmental aspects of mother-child communications. *Developmental Psychology, 11,* 763-768.

Slobin, D., & Welsh, C. (1973). Elicited imitation as a research tool in developmental psycholinguistics. In C. A. Ferguson & D. I. Slobin (Eds.), *Studies of child language development.* New York: Holt, Rinehart & Winston.

Snow, C. (1981). The uses of imitation. *Journal of Child Language, 8,* 205-212.

Snow, C. (1989). Imitativeness: Trait or skill? In G. Speidel & K. E. Nelson (Eds.), *The many faces of imitation in language learning.* New York: Springer-Verlag.

Snow, C., & Dickinson, D. (1991). Skills that aren't basic in a new conception of literacy. In A. Purvis & T. Jennings (Eds.), *Literate systems and individual lives.* Albany: SUNY Press.

Snyder, L., Bates, E., & Bretherton, I. (1981). Content and context in early lexical development. *Journal of Child Language, 8,* 565-582.

Sokolov, J. L. (1991). The CHIP Manual. In B. MacWhinney, *The CHILDES Project: Computational tools for analyzing talk.* Hillsdale, NJ: Lawrence Erlbaum Associates.

Sokolov, J. L. (1992). Linguistic imitation in children with Down syndrome. *American Journal on Mental Retardation, 97:2,* 209-221.

Sokolov, J. L., & MacWhinney, B. (1990). The CHIP framework: Automatic coding and analysis of parent-child conversational interaction. *Behavior Research Methods, Instruments, and Computers, 22:2,* 151-161.

Tager-Flusberg, H., & Calkins, S. (1990). Does imitation facilitate the acquisition of grammar? Evidence from a study of autistic, Down syndrome, and normal children. *Journal of Child Language, 17,* 591-606.

Whitehurst, G., & Vasta, R. (1975). Is language acquired through imitation? *Journal of Psycholinguistic Research, 4,* 37-59.

Wolf, D., & Gardner, H. (1979). Style and sequence in symbolic play. In M. Franklin & N. Smith (Eds.), *Early symbolization*. Hillsdale, NJ: Lawrence Erlbaum Associates.

Appendix A: The CHIP Framework

A.1. The CHIP Coding System

The CHIP program codes pairs of utterances. The first utterance is called the *source* utterance, and the second utterance is the *response* utterance. CHIP compares the response utterance to the source utterance and inserts special codes into the language transcript as a distinct coding tier. In addition, the program tabulates a series of descriptive statistics as it processes a data set, and these are output following transcript coding.

The following example should provide the reader with a gentle introduction to the coding system. Given the following mother-child interchange:

```
*CHI:      Truck red.
*MOT:      The truck is red.
```

the CHIP system would produce the following tiers:

```
*CHI:      Truck red.
*MOT:      The truck is red.
%adu:      $EXA:truck $EXA:red $ADD:the $ADD:is $EXPAN $DIST = 1
           $REP = 0.50
```

The coding tier indicates that the adult response contained discontinuous EXAct repetitions of both *truck* and *red*, and ADDitions of both *the* and *is*. Since there are repetitions and additions but no deletions, the response is also coded as an EXPANsion. The distance between the source and the response is one utterance as indicated by the $DIST variable. Finally, a repetition index is computed for the amount of lexical overlap between the source and response utterances. The repetition index is 0.50 (2 overlapping stems divided by 4 total stems in the response).

The relevant codes are as follows:

$ADD: additions of N continuous words
$DEL: deletions of N continuous words
$EXA: exact repetitions of N continuous words

$EXACT: Source-response pairs with no changes (e.g., no additions or deletions).
$EXPAN: Source-response pairs with exact-matches and additions but no deletions.
$REDUC: Source-response pairs with exact-matches and deletions but no additions.

$DIST: The distance between the source and response utterances.
$NO_REP: There is no repetition between the source and response utterances.
$REP: The proportion of exactly repeated words in the source and response over the total number of words in the response.

A.2. The Automated Coding Process

When CHIP is invoked, it is told by a series of flags who the child and adult participants are and what options to code. CHIP then moves through transcripts of conversational interaction looking for utterance pairs to code. When a response utterance is encountered, the program looks backward for the most recent and only the most recent potential source utterance. Potential source utterances are located according to speaker type. For example, if an adult response to a child utterance is being coded, only the most recent child utterance is counted as the source. Once a source utterance is encountered, the search is terminated, regardless of the presence or absence of overlapping elements. Only one source utterance is coded for each response utterance. Once a source-response pair has been found, a simple matching procedure is performed. After the matching has been performed, if the amount of lexical overlap is zero, then no statistical information is computed and the code $NO_REP (no repetition) is inserted into the transcript. It is important to note that if the same speaker produces two sequential responses, the same source utterance may be coded for each one. Presumably the second response is a modification of the first, so the codes for this source-response pair should represent new information.

For the purposes of the present analysis, a window of seven utterances was utilized. The utterance window includes the response utterance and six preceding utterances. CHIP cannot search beyond this window. If a source utterance cannot be found within this window, the program simply moves forward in the file looking for a different response. The number 7 was selected to remain within range of the child's short-term memory capabilities. This is based on the assumption that children will not be able to process information outside their short-term memory capacity. In fact, very few source-response pairs fell outside the six utterance window, which includes the target and five utterances above the target, that is used more traditionally within the imitation literature (cf. Bloom, Hood, & Lightbown, 1974). The average distance between source and response utterances for these three corpora was 1.27 utterances.

In addition, CHIP is instructed to ignore the interactional words listed in the Appendix B. For example, if the mother said *oh look* and then the child said *look*, the child's response would still be coded as an exact imitation. Finally, the current version of CHIP differs from the one cited in Sokolov and MacWhinney (1990) in using the total number of utterances as the denominator for the proportions rather than the number of CHIP-defined responses. This change was also intended to bring the CHIP coding system into conformation with past research concerning linguistic imitation.

Appendix B: The Exclude List

aah, ah, ahah, ahem, ahhah, alas, amen, anyway, atta-boy, aw, awoh, bah, bong, boom, boom-boom-boom, bravo, bye, c'mon, chrissake, christ, crap, creepers, da-da-da-dum, dammit, damn, darling, darn, dear, doggone, eek, eh, fiddlesticks, gawdamighty, gee, glory-be, god, godamit, goddamit, goddammit, goddamn, golly, good-by, good-bye, good-morning, good-night, goodby, goodbye, goodmorning, goodnight, goody, gosh, guck, gucky, ha, haha, hallelujah, haw, heehee, hell, hello, hey, hi, hmm, hmpf, honey, hooray, howdy, hubba, huh, huh-uh, hunhunh, hunmmm, hurrah, hurray, hush, ick, icky, indeed, jeepers, jesus, kaboom, ma'am, mmmm, mmmmm, mornin', mush, mushy, nah, nuhuh, oh, oh-good-right, oh-nuts, oh-oh, oh-yeah, ok, okay, oops, ouch, ow, presto, pss, pugh, roger, scrunch, shh, shucks, sir, smoosh, sonuvabitch, ssh, sure, sure-sure, sweetie, thank-you, toot, toot-toot, truly, tsk, ugh, uh, uhhuh, uhhum, uhoh, uhuh, um, umm, very-often, whee, whoa, whoosh, wow, yay, yeahhuh, yeek, yesiree, yick, yicky, yikes, yuck, yucky, yum, yummy, yumyum, yup, zounds, zowie

Appendix C: Reductions for the File eve15a.cha

```
@Comment:   ----------------------------------------
@Comment:   *** File pipeout. Line 663. Keyword: $reduc
*MOT:   what did he forget and where is it ?
*CHI:   an(d) it in my toy box .
*MOT:   d(o) you know what it is ?
*CHI:   what ?
%chi:   $EXA:what $DEL:do-you-know $DEL:it-is $REDUC $DIST = 1
        $REP = 1 .00
@Comment:   ----------------------------------------
@Comment:   *** File pipeout. Line 878. Keyword: $reduc
*MOT:   well blow your nose first .
*MOT:   that-'is it .
*MOT:   alright # now you can get in .
*CHI:   now .
%chi:   $EXA:now $DEL:alright $DEL:you-can-get-in $REDUC $DIST =
        1 $REP = 1 .00
@Comment:   ----------------------------------------
@Comment:   *** File pipeout. Line 1655. Keyword: $reduc
*CHI:   eh ?
*MOT:   the airplane was there .
*MOT:   we saw it # did-'nt we ?
*CHI:   we saw it .
%chi:   $EXA:we-saw-it $DEL:did-n't $REDUC $DIST = 1 $REP = 1 .33
@Comment:   ----------------------------------------
@Comment:   *** File pipeout. Line 1731. Keyword: $reduc
*MOT:   no # those do-'nt bend .
*MOT:   do-'nt break those .
*MOT:   it only come-es apart right there and right there .
*CHI:   oh # it only come-es apart +...
%chi:   $EXA:it-only-come-apart $DEL:right-there-and-right-there
        $REDUC $MEXA:-es $DIST = 1 $REP = 1 .00
@Comment:   ----------------------------------------
@Comment:   *** File pipeout. Line 1866. Keyword: $reduc
*MOT:   this is the track .
*CHI:   that a railroad .
*MOT:   and that-'is the train .
*CHI:   oh # that-'is the train .
%chi:   $EXA:that-the-train $DEL:and $REDUC $MEXA:-'is $DIST = 1
        $REP = 1 .00
```

```
@Comment:  -----------------------------------------
@Comment:  *** File pipeout. Line 1996. Keyword: $reduc
*MOT:   that-'is it .
*CHI:   an(d) we need some more more track .
*MOT:   more track # yeah .
*CHI:   more track .
%chi:   $EXA:more-track $DEL:yeah $REDUC $DIST = 1 $REP = 1 .00
@Comment:  -----------------------------------------
@Comment:  *** File pipeout. Line 2336. Keyword: $reduc
*CHI:   my blanket # not my blanky .
*MOT:   not your blanky .
*MOT:   no # blanket .
*CHI:   blanket .
%chi:   $EXA:blanket $DEL:no $REDUC $DIST = 1 $REP = 1 .00
@Comment:  -----------------------------------------
@Comment:  *** File pipeout. Line 2406. Keyword: $reduc
*MOT:   well # I do-'nt have any more .
*MOT:   it-'is empty .
*MOT:   woops # there-'is one right in the bottom .
*CHI:   there one right in bottom .
%chi:   $EXA:there-one-right-in-bottom $DEL:woops $DEL:the $REDUC
        $MDEL:-'is $DIST = 1 $REP = 1 .00
@Comment:  -----------------------------------------
@Comment:  *** File pipeout. Line 2415. Keyword: $reduc
*MOT:   woops # there-'is one right in the bottom .
*CHI:   there one right in bottom .
*MOT:   right in the bottom # and that-'is all .
*CHI:   an(d) that-'is all .
%chi:   $EXA:and-that-all    $DEL:right-in-the-bottom    $REDUC
        $MEXA:-'is $DIST =1 $REP = 1 .00
```

8

Early Morphological Development: The Acquisition of Articles in Spanish

Beatrice Schnell de Acedo
Harvard Graduate School of Education

In this chapter, you will learn the following skills:

- To use CHAT to transcribe Spanish data.

- To code for language forms that have the same surface structure, but have different grammatical functions.

- To create include files with the language structures you wish to study, in this case, articles.

- To examine the emergence of articles in the child's speech by running the CLAN program FREQ with include files.

- To use KWAL to analyze the mother's responses to the child's errors and to determine whether the child's use of an article is either imitative or spontaneous.

To replicate the analyses and to do the exercises at the end of this chapter, you will need the Spanish language data contained in a file called **morela16.cha** found in the **acedo** directory.

8.1. Introduction

Children's first utterances consist mainly of words that in the adult language correspond to the categories of nouns, verbs, and adjectives. As soon as children start to produce their first word combinations, words such as articles, prepositions, and inflections, "like an intricate sort of ivy, begin to grow up between and upon the major construction blocks" (Brown, 1973, p. 249). These language structures, known as *grammatical morphemes,* often do not carry any meaning in isolation.

Morphological Development in Spanish 211

When they are attached to nouns, verbs, or adjectives, they affect the meaning of sentences in subtle ways. Most of our present knowledge of how children acquire the morphology of their language stems from the study of English-speaking children, beginning with the seminal work on the children Adam, Eve, and Sarah by Brown and his colleagues (1973). Although there are a number of studies on the acquisition of morphology in other languages (e.g., see chapters in Slobin, 1985), none is as detailed and complete as the account of the emergence of English morphology.

The purpose of this chapter is to describe how CHILDES can be used to explore the acquisition of one of the morphemes studied by Brown – the article – in a child learning Spanish as a first language. A brief summary of Brown's methodology and overall findings with English-speaking children is presented first. A discussion of what the research on the acquisition of articles in children learning Spanish has revealed, as well as some of the limitations of these studies, follows. Next an explanation of how CHILDES can be used to both transcribe and analyze Spanish data is provided, ending with several exercises to give the reader hands-on experience working with Spanish data.

8.2. Background

8.2.1. Brown's Findings with English-Speaking Children

For their study of English morphology, Brown (1973) and Cazden (1968) selected a subset of 14 highly frequent morphemes whose obligatory contexts could be easily identified (i.e., contexts in which the use of a morpheme would be required for the adult speaker of English). The subset of morphemes consisted of two articles (*a, the*); two prepositions (*in, on*); the noun inflections for marking plural and possession (*s, 's*); the verb inflections for marking third-person singular of regular (e.g., she talk*s*) and irregular verbs (e.g., he *goes*); the past tense of regular (e.g., she talk*ed*) and irregular verbs (e.g., he *went*); the present progressive (e.g., talk*ing*); the use of *be* as a contractible (she*'s talking*) or uncontractible auxiliary (she *was talking*) and as a contractible (she*'s* good) or uncontractible (this *is* hers) main verb or copula.

Brown and Cazden analyzed the transcripts of their three subjects using both the *linguistic* context (the meaning of either the child's utterance or the preceding/following adult utterance) and the *nonlinguistic* context (e.g., if the child pointed at something while speaking) to determine when a morpheme was correctly supplied versus when it was either incorrect or omitted. For example, if in referring to a given book for the first time a child produces an utterance such as "there book," while pointing at it, we know that his utterance is missing an article (*a*) and the contracted copula of the verb to be (there*'s*). The criterion for mastery of a given morpheme was established at the point at which the child was able to supply it in at least **90%** of the contexts in which it was needed in three successive language samples (Brown, 1973).[9]

Brown's (1973) analyses revealed that, although morphemes begin to emerge early (when MLU=2.0), the process is long and gradual. In fact, the children he studied had not achieved the criterion of full mastery for all the morphemes studied by Stage V (MLU=4.00+) of their syntactic development. The most important finding of this study was that the developmental order of the 14 morphemes was remarkably consistent across the three children.[10]

This consistency, as Brown (1973) pointed out, was an unexpected finding considering that the results were obtained from spontaneous speech samples of three unrelated children. Although the *order* was constant, the *rate* of development varied greatly. For example, at age 2;3, Eve, the fastest learner, had a Stage V MLU and had achieved full mastery of six of the morphemes, while Adam and Sarah, at the same age, had a Stage I MLU and still had not reached criterion for any of the morphemes (Brown, 1973).[11]

Why is it that English-speaking children seem to acquire grammatical morphemes in a similar order? Brown (1973) argued that, in his data, acquisitional

---

[9] As de Villiers and de Villiers (1985) pointed out, using obligatory contexts as a measure of acquisition provides a more accurate picture of a child's language skill than simply estimating frequencies or time of first use. They argued that "since the morpheme is required by the grammar, its presence or absence indicates what the child is *able* to say rather than what he *chooses* to say" (de Villiers & de Villiers, 1985, p. 67, italics added).

[10] de Villiers and de Villiers (1974) confirmed Brown's findings in a cross-sectional study that examined the emergence of the same group of morphemes in a sample of 21 children.

[11] But see Lahey, Liebergott, Chesnick, Menyuk, and Adams (1993) for a recent study of 42 children that suggests that this often quoted order of acquisition of morphemes is not as consistent as the earlier studies indicated.

order did *not* seem to be related to how frequently a morpheme appeared in the parents' speech, but rather to the *linguistic complexity* of the morpheme.[12] To compare the order of acquisition of different morphemes, he introduced the notion of *cumulative complexity* (Brown, 1973, p. 185). That is, a morpheme that involves knowledge of x is less complex than a morpheme that requires knowledge of both x and y. For example, the plural marker (e.g., book-book*s*) encodes number only, whereas the uncontractible copula encodes both number and tense (e.g., this *is* a book, these *were* books). Thus, according to Brown's hypothesis of cumulative complexity, we would expect the plural marker to be acquired earlier than the copula, which in his study was, in fact, the case.

To date few studies on the acquisition of Spanish have used Brown's detailed methodology to examine morphological development in spontaneous speech (Beléndez-Soltero, 1980; Kvaal, Shipstead-Cox, Nevitt, Hodson, & Launer, 1988; Tolbert, 1978). Of these, most have been unpublished doctoral dissertations. It is particularly interesting to explore, using Brown's linguistic complexity hypothesis, how morphemes are acquired in a language that, in contrast to English, is as highly inflected as is Spanish. This kind of analysis enables us to determine whether, for example, Spanish-speaking children take longer to achieve mastery in the use of articles than their English-speaking counterparts, given that Spanish articles also encode number and gender in addition to what Brown termed *specific-nonspecific meanings* (1973, p. 369).

Specific and *nonspecific* are terms that Brown employs to explain the semantic distinction between the uses of the definite versus the indefinite article. It is important to note that there is no one-to-one correspondence between definite and indefinite forms and specific and nonspecific meanings (e.g., specific reference does not entail use of the definite article *the* in all cases). The choice of reference in the article is determined by "the speaker's conception of speaker and listener" (Brown, 1973, p. 341). When the reference is specific for both speaker and listener, the English rule calls for the speaker to use the definite form *the* (e.g., "Hand me *the*

---

[12] However, more recent studies suggest that input frequency can affect children's use of some morphemes (Bybee & Slobin, 1982; Moerk, 1980). Moerk cited a study by Foerner (1977) that revealed high correlations between the order of acquisition of a group of bound morphemes and their frequency in parental speech. Bybee and Slobin (1982) found that the number of times the adult caretakers used an irregular verb form was negatively associated with the number of times such a form was overregularized by the children.

pen," while pointing at it), whereas when the reference is nonspecific for both speaker and listener, the rule calls for the speaker to use the indefinite form *a* (e.g., "I need to buy *a* pen). However, when the points of view of speaker and listener differ, the speaker needs to use the indefinite article *a* (e.g., I saw *a* strange man today," is the case of a referent specific only to the speaker; "you once wrote *a* book about cats," is the case of a referent specific only to the listener; Brown, 1973).[13]

8.2.2. Findings with Spanish-Speaking Children

Difficulties in Studying the Acquisition of Spanish as a First Language

Lack of studies or lack of access to studies? Although Spanish is the third most widely spoken language in the world (Crystal, 1987), there is no comprehensive overview of what existing research tells us on its acquisition as a first language. In her review chapter on the acquisition of Romance languages, Clark (1985) reported that for Spanish, with the exception of several older observational studies (e.g., Montes Giraldo, 1974) and some recent doctoral dissertations (e.g., Eisenberg, 1982), "... many of the studies available are rather sketchy" (p. 698). She also pointed out that "... there is still relatively little published research available on Spanish as a first language" (Clark, 1985, p. 698).

Spanish researcher López-Ornat (1988) believes that the problem with the existing information on Spanish acquisition is not one of restricted scope, but rather one of reaching international audiences. In a bibliography that she provides of all the published studies available in Spain, one can see that a considerable number of sources on the acquisition of Spanish as a first language exists. Among them is Hernández-Pina's (1984) longitudinal study of her son Rafael from birth to 4 years, the most extensive published study on the spontaneous acquisition of Spanish. The problem of reaching international audiences, however, is twofold: (a) these sources are not easily accessible to researchers outside of Spain and (b) as López-Ornat indicates, they are usually only published in Spanish, and thus cannot be read by

---

[13] As Brown (1973) pointed out, instances of referents that are specific only to the listener are rare in adult language and, according to his study, non-existant in early child language.

researchers "whose native or adopted scientific language is English" (López-Ornat, 1988, p. 679).

Because of these problems, the data on Spanish language acquisition are often contradictory and inconclusive. As Kvaal et al. pointed out, "this has been particularly true for the study of Spanish morphology" (Kvaal et al., 1988, p. 384). The contradictory data on Spanish grammatical morphemes greatly contrasts with the relatively consistent order of acquisition that Brown and others have described for English morphemes (Kvaal et al., 1988). It is clear that more studies are needed, in addition to a comprehensive review of existing ones, to obtain adequate normative data on the acquisition of Spanish, especially its morphology.

Spanish Language Varieties. In studying the acquisition of Spanish, we also need to consider another issue, namely that it is not a monolithic language. The Spanish spoken in the different countries of Central and South America, in different parts of the United States, in Equatorial Guinea and Spain have distinct features that are immediately evident to native speakers (López-Ornat, 1988). Although there are norms for spelling and grammar that are common to all, there are clear differences in vocabulary use and meaning, in word order, as well as in pronunciation. This is also characteristic for such widespread languages as English. However, as López-Ornat (1988) pointed out, the Spanish language varieties "tend to be treated as one language in the United States under the label 'Hispanic'" (p. 608).

Failure to differentiate among language varieties can lead to inaccurate descriptions of the acquisition of Spanish. For example, in describing the appearance of temporal markers in the child's speech, Clark cited a study by González (1980) that identified phrases such as *hasta la noche* – translated as 'toward evening' – as the type of structure that young Spanish speakers begin to use at around age 2;6. López-Ornat (1988) pointed out that it is difficult to judge the grammaticality of such a temporal marker because in Iberian Spanish the preposition *hasta* means "a limitation – of either space or time – to the action expressed in the verb" (p. 682) and is therefore equivalent to either *up to* or *until*, but never *toward*. In fact, the equivalent of the preposition *toward* is *hacia* in most Spanish varieties. However, in Mexico the meaning of *hasta* has changed to *toward*. López-Ornat (1988) therefore argued that, before one makes generalizations about the order of acquisition of prepositions and other language features, one needs to distinguish carefully between "normative and specifically varietal data" (p. 683).

Not differentiating between common and specific features of language varieties can have serious consequences when a Spanish-speaking child's language development needs to be clinically evaluated (e.g., Cummins, 1984; Omark & Good Erickson, 1983). It is a particular problem when clinicians use standardized diagnostics – particularly vocabulary tests – normed on a group of children that speak a different Spanish variety than that used by those being assessed (Toronto & Merrill, 1983). Hence, it is of crucial importance that researchers not only identify the region or country where their language samples were collected (or where their language tests were developed), but also alert the reader to possible regional differences.

The Acquisition of Spanish in Monolingual Versus Bilingual Children: Same or Different? An additional problem, related to the one previously discussed, is that researchers often fail to make a clear distinction when they are describing the acquisition of Spanish in children growing up in monolingual versus bilingual speech communities. Both Clark (1985) and López-Ornat (1988) describe this lack of a distinction as a frequent methodological problem in studies conducted with Spanish speakers growing up in the United States, where researchers describe their subjects as native speakers of Spanish and do not take into account the influence English may have on the order of acquisition of certain grammatical structures, on vocabulary, or on the types of errors children make. In fact, some studies have found that children learning Spanish in the United States may even experience arrested development or loss of their Spanish skills as they get older (Merino, 1979). Describing Spanish acquisition patterns without acknowledging, as Clark (1985) does, that "data collected in the U.S. have mostly been collected from children who are, or are becoming, bilingual" (p. 698), can therefore be misleading.

Although it *may be* that monolingual and bilingual Spanish speakers acquire language in similar ways, one should not simply assume this to be the case for all language features. Before one can assert that the acquisition of a particular language feature is common to all speakers of Spanish, that acquisition first needs to be systematically explored.

The Acquisition of the Spanish Article System: What do We Know?

Forms that Need to be Learned. Definite and indefinite articles in Romance languages such as Spanish take different forms depending on the number and gender of the noun they precede. A child acquiring Spanish has to master nine different articles: five definite and four indefinite forms (as shown in Table 8.1 below).[14]

Table 8.1 reveals that, in addition to the masculine and feminine articles, there is also a neuter singular form (*lo*) in Spanish. In contrast to the others, *lo* is used exclusively before adjectives, adverbs, and participles that are nominalized (e.g., *es lo bueno*, "that's the good thing"; Quilis et al., 1989). This study therefore only examines the acquisition of feminine and masculine articles.

Correct article use also involves mastery of special cases. In Spanish, singular feminine articles (*la, una*) are replaced by a masculine article when a feminine noun begins with a stressed *a* or *ha* (e.g., *el agua*, "the water"; *un hacha*, "an ax"), but not when it is used in its plural form (e.g., *las aguas; unas hachas*) or with a proper noun (e.g., *La Haya*, "The Hague"). Children also need to learn that when the masculine singular definite article *el* is preceded by the prepositions *a* (at, to) or *de* (of, from), its form changes to *al* and *del*, respectively (e.g., *ella fue al (a el) colegio*; "she went to school"; García-Pelayo, 1983).

In addition, Spanish speakers need to be aware of the homonymy (i.e., same structure but different meanings) of several forms. The masculine definite article *el* is a homonym of the masculine pronoun *él*; the definite forms *la, las*, and *los* are also the forms of direct-object pronouns. *Un* and *una*, the singular indefinite

Table 8.1: Spanish articles.

	Definite Articles		Indefinite Articles	
	Singular	Plural	Singular	Plural
Masculine	el	los	un	unos
Feminine	la	las	una	unas
Neuter	lo			

---

[14] There is presently no consensus among Spanish linguists as to how indefinite articles should be classified. Many have argued against the traditional contrast of definite versus indefinite articles. For discussion of alternative classifications of indefinite articles see García (1991) and Quilis, Esgueva, Gutierrez, and Ruiz-Va (1989). Because of the lack of consensus, this study will adhere to the traditional terminology, as Soler (1984) and others have done in studying the acquisition of articles.

articles, are homonyms of *un* and *una*, the cardinal numbers (Quilis et al., 1989). *Un*, the indefinite form, functions as the English indefinite article "a", such as in *te estás portando como un niño*, "you are behaving like a child"; whereas *un*, the cardinal number functions as the English "one", such as in *sólo asistió un padre*, "only one parent attended." Which form is used can usually be determined from the context, although in early child speech they are sometimes difficult to differentiate.

Contexts in which articles need to be used (in contrast to English)

Definite articles. According to García-Pelayo (1983, p. ii-iii), definite articles are used more frequently in Spanish than in English, particularly when the noun is qualified as in *la Europa de la posguerra*, "post-war Europe"); before titles (*la Reina Isabel*, "Queen Elizabeth"); with parts of the body and articles of clothing, where in English the possessive adjective is more commonly used (*levantó la mano*, "he raised *his* hand"); before infinitives (*el comer*, "to eat"); in certain expressions of time (*son las cinco*, "it's five o'clock"); with nouns used generically (*los profesores están mal pagados*, "teachers are underpaid"); with names of certain countries (*el Canadá*), among others.

Indefinite articles. The opposite seems to be true for indefinite articles; they are used less frequently in Spanish than in English. Like English, indefinite articles are used when nouns are first introduced. But, in contrast to English, they cannot be omitted in constructions such as "a shirt and tie" (*una camisa y una corbata*); they also precede qualified abstract nouns (*reinó un silencio total*; "there was total silence") (García-Pelayo, 1983).

Acquisition studies: When are articles learned?

There has been little or no research to date on the acquisition of article systems in the Romance languages aside from French (Clark, 1985). The few studies that have been conducted suggest that, in Romance languages, articles start to appear in young children's speech as early as the one-word stage. MacWhinney and Bates (1978) report that, in Italian, for example, articles emerge at this stage "as 'schwas' preceding nouns" (p. 545). Despite this precocious emergence, Clark (1985) points out that children acquiring Romance languages may take six or more years to acquire adult-like use of articles. This is presumably because in these languages articles are complex morphemes. As was noted earlier, in Spanish, articles encode gender, number and, as in English, specific versus nonspecific reference. The studies discussed in this section illustrate some of the contradictions in the existing data on Spanish morphology (see Table 8.2 for a summary of the data). The studies that examined children at different ages, either longitudinally or cross-sectionally, all found that children go through several stages in the process of acquiring articles and that they make different types of errors. Furthermore, all reported that errors were few when compared to the total number of productions and that age of mastery was quite early. Other studies, however, found no evidence of stages, reported a high frequency of gender agreement errors, and provided a much later age of mastery.

Stages of Acquisition. Some Spanish acquisition studies suggest that young children go through several stages before achieving mastery in their article use (e.g., González, 1970; Hernández-Pina, 1984; Kvaal et al., 1988; Soler, 1984; Tolbert, 1978). Evidence from Hernández-Pina's (1984) study of her son indicates that the earliest attempts at article use were recorded at the end of the boy's one-word stage, between the ages of 16 and 18 months (during what some researchers call the "holophrastic stage"). According to Hernández-Pina (1984), these early forms resemble the definite singular articles *el* and *la*, but seem to be produced as part of the noun (e.g., *e(l)nené*, "the baby"; *ta táta* (la puerta), "the door"; *ka kaka* (la jaca), "the pony"; p. 232). Once articles were used productively, the definite, singular forms – *el* and *la* – seemed to be acquired before the singular, indefinite forms – *un* and *una*. Plural and contracted forms (*al* and *del*) were not used by the child until around 29 months. Like the singular forms, definite plural articles (*los* and *las*) emerged before indefinite ones (*unos* and *unas*; Hernández-Pina, 1984).

Error Types. During the earliest stage of article use, children learning Spanish make almost no errors in article+noun agreement. When they begin to form their first word combinations, and thus discover that articles and nouns operate independently (usually between 2 and 2;6 years of age), this apparent "error-free" stage is followed by what López-Ornat (1988) refers to as the "erratic stage" because of children's inconsistent use of Spanish agreement rules (p. 681).

Aside from omission errors, lack of gender agreement seems to be the most common error in the early stages of article use in Spanish. Number agreement errors appear much later because, as we saw above, children initially do not use plural forms. According to Clark (1985), the latter type of agreement error seems

Table 8.2: Summary of existing data on the acquisition of Spanish articles.

Investigator	Type of Study	Language Environment	Error Frequency	Age of Mastery
Hernández-Pina (1984)	Longitudinal	Monolingual	Few errors of any type (omission, gender, number, overext. of definites in all studies) (numbers not available)	31 mos.
Tolbert (1978)	Longitudinal	Monolingual		S1: 25.0 mos. S2: 30.5 mos.
González (1970)	Cross-sectional	Monolingual*		≈ 39 mos.
Soler (1984)	Cross-sectional	Monolingual		≈ 36 mos.
Brisk (1976)	Single-age Group	Bilingual	overext. fem. article to 76% of masc. nouns	> 5 yrs.
Kvaal et al. (1988)	Cross-sectional	Bilingual	Group I (24-32 months): pref. for masc. article: 63% of total for subjects with MLUs below 3.6	MLU = 2.6
Mazeika (1973)	Longitudinal	Bilingual	53 fem. articles/2 masc. articles	Not available

* Although González's subjects were Mexican-American, he reported that they spoke primarily Spanish until age 3.
** Studies used different criteria for judging mastery. Tolbert and Kvaal et al. provide specific criteria for how children's productions were judged: Tolbert's ages are based on 90% correct use in obligatory contexts, whereas Kvaal et al.'s ages are based on 80% correct us. Others as Hernández-Pina, González, and Soler only give age at which children were using all forms, making it difficult to know whether authors mean error-free use or not.

to be rare, although children have to learn to mark number in both articles and nouns. In regard to the use of specific versus nonspecific reference, the evidence suggests that children acquiring Spanish initially also make few errors (Tolbert, 1978). Brown (1973) reported similar findings for his English-speaking sample. Considering that at a very young age children talk mostly with familiar adults about referents that are in sight of both speaker and listener, it is not surprising that these studies suggest correct use of the reference distinction at an early age. However, as Maratsos (1974) pointed out, true command of this distinction must involve correct use in "situations where referents are introduced and known *only verbally*" (p. 448, italics added). It is in these situations that Maratsos finds that even 4-year-olds tend to use definite articles when introducing noun phrases (i.e., nonspecific referents), treating facts as if they were known to their listeners. Thus, proper use of the reference system requires that the speaker be able to take into account the listener's referential knowledge (Maratsos, 1974).

Error patterns and age of mastery. In most studies, gender agreement errors are observed in children's spontaneous productions for quite some time, yet conflicting results have been reported in regard to the frequency of gender agreement errors (compared to the child's total number of article+noun productions) and in regard to the age at which gender agreement is mastered. Evidence from two studies conducted with Spanish-English bilinguals in the U.S. (Brisk, 1976; Mazeika, 1973) suggest that gender agreement errors are a highly frequent phenomenon in children acquiring Spanish. According to one of the studies (Brisk, 1976), this phenomenon continues well into the early school years. In studying the spontaneous speech of a bilingual child from age 26 to 30 months, Mazeika (1973) found that when the boy used articles, he almost always used the feminine singular article *la*. In fact, Mazeika reported a 53 to 2 ratio for the Spanish corpus he analyzed. The other study, done with older children, seems to confirm this pattern of overgeneralization. Brisk (1976) found that, in their spontaneous speech, a group of 5-year-old New Mexico children used the feminine article for 76% of masculine nouns. She described a similar over-dependence on the feminine article in children 6 to 7;9 years old on an elicitation task.

However, López-Ornat (1988) argued that "such a pervasive [gender agreement] error has not been observed in Spanish children" (p. 681). Studies done with monolingual children in Spain indicate that gender agreement errors seem to occur with *both* masculine and feminine nouns, and in only a small number of the total article+noun combinations (Hernández-Pina, 1984). Hernández-Pina reported that at 23 months, when her son began to use singular indefinite articles, he tended to overgeneralize them. In contrast to Mazeika's and Brisk's subjects, however, the child first marked the gender of most nouns used as nonspecific referents with the masculine article *un* (e.g., **un llave,* "a key"), and then a short time later, began to systematically use the feminine article *una* (e.g., **una paraguas,* "an umbrella") for these nouns (p. 236). In addition, Hernández-Pina recorded the use of this strategy in only a limited number of article+noun combinations. Because she only provided descriptive data on her son's article use, however, we do not know what percentage of article+noun productions had gender agreement errors.

Tolbert (1978) reported similar findings in her study of a group of Latin-American children acquiring Spanish as a first language. Using the same methodology and acquisition criterion that Brown (1973) and his colleagues had used, Tolbert studied the acquisition of 12 of the original 14 morphemes.[15] She collected both longitudinal and cross-sectional data. The longitudinal sample included two children from middle-class families that were followed from the time they began to produce their first word combinations at around 23 months of age. Pishu, a Guatemalan girl, was followed until age 28 months, whereas Fanny, a Peruvian girl, was followed until she was 3 years old.

Like Hernández-Pina (1984), Tolbert found that the errors that influenced acquisition were those of gender, number, and omission, yet the frequency of these errors varied greatly from one child to another and, consequently, so did the point of acquisition. Pishu's errors were of all three types, but she made fewer mistakes after the first sample. Errors of gender agreement accounted, surprisingly, for only 4% of Pishu's errors. Fanny also made errors of the three types, with omissions being considerably more frequent, followed by gender agreement errors, which accounted for 28% of the errors. Tolbert reported that error types for gender did not follow any particular rule: The two children had gender agreement errors in both masculine and feminine words.

In regard to the age at which article+noun agreement is mastered, Hernández-Pina (1984) reported that, at 31 months, Rafael made use of the full repertoire of

---

[15] As Tolbert (1983) pointed out, only "twelve of the morphemes studied in English have equivalents in Spanish" (p. 74). The two morphemes that are specific only to English are the contractible copula (she's good) and the contractible auxiliary (she's talking).

articles without difficulty. Tolbert's results (as shown in Figure 8.1) indicate that one of her subjects, Pishu, was already able to supply the correct article 65% of the time in the first sample, and had reached the 90% criterion level in the second sample, at 25 months. These results suggest that Pishu may already have been well past the initial stages of article acquisition when Tolbert began to observe her. Results for Fanny suggest that her age of mastery was much later than Pishu's. Figure 8.1 indicates that at 23 months she was able to provide the correct article only 39% of the time, but 2½ months later, she provided articles 82% of the time. However, like Rafael, Hernández-Pina's son, plural forms entered Fanny's repertoire at about this age, which resulted in her making number errors. She did not reach acquisition criterion until 30½ months, at almost the same age as Rafael.

Explaining conflicting results: Bilingual versus monolingual acquisition? The contrasting evidence of Mazeika and Brisk lead one to ask whether article acquisition in monolingual Spanish-speaking children might be different from that of bilingual speakers growing up in the U.S., and if so, why. Results of a cross-sectional study by González (1970), using spontaneous speech samples from a group of Mexican-American children (ranging in age from 2 to 5 years), indicates that article acquisition in bilingual Spanish-speaking children can resemble that of monolingual children. In fact, González's (1970) 2-year-old subjects showed error patterns similar to those described by Hernández-Pina and Tolbert: (a) use of feminine articles for masculine nouns and vice versa; and (b) omission of the article altogether (p. 18). Like Hernández-Pina (1984), González (1970) found no evidence of plural articles in the 2-year age group. However at 2;6 years of age, the use of plural articles had become widespread. In regard to error frequency, González reported only two gender agreement errors for one of the three subjects in the latter age group. Interestingly, at 3 years of age, all of González's subjects showed gender agreement errors (ranging in number from 1 to 6). He also reported another type of error in children's use of indefinite articles: All of his 3-year-old subjects had difficulty differentiating the use of *un* versus *uno*, producing utterances such as **uno señor*, instead of the correct *un señor*, an indication that at this age children seem to be struggling with the use of *un* and *una* as articles versus *un* and *una* as quantifiers. From 3;3 years on, González detected no errors in his subjects' article use.

Results of a more recent cross-sectional study with Mexican-American children in the same age range as those studied by González (2;0 to 4;8 years), also suggest that bilingual Spanish speakers acquire articles in a manner similar to that of

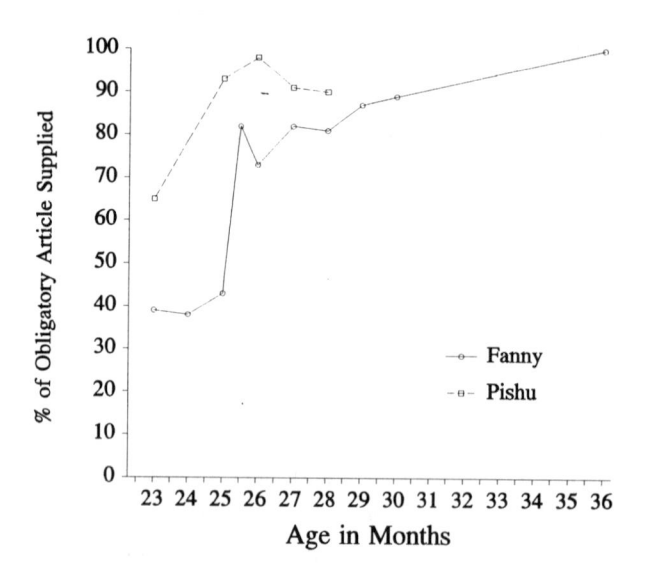

Figure 8.1: Article acquisition for the children in Tolbert's (1978) longitudinal sample.

monolingual speakers. Kvaal et al. (1988) divided their 15 subjects into three groups, according to MLU levels. Contrary to the researchers' expectations, articles were among the 10 earliest morphemes acquired (the morphemes were chosen based on their semantic similarity to those studied by Brown). Articles were acquired (defined as 80% accuracy) by all subjects except one, who only reached the productivity criterion (minimum of 3 productions). MLU at time of acquisition for the youngest subject was 2;6, equivalent to a chronological age of approximately 24 months. Similar to Hernández-Pina and Tolbert, Kvaal et al. (1988) reported that subjects with lower MLUs produced definite articles more often than indefinite articles, and masculine forms more often than feminine ones. In addition, use of plural articles was found to progressively increase from Group I to Group III.

Hence Spanish acquisition studies, with the exception of Brisk's, suggest that around age 3 children are able to use the full repertoire of articles and to exhibit command of gender and number agreement in their article-noun combinations. Results of a study of 66 Spanish children between the ages of 3 and 6 years confirms this (Soler, 1984). Using an elicitation task, Soler found that 3-year-old monolingual children did not make mistakes in gender or number agreement between nouns and articles. However, like Tolbert (1978), Soler (1984) did find an overdependence on the use of definite articles in her younger subjects, an indication that children take longer to learn the specific/nonspecific use of articles. Given that definite articles are used more frequently than indefinite ones in Spanish (García-Pelayo, 1983), it is not surprising that children would overgeneralize their use. It may also be, as Maratsos (1976) suggested for English-speaking children, that learning the difference between specific and nonspecific reference is a more complex cognitive task than learning gender and number. In addition, it is important to note that although children have acquired article-noun agreement at this age, they are still learning the agreement of article+noun+adjective combinations (López-Ornat, 1988; Pérez-Pereira, 1991). As López-Ornat pointed out, "these new errors... should not be confused with the earlier article+noun ones" (p. 682).

How can we explain the discrepancies between the language data collected by González, Hernández-Pina, Soler, and Tolbert versus that collected by Mazeika and Brisk? López-Ornat (1988) suggested that Brisk and Mazeika may have failed to distinguish among the different stages that other researchers observed in their subjects' article acquisition. She suggests that in Brisk's case, the high error frequency may have been found because Brisk did not adequately separate article+noun agreement errors from the later article+noun+adjective ones. López-Ornat's criticism may well be justified, since Brisk's and Mazeika's studies were neither longitudinal (as were Hernández-Pina's and Tolbert's studies) nor cross-sectional (as were González's and Soler's studies).

Yet the latter explanation fails to explain why Brisk's subjects made errors well after 3 years of age. One reason for this apparent age difference may be that Brisk's subjects were exposed to these two very different article systems (of Spanish and English) early on and thus may have taken longer to master article+noun agreement. In contrast, González's subjects spoke primarily Spanish until age 3, and thus may have had full command of Spanish article use by the time they entered a bilingual preschool. This, in fact, seems to have been the case. The overgeneralization of the feminine article in Brisk's studies was more widespread in subjects whose Spanish skills were *least* developed. But there are other features in Brisk's study that may have led to these results, such as her testing instrument. Brisk's noun recognition test not only included Spanish nouns, but also nouns borrowed from English that are typical of the Spanish variety spoken in Puerto Rico. Six of these followed Spanish morphology (e.g., *la furnitura*, "the furniture", *el rufo*, "the roof"), while seven others did not (e.g., *popcorn, hamburger*). Not surprisingly, children had more difficulty in providing the correct gender for articles accompanying the English loan words.

226   Chapter 8

In sum, the shortcomings of Spanish child language research are clearly illustrated by the studies on the acquisition of the article system. What emerges is the impression that whether or not a pattern like pervasive gender overgeneralization or high error frequency is observed seems to be influenced by how the data are collected (longitudinal, cross-sectional, or single-age group), by the Spanish-speaking child's command of the language (monolingual or bilingual), by how command of the language is assessed (elicitation or spontaneous production), by the Spanish variety he or she speaks, and sometimes, as in the case of Brisk's subjects, by all four factors.

8.3. Research Questions

The available evidence on the acquisition of the Spanish article system is limited and difficult to systematize. Longitudinal naturalistic study is a costly and labor-intensive method, yet it provides the researcher with the most complete and accurate picture of the process of language acquisition. The work of Brown and many others has provided this kind of invaluable data for English, but so far only one researcher, Hernández-Pina, has provided us with a complete account of one child's acquisition of Spanish. There is a clear need for more longitudinal studies on the acquisition of Spanish to shed light on conflicting results. This study attempts to do just that. Longitudinal language data from a Spanish-speaking child will be used to explore the following questions:

Question 1: *What forms seem to appear earlier? What do these early forms tell us about when number and gender agreement are mastered in article+noun combinations? When is the definite/indefinite contrast learned?*

Question 2: *What kinds of errors are more common when children learn to use articles? How prevalent are gender agreement errors: highly frequent, as Brisk and Mazeika suggest, or sporadic, as Hernández-Pina, Tolbert, and González found?*

Question 3: *Can the acquisition of these morphemes be compared to their equivalent in English? Do the morphemes under study emerge earlier in one of the languages? Are they acquired earlier in one of the languages? If this is the case, to what can we attribute such a difference in acquisition?*

8.4. Method

8.4.1. Subject

The subject of this study was a monolingual Venezuelan girl, Morela, whose language development was followed on a monthly basis between the ages of 16 and 33 months. Morela was videotaped during freeplay interactions with her mother every 3-4 weeks in sessions of 30-45 minutes. During each of these play sessions, age-appropriate materials were supplied by the experimenter (picture books, family pictures, toy animals). Some of the video recordings also involve interactions with her three older siblings, and her cousins, aunts, and uncles.

8.4.2. Language Samples

For this study we used data from 3 of the 18 videorecordings that were made of the child and her mother. The speech samples that were transcribed correspond to child ages 16, 23, and 29 months.

8.4.3. Transcription Procedure

All maternal and child utterances were transcribed using CHAT, the standard transcription system of The Child Language Data Exchange System (CHILDES; MacWhinney, 1991). Since we are dealing with non-English data, I want to bring to your attention several CHAT conventions you may not have encountered before. There are no symbols in basic ASCII to indicate the presence of a diacritic on a letter, such as we find in Spanish and many other languages. To represent diacritics MacWhinney (1991) suggested placing a carat (^) before the letter and the diacritic after the letter [see section on "ASCII Symbols for Diacritics and non-Roman Characters" in MacWhinney (1991, p. 69)]. In Spanish there are three types of diacritics:

1. ñ: a sound similar to 'n', that appears in words such as *niño* (child), *paño* (towel). In CHAT format, this sound is transcribed as ^n~ .

2. accented vowels to indicate stressed syllables: In Spanish, this marker is very important because it differentiates minimal pairs such as *"papá"* (father) *versus papa* (potato), *cayó* (it fell) versus *callo* (I remain silent). In cases such as these, the stressed syllable is transcribed as **pap^a'** or **cay^o'**.

3. a diaresis as in *bilingüe* (bilingual), which is transcribed as **biling^u"e**.

8.4.4. CLAN Procedures

In this section, the different CLAN programs used to answer the research questions are demonstrated. In order for you to be able to replicate the analyses, the procedures and results for Morela at 16 months are described in detail. Results comparing the three age points are presented in the Discussion section.

MLU

Since the focus of this study is morphology, the initial language analysis involved one of the most common measures of productive syntax in the assessment of natural language: mean length of utterance (MLU; see Pan, this volume). For nearly all the English language samples you will work with in this handbook, the speech has been morphemicized. In the case of the Spanish data, however, it was decided against this because of the lack of adequate morphemicization rules for Spanish child language. For a discussion of some of the problems in using MLU in morphemes in a language other than English see Appendix A.

To obtain the mean length of utterance in words for Morela at 16 months, we used the following command string:

Morphological Development in Spanish 229

mlu +t*CHI morela16.cha

+t*CHI	Analyze the child speaker tier only
morela16.cha	The child language transcript to be analyzed

Command Box 8.1

To obtain the mean length of utterance for all three files at the same time use **morela*.cha**, in place of **morela16.cha**. You can do this for the other CLAN analyses as well.

> If Morela's transcript was morphemicized, you would have to include the command **–c&-#^** in the command string for CLAN to ignore morpheme markers. See documentation for MLU in MacWhinney (1991) for more detail.

In addition to looking at the child's mean length of utterance, we were interested in examining whether there were differences in the mother's speech to the child across time. To do this we used the same command string for the child but replaced the speaker tier option with **+t*MOT**. Results of the MLU analyses for Morela and her mother at 16 months are summarized in Table 8.3:

Table 8.3: Mean utterance length in words (MLUw) for child's and mother's speech.

Child's Age	Child	Mother
16 months	1.35	2.91

FREQ

To determine how often each of the articles appeared in the child's and the mother's speech, we used the CLAN program FREQ. In its simplest form, FREQ would list frequencies for *all* the words in the file. Yet, one can also use it to obtain the frequency of *a given word or set of words*, such as a child's article use. To do this, you first create an include file that contains the group of words under study, in this case, definite and indefinite articles (in Table 8.1), as well as contractions *al* and *del*. Then you need to indicate that the CLAN analysis should focus on those words by adding the name of the include file (in this case called **articles.inc**), preceded by the **+s** option, to the command string (i.e., **+s@articles.inc**).

However, in this study there was a potential problem that also needed to be addressed: as was pointed out earlier, in Spanish *el, la, los,* and *las* are not only the language forms for definite articles, but also the forms for personal pronouns. For example, in the sentences below *los* is used as an *article* by the child (it is preceding a noun), but as an *object pronoun* by the mother (it is preceding a verb):

```
*CHI:      poneme xx los zarcillos!
%eng:      put on the earrings
*MOT:      te los pongo?
%eng:      should I put them on?      (Morela at 29 months)
```

In order to get CLAN to omit the instances in which these items were not articles, we did two things: (a) added a code ([$PP]) to the main tiers, following each of the forms we wanted FREQ to ignore; (b) added the option –s" <$PP> " to the command string, so that FREQ would not count instances followed by the code. Thus, the example listed above would be coded as follows:

```
*MOT:      te los [$PP] pongo?
%eng:      should I put them on?
```

The complete command to estimate the frequencies of the articles for Morela at 16 months, would be:

freq +t*CHI +o +s@articles.inc –s" <$PP> " morela16.cha

+t*CHI	Analyze the child speaker tier only
+o	Give frequencies in descending order
+s@articles.inc	Search for words in the include file **articles.inc**
–s" <$PP> "	Exclude all forms followed by this symbol
morela16.cha	The child language transcript to be analyzed

Command Box 8.2

Table 8.4: Both the child's and mother's use of articles at 16 months.

Child's Article Use	Mother's Article Use
4 el	16 un
3 un	12 el
1 una	10 la
	9 los
	2 una
	1 las
	1 del
8 Total	51 Total

To examine how the mother's use of articles compares to that of the child, use the same command string as above, but replace +t*CHI with +t*MOT. The results for Morela at 16 months of age and her mother are listed in Table 8.4.

FREQ was also used to estimate the number of instances in which the subject omitted an article in an obligatory context. For this it was necessary to first code all the omissions on the main tier. In CHAT, omitted words are coded with the zero symbol before the word or part of speech (see MacWhinney, 1991, chapter 4). Since the topic of this study was the use of articles, the code Øart was chosen. Note that mother's omissions were also coded. The FREQ command for the child's omissions at 16 months was:

freq +t*CHI +s"Øart" morela16.cha

+t*CHI	Analyze the child speaker tier only
+s"Øart"	Search for the keyword Øart
morela16.cha	The child language transcript to be analyzed

Command Box 8.3

KWAL

KWAL was used to search for particular instances in the transcript in which the child or the mother either used or omitted an article. With regard to omissions, we wanted to determine whether there was a pattern in how the mother responded to them, whether she also tended to omit the article in her response to the child, or whether she consistently provided the corresponding article. To obtain this information we used the following command:

kwal +t*CHI +s"Øart" +w5 +f morela16.cha

+t*CHI	Analyze the child speaker tier only
+s"Øart"	Search for the keyword **Øart**
+w5	Output window of five utterances after target
+f	Save the results in a file with the default extension **.kwa**
morela16.cha	The child language transcript to be analyzed

Command Box 8.4

KWAL was also useful for discovering how often the child's use of an article was either an *imitation* of the mother's previous utterance or a *spontaneous* production. Results for this analysis are not given here because it is one of the suggested exercises at the end of the chapter.

8.5. Results and Discussion

8.5.1. Mean Length of Utterance: An Overall Measure of Morphological Development

Table 8.5 shows that an important developmental change in Morela's language skills occurred between 16 and 23 months. During this period she made the transition from single-word utterances to multiple-word combinations. From 23 to 29 months, the MLU reveals only very minor progress, suggesting that the changes that were occurring in the child's speech may not have been picked up by this measure. If we examine the transcripts for the later ages, it becomes evident that the child was producing both longer and more sophisticated sentences at 29 months. But, because she engaged in frequent bookreading during the 29-month recording, her speech also contained a large number of one-word labeling utterances. Since MLU provides an average value, the one-word utterances probably brought her MLU word count down at this age.

Table 8.5: The results for mean length of utterance in words (MLUw) for the child's and mother's speech.

Child's Age	Child	Mother
16 Months	1.35	2.91
23 Months	2.15	3.53
29 Months	2.26	3.69

If we compare the child's and the mother's MLU for each of the child's ages we see that the mother is clearly attuned to the child's language capacity, increasing her utterance length as the child increases hers.

8.5.2. The Acquisition of Articles in Spanish

Question 1: *What articles seem to appear earlier? What do these early forms tell us about when number and gender agreement are mastered in article+noun combinations? When is the definite/indefinite contrast learned?*

The results for Morela's article use, summarized in Table 8.6, lend support to the patterns of use described in longitudinal and cross-sectional studies of young Spanish speakers (e.g., González, 1970; Hernández-Pina, 1984; Soler, 1984; Tolbert, 1978). At 16 months of age (MLUw= 1.35), we can see that articles have just begun to emerge in Morela's speech. At this age there is a clear disparity between the child's and the mother's frequency of use (8 versus 51 instances). Following Brown's (1973) method of analysis, we find that at this age Morela was able to supply the corresponding article in only 15% of obligatory contexts. The eight articles that the child produced accompanied either very familiar nouns, that she used on a daily basis, such as *papá* ("father"), *tetero* ("baby bottle"), and *gato* ("cat"), or nouns that had been introduced by the mother as topics of conversation earlier in the session, such as *caballo* ("horse").

During this early recording the child did not use articles until the end of the session, except for one instance (**una papá*, "a [fem] Daddy"). Since Morela produced only one feminine article (*una*) at 16 months, it is difficult to determine

234   Chapter 8

Table 8.6:   Child's and mother's use of articles.

Age of Child	Child's Article Use	Mother's Article Use
16 Months	4 el 3 un 1 una 8/47 7 correct / 47 Total Oblig. Contexts (15%)[a]	16 un 12 el 10 la 9 los 2 una 1 las 1 del (de el) 51/64 Total Oblig. Contexts (80%)
23 Months	10 los 5 la 1 el 1 al (a el) 1 las 18/24 Total Oblig. Contexts (75%)	7 los 5 la 4 un 2 el 2 una 1 al (a el) 1 las 22/23 Total Oblig. Contexts (96%)[b]
29 Months	31 un 13 la 12 una 8 el 2 unos 1 los 67/67 Total Oblig. Contexts (100%)	22 la 17 el 16 una 13 un 2 los 1 las 71/71 Total Oblig. Contexts (100%)

[a]   Although Morela produced eight articles at this age, one of them (*una*) was incorrect.
[b]   The low number of articles in this cell is due to the presence of other interlocutors.

whether she was at this age truly aware of gender markers. The other seven articles were all masculine and were in agreement with the nouns they accompanied, yet based on what Hernández-Pina (1984) describes for this early age, these article+noun combinations could have been acquired as unanalyzed or frozen strings. The results suggest that Morela had not mastered number markers either. In fact, all of her articles at this age were **singular**. This lack of plural forms is consistent with the article use that González (1970) and Hernández-Pina (1984) report for children at or below 2 years of age. One of Morela's omission errors provides further evidence for this difficulty. Upon seeing a **pair** of shoes in a picture book, she excitedly identified them as (za)*pato* (shoe), to which the mother responded *si, los zapatos* (yes, the shoes), an expansion that provided the correct number marking for both the article and the noun.

At 23 months of age, Morela has clearly begun to use articles more consistently. She now spontaneously supplies them in 75% of obligatory contexts. As is seen in Table 8.6, she uses both feminine and masculine forms, as well as singular and plural ones. She is able to produce the contracted forms of the singular masculine article *el*, such as *al* (*a el*). Note, however, that as Hernández-Pina (1984) observed in her son Rafael, at this age Morela still does not use plural indefinite forms (*unas, unos*). In addition, all of the instances of article use at 23 months were **definite** forms. If we examine the context in which the articles were produced, we note that they were instances that clearly called for the use of definite forms. Indeed, most of the topics that were discussed by the child with her mother and her siblings repeatedly involved the same articles of clothing. If we look at Morela's omission errors (discussed in more detail in the next section), we do find evidence that points to a possible difficulty with indefinite article use. Most of the omissions (five out of seven) occurred when the child was labeling objects, an activity that usually requires the use of indefinite articles. In short, the results for this age suggest that Morela is close to mastering number and gender agreement in article+noun combinations, but still seems to be struggling with the appropriate use of indefinite articles (when used with nonspecific referents).

At 29 months, Morela appears to be in command of the full inventory of forms. The results in Table 8.6 show that she is able to correctly produce gender and number markers for both definite and indefinite articles. Furthermore, at this age there are proportionately very few instances of article use that are direct imitation of the mother's utterances (3/48). There was also no evidence of any omission errors. If we compare Morela's article use with that of Tolbert's (1978)

236   Chapter 8

longitudinal subjects, we find that the article acquisition of the three children is quite similar (Figure 8.2). The pattern of acquisition in all three cases shows a low starting point, followed by an abrupt increase in article use, that for Morela and Pishu took place at 23 months and for Fanny somewhat later, at 25½ months, followed by a slow increase until the 90% acquisition criterion was reached. With regard to the age at which the children reached this acquisition criterion, there seemed to be more of a difference: Pishu reached it at 25 months, Fanny at 30½ months (although she was close to it from 28 months on), and Morela, based on the limited data presently available, at 29 months. It still needs to be determined if Morela's data for other ages show that article mastery occurred earlier.[16]

In contrast to Morela's article use at 23 months, we find that at 29 months she produced indefinite articles almost twice as often (31 indefinite/17 definite). This seems to be a result of the context in which most of the interactions with her mother took place. The materials she was most interested in during this recording were new

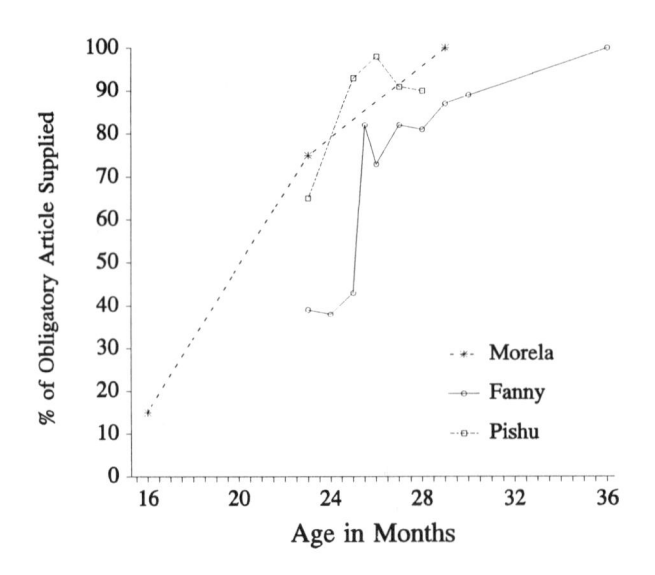

Figure 8.2: A comparison of article acquisition between Tolbert's (1978) longitudinal sample and Morela.

---

[16] Speech samples for ages immediately before and after 29 months are presently being analyzed to obtain a more precise estimate of when Brown's criterion of stable acquisition was met.

books. Since most of the talk around these books involved identifying different animals and objects, she correctly used more indefinite articles in her answers to her mother's questions. Thus, the progress in Morela's article use is evident. Labeling, as we saw earlier, was a task during which most of Morela's omissions occurred 6 months earlier.

In sum, Morela's spontaneous production data seem to suggest that number and gender agreement in article+noun combinations had been mastered by 29 months. This is consistent with the age at which González (1970), Hernández-Pina (1984), Soler (1984), and Tolbert (1978) reported stable acquisition of articles for their samples. However, from these data it is difficult to determine which of the two notions was acquired first: number or gender? Hernández-Pina's (1984) data on her son Rafael suggest that young Spanish speakers master number first. Clark (1985) provided further support. She argued that the plural marker may be easier to learn because most nouns in Spanish end in either the vowel -a (feminine) or -o (masculine; and, if not, children often overregularize these endings). Young Spanish speakers, therefore, only have to add -s at the end of all nouns and the feminine articles (la, las; una unas). The only clearly different form they have to learn is *los*, the plural form of singular masculine article *el*. Thus, from the standpoint of Brown's (1973) cumulative complexity hypothesis it would also seem that number markers, because they are less complex, should be acquired before gender markers.

With regard to the specific/nonspecific distinction, although the findings in this study do not reveal any errors at 29 months, we cannot be certain whether the child had at this age truly mastered it. Like Tolbert's (1978) and Brown's (1973) subjects, Morela's spontaneous use of the definite and indefinite singular forms suggests that she was able to adequately make the distinction. However, the data for this contrast was particularly limited in the case of the plural forms: Morela produced only one definite (*los*) and one indefinite plural article (*unos*). Given that spontaneous speech data only provide information on the forms children *choose* to use, elicitation studies, which test the entire inventory of forms, may be more helpful in determining when such a contrast has been attained. Thus, findings of this study and others strongly suggest that number and gender of Spanish articles are acquired around age 3, and prior to specific/nonspecific reference. However, more studies are needed to determine when and how young Spanish speakers acquire command of the latter.

8.5.3. Errors in the acquisition of Spanish articles

Question 2: What kinds of errors do children make when learning to use articles? How prevalent are gender agreement errors: highly frequent, as Brisk and Mazeika suggest, or sporadic, as López-Ornat and González found?

During acquisition, children make errors of both commission and omission. Yet, as Clark (1985) pointed out, most studies of acquisition errors have usually focused on errors of commission. This is mainly because omission errors are very difficult to study. In fact, it is not only difficult to determine precisely what structure the child has omitted in some contexts, but also why such an avoidance has occurred. Omission of a particular structure may be evidence of cognitive or linguistic constraints, but it could also be a strategy chosen by a cautious learner (Clark, 1985).

In this study, the subject's error pattern did not allow for much choice as to what type of error to analyze. Inspection of the transcripts revealed that, across all three speech samples, Morela made a single commission error. This error (**una papá*, "a[fem] Daddy") was also her only gender agreement error. The article Morela chose to use in this utterance – singular feminine *una* – is the appropriate one based on the ending of the noun (i.e., nouns ending in *-a* are usually feminine), but *papá* is, obviously, an exception to the rule. However, this error could also be interpreted as an attempt to say *uno* (one) *papá*, since, as the mother points out in the transcript, Morela referred to all men as *papá* at this age. All other errors in article use that were recorded at 16 and 23 months were errors of *omission*. These errors were particularly prevalent at the earliest age. In Table 8.7 we can see that Morela omitted articles in 39 of the 47 utterances requiring an article (83%). These results are consistent with the error patterns that Tolbert (1978) and González (1970) identified in the spontaneous speech of their 2-year-old subjects.

When looking at error patterns, it is also interesting to analyze maternal responses. Clark (1985) pointed out that "both agreement and article errors are corrected automatically by adults in any repetitions or expansions of what the child says" (p. 706). If we examine Morela's mother's responses, we find that this was indeed the case, particularly at 16 months. Yet, she did not always respond to th e child's omission with an expansion that included the corresponding article. In

Morphological Development in Spanish 239

Table 8.7: Child's article omissions broken down according to type of maternal response: (a) noun with article omitted; (b) noun with corresponding article; (c) first noun without and then with article.

Child's Age	Total Child Omissions	Response with Omission	Response with Article	Response with Omission + Article
		\multicolumn{3}{c}{Type of Maternal Response}
16 Months	39/47 (83%)	4	11	12
23 Months	6/24 (25%)	1	1	0
29 Months	0	0	0	0

fact, a more detailed analysis of the mother's speech directed to the child suggests three types of maternal responses: (a) instances in which the child's omission was followed by a maternal utterance with the same article omission; (b) instances in which the mother expanded the child's utterance with the corresponding article; and (c) instances in which the mother provided a more elaborate response: first repeating the child's omission and then providing the corresponding article (Table 8.7). The first type of maternal response appeared to follow nouns that seemed to be either unfamiliar to the child or difficult to pronounce, for example:

```
*MOT:    y éste que es?
%eng:    and this one what is it?
*CHI:    Øart ca(ba)llo.
%eng:    horse
*MOT:    Øart caballo! (16 mos. transcript)
```

Caballo (horse) was a word the child had difficulty with throughout the session, both with its pronunciation and with its correct meaning (she was at this point calling all animals *gato* "cat"). As you will see when you do the exercise on comparing spontaneous and imitated article use in the child's speech (at the end of this chapter), utterances with the noun *caballo* were often imitations. However, this type of response – simply repeating the same omission – only occurred in four instances.

240   Chapter 8

In contrast, 11/39 of the child's omissions were followed by the second type of response, an expansion with the corresponding article, as in the following example:

>   *MOT: mira este.
>   %eng: look at this one
>   *MOT: este que es?
>   %eng: what is this
>   *CHI: Øart tato !
>   *MOT: **un** gato.
>   %eng: a cat   (16 mos. transcript)

The third type of response, which was also the more frequent one (12/39), was a combination of the other two. As the example below indicates, these responses consisted of a repetition of the child's omission followed by an expansion that included the corresponding article:

>   *MOT: mira # que es eso [= baby carriage]?
>   *CHI: Øart cochco [* cochco = coche].
>   *MOT: Øart coche [= laughs]!
>   *CHI: Øart coche.
>   *MOT: muy bien # **un** coche. (16 mos. transcript)

This intensive modeling, which the mother did after almost every error that the child made at 16 months, appears to serve a number of purposes: It provides the child with the appropriate pronunciation of a word, it corrects the meaning of the words and it supplies the missing morphological markers (i.e., number and gender of both article and nouns). Yet, as the sequence in the third and more common type of response suggests, when the child is very young, the mother tends to pursue each of these goals one after the other.

Typical errors in Morela's article use at 23 months were also omission errors, though they were not as frequent at this age (6/24 or 25%). Most of these omissions occurred when the child had difficulty providing a label for an object (e.g., *taco*, "block"; *cuchillo*, "knife"), judging from the repeated queries that were directed at her, before she was able to supply the correct name. These omission errors could be an indication that Morela was still struggling with the use of indefinite nouns, as was suggested earlier. Yet, it could also be that she was unable to correctly mark morphology because she was focusing all of her efforts on meaning instead.

Two of the omissions, however, seemed to be of a very different type: They occurred in the context of Morela's more complex sentences. One instance, for example, occurred when Morela explained to the experimenter why she would not comply with the experimenter's request:

*EXP:	oye More y ahora llama a Padrino.
%eng:	listen More now call your godfather
*CHI:	que?
%eng:	what?
*EXP:	llama a Padrino.
%eng:	call Godfather
*CHI:	aho(r)a no!
%eng:	not right now
%act:	CHI tries to put her sister's shoes on while holding telephone receiver in left hand.
*CHI:	+^ quie(r)o pone(r)me Øart zapatos [*]!
%eng:	I want to put shoes on
%err:	quieo poneme zapatos = quiero ponerme *los* zapatos

Note that the child's utterance expresses her desire to engage in another activity in a quite sophisticated way. Yet, because she seems to be focusing on getting the meaning across, she fails to produce the article *los* that needs to accompany *zapatos*, in spite of having produced it earlier, with no apparent difficulty in several of her more simple noun phrases.[17]

At 29 months Morela was able to produce complex sentences with correct morphological markings such as the following (although note that she was still having difficulty with the verb *poner*, to put on):

---

[17] As MacWhinney (1991) pointed out, "...the identity of the omitted word is always a guess" (p. 26). In this case, the definite article *los* is our best guess, because the child and the mother were continuously talking about the same pair of shoes. But the child could have also used other determiners, such as the demonstrative *estos* ("these") or the possessive *mis* ("my").

```
*CHI:      <p^o'neme> [*] xx los za(r)cillos.
%eng:      put the earrings on
%err:      p^o'neme = ponme   (29 mos. transcript)
```

How the mother corrects the child's errors appears to vary with age. Indeed, the type of consistent feedback that the mother provided at 16 months was not observed in the case of Morela's omission errors at 23 months. In the labeling activities, only two out of six of the child's omissions were followed by a maternal response, and, when the omission occurred in the more complex sentences, the child received no feedback at all.

Although these results are preliminary, we can say that there is so far no evidence of some of the errors that Brisk and Mazeika described for their Spanish-English bilinguals. Results of Morela's article use did not show a marked overgeneralization of the feminine singular article *la*. In fact, the rare occurrence of gender errors in her speech agrees with González's and Hernández-Pina's findings that this type of error appears in only a small set of Spanish children's article+noun combinations. Furthermore, in contrast to Brisk's first graders, Morela seemed to have full command of gender and number agreement at 29 months, as González and Soler reported as well. These results were to be expected given that Morela's command of Spanish, as a monolingual speaker, more closely resembles that of the children studied by González, Hernández-Pina, Soler, and Tolbert than that of the children studied by Brisk and Mazeika.

8.5.4. A Cross-Linguistic Comparison of the Acquisition of Articles

Question 3:   Can the acquisition of these Spanish morphemes be compared to their equivalent in English? Do the morphemes under study emerge earlier in one of the languages? Are they mastered earlier in one of the languages? If this is the case, to what can we attribute such a difference in acquisition?

As this study has shown, in Spanish, articles encode number, gender, and specific/nonspecific reference. In English, articles only encode the last. In line with Brown's (1973) cumulative complexity hypothesis, one might expect articles to emerge later in the speech of children learning Spanish than in that of children learning English, since the former have to learn several different notions and the latter only one. In addition, as Kvaal et al. (1988) suggested, Spanish articles might also be expected to appear later because of the homonymy of several forms (see above for more details). However, studies have shown the opposite to be true. Although the language development of English and Spanish speakers cannot be compared based on their MLU levels (see Appendix A for a discussion of this issue), results from this study and others (e.g., González, 1970; Hernández-Pina, 1984) strongly suggest that, in Spanish, articles emerge in children's earliest word combinations (between 16 and 18 months), whereas in English this is not the case. Studies by Brown and others have found that English articles are late-emerging morphemes. Brown (1973) reported that the two articles appeared in his subjects' spontaneous speech between 32 and 41 months, depending on their linguistic rate of development.

How can this difference be explained? As we saw earlier, number seems to be the first notion that young Spanish speakers master, followed closely by gender. Pérez-Pereira (1991) argued that "the more extensive and productive the system of gender marking in a language, the easier is its learning" (p. 585). This is precisely the case of the Spanish gender system: It is extensive because gender is marked in many different parts of speech (articles, nouns, adjectives, pronouns), and it is productive because it involves the clear and systematic marking of two genders. The same can be said of the Spanish number marker: It is both simple and extensively used. Contrary to what one might predict, gender and number seem to make articles more salient for the young Spanish speakers, and, thus, easier to learn, which may in part explain their early emergence. Yet, one could also argue that in a language with a rich morphological system such as Spanish, articles serve a more important function than in a language with relatively weak morphology (such as English), and therefore are needed earlier. In this study, the intensive modelling by the mother after almost every child omission or commission error, at 16 months, clearly illustrates the importance of articles in Spanish. A recent cross-linguistic study on language loss provides even stronger evidence for this. Bates, Friederici, and Wulfeck (1987) found that the same cortical lesion (leading to Broca's aphasia) caused adult speakers of English to leave out articles in 70% of obligatory contexts, but caused speakers of Italian – a language whose articles, like Spanish, also encode gender and number – to leave out articles only 25% of the time. Thus, it appears that the more information articles carry in a language, the more a speaker will struggle to produce them, in spite of linguistic constraints.

Although Spanish articles are among the earliest morphemes that emerge, studies show that young children learn the specific/nonspecific notion they encode later. As researchers of both Spanish (Soler, 1984) and English (Maratsos, 1976) have suggested, the reason for this may be that the specific/nonspecific contrast is the notion most clearly linked to children's cognitive abilities. Maratsos (1976) points out that to master this contrast, children need to take into account the referential knowledge of their listener. Using experimental means, Maratsos found that only linguistically advanced 4-year-olds were able to do this error-free. It is therefore not surprising that English articles, which only encode this specific/nonspecific notion, have been found to be late emerging morphemes. It may also explain why Brown (1973) found that parental input frequency seemed to have no effect on the acquisition of English articles. Children probably do not learn this contrast until they are cognitively ready to do so. Thus, although articles *appear earlier* in Spanish, it seems that *mastery* of the article system is attained at about the same age in both languages.

8.6. Exercises

8.6.1. Besides calculating mean length of utterance for an entire transcript of a child, researchers have also found it helpful to compute the length of the child's five longest utterances, to determine what the upper limits of his or her language ability are (for more details, see Pan, this volume). In this exercise you will use file **morela16.cha** to estimate the MLU for the child's five longest utterances at 16 months. **Hint:** The CLAN program you need to perform this analysis is MAXWD. Remember to use the **+g2** option in your CLAN command string so that the MLU is computed in words rather than morphemes. In examining your output, consider the following:

1. How does the length of the child's MLU for the entire transcript compare to that of her five longest utterances?

2. What characterizes the child's longest productions at this age? Are they mostly unanalyzed strings? Are they imitations of her mother's previous utterances? Do they include articles?

Morphological Development in Spanish   245

3. What activity was the child engaged in when she produced them (e.g., book reading, free play)?

8.6.2. Analyze Morela's article use to determine whether utterances that included articles were imitated or were spontaneous productions. For this analysis you should use **KWAL**. Keep in mind that you need to run a KWAL on *every* form Morela used at 16 months. To obtain this information you will need to look at Table 8.6. To get KWAL to provide you with the mother's previous utterance you need to use the –w option in the command string. You should look at the *five* preceding utterances, because it often took the mother several attempts to get Morela's attention. Once you have completed your analysis, answer the following:

1. How many instances of article use were direct imitations of the mother's preceding utterance?

2. How many articles seem to be used spontaneously by the child?

3. Compare the nouns that were part of the imitated noun phrase. Are they different in some way? For example, do imitated nouns seem to be newer words in the child's vocabulary (consider the mother's response to the child's difficulty with pronunciation and meaning?)

8.6.3. If you have a fair command of Spanish, you can also use the present language data on Morela to study the emergence of possessive structures in Spanish-speaking children. For more background information on the acquisition of possessives forms see Clark (1985), Muñoz and Vila (1985), Padilla and Lindholm (1976) and Sebastián (1984). Use Table 8.8 in Appendix B as a guide to carring out the following analyses.

1. Use **FREQ** to find out what possessive adjectives and pronouns Morela and her mother used when the child was 16 months old. You should know that, in adult speech, the presence of a noun helps us make the distinction between adjectives and pronouns. For example, if a person says *esa es la casa mía* (that's my house), we know that, although *mía* could also be a possessive **pronoun** (such as in *esa es mía*, that is mine), in this case it is an **adjective** because it is preceded by a noun (*casa*). However, the frequent omissions that characterizes the speech of young children often make it difficult to determine whether a possessive form is a pronoun or an

adjective. Thus, for the purpose of this exercise all child forms are considered adjectives. Based on your results, answer the following questions:

Does Morela use forms indicating one possessor (e.g., *mi*, my; *tu*, your) or multiple possessor (e.g., *nuestro*, our)?

Are first person forms more frequently used at this early age?

Within the one possessor forms the child produced, does she use singular or plural forms?

How does the mother's use of possessive structures compare with that of the child? That is, does the mother only use forms the child is able to produce?

2. Use KWAL to examine, whether at 16 months, Morela's use of possessive forms was mostly imitative or whether she was also capable of spontaneous use at this age.

8.7. Suggested Project

In this chapter you have learned that there are conflicting data on how Spanish-English bilinguals acquire the Spanish article system. A number of factors seem to influence this process, such as the variety of Spanish a child speaks and the command the child has of the Spanish language. Collect spontaneous speech data from a Spanish-English bilingual child. Carefully note the child's early language environment: Does the child hear mostly Spanish or is he or she exposed to both languages? What Spanish variety is the child learning? Note if it is a variety that has many English loan words. Ask the parent for any particular errors the child makes. Then transcribe your data using CHAT and examine the errors in the child's article use. Do they seem to follow a specific pattern? For example, are article errors frequent? Are they mostly gender marking errors (overgeneralization of one form)? Does the child appear to have difficulty with the specific/nonspecific contrast?

Use the same language corpus to look at the child's use of possessive forms. Describe the forms present in the child's speech.

Acknowledgments

I am grateful to the mother and child dyad who participated in this study for allowing me to record their interactions for a period of 2 years. Special thanks go to Jane Herman, David Poeppel, and Ann Robyns for valuable comments on earlier versions of this chapter. Thanks also to Anamaría Rodino for help in coding and reliability.

References

Bates, E., Friederici, A., & Wulfeck, B. (1987). Grammatical morphology in aphasia: Evidence from three languages. *Cortex, 23*, 545-574

Beléndez-Soltero, P. (1980). *Repetitions and the acquisition of the Spanish verb system.* Unpublished doctoral dissertation, Harvard Graduate School of Education, Cambridge, MA.

Brisk, M. E. (1976). The acquisition of Spanish gender by first-grade Spanish-speaking children. In G. D. Keller, R. V. Teschner, & S. Viera (Eds.), *Bilingualism in the bicentennial and beyond.* Jamaica, NY: Bilingual Review Press.

Brown, R. (1973). *A first language: The early stages.* Cambridge, MA: Harvard University Press.

Bybee, J.L., & Slobin, D.I. (1982). Rules and schemas in the development and use of the English past tense. *Language, 58*, 265-289.

Cazden, C. (1968). The acquisition of noun and verb inflections. *Child Development, 39*, 433-448.

Clark, E. V. (1985). The acquisition of Romance, with special reference to French. In D. I. Slobin (Ed.), *The crosslinguistic study of language acquisition: Vol. I The Data.* Hillsdale, NJ: Lawrence Erlbaum Associates.

Crystal, D. (1974). Review of R. Brown *A first language. Journal of Child Language, 1*, 289-307.

Crystal, D. (1987). *The Cambridge encyclopedia of language.* New York: Cambridge University Press.

Cummins, J. (1984). *Bilingualism and special education: Issues in assessment and pedagogy.* San Diego: College Hill Press.

de Villiers, J. G., & de Villiers, P. A. (1973). A cross-sectional study of the acquisition of grammatical morphemes in child speech. *Journal of Psycholinguistic Research, 2*, 331-341.

de Villiers, J. G., & de Villiers, P. A. (1985). The acquisition of English. In D. I. Slobin (Ed.) *The crosslinguistic study of language acquisition: Vol. I The Data.* Hillsdale, NJ: Lawrence Erlbaum Associates.

Dromi, E., & Berman, R. (1982). A morphemic measure of early language development: Data from modern Hebrew. *Journal of Child Language*, *9*, 403-424.

Eisenberg, A. R. (1982). *Language acquisition in cultural perspective: Talk in three Mexican homes.* Unpublished doctoral dissertation, University of California, Berkeley.

García, S.M. (1991). Estudios gramaticales (V): El "artículo" castellano [Studies of grammar: The Spanish article]. Buenos Aires: SyF.

García-Pelayo, Ramón (1983). *Diccionario moderno español-inglés.* Mexico: Ediciones Larousse

González, G. (1970). *The acquisition of Spanish grammar by native Spanish-speaking children.* Unpublished PhD dissertation, University of Texas.

Hernández-Pina, F. (1984). *Teorías psicosociolingüísticas y su aplicación a la adquisición del español como lengua materna* [Psycholinguistic theories and their application to the acquisition of Spanish as a mother tongue]. Madrid, Spain: Siglo XXI.

Hickey, T. (1991). Mean length of utterance and the acquisition of Irish. *Journal of Child Language*, *18*, 553-569.

Johnston, J., & Kamhi, A. (1984). Syntactic and semantic aspects of the utterances of language-impaired children: The same can be less. *Merrill-Palmer Quarterly*, *30*, 65-86.

Klee, T., & Fitzgerald, M. (1985). The relation between grammatical development and MLU in morphemes. *Journal of Child Language*, *12*, 251-269.

Kvaal, J. T., Shipstead-Cox, Nevitt, S. G., Hodson, B. W., & Launer, P. B (1988). The acquisition of 10 Spanish morphemes by Spanish-speaking children. *Language, Speech and Hearing Services in Schools*, *19*, 384-394.

Lahey, M., Liebergott, J., Chesnick, M., Menyuk, P., & Adams, J. (in press). Variability in children's use of grammatical morphemes. *Applied Psycholinguitics*.

Linares, N. (1975). *The language evaluation of preschool Spanish-speaking Puerto Rican children.* Unpublished doctoral dissertation, University of Illinois, Urbana. (MLU rules are also published as Appendix B in J. Good Erickson, & D. R. Omark (1981). *Communication assessment of the bilingual-bicultural child: Issues and guidelines.* Baltimore: University Park Press).

López-Ornat, S. (1988). On data sources on the acquisition of Spanish as a first language. *Journal of Child Language*, *15*, 679-686.

MacWhinney, B. (1991). *The CHILDES Project: Computational tools for analyzing talk.* Hillsdale, NJ: Lawrence Erlbaum Associates.

MacWhinney, B. & Bates, E. (1978). Sentential devices for conveying givenness and newness: A cross-cultural development study. *Journal of Verbal Learning and Verbal Behavior, 17,* 559-572.

Maratsos, M. P. (1974). Preschool children's use of definite and indefinite articles. *Child Development, 45,* 446-455.

Maratsos, M. P. (1976). *The use of definite and indefinite reference in young children.* New York: Cambridge University Press.

Mazeika, E. J. (1973). *A comparison of the grammar of a monolingual and a bilingual (Spanish-English) child.* Paper presented at the biennial meeting of the Society for Research in Child Development, Philadelphia, PA.

Merino, B. J. (1979). *Order and pace in the acquisition of Spanish syntax in a monolingual setting.* Paper presented at the Conference on the Exceptional Child, Phoenix, AZ.

Moerk, E. L. (1980). Relationships between parental input frequencies and children's language acquisition: A reanalysis of Brown's data. *Journal of Child Language, 7,* 105-118.

Montes-Giraldo, J. (1974). Esquema ontogenético del desarrollo del lenguaje y otras cuestiones del habla infantil [A developmental outline of language acquisition and other issues about child speech]. *Thesaurus: Boletín del Instituto Caro y Cuervo, 29,* 254-270.

Muñoz, C. & Vila, I. (1985). *The emergence and use of first and second person reference in Spanish.* Paper presented at the Child Language Seminar, University of Reading, England.

Omark, D. R., & Good Erickson, J. (1983). *The bilingual exceptional child.* San Diego, CA: College-Hill Press.

Padilla, A. M., & Linholm, K. (1976). Acquisition of bilingualism: A descriptive analysis of the linguistic structures of Spanish/English-speaking children. In G. D. Keller, R. V. Teschner, & S. Viera (Eds.), *Bilingualism in the bicentennial and beyond.* Jamaica, NY: Bilingual Review Press.

Pérez-Pereira, M. (1991). The acquisition of gender: What Spanish children tell us. *Journal of Child Language, 18,* 571-590.

Quilis, A., Esgueva, M., Gutiérrez, M. L., & Ruiz-Va, P. (1989). *Lengua española* [Spanish language]. Madrid, Spain: Editorial Centro de Estudios Ramón Areces.

Repiso-Repiso, S. (1990). *Los posesivos* [The possessives]. Colección 'Problemas fundamentales del español'. Publicaciones del Colegio de España. Salamanca, Spain: Imprenta Kadmos, S.C.L.

Sebastián, M. E. (1984). Un estudio sobre el lenguaje infantil: Adquisición de las formas de posesión [A study on child language: Acquisition of possessive forms]. In P. del Río (Ed.), *Monografía de Infancia y Aprendizaje: La Adquisición del Lenguaje*. Madrid: Aprendizaje, S.A.

Soler, M.R. (1984). Adquisición y utilización del artículo [Acquisition and use of the article]. In M. Siguán (Ed.), *Estudios sobre psicología del lenguaje infantil*. Madrid: Pirámide.

Tolbert, K. (1978). *The acquisition of grammatical morphemes: A cross-linguistic study with reference to Mayan and Spanish*. Unpublished doctoral dissertation, Harvard University, Cambridge, MA.

Toronto, A. S., & Merrill, S. (1983). Developing local normed assessment instruments. In D. R. Omark & J. Good Erickson (Eds.), *The bilingual exceptional child*. San Diego, CA: College-Hill Press.

Appendix A

Is MLU a Useful Measure of Syntactic Growth When Analyzing Spontaneous Language Performance in a Language Other Than English?

Most of the measures that are commonly used to analyze spontaneous language production were originally developed for English-speaking subjects. This is a particular problem in the case of an index such as the mean length of utterance or MLU, which is used to assess grammar and morphology, because it measures performance in domains that vary greatly among languages. In studies on the acquisition of English syntax, MLU is the most widely used and accepted estimate of a child's general syntactic performance level, though some have questioned its validity and interpretation (e.g., Crystal, 1974; Klee & Fitzgerald, 1985). Most studies describe syntactic development in terms of stages delimited by mean length of utterance values, based on Brown's (1973) findings that children who are matched for MLU are more likely to have speech at the same level of complexity than children of the same age. MLU is also the preferred developmental index for matching language-impaired children and their normal controls in clinical studies (e.g., Johnston & Kamhi, 1984; Rollins, this volume).

However, since MLU in morphemes became the standard index, its applicability to the study of other languages has been under heated debate (e.g., see

Crystal, 1974, and more recently, Hickey, 1991). Brown (1973) himself acknowledged that "studies of highly inflected languages, like Finnish, Swedish, and Spanish, all report some difficulty in adapting [the] rules of calculation, invented for English" (p. 68). Researchers are far from reaching a consensus in regard to how useful MLU is for describing the acquisition of Spanish (Barrera & Barrera, 1989). There are no studies that have truly evaluated the applicability of MLU in morphemes to the particular characteristics of Spanish, as has been done for other languages (e.g., Dromi & Berman, 1982, for Hebrew; Hickey, 1991, for Irish). Thus far there is only one published attempt to adapt Brown's rules for calculating MLU in Spanish: in Linares (1975), who developed these rules for his dissertation on the language development of Spanish-speaking Puerto Rican preschoolers.

In reviewing Linares' morpheme counting rules, I found several instances in which Spanish acquisition researchers might disagree with his interpretation of Brown's (1973) original rules, in particular, Linares' criteria for counting verb inflections. In his language samples, Linares (1981) counted all verbs that were correctly inflected, and were not infinitive, participial, or gerund, as having five morphemes ("one for the root, one for the number inflection, one for the person inflection, one for the tense inflection, and one for the mood inflection," p. 295). He also considered the feminine article *la* as having two morphemes, but the masculine article *el* as having only one.

Although Linares' proposal is a valid effort toward devising morpheme-counting rules for Spanish, these examples illustrate what Crystal (1974) and others have described as "the danger" of researchers being forced to make arbitrary, ad hoc decisions in their attempt to use MLU for non-English data (p. 300). But, as Brown (1973) said of another's researcher's attempt to adapt MLU to German, "...we cannot afford to be critical of him because [the] counting rules [in English] are not really very well rationalized" (p. 71).

A recent study proposes an alternative. After comparing the usefulness of MLUm (in morphemes) and MLUw (in words) for Irish, Hickey (1991) concluded that MLU based on word counts is a preliminary developmental index that "...is not burdened by decisions concerning productivity and morphemic status," and is therefore the most reasonable choice when doing research in a language whose acquisition has still not been fully described (p. 568). The present study therefore followed Hickey's (1991) recommendations, providing the subject's MLU only in words.

Another important issue that Hickey (1991) raised is that "MLUm [in morphemes] gives the impression that it can be used for cross-linguistic comparison on the assumption that *like is being compared with like*, when in fact that is generally not the case" (p. 569, italics added). In fact, presently most researchers concur that MLU is best used for *intralinguistic* comparisons of a child's progress over time, or for comparison of children speaking the same language, as Brown (1973) did with Adam, Eve, and Sarah.

Appendix B

The Acquisition of Possessive Structures in Spanish

Children acquiring Romance languages need to master several different subsystems for the expression of possession (Clark, 1985). In Spanish there are possessive *adjectives* that can be used before (*mi casa*, mi house) or after (e.g., *la casa mía*, the house of mine) nouns (see Table 8.8). Possession can also be

Table 8.8: Spanish possessive forms (from *Los Posesivos*, p. 15, by Sigifredo Repiso-Repiso. Publicaciones del Colegio de España, Salamanca, Spain, 1989).

Possessor		Object Possessed	
Number	Person	Singular	Plural
One	first	mi; mia, mio (my)[a]	mis; mios, mias (my)
	second	tu; tuyo, tuya (your)	tus; tuyos, tuyas (your)
	third	su; suyo, suya (his, her, its)	sus; suyos, suyas (his, her, is)
Several	first	nuestro, nuestra (our)	nuestros, nuestras (our)
	second	vuestro, vuestra (your)	vuestros, vuestras (your)
	third	su; suyo, suya (their)	sus; suyos, suyas (their)

[a] In Spanish, one possessor adjective takes on two forms; which one is used depends on whether the adjective precedes or follows the noun. Forms that appear before the semicolon are adjectives that *precede* the noun (e.g., *mi casa*, my house), forms that appear after the semicolon are adjectives that *follow* the noun (e.g., *la casa mia*, the house of mine). The latter are also the forms of the possessive pronouns.

expressed by using possessive *pronouns* on their own. Unlike their English equivalents, these pronouns are often used with definite articles (e.g., *el mío*). *Both adjectives and pronouns agree in person with the possessor, and in gender and number with the object possessed.* The third subsystem is the nominal or analytic form of expressing possession, which in Spanish is expressed with the preposition *de* (*de ella, de ellos*). This nominal form is more frequently used in substitution of adjectives and pronouns in the third-person (e.g., *su, suyo*, respectively), because of the ambiguity that may arise from the use of these forms. As García-Pelayo (1983) explains, third person adjectives and pronouns do not differentiate between the gender and the number of the possessor as they do in English (i.e, his, her, its, and their), so to avoid this ambiguity Spanish speakers tend to replace them by using the structure 'article + noun + de ella, de él, etc.' (e.g., saying *la casa de ella* in place of *su casa*) or by adding '*de ella, de él*, etc.' at the end (e.g., *su libro de él*).

9 Young Children's Hypotheses about English Reflexives

Margaret Thomas
Boston College

In this chapter, you will learn the following skills:

- To tabulate the frequency of reflexives in child language transcripts using the FREQ program.

- To locate anomalous forms of reflexives (e.g., *hisself*) using wildcards.

- To collect contextually based examples of children's use of reflexives using the KWAL program and to analyze their syntax.

- To use include files to search for reflexives in multiple corpora.

To replicate the analyses and conduct the exercises, you will need the **adam55.cha** file found in the **thomas** directory.

9.1. Introduction

In the past 30 years, a great deal has been written about the properties of the class of words known as **anaphors**, which includes reflexives like *myself* and *themselves*. The task of analyzing the grammar of these words has captured the imagination of linguists for a number of reasons. First, although certain general properties seem to be shared by reflexives in all languages, specific details of these properties differ from language to language. This offers child language researchers an opportunity to study the emergence of both universal and language-particular linguistic features. Second, the behavior of reflexives is often cited as representative of innate knowledge of language, since the syntactic constraints that bear on their distribution are highly abstract and detailed, and there is no evidence that child language learners receive explicit tutoring about the production or comprehension of reflexives. Therefore, research into the emergence of reflexives serves as a microcosm in which to study the growth of language skills purportedly guided by principles of universal grammar.

This chapter investigates the contribution of spontaneous production data to our understanding of how children arrive at the adult grammar of English reflexives. The discussion is organized as follows. Section 9.1 summarizes some key properties of the grammar of reflexives, discusses relevant experimental research, and defines two specific issues to be investigated. Section 9.2 describes how information about reflexives in the spontaneous speech of child language learners was gathered from the CHILDES data files. Section 9.3 presents the results, which in Section 9.4 are discussed in the light of their contribution to our understanding of the grammar of anaphora. The chapter concludes in Section 9.5, with some suggestions for further research.

9.1.1. Background

A significant constraint on the distribution of reflexives consists in the fact that they must be "bound within their governing category." That a reflexive must be *bound* means it must appear along with another noun or pronoun on whose identity the reflexive depends. For example, the sentence in (1) is acceptable because the subject *Paul* binds the reflexive *himself*; and thus (1) means that Paul bought a bicycle for *Paul*. But the sentence in (2) is unacceptable, because there is no binder for the reflexive *herself*.

(1)   Paul bought a bicycle for himself
(2)   *Herself reads the newspaper every day

A noun or pronoun that binds a reflexive is known as its *antecedent*. In addition to the requirement that the reflexive be bound by an antecedent, the antecedent must be within the *governing category* of the reflexive. In English, the governing category of a reflexive is its minimal clause. In other words, the antecedent of a reflexive and the reflexive itself must be members of the same clause.[18] Evidence for this fact derives from sentences like (3), which can only mean that Paul bought

---

[18] This presentation simplifies numerous aspects of the grammar of reflexives in English. For a more complete discussion, see Chomsky (1986). Useful secondary sources include van Riemsdijk and Williams (1986) and Lasnik and Uriagereka (1988).

a bicycle for *Paul*. This is because *Paul* is in the same minimal clause as the reflexive, and therefore serves as its antecedent.

(3) Steve said that Paul bought a bicycle for himself

But (3) cannot mean that Paul bought a bicycle for Steve, because *Steve* is not within the governing category of the reflexive. *Steve* is a member of the higher clause and therefore cannot serve as the antecedent of *himself*. Figure 9.1 shows in simplified form the syntactic structure of (3), with a dotted line delineating the domain within which the reflexive must find its antecedent.

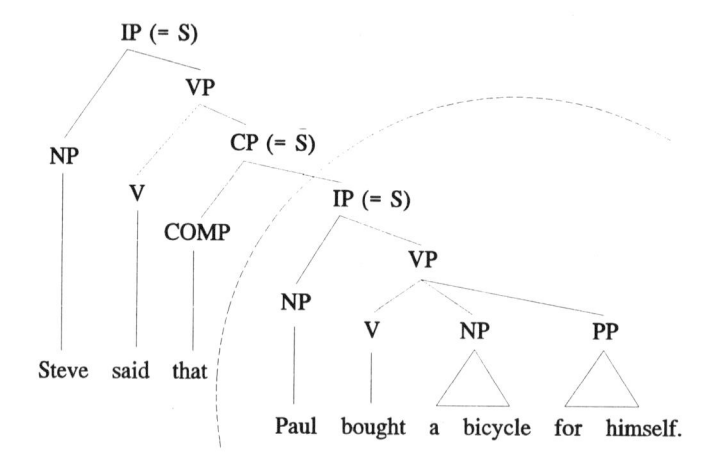

Figure 9.1

Different languages define governing categories differently. In Japanese, for example, the reflexive *zibun* ('self') and its antecedent need not be in the same clause. Sentence (4) illustrates this property.

(4)   Yoko wa Mika ga zibun o aisite iru to omotte iru
        Yoko TOP Mika NOM self ACC love is COMP think is[19]
        'Yoko thinks that Mika loves self'

Either *Yoko* or *Mika* may serve as the antecedent of *zibun*; that is, the Japanese sentence in (4) can mean either that Yoko thinks that Mika loves *Mika*, or that Yoko thinks that Mika loves *Yoko*.[20] Thus, the definition of the domain within which a reflexive must be bound varies from language to language. Since in English a reflexive and its antecedent must be members of the same clause, the language is said to allow only "local" binding of anaphors. In contrast, Japanese allows "long-distance" binding, since the antecedent of *zibun* may be in a higher clause than the reflexive.

Cross-linguistic variation, such as that illustrated here between English and Japanese, introduces a learnability problem that has attracted considerable attention. How do child learners establish the appropriate definition of the governing category of reflexives in the language they are learning, assuming that they have access only to positive evidence in the form of sentences like (3) or (4)? Extending a notion developed by Berwick (1985), Manzini and Wexler (1987) proposed that children's hypotheses about the domain within which a reflexive must be bound is guided by a *subset principle*. The subset principle claims that child learners start out with a maximally narrow definition of the governing category of a reflexive, adopting a more inclusive definition if and only if they encounter data that contradict their initial hypothesis. That is, Manzini and Wexler suggest that children first assume that reflexives must be strictly locally bound. Since reflexives in the input to learners of English are always locally bound, children do not have reason to abandon their initial assumption and hence never bind reflexives to long-distance antecedents. The subset principle would predict that learners of Japanese also first assume that reflexives in that language are locally bound. However, on observing a sentence like (4) in a context where *zibun* is bound by *Yoko*, learners of Japanese revise their definition of governing category to allow either local *or* long-distance binding. If the subset principle accurately represents how child language learners

---

[19] The following abbreviations are employed: ACC accusative, COMP complementizer, GEN genitive, NOM nominative, OBJ objective, TOP topic marker.

[20] Again, this statement simplifies certain facts about the reflexive *zibun*. See Kuno (1973), Yang (1983), Manzini and Wexler (1987), and Katada (1991).

construct the grammar of anaphora, it ensures that children will not create overly inclusive grammars. This is important because it is unclear how a child would retreat from a grammar that allows both local and long-distance binding to a grammar that allows only local binding, without access to explicit negative evidence (that is, without receiving explicit evidence that reflexives cannot be bound across clause boundaries).

9.1.2. Research on the Acquisition of the Grammar of Reflexives

With these proposals in mind, let us turn to research on how child learners interpret reflexives in their native languages. Most of this work has been carried out using experimentally elicited data, gathered via act-out or grammaticality judgment tasks. Chien and Wexler (1990) reported a series of experiments designed to investigate how child learners define the governing category of English reflexives. The task involves a game in which they used a male puppet ("Snoopy") with boys, and a female puppet ("Kitty") with girls. Chien and Wexler asked their subjects, children between the ages of 2;6 and 6;6, to act out the instructions of the puppet in response to sentences like "[Puppet's name] says that [child's name] should point to [himself/herself]." The experimenters gleaned the child's interpretation of the reflexive according to whether the child pointed to the puppet or pointed to himself or herself. Their results show that after 5;6 about 90% of children's interpretations of reflexives are consistent with the adult grammar, that is, by that age most children consistently bind reflexives to local antecedents and not to long-distance antecedents.[21] Other researchers (e.g., Jakubowicz, 1984; Otsu, 1981; Read & Chou Hare, 1979; Solan, 1983, 1987) report similar results for children around age 5 or 6.[22]

However, it is not the case that children younger than 5;6 necessarily also bind English reflexives locally. In fact, Chien and Wexler found that many of them

---

[21] The figure given here averages the results of four separate experiments that Chien and Wexler conducted. The actual percentage of local binding of reflexives varies depending on the specific design of comprehension task, and on whether the subordinate clause containing the reflexive is tensed or infinitival.

[22] Research on other languages that, like English, require reflexives to have local antecedents yields similarly high levels of local-only binding among children at this age. See Solan (1986) for Spanish, and Crain and McKee (1987) for Italian.

allowed long-distance binding. At age 2;6 only about 40% of their responses bind reflexives to local antecedents; this figure rises to around 60% at age 4;0 and continues to increase with age. Not many other researchers have tested children as young as Chien and Wexler's subjects, but one study by Otsu (1981) found that 3- and 4-year-olds bind only about 20% of reflexives locally.[23]

Let us assume that experimental evidence shows that children older than 5;6 assign only local antecedents to English reflexives, but younger children frequently allow either local or long-distance binding.[24] This creates a dilemma for Manzini and Wexler's account of the development of the grammar of reflexives. If children learning English initially judge that reflexives can be bound either locally or long-distance, but subsequently retreat to a grammar in which reflexives must be bound locally, then these data do not accord with the predictions of the subset principle. However, Chien and Wexler developed a different interpretation of their findings. They claimed that child learners of English younger than 5;6 may not recognize that reflexives belong to the class of anaphors, and therefore their interpretations of the test stimuli are irrelevant to how they define the governing category of reflexives. But by 6;0 most children have grasped that reflexives are anaphors. At that point they bind reflexives exclusively to local antecedents (in accord with the subset principle), and thus arrive at the appropriate adult grammar.

This post-hoc interpretation of Chien and Wexler's results raises some important questions. If children younger than 5;6 do not recognize reflexives as reflexives, how do they classify these words? Although Chien and Wexler do not explore this issue, research by McDaniel, Smith Cairns, and Ryan Hsu (1990)

---

[23] The results of Jakubowicz (1984) differ in that she found children as young as 3 years old already bind reflexives locally at rates above 90%. (This is an approximation based on her Figure 1.)

[24] It is important to keep in mind the limits of empirical work on children's acquisition of anaphors. The research adverted to in the previous two paragraphs is based on act-out tasks, which may under-represent the range of children's interpretations of sentences with reflexives. For example, if a child responds to *Snoopy says that [child's name] should point to himself* by pointing to himself, Chien and Wexler would code this as evidence that the subject locally binds English reflexives. But since the task only requires the child to give one interpretation of the stimulus, it is not impossible that his grammar also allows an additional reading in which the long-distance antecedent *Snoopy* binds *himself*. Strictly interpreted, the observed lack of long-distance binding of reflexives does not mean that this option is *disallowed* in children's grammars. It may only be dispreferred.

provides some relevant experimental data. The authors report the results of several act-out and grammaticality judgment tasks aimed at determining at what age children exhibit adultlike control of the properties of reflexives, pronouns, and referential nouns. The subjects were English-speaking children between 2;9 and 6;7. In two related experiments, McDaniel et al. found that a few children (all younger than 4;1) seem to allow English reflexives to refer to either local or long-distance antecedents, or even to antecedents not syntactically present in the sentence. For example, in the first of their experiments, 4 subjects out of 20 allowed the reflexive in (5) to refer to Cookie Monster or to Grover, or to another puppet (Bert), which was not mentioned in the sentence, but was present in the experimental environment.

(5)   Grover says that Cookie Monster is patting himself

This suggests that these children do not treat *himself* as a reflexive at all in (5). McDaniel et al. interpreted this result to mean that such children analyze reflexives as noun phrases consisting of a genitive determiner plus the (nonanaphoric) noun *self*, which has "a meaning much like *his self*, analogous to *his body*" (p. 131). Their second experiment turned up another 4 children who exhibited similar interpretations of sentences like (5). McDaniel et al.'s speculation that reflexives are analyzed as "genitives + *self*" gains support from the additional evidence that all 4 of these children in the second experiment accept (6), and 3 out of 4 accepted (7).

(6)   I am washing himself
(7)   Grover draws a picture of Cookie Monster's self

If children understand *himself* to be structurally parallel to a noun phrase like *his body*, then their judgments of (6) and (7) do not reveal how reflexives are constrained in their grammars. Therefore, neither the interpretations of (5) that bind *himself* to Grover or to Bert nor the acceptance of (6) poses a problem to Chien and Wexler's claim that children first assume reflexives to be locally bound. Children younger than 5;6 do not bind reflexives locally because they do not recognize these words as anaphors.

9.1.3. Research Questions

The proposal that young children who do not observe the adult grammar of reflexives fail to do so because they misclassify reflexives as "genitives + *self*" fits nicely with Chien and Wexler's interpretation of their own experimental findings. But McDaniel et al.'s data do not rule out other accounts of young children's treatment of reflexives, accounts less consistent with Chien and Wexler's claims. For example, perhaps children correctly classify reflexives as reflexives but, contrary to the subset principle, first assume that reflexives may be bound by either local or long-distance antecedents.[25]

A problem in evaluating this or other imaginable accounts of the experimental data is that the approach of both Chien and Wexler and McDaniel et al. is more adapted to discovering whether or not children treat reflexives as adults do than it is adapted to discovering exactly how children *do* treat reflexives. To accomplish the latter goal, we need to investigate spontaneous production data as a complement to experimental work. For example, is there evidence in children's usage of reflexives that supports the hypothesis that they analyze them as "genitives + *self*"? Production data may also shed some light on an additional question not addressed in previous experimental work; namely, if young children initially treat reflexives as noun phrases consisting of genitive determiners + *self*, what motivates them to re-analyze the properties of these words? That is, why do children abandon their earlier hypothesis in favor of the adult grammar in which reflexives are classified as anaphors, and thus subject to the requirement of being bound in their governing categories? In the remainder of this chapter I focus on these two research questions, summarized in (8) and (9).

---

[25] McDaniel et al.'s report that four of the children in their first experiment allowed the reflexive in (5) to refer to Grover, Cookie Monster, or to Bert (p. 129) does not make it clear whether the four children consistently allowed all three readings of (5). In the act-out part of the experiment, two of these children did not bind reflexives to sentence-external antecedents, and thus may have had grammars in which reflexives must be bound by sentence-internal antecedents. If so, these children had correctly identified reflexives as anaphors, but had incorrectly defined their governing category. However, the four children in McDaniel et al.'s second experiment who accepted (6) do not seem to treat reflexives as anaphors at all.

(8) Is there evidence in the spontaneous production data that supports the hypothesis that young children classify English reflexives as consisting of genitive determiners plus the nonanaphoric noun *self*?

(9) Assuming that production data support this hypothesis, what triggers children's eventual re-analysis of reflexives as belonging to the class of anaphors?

9.2. Method

9.2.1. Subjects

I investigated nine children's spontaneous use of reflexives. Subjects were selected from CHILDES as representative of English-speaking children in the appropriate age range, from very young up to around Chien and Wexler's criterial age of 5;6. The sample includes four females and five males, from ages 1;2 to 5;4: Adam, Eve, and Sarah from Brown (1973), Shem from Clark (1978), Abe from Kuczaj (1976), Ross from MacWhinney (1991), Naomi from Sachs (1983), Nathaniel from Snow, and Nina from Suppes (1973). Since reflexives are relatively rare in spontaneous speech, it was necessary to work with a large pool of data. For pedagogical purposes, this section shows how to gather data on children's use of reflexives by using as an example a single file from the Brown directory, **adam55.cha**. Section 9.2.2 also reviews how this search was expanded to include the full set of corpora from these nine children, comprising more than 200,000 child utterances (see Table 9.1).

9.2.2. CLAN Tools and Procedures

My aim in using the CHILDES database was to search through it for reflexives used in early child speech, and to examine their syntactic and semantic contexts for clues to the subjects' underlying grammars. I also gathered data about input to child learners by examining reflexives used in adult speech directed to children.

Table 9.1: The number of child utterances in each of the nine corpora.

Adam	46,478	Shem	17,881
Eve	12,484	Ross	20,462
Sarah	37,079	Nath	13,371
Abe	22,462	Nina	31,884
Naomi	16,678		

The first step was to determine what forms of reflexives appear in child speech. The following eight reflexives are present in the standard adult grammar of English.

(10) *myself, yourself, herself, himself, itself, ourselves, yourselves, themselves*

However, it would be inadequate to search the transcripts for the occurrence of these forms alone. Previous research shows that children use reflexives that deviate from the morphology of the adult inventory in various ways, e.g., *self* (McDaniel et al., 1990); *hisself* (Huxley, 1979; p. 155, among others); *themself, ourselfs* (extrapolating from Chiat, 1981). A search through the CHILDES transcripts that looked only for the adult reflexives would miss all such forms. In order to locate instances of both conventional adult reflexives and morphologically deviant child-generated forms, I created an **include file** using a standard text editor, which listed the following three items:

(11) **self, *selves, *selfs*

Each item in the include file is typed on a separate line, ending with a carriage return. The asterisks ("wildcards") will match any word that ends in *-self*, *-selves*, or *-selfs* as a target form (including independent words such as *self*, *selves*, and *selfs*). I named this include file **find.rfl**, and used it, along with the CLAN program FREQ, to search for the reflexive forms generated by the child in the **adam55.cha** transcript. The search was performed by issuing the command listed below. This command initiates a search of the file **adam55.cha** for instances of Adam's use of the target forms defined in (11).

freq +t*ADA +s@find.rfl adam55.cha

+t*ADA	Analyze Adam's speaker tier only
+s@find.rfl	Search for the words in the include file **find.rfl**
adam55.cha	The child language transcript to be analyzed

Command Box 9.1

This analysis can be replicated using the data that accompany this volume by typing the exact command. As usual, this CLAN command consists of three parts. The word FREQ, placed at the beginning of the command, names the program to be run. The FREQ program searches for and counts the incidence of a specific target word or set of words, which are defined by the options appearing after the FREQ command. The output of FREQ will be a tabulation of the number of occurrences of each of the target words. Second, the filename **adam55.cha** at the end of the command directs the program to carry out the tabulation on this CHAT-formatted file.

Third, between the FREQ command and the **adam55.cha** filename, there appear two options. These options define the nature of the FREQ operation that the program performs. The option **+s@find.rfl** instructs FREQ to tabulate the appearance of every member of the file named **find.rfl**. Thus, each lexical item defined by the include file – each word ending in *-self*, *-selves*, *-selfs*, and each instance of *self*, *selves*, and *selfs* as independent words – is to be tabulated. The option **+t*ADA** directs FREQ to carry out the frequency count on each of the main tiers produced by the speaker Adam, that is, on all verbal productions of the target child.

The output from this FREQ command indicates that Adam produced two instances of *myself* and one instance of *self*:

```
FREQ.EXE +t*ADA +s@find.rfl adam55.cha
FREQ.EXE (04-MAY-93) is conducting analyses on:
  ONLY speaker main tiers matching: *ADA;
*****************************************
From file <adam55.cha>
  2 myself
  1 self
-------------------------------
    2   Total number of different word types used
    3   Total number of words (tokens)
0.667   Type/Token ratio
```

It is also possible to tabulate the reflexive forms in Adam's speech across the complete corpus of 55 samples by issuing a single command:

freq +t*ADA +s@find.rfl +u adam*.cha

+t*ADA	Analyze Adam's speaker tier only
+s@find.rfl	Search for the words in the include file **find.rfl**
+u	Merge all input files into a combined analysis
adam*.cha	Analyze all files beginning with **adam** and ending with **.cha**

Command Box 9.2

This command differs from the previous one in that the filename **adam*.cha** uses a wildcard (an asterisk) to direct FREQ to carry out the frequency count over every **adam** transcript, that is, over adam01, adam02, adam03, up to and including the final recording session, adam55. The other difference is that the +u option is employed to indicate that we wish to pool the results from all 55 samples into one comprehensive frequency count. The results (minus the header information) from this analysis are as follows:

```
 1 deirselves
 1 demselves
 2 herself
 4 himself
 2 hisself
16 itself
87 myself
26 self
 1 selfs
 2 selves
12 yourself
-------------------------------
   11  Total number of different word types used
  154  Total number of words (tokens)
0.071  Type/Token ratio
```

This same analysis was performed for each of the other eight children in the sample of longitudinal data. To calculate the frequencies of reflexive forms in the transcripts from another child, one needs to make three changes: (a) change the working directory to the one in which the data are stored; (b) replace the **adam** in **adam*.cha** with the prefix from the names of the other files (e.g., to analyze the data for Eve, you would specify the input files as **eve*.cha**); and (c) replace the **ADA** in the option **+t*ADA** with the three-letter code designating the new target child (e.g., for Eve that would be **EVE**).

When merging all of the input files into a single analysis, the output filename is given the name of the first input file with the appropriate extension. In this case, this would be **adam01.frq**. Since this is not a very informative filename, it is often better to specify the complete filename yourself. To do this, you must use the redirect symbol ('>') before specifying the new filename. In this case, the command would be as follows: **freq +t*ADA +s@find.rfl +u adam*.cha > adam.rfl**.

In all, 22 different reflexive forms appeared in all the samples for all nine children. Table 9.2 lists these forms, and their frequencies by the name of the child. (The table conflates certain phonetic variants, e.g., *demselves* and *themselves*, *deirselves* and *theirselves*.)

Table 9.2: The incidence of reflexive forms in all nine corpora.

	Adam	Eve	Sarah	Abe	Naomi	Shem	Ross	Nath	Nina	Total
myself	87	3	39	71	13	19	37	9	12	290
meeself									3	
yourself	12	3	2	26	8	5	6	4	11	77
himself	4		1	7			5	4	6	27
heemself		1								1
hisself	2		4	4		1	1	1		13
herself	2		3	1	1				11	18
itself	16	4		2		3	2	2		29
ourselves			1	7			4			12
ourselfs				2		1				3
ourself										
themselves demselves	1			1			2			4
themselfs				1						1
themself			1	1						2
theirselves deirselves	1				2	1				4
theirself deirself							2		1	3
self	26	5	1	6		3	2		2	45
selves	2						1			3
selfs	1									1
Total	154	16	52	129	24	35	61	20	48	539

Having determined the inventory of reflexives in the speech of these nine children, the next step is to locate and examine the contexts in which each of these forms appears. To do so, I created another include file, which I named **reflex**. This file contains each of the 22 reflexive forms listed in Table 9.2, with each one appearing on a separate line followed by a carriage return. I then used the CLAN program KWAL to search for the appearance of every item in this list within the complete set of files from the nine corpora specified in Section 9.2.1. Again, the reader can replicate this analysis for a sample from Adam's corpus. For example, to search for the contexts of all the reflexives in Adam's speech in the **adam55.cha** file, one would use the following command:

kwal +t* +s@reflex −w4 +w4 +f adam55.cha

+t*	Analyze all speaker tiers
+s@reflex	Search for the reflexives in the include file **reflex**
−w4	Output a window of 4 utterances before the target
+w4	Output a window of 4 utterances after the target
+f	Save the results in a file with the default extension **.kwa**
adam55.cha	The child language transcript to be analyzed

Command Box 9.3

The KWAL program locates the line in which a specific keyword or keywords appears, and indicates the filename and line number in which that keyword appears. Once again, by specifying the filename as **adam55.cha**, we direct the program to carry out the search on that file only.

The options that appear between the KWAL command at the beginning and the **adam55.cha** filename at the end define the nature of the keyword search that KWAL is to perform. The option **+t*** ensures that the search is carried out on all speaker tiers. Though this option is not strictly necessary (since it is the default), including it helps to emphasize that this analysis includes the speech of adults as well as children (since adult input to children is also of interest). The option **+s@reflex** instructs KWAL to search the transcripts for the appearance of every item in the **reflex** file. Thus, every element listed in this include file serves as a keyword in the search. The options, **−w4** and **+w4**, direct KWAL to display each instance of a keyword along with a portion of its preceding and following context, as an aid to

English Reflexives 269

interpreting the role of the keyword in its discourse setting. The option –w4 indicates that the four utterances preceding the keyword are to be included and the +w4 option specifies that the same number of utterances following the keyword are to be included. The option +f instructs CLAN to save the output of KWAL in a file, rather than display it on the screen. Since no file extension appears after the +f, the output file will bear the filename **adam55.kwa**, with the extension of the new filename taken from the command that created it.

> If you were interested in analyzing the mother's use of reflexives separately from the child's, you might wish to store them in a different file. To specify the mother's reflexives, you would add the option **+t*MOT** and then give the output filename a specific extension such as **.mot** using the +f option as in **+fmot**. For the present analysis, this would result in the creation of a file named **adam55.mot** containing all of the reflexives produced by Adam's mother.

Since the output from this analysis is quite long, we will show you only the first two examples:

```
*** File adam55.cha. Line 175. Keyword: self
*ADA:   then buy another one .
*ADA:   so much rings .
*URS:   what ?
*ADA:   I've got so much rings .
*ADA:   hey # you gon (t)a make your own self a ring?
*URS:   shall I ?
*URS:   what color ?
*ADA:   see if I got any green .
*ADA:   I got green .
-----------------------------------------
*** File adam55.cha. Line 535. Keyword: yourself
*ADA:   tell me what they taste like .
*URS:   they taste salty and delicious .
*ADA:   yes # they do .
*ADA:   slowly in the pipe .
*URS:   brush yourself off .
*URS:   let's see if we can rescue some of this # alright ?
*ADA:   what's that mean ?
*URS:   that means you can grind this up again .
*ADA:   we could have some paper dere and then when it spills ?
-----------------------------------------
```

As before, it is possible to collect the context of all reflexive forms in Adam's speech across the complete corpus of 55 samples by issuing a single command. The following command performs this operation:

kwal +t* +s@reflex –w4 +w4 +u +f adam*.cha

+t*	Analyze all speaker tiers
+s@reflex	Search for the reflexives in the include file **reflex**
–w4	Output a window of 4 utterances before the target
+w4	Output a window of 4 utterances after the target
+u	Merge all input files into a combined analysis
+f	Save the results in a file with the default extension **.kwa**
adam*.cha	Analyze all files beginning with **adam** and ending with **.cha**

Command Box 9.4

This command differs from the previous one in that it uses a wildcard within the filename **adam*.cha** to direct KWAL to conduct the search over every one of the fifty-five samples in the Adam corpus. In addition, the option **+u** directs KWAL to pool the results of the keyword search across all "adam" transcripts into a single output, rather than presenting one output for adam01, one for adam02, etc. Since the transcripts are numbered in the order in which they were taped and KWAL searches them in order, this results in a convenient chronological record of the appearance of reflexives throughout the period during which recording sessions were held.

As with the previous FREQ analysis, this analysis can easily be performed for each of the other eight children in the sample of longitudinal data. All one needs to do is follow these three steps: (a) change the working directory; (b) change the input filenames; and (c) change the child speaker identification.

Analyses such as these across large longitudinal corpora are extremely computation-intensive. Depending on the type of computer you have, they may take several hours to complete. An alternative to waiting for the analysis of a single corpus to finish and then typing in the command for the next corpus, is to list all of the commands in a batch file (for DOS machines) or a shell script (for UNIX machines) and then simply execute the batch file. See Rollins (this volume) for a description of batch files.

9.3. Results

Because reflexives are relatively rare in spontaneous speech – and even more rare in contexts that bear on our Research Questions – this section discusses the results of the KWAL search performed across all nine corpora. For analysis of the results of the replication file adam55.cha, see Exercise 9.5.1.

9.3.1. Production Data versus Data from Experimental Studies

Naturally, the production data culled from the CHILDES database differ greatly from data available through experimental studies of the acquisition of reflexives. Production data are not a good source of insight into children's definitions of the governing category of reflexives, since the elaborate syntactic contexts required to tap this knowledge very rarely appear in spontaneous speech. Experimental stimuli (e.g., (3)) are typically bi-clausal sentences with two full noun phrase subjects that serve as candidate antecedents, one local and one long-distance. The reflexive must be third-person singular, so that its morphology does not prevent either of the clausal subjects from serving as its antecedent. In contrast, the bulk of reflexives in children's spontaneous speech consist of first- and second-person singular forms, in single-clause sentences with pronominal subjects.[26] Those few multiclausal sentences that emerged frequently contained control verbs (e.g., *want, like*) in which the subject argument of the subordinate clause was not overt. About half of the reflexives in the production data appeared in an adverbial phrase meaning "alone" or "without assistance," as the object of an optional preposition *by*. This is illustrated in (12).[27]

---

[26] Table 9.2 shows that 53.8% ($n=290$) of the total number of child-produced reflexives are first-person singular *myself*, and 14.3% ($n=77$) are second-person singular *yourself*.

[27] Certain CHAT symbols have been removed from the data cited in the text, including indicators of pauses, retracings, and "best guess" markers. Utterance terminators are those given in the CHILDES files.

272   Chapter 9

(12) a. I want choose it myself. (Eve 2;3)
 b. Yes sure can she eat by herself. (Nina 2;5)
 c. I'm gon (t)a put these away and then tell how the hippo goes by himself ok? (Abe 2;11)
 d. No you do it by yourself. (Naomi 3;5)

Most of the remainder of reflexives in young children's speech are direct or indirect objects of verbs, or complements of prepositions. Some examples appear in (13).

(13) a. And my you brush yourself. (Nina 2;1)
 b. I hurting myself. (Naomi 2;9)
 c. Look I made myself a stethoscope. (Adam 3;5)
 d. I want wine in myself. (Ross 3;0)
 e. We would just go to a store with a badge on ourselves. (Abe 4;1)

These data indicate that children as young as 2 or 3 years can use reflexives appropriately in certain syntactic and semantic contexts. However, there is also evidence that children's grammars differ from adults' grammars in ways congruent with the results of previous experimental work. For example, we have reviewed experimental evidence that some children allow reflexives to appear in structures where they are not locally bound; (14) illustrates a number of such sentences among the spontaneous production data.

(14) Reflexives lacking sentence-internal antecedents
 a. You dress myself. (Sarah 2;3)
 b. This is myself. (Ross 2;10)
 c. Mother: We need keys to lock ourselves in and other people out.
    Abe: And other people out lock ourselfs in and other people out.
    (Abe 2;11)
 d. Don't cut myself. (Ross 3;0)
 e. So it won't hurt yourself. (Shem 3;0)
 f. It didn't roll down to myself. (Sarah 4;3)

McDaniel et al. also reported that some children accept reflexives in subject position inside tensed clauses, although these structures are not generated in the adult grammar.[28] The CHILDES database includes a few such sentences, confirming this experimental finding; (15) illustrates some examples.

(19) Reflexives in subject position of tensed clauses
    a. But first deirself moved de furniture in dough. (Shem 3;0)
    b. Yourself would hate you. (Abe 3;10)
    c. Now myself has to park. (Adam 4;3)
    d. Which one myself would like huh? (Adam 4;3)

In short, although the nature of production data and experimental data differ, the former are consistent with certain claims made on the basis of the latter. Sections 9.3.2 and 9.3.3 show how spontaneous production data may reveal aspects of children's knowledge of reflexives unavailable in experimental studies.

---

[28] A few of McDaniel et al.'s subjects persisted in allowing sentences like *Himself is patting Grover*, even after they required reflexives to have sentence-internal antecedents (and thus can be assumed to have abandoned the genitive + non-anaphoric *self* analysis of reflexives). McDaniel et al. attribute this to incomplete acquisition of emphatic reflexives. The focus in this chapter is on children who McDaniel et al. would assign to an earlier developmental stage (i.e., those who have not yet identified reflexives as reflexives). In any case, there is little among the CHILDES data to support McDaniel et al.'s proposal about the acquisition of emphatic reflexives. Notice that in (15c) Adam marks the verb for third-person singular agreement, whereas an emphatic reflexive, at least in the adult grammar, would require first-person singular agreement. But if Adam analyzes *myself* in (15c) as consisting of a genitive + *self*, third-person singular agreement is appropriate. In addition, the CHILDES data files I searched yielded very few examples of emphatic reflexives in adult speech to children: one instance in which a reflexive appeared in apposition to a noun (mother reading aloud to Nathaniel at 3;9: *T.E. Eastman....By the cat himself and T.E. Eastman.*); three unambiguous instances of emphatic reflexives in which the reflexive is moved rightward (e.g., mother to Nina at 2;4: *I haven't seen this book myself.*). (In general, sentences in which the reflexive has shifted rightward may be ambiguous between an emphatic reflexive reading and a reading in which the reflexive is the complement of a deleted preposition *by*. When Adam's mother says *Yes you have some yourself.*, the utterance may mean 'Even you [may] have some' or it may mean 'You [may] have some by yourself.' This ambiguity may introduce additional complexity for learners.) The scarcity of emphatic reflexives in adult input, especially those in apposition to subject NPs, does not mean that children do not hear them, but it casts doubt on the key position McDaniel et al. grant to these structures in the acquisition of the grammar of reflexives. Only one emphatic reflexive appeared in child speech among the CHILDES transcripts I searched, when Adam at 3;6 said *I hope so myself too*.

9.3.2. How Do Young Children Classify Reflexives?

McDaniel et al.'s proposal about young children's classification of reflexives encompasses two subclaims: first, that children analyze *self* as an independent, nonanaphoric noun; and second, that words that adults identify as reflexives children consider to consist of a genitive determiner plus the noun *self*. There is evidence compatible with both of these subclaims among the production data.

The status of *self* as an independent noun is supported by three observations. First, *self* appears alone in reflexive contexts, exemplified in (16).

(16) Bare *self* appearing in reflexive contexts
    a. Look hurt self. (Eve 1;7)
    b. Put it by self. (Adam 2;6)
    c. Investigator: You'll get them out yourself?
       Shem: By self. (2;5)
    d. Mother: Did you bake that yourself?
       Adam: Bake it self. (2;7)

Most instances of bare *self* occur in the speech of children younger than 3;0 in utterances where the reflexive lacks an overt antecedent. Because these are often sentences where the subject position is empty, it is not clear whether *self* in these contexts is an anaphoric or a nonanaphoric noun. But as Section 9.3.1 points out, the existence of utterances like those in (14) and (15) supports the experimental claim that children do not attribute anaphoric properties to *X+self* structures, at least at some stages of development.

Second, in the Adam and the Abe transcripts, *self* appears at a later age in the productive idiom, *X's own self*. Examples are shown in (17).

(17)   a. You put em on your own self. (Abe 3;7)
       b. No let me do it my own self. (Adam 4;3)
       c. Hey you gon (t)a make your own self a ring? (Adam 4;10)

Third, bare *self* appears in some children's speech as a semantic equivalent of "body" or "(unspecified) body part;" (18) gives some examples.[29]

(18) a. We all bumped self and noses. Do you have selfs and noses? (Adam 3;4)
b. Marky get foot under self. (Ross 3;6)

On the other hand, the data lack one potential source of evidence in support of the proposal that children treat *self* as an independent noun, namely, examples of *self* appearing with full noun phrase determiners as in (7). No expressions like *Cookie Monster's self* appear in the CHILDES transcripts I searched. Given the nature of production data, this lack does not contradict the claim that such expressions are acceptable to some children; it merely means that the data fail to confirm this particular experimental finding.[30]

If *self* constitutes an independent noun, do children analyze reflexives as consisting of genitive determiners + *self*? The spontaneous production data offer some support for this hypothesis. The key evidence is that children generalize the genitive prefix across the entire inventory of reflexives. In the adult grammar, the first morpheme of *myself*, *yourself*(*-ves*), and *ourselves* consists of (or at least is homophonous with) the genitive determiners *my*, *your*, and *our*. *Himself* and *themselves* are exceptional in that the first morpheme is objective. *Herself* could be analyzed as either objective or genitive, since in this instance the two case forms coincide. *Itself* is similarly opaque, as it might consist of *it* $_{[OBJ]}$ + *self* or *its* $_{[GEN]}$ + *self*. Children seem to level this heterogeneous paradigm in favor of the genitive

---

[29] The transcripts also abound in children's use of genitive + *self* structures that admit the interpretation that *self* means "(unspecified) body part" (e.g., Adam at 3;5 *I fell down and broke myself.*; Abe at 3;6 *Daddy when I call you that means you need to wipe myself OK?*; Abe at 3;11 *He ate hisself...he likes meat so he ate it from hisself...*; Sarah at 4;5 *You want me to color myself?*).

[30] Of course, *self* exists as an independent noun in the adult lexicon, but in modern English it does not appear in contexts like those in (16) or (18). The structure *X's own self* is interesting because it takes a true genitive in the third-person singular masculine (*his own self*) and third-person plural (*their own selves*), contrasting with the standard adult reflexives, *himself* and *themselves*.

forms, creating *hisself* and *theirself(-ves)*, even where the input data clearly contradict this hypothesis, as in the exchanges in (19).[31]

(19) a. Father: Well they sort of broke by themselves.
Naomi: They broke by theirselves. (2;11)
b. Mother: What's he gonna do all by himself?
Nathaniel: Eh eh put put out all by hisself. (3;0)
c. Mother: He's looking at himself in the mirror.
Nina: Yup.
Mother: So he doesn't cut himself.
Nina: Uhhuh. Did he cut his self? (3;0)

Additional examples of hisself and theirself(-ves) appear in (20).

(20) a. But first deirself moved de furniture in dough. (Shem 3;0)
b. They're swimming all by their self. (Nina 3;1)
c. Yeah an' dey do funny things to theirselves an' pour ev'ything on deir face! (Shem 3;2)
d. He got paint all over hisself. (Nathaniel 3;4)
e. Mom why does this pirate have rings on his self? (Abe 3;4)
f. He check hisself. (Adam 3;5)
g. No wonder animals can box their selves. (Adam 4;6)
h. Well, someone hurts hisself (a)n(d) e(ve)rything. (Sarah 4;8)

Every child in the corpus except Eve (who contributed the smallest number of utterances) produced at least one token of either *hisself* or *theirself (-ves)*. The standard adult forms, *himself* and *themselves*, also appear in children's spontaneous production, often alongside *hisself* and *theirself(-ves)*.[32] Chiat (1981; pp. 85-7) pointed out the complexity of the genitive paradigm in English, and noted that

---

[31] Some of the transcripts represent *hisself* and *theirself(-ves)* as *his self* and *their self(-ves)*, although there is no indication of the significance of this orthographic convention, nor is it consistently observed within a single transcript. (19) and (20) preserve the spelling used in the CHILDES files.

[32] Among reflexives produced by the child subjects studied in this paper, 31.7% ($n=13$) of third-person singular masculine forms are *hisself*, and 46.7% ($n=7$) of third-person plural forms are *theirself(-ves)*. See Table 9.1.

children acquiring the paradigm may use (inter alia) *him* and *them* in genitive contexts. Example (21) illustrates one incidence of this in the CHILDES data.

(21)   I a hurt myself. (...) My daddy go up. He hurt him hand.   (Sarah 3;1)

Thus, it is possible that even some children's use of the adult forms *himself* and *themselves* constitutes genitive + *self* structures in their grammars, although production data can neither confirm nor disconfirm this speculation.

9.3.3. What Triggers Re-Analysis of Reflexives?

If children first treat reflexives as genitive determiners plus the independent, nonanaphoric noun *self*, what might cause them to abandon this hypothesis for the adult grammar, whereby reflexives are classified as anaphors, and therefore must be bound within their governing categories? Most research on the acquisition of reflexives proceeds from the assumption that children can recognize *myself, himself*, etc. as belonging to the class of anaphors. But it is not at all clear how this recognition is accomplished. It is inadequate to presume that children can assign to reflexives the lexical feature [+anaphor] because positive evidence informs them that reflexives lack independent referential properties. For example, the expressions *my foot* or *my mother* also lack independent referential properties in that the specific identity of the foot or the mother varies with the identity of the speaker. What distinguishes *myself* from *my foot* is that the former must appear in the context of a coreferential NP; the latter may appear in such a context but need not do so. This means that, in effect, the contexts in which *myself* may appear form a subset of those in which *my foot* may appear. If, as suggested both by the spontaneous production data presented here and by the experimental data reviewed in Section 9.1.2, children start out classifying *self* as a nonanaphoric noun like *foot*, how do they come to abandon this hypothesis? Perhaps they can make use of indirect negative evidence, by noticing that in the input data genitive + *self* structures always appear with antecedents. That is, perhaps children eventually recognize that although utterances like *My foot hurts* or *She's looking at my foot* abound, *myself* only appears in the context of another nominal, which identifies its referent. For example, the alternations exhibited in (22a, b) might serve to signal to a child that *myself* and *yourself* do not have the same distribution as *my foot* and *your foot*.

278   Chapter 9

(22) a. I wash *myself*; I wash *you* (cf. I wash my foot; I wash your foot)
b. You wash *yourself*; You wash *me* (cf. You wash your foot; You wash my foot)

On this realization, children assign the feature [+anaphor] to reflexives. Presumably, the language faculty apprises children of the consequences of this lexical feature, disposing them to stop producing utterances like those in (14) and (15). Once learners reach the realization that genitive + *self* structures are anaphors, the subset principle then informs them that the domain within which an anaphor must find its antecedent is its minimal clause. For learners of English this assumption is not challenged by input data. Input data also eventually disabuses children of *hisself* and *theirselves* in favor of the suppletive forms *himself* and *themselves*. At this point, the adult grammar of English reflexives has been acquired.

9.4. Discussion

In short, I propose along with McDaniel et al. that children's first hypothesis about reflexives is that they constitute genitive determiners plus the nonanaphoric noun *self*. As long as children maintain this analysis, they may (a) allow reflexives to have long-distance or extra-sentential antecedents; (b) permit reflexives in subject position of tensed clauses; and (c) produce *hisself* and *theirself*(-*ves*). Chien and Wexler's subjects under the age of 5;6 may be at this stage of development, as may McDaniel et al.'s subjects who accept sentences like (6) and (7) and who identify the reflexive with Grover or with Bert in (5). However, children come to realize that genitive + *self* forms appear only in the environment of a coreferential NP, causing them to assign the feature [+anaphor] to *self*. Innate knowledge of language informs learners that anaphors must be bound in their governing categories, and by the subset principle children set the definition of governing category as the minimal clause including the reflexive.

This proposal is consistent with the experimental evidence that children may initially fail to bind reflexives locally, but that as their grammars mature they adopt the adult system apparently without access to explicit tutoring. The proposal does not conflict with Manzini and Wexler's subset principle, since it attributes early long-distance binding of English reflexives to hypotheses irrelevant to the grammar of anaphors.

However, the production data do not uniquely support Manzini and Wexler's assumptions. The facts about children's use of reflexives reported above, and the interpretation of those facts proposed in this section, are also consistent with a competing hypothesis about the grammar of anaphors. This hypothesis is adverted to in Chomsky (1986), and developed by Cole, Hermon, and Sung (1990), Lebeaux (1983), and Pica (1987), among others. It focuses on accounting for cross-linguistic differences among anaphors, including the differences between English and Japanese cited in Section 9.1.1. Its gist is the claim that all reflexives essentially take local antecedents; in languages with apparent long-distance binding, a reflexive in a subordinate clause moves into a higher clause at an abstract level of linguistic structure known as "logical form." Such movement allows *zibun* in (4) to be bound by the subject of the higher clause, since *Yoko* and the reflexive become clausemates after movement has taken place. Reflexives in languages like English lack this kind of movement and therefore may be bound only by noun phrases that are their immediate clausemates. A learnability problem that the movement hypothesis must face is the question of how learners determine whether or not the language they are learning allows long-distance movement of anaphors. Pica points out that reflexives that require local antecedents (that is, ones that do not undergo long-distance movement) are morphologically complex; that is, they are obligatorily marked for features like number, gender, or person. In contrast, reflexives that can be bound long-distance are morphologically simple: Japanese *zibun*, for example, is not inflected to agree with its antecedent in number, gender, or person. (The correlation between morphological and syntactic facts is not coincidental, since in Pica's analysis it is the morphological simplicity of *zibun* that allows it to move long distance, although I do not discuss these mechanics here.)

Thus according to Pica's version of the movement hypothesis, it is a reflexive's morphological properties that inform learners about its syntactic properties. This notion forges an interesting link with the proposals presented in this chapter. Again, let us say that young children first treat English reflexives as noun phrases containing genitive determiners plus the non-anaphoric noun *self*. At this stage learners do not identify reflexives as anaphors, and therefore do not require that they be bound at all, much less strictly locally. But by the time *self* is re-classified as an anaphor, children will already have established an analysis of English *myself*, *yourself*, etc. as morphologically complex lexical items with genitive determiners in specifier position of the head noun *self*. Therefore, they should locally bind reflexives as soon as they re-classify *self* as an anaphor, which may take place by around 5;6, as Chien and Wexler's experimental results suggest. Thus, the data reviewed in this chapter are compatible with the hypothesis that the syntactic properties of reflexives are keyed to their morphological properties, since children's early failure to observe the adult grammar of English reflexives stems not from incorrect morphological analysis, but from failure to identify *self* as an anaphor.

In conclusion, we have seen that the production data as they are analyzed here make sense in the light of Manzini and Wexler's account of the grammar of anaphors, and also in the light of the movement hypothesis as developed by Pica and others.[33] In either case, inspection of children's spontaneous use of reflexives proves to be a useful complement to experimental evidence in research on the development of learners' grammars of anaphora.

9.5. Exercises

9.5.1. Analysis of Data from adam55.cha

Create a copy of the **include file** described in Section 9.2.2, and then use it to replicate the search for reflexives within the file **adam55.cha**. What is the syntactic context of Adam's use of *myself* and of the adults' uses of *yourself*? What is the significance of Adam's mother's response to his use of *myself*?

9.5.2. How Do Children Revise Hypotheses about the Grammar of Reflexives?

Examine this exchange between Sarah and her mother. Sarah was 2;3 years old at the time.

(23)   a.   Mother: Can't you dress yourself?
         b.   Sarah: You dress myself.
         c.   Mother: Huh?

---

[33] On the other hand, research by Hyams and Sigurjónsdóttir (1990) on the acquisition of Icelandic (a language that allows long-distance binding of reflexives) turns up evidence compatible with the movement account of the grammar of anaphors, and incompatible with Manzini and Wexler's proposals.

d.	Sarah:	You dress me.
e.	Mother:	What?
f.	Sarah:	You dress myself.
g.	Mother:	Do what? What do you want me to do?
h.	Sarah:	You dress myself.
i.	Mother:	What?
j.	Sarah:	You dress my.
k.	Mother:	Pull up your what?

There are at least two issues of interest in (23). One concerns the nature of Sarah's hypotheses about the properties of reflexives. When her mother fails to understand her request in (23b), how does Sarah revise the message in succeeding attempts at communication? Describe what this dialogue reveals about Sarah's grammar of anaphors.

Second, notice that Sarah's mother responds similarly to (23d) as to (23b, f, h). What significance might these facts hold for a child's construction of the grammar of anaphora?

9.5.3. Case Marking and the Structure of Reflexives

Chiat (1981) described some typical errors children make in the course of acquiring the full adult paradigm of genitive forms: (21) gives an example of a child who uses an accusative pronoun in a genitive context, suggesting that at a certain stage some children may construe the adult reflexives *himself* and *themselves* as genitive + *self* constructions. Use the KWAL command to look for evidence that children use accusative *him* and *them* in genitive contexts. Start by creating a list containing the forms you wish CLAN to search for. Then create a KWAL command which will locate the keyword(s) listed in your include file. Run this program on a file available to you within the CHILDES database and analyze the results. If you found no instances of nongenitive forms (e.g., *him*) in genitive contexts (e.g., *hurt him hand*), how might you interpret this result? In other words, how would you interpret a negative result?

9.6. Suggested Project

9.6.1. Young Children's Hypotheses about English Reciprocals

Most treatments of reciprocals such as English *each other* assume that, like reflexives, they must be bound within their governing categories. Simplifying this constraint somewhat, it means that a reciprocal must appear along with a (morphologically appropriate) antecedent within the same clause which identifies its referent(s). Example (24) shows that the distribution of English *each other* is in many ways parallel to the distribution of reflexives like *herself*.

(24) a. Paul and Tom bought bicycles for each other
      b. *Each other reads the newspaper every day
      c. Steve and Tom said that their parents bought bicycles for each other

Like (2), (24b) is ungrammatical, because *each other* lacks an antecedent. The reciprocal in (24c) can be bound to *their parents*, not to *Steve and Tom* since only the former noun phrase is within the governing category of *each other*. Thus (24c) can only mean that the parents bought bicycles for the parents.

Despite these similarities, Lebeaux (1983) pointed out several differences in the syntactic properties of reciprocals and reflexives, two of which are illustrated in the contrast between the (a) and (b) sentences in (25) and (26) (from Lebeaux, 1983; pp. 723-725).

(25) a. John and Mary brought some friends for each other to meet
      b. *John would like some books for himself to read
(26) a. John and Mary like each other's parents
      b. *John likes himself's parents

Lebeaux uses these data to anchor his claim that reciprocals and reflexives are subject to quite different grammatical constraints: at an abstract level of representation reflexives move out of their surface-structure positions, as adverted to in Section 9.4, whereas reciprocals do not.

It would be worthwhile to investigate how young children acquire English reciprocals. Although reciprocals are even less frequent in spontaneous speech than reflexives, try to reach a descriptive generalization about their distribution in early child language. In order to search for reciprocals, you will need to use the COMBO program. For example, to search for examples of *each other* in the **adam55.cha** file, you would use the following command:

combo +t* +s"each^other" −w4 +w4 adam55.cha

Start by generating possible combinations of the lexical items that represent plausible child forms of reciprocals (e.g., *each others*, *each another*, etc.). Use wildcards if appropriate. Then you may create two include files: one for the lexical items in the first position (call it **pos1**) and one for the lexical items in the second position (call it **pos2**). Use these include files to search CHILDES transcripts for examples of reciprocals in children's language, and in the language of adults addressed to children. The following is an example command for doing so:

combo +t* +s@pos1^@pos2 −w4 +w4 adam55.cha

Do the data show that child learners produce reciprocals that lack sentence-internal antecedents or which appear in the subject position of tensed clauses? Do the data include any examples of sentences like (29a) or (30a)? Are there learnability issues raised by the data similar to those raised by data on children's production of reflexives?

References

Berwick, R. (1985). *The acquisition of syntactic knowledge.* Cambridge, MA: MIT Press.

Brown, R. (1973). *A first language: The early stages.* Cambridge, MA: Harvard University Press.

Chiat, S. (1981). Context-specificity and generalization in the acquisition of pronominal distinctions. *Journal of Child Language, 8,* 75-91.

Chien, Y.-C., & Wexler, K. (1990). Children's knowledge of locality conditions in binding as evidence for the modularity of syntax and pragmatics. *Language Acquisition, 1,* 225-295.

Chomsky, N. (1986). *Knowledge of language: Its nature, origin, and use.* New York: Praeger Press.

Clark, E. V. (1978). Awareness of language: Some evidence from what children say and do. In A. Sinclair, R. J. Jarvella, & W. J. M. Levelt (Eds.), *The child's conception of language* (pp. 17-43). Berlin: Springer-Verlag.

Cole, P., Hermon, G., & Sung, L.-M. (1990). Principles and parameters of long-distance reflexives. *Linguistic Inquiry, 21,* 1-22.

Crain, S., & McKee, C. (1987). *Cross-linguistic analyses of the acquisition of coreference relations.* Paper presented at the 12th Annual Boston University Conference on Language Development, Boston, MA.

Huxley, R. (1970). The development of the correct use of subject personal pronouns in two children. In G. B. Flores d'Arcais & W. J. M. Levelt (Eds.), *Advances in psycholinguistics* (pp. 141-165). Amsterdam: North-Holland Publishing Co.

Hyams, N., & Sigurjónsdóttir, S. (1990) The development of "long-distance anaphora": A cross-linguistic comparison with special reference to Icelandic. *Language Acquisition, 1,* 57-93.

Jakubowicz, C. (1984). On markedness and the binding principles. *Proceedings of the North Eastern Linguistic Society, 14,* 154-182.

Katada, F. (1991). The LF representation of anaphors. *Linguistic Inquiry, 22,* 287-313.

Kuczaj, S. (1976). *-ing, -s, and -ed: A study of the acquisition of certain verb inflections.* Unpublished doctoral dissertation, University of Minnesota.

Kuno, S. (1973). *The structure of the Japanese language.* Cambridge, MA: MIT Press.

Lasnik, H., & Uriagereka, J. (1988). *A course in GB syntax.* Cambridge, MA: MIT Press.

Lebeaux, D. (1983). A distributional difference between reciprocals and reflexives. *Linguistic Inquiry, 14,* 723-730.

MacWhinney, B. (1991). *The CHILDES project: Tools for analyzing talk.* Hillsdale, NJ: Lawrence Erlbaum Associates.

Manzini, M. R., & Wexler, K. (1987). Parameters, binding theory, and learnability. *Linguistic Inquiry, 18,* 413-44.

McDaniel, D., Smith Cairns, H., & Ryan Hsu, J. (1990). Binding principles in the grammars of young children. *Language Acquisition, 1,* 121-138.

Otsu, Y. (1981). *Universal grammar and syntactic development in children: Toward a theory of syntactic development.* Unpublished doctoral dissertation, MIT.

Pica, P. (1987). On the nature of the reflexivization cycle. *Proceedings of the North Eastern Linguistic Society, 17*, 483-499.

Read, C., & Chou Hare, V. (1979). Children's interpretations of reflexive pronouns in English. In F. Eckman & A. Hastings (Eds.), *Studies in first and second language acquisition* (pp. 98-116). Rowley, MA: Newbury House.

Sachs, J. (1983). Talking about there and then: The emergence of displaced reference in parent-child discourse. In K. E. Nelson (Ed.), *Children's language: Vol. 4* pp. 1-28). Hillsdale, NJ: Lawrence Erlbaum.

Solan, L. (1983). *Pronominal reference: Child language and the theory of grammar*. Dordrecht: D. Reidel.

Solan, L. (1986). Language acquisition data and the theory of markedness: Evidence from Spanish. In F. Eckman, E. Moravcsik, & J. Wirth (Eds.), *Markedness* (pp. 257-269). New York: Plenum.

Solan, L. (1987). Parameter setting and the development of pronouns and reflexives. In T. Roeper & E. Williams (Eds.), *Parameter setting* (pp. 189-210). Dordrecht: D. Reidel.

Suppes, P. (1974). The semantics of children's language. *American Psychologist, 29*, 103-114.

van Riemsdijk, H., & Williams, E. (1986). *Introduction to the theory of grammar*. Cambridge, MA: MIT Press.

Yang, D.-W. (1983). The extended binding theory of anaphors. *Language Research, 19*, 169-192.

10

Children's Acquisition of Different Kinds of Narrative Discourse: Genres and Lines of Talk

Dennie Wolf
Joy Moreton
Linda Camp
Harvard Graduate School of Education

In this chapter, you will learn the following skills:

- To use the CLAN program FREQ to compare the frequency of different discourse features in two narrative genres.

- To get a clause-by-clause diagram of a narrative performance using the CLAN program CHAINS, which shows the progression of the narrative across different lines of talk and different speakers.

- To use the LINES program to generate a line-numbered transcript.

To replicate the analyses, you will need the six files found in the **narrativ** directory: **sc5.cha, pa5.cha, sc7.cha, pa7.cha, pp5.cha, codes.ord**.

10.1. Overview

Making up stories, sharing plans, giving instructions, reporting what happened. Each of these are different types of "event-talk" – varied forms of discourse that form part of the social fabric of any culture. Children everywhere grow up learning and practicing the kinds of narration that are important to their particular speech community. But what makes these different kinds of discourse distinctive and recognizable? What are the social consequences of having a repertoire of discourse forms to draw upon? How do different kinds of telling affect the relationship between speaker and listener, suggest different conversational roles for participants, or even change the way utterances are interpreted? Most importantly, how do children acquire the skills for participating in different kinds of discourse contexts?

This chapter begins to address these questions by focusing on aspects of young children's narration that provide the distinctions among types of narrative discourse, and that make those forms recognizable to other members of a speech community. Our goals are to examine whether kindergarten-aged children are capable of producing different varieties of narrative, and if so, what linguistic and performative resources they exploit for doing so. The analysis will also explore how children's strategies for engaging in different kinds of event-talk change as they become older and more experienced members of their culture.

Our approach involves performing a detailed analysis of a restricted number of narratives using several of the tools available within CHILDES. Section 10.2 begins with a background discussion that motivates the specific set of research questions guiding the analysis. Section 10.3 describes how to use the transcription, coding, and data analysis tools provided by CHILDES to address these issues. Section 10.4 discusses the results and how they relate to the research questions. The chapter concludes in Section 10.5, and there are suggestions for exercises and additional analysis in Section 10.6.

10.2. Introduction

10.2.1. The Importance of Acquiring Narrative Skills

In much of the early history of child language study, researchers were concerned with how young speakers acquired either the vocabulary or the sentence-level syntax that made them recognizable as members of a particular language community. But recently, it has become increasingly clear that vocabulary and syntax, while undeniably important, are only two types of development in a much more complex network of acquisitions (Tager-Flusberg, 1985). In particular, contemporary research on pragmatics and discourse strategies have enriched the understanding of all that it takes to become a competent language user (Bates, 1976, 1990; Miller, 1982, 1988; Nelson, 1988; Nelson & Gruendel, 1986; Ninio & Wheeler, 1984; Ochs & Schieffelin, 1984; Pan, Rollins, & Snow, 1991).

As early as their second year, children can represent and render experience through a series of utterances that capture not only a sequence of events and their consequences, but also the point of view of the teller and the experiences of more than one character. In short, they can produce the bare bones of a narrative. This capacity for narrative plays a major role in many areas of children's personal lives. Recent work on the formation of a coherent autobiography and sense of self suggests that the capacity to tell narratives, and thereby probe the meaning of events, is a central element in life-span adaptation (Bruner, 1990; Linde, 1987). Developmental researchers have begun to explore how early this process begins. For example, as a part of playing, either through night-time crib monologues or everyday discussions of "what happened," children use their narratives to produce order and understanding of both the commonplace and the signal events in their lives (Nelson, 1988; Sachs, 1983; Snow, 1990). In this way, they come to grasp both the predictable contours of human routines and the distinctive events that mark their personal histories.

Producing narratives becomes particularly important from the second year on, when the advent of walking and other forms of autonomy mean that young children spend portions of their days apart from the immediate presence of caregivers. If significant others are to keep in touch with the unfolding life history of a small child, the spoken narratives that crop up in the midst of ongoing conversation become increasingly important: they can make vivid what happened earlier that morning, three miles away at school, or in the otherwise secret and wholly internal worlds of the mind and heart.

In fact, the mastery of narrative forms has more than intimate and familial significance. It is also a kind of preparation and proving ground for the framing of experience essential to the presentation of self in public. In their first 3 years, children learn the conventions of their particular family and culture for forming and conducting different kinds of narratives. Thus, even 2- and 3-year-olds participate in such different narrative activities as make-believe play, the sharing of recent personal experiences, family fables that mix fact and myth, and simple future planning narratives ("When you get up from your nap, Katie will take you to Nana's"; "You can do that when you are bigger"; etc.). While engaging in these narratives, children assimilate a deep-running set of values and forms for how one presents the self and experience through the practices and language forms of an original community (Heath, 1983; Michaels, 1981; Wolf, in press). Like the syntax of their first language, these *genres of narrative* are not questioned; everyone in the speech community recognizes and responds to them. In effect, early narratives provide a remarkably sensitive indicator for the ways in which young speakers learn the values and conventions of their particular speech communities (Cummins, 1981; Gee, 1989; Goodwin, 1982; Heath, 1983; Michaels, 1981).

However, once children enter public institutions outside the original community – whether preschool, Head Start, kindergarten, or a clinic – the ways in which their narrative skills match or depart from the public institution's expected patterns of discourse will play a significant role in the perception of them as "healthy," "well-adjusted," "ready for school," or "at risk." Such assessments directly influence whether children are viewed as having sufficient or delayed control of the language, experiences, and behaviors needed to succeed in public settings (Feagans & Farran, 1981; Heath, 1983; Michaels, 1981). Consequently, varying styles of narrative rendition among children have often been the ground for debate over models of early discourse performance that stress the differences versus the deficiencies of varied narrative styles, and that highlight the presence of both multiple paths and endpoints in language development.

More broadly, the study of children's narrative discourse is an important aspect of the construction of a broader understanding of the processes and the developmental course of language acquisition. For one thing, narrative performances tap aspects of language development, such as the capacity for organizing complex chains of information (e.g., sequences of events, references to characters) that can be less prominent in simple, here-and-now conversations. Thus, if narrative development is monitored in contrast to other aspects of language growth, such as syntax or pragmatics, the question of whether language development is unified versus fundamentally componential can be addressed. In addition, because it places such high demands on young speakers, narrative turns out to be an effective tool for tracking both manifest and more subtle forms of language difficulties. Telling a narrative demands the coordination of many levels and aspects of performance. A narrative requires an understanding of how to use words to conjure up a world that is distant in time and space, of how to create an overarching structure for some specific kind of telling (a story, an account, a plan), and of how to negotiate and maintain a compelling relationship between teller and listener. Because of this complexity, narrative discourse and control over distinct genres of narration emerge slowly and are mastered later than the pragmatic rules governing conversation or the basics of sentence formation.

10.2.2. Re-Thinking Genre: From Individual Speakers to Social Performances

In much of the research literature, narrative genres have traditionally been distinguished from one another on structural grounds. For instance, *stories* are structured into a beginning, a middle (high point), and an end (resolution) and, by contrast, *scripts* and *explanations* have a "flatter," less contoured organization. However, Goodman (1978) pointed out that genres might better be understood as "ways of worldmaking," in which the speaker varies language and performance on a number of dimensions in order to create a particular universe for the self and for a listening and participating other. These universes vary along dimensions such as generality/specificity, truth/fiction, and personal exposure/veiled presence. Consider, for instance, the highly generalized, abstracted world suggested by a "script for what happens at a restaurant":

> you go in and wait to be seated
> you get taken to your table and they give you a menu
> the waiter takes your order
> you get your food
> when you finish, the waiter brings the check
> you pay and then you leave

This restaurant script has several distinct characteristics: (a) people appear as "the waiter" and "the customer" or as a universal "you"; (b) only observable actions are narrated to the exclusion of internal thoughts or feelings; (c) the narrator reveals nothing about his or her attitude toward the unfolding events; and (d) those events occur in an entirely predictable (and unaccented) sequence.

Compare with this restrained script the highly detailed, perspectival, and dramatic world most speakers create in the telling of a personal anecdote. The linguistic means for creating such different worlds are many: varying from the choice of **pronouns** and **verb tense** to the relative prominence of different kinds of **narrative information** (e.g., event clauses: "He came downstairs"; durative-descriptive information: "with the music still going"; and evaluative remarks that reveal the stance or perspective of the narrator: "just as crazy as ever"). Conceivably, the "same" event (a restaurant experience) could be represented in two very different ways (as a general script or as a dramatic personal anecdote).

In effect, genres are socially invented linguistic spaces that encourage different forms of human exchange, varying in the roles they suggest for speaker and listener, the amount of revelation they permit or forbid, and the way they open up or limit the range and intensity of emotion and/or intimacy carried by the act of narrating. It is in this way, as a means of control, that narrative genres are like other social frames for interaction, such as those governing medical examinations, classrooms, or locker rooms. In this chapter, we employ the term *narrative genre* to refer to the variety of performance types that a community of speakers recognizes and uses to accomplish different sorts of tellings. These may include such forms as accounts of personal experience, recounts of other people's experiences, generalized scripts for well-known events (e.g., what happens in a restaurant), and stories (which, in turn, might be broken up into fairy tales, parables, and myths). Because the term *genre* has been borrowed from the study of written, and especially, literary work, there is a tendency to treat these kinds of discourse performances as if they were fixed and stable forms. However, most naturally occurring discourse simply does not occur in sharply outlined genres. Rather, participants in a conversational setting move among different genres, using even those moves to carry some of the meaning. For instance, consider the following dialogue between a mother and her 3-year-old son as they jointly narrate a picture book about a boy and a frog:

Mother: (looking at illustration) What's this?
Child: He's a frog.
Mother: Right, frogs live in ponds just like this one (etches rim of pond with her fingertip).
Child: He gonna jump in the water. He's gonna be sad (makes an emphatic sad facial and vocal expression, mimicking frog in illustration).
Mother: Why's he gonna be sad? (She takes up the sad expression and voice tone.)
Child: Because *he* don't like the water. (He looks up at mother.)
Mother: Not like *you*. (She looks at him.)
Child: Because *he* don't fall in the duck pond.
Mother: That's right. Like you. You fell in the pond when we went to the farm. And got all wet. But you liked it, remember, crazy boy?
(Child laughs and crawls almost into her lap from where they go on looking at the illustrations and narrating.)

Here, although mother and son have been asked to tell a fictional story based on book illustrations, they actually zig-zag among different genres, starting with a kind of teaching explanation, moving to a moment of fiction, and ending in a sequence of personal, remembered anecdote. It is important to recognize that it is not only the linguistic markers (e.g., tense, grammatical person) or the small structures of these short passages that differ. Each of these genres, subtle as the shift between them is, brings the pair into quite different social relations: pupil and teacher, co-authors of a fiction, and then joint participants in the evocation – or perhaps even the creation – of a shared moment in family history. Not surprisingly, the form and content of their turns in each of these genres is different – as is the intimacy, the affect, and the amount of personal revelation that occurs. Correspondingly, their behavior also shifts, becoming increasingly responsive, intimate, and positive.

In much of the research on narrative discourse, the emphasis has been more on what a *solo* speaker must be able to do, and consequently, less on the social and mutual qualities of the performance. Since our interests in this analysis are to explore the social implications of shifts among different kinds of narrative discourse, our definitions for *narrative* and *discourse* acknowledge the participation of a listening other. We use *narrative* to describe the *mutual* rendition of experience over time (Holt, 1990; Labov, 1972; Peterson & McCabe, 1983; Ricoeur, 1984) as a speaker selects and shapes it for an audience. By *discourse* we mean stretches of talk in which the speaker and listener *jointly* formulate and sustain connections between earlier and later units of speech, whether by distinguishing between old and new information, by constructing and maintaining chains of temporal and referential links, or by moving through the expected parts of a well-known form such as a story, where an introduction forecasts later problems and a resolution ties up loose ends. Our goal in this chapter is to allow these broader definitions to inform an analysis of whether, and how, young children manifest distinctions among varieties of narrative discourse.

10.2.3. Genres in Conversational Context

Consider the following example of a conversation between an experimenter and a 5-year-old girl, in which both participate in formulating and sustaining a passage of narrative discourse:

> Experimenter: Tell me about what happens when you go out on the playground?
> Child: About my school? Where I go, the Harrington?
> Experimenter: Yeah, about your school.
> Child: Okay...when you're all done with recess

>   you go outside to the playground
>   and you can play in the field
>   or on the swings
>   or the jungle gym
>   Experimenter: what? the what?
>   Child: you know, the climbing thing, the jungle gym
>   Experimenter: oh, okay, the jungle gym
>   Child: ya
>   then you stay out there
>   until Bisse...your teacher... rings the bell and says
>   "Everyone to come in"
>   Child: But one time something happened there
>   Experimenter: Yeah?
>   Child: my friend Alyssa was going out to recess
>   and she said to meet her on the jungle gym
>   so I did
>   I started climbing and doing this trick
>   see
>   like this with my hands (demonstrates hand over hand climbing)
>   Experimenter: ya
>   Child: so I was doing that trick
>   only I missed with one hand
>   and so then I fell
>   and conked my head
>   and it was bleeding
>   and Alyssa went to get the nurse
>   saying like "Hurry, hurry."
>   there was blood all over the cement
>   what a mess

This somewhat jolting performance shows a clear shift in genre midway through, when the child moves from sketching the events that typify a visit to the playground to telling an anecdote about an accident she once had ("But one time something happened there."). She initially indicates the generality of her account by employing the genre of a script, with regular use of the historical present ("you go outside"), the second person ("you"), and simple connectives like "and" and "and then." These linguistic resources help provide her listener with a chronological, evenly paced rendition of events, in which no particular incident stands out above others. Thus, at the outset, there is little use of either descriptive information or evaluative comment to underscore any particular event as central or especially significant.

But once the conversation warms up, the child moves on to tell what happened to her once when she had a playground accident. She relates a sharply focused personal anecdote in which the tense and person of the individual clauses, as well as the overarching structure of the whole, are starkly different from her earlier way of talking. Her anecdote has what is often referred to as a high-point structure, in which the cardinal event (hitting her head) stands out from the prologue and the conclusion – in direct contrast to the earlier script. She uses various aspects of discourse (tense, person, and overall structure) to underscore her experience of being surprised and upset, as well as added gestures of the performance (such as miming the actions of climbing) and a deeper descriptive/evaluative pool ("conked" "all over the cement" "what a mess") which reveal her involvement in and attitude toward the events. Not only is this 5-year-old capable of producing two distinct and recognizable forms of narrative discourse, but the excerpt provides an example of some of the linguistic and performative strategies she has for doing so. The purpose of our analysis will be to look in greater detail at how these genre contrasts are formed and to characterize the nature of any developmental changes that occur.

While one kind of shifting in the previous child-experimenter discourse relates to genre, the same passage contains transitions of a different kind. In several locations, the discourse contains conversational asides in which the speaker and listener clarify meaning, thus juggling moments of **real-world conversation** ("about my school?" "what? the what?" "ya") with the narration of **events**. In the anecdote about her accident on the jungle gym, the teller weaves in a third kind of talk – a line of **description and evaluation** in which she adds information and relates her feelings about the experience ("and it was bleeding" "what a mess"). Similar to genre, these shifts to conversation and descriptive commentary create transitions in the social qualities of the performance. However, they are transitions that reflect the on-line, participatory process of negotiating and texturing meaning, rather than the more general structural changes in the context of telling that are brought by shifts in genre. For example, the playground example shows a shift from an ongoing line of event narration ("you go outside..." "you can play...") to the conversational line of talk that had been active initially ("the what?" "you know, the climbing thing"). This occurred as a result of the listener's need to clarify the meaning of "jungle gym." Once this clarification has taken place, the line of event narration resumes ("then you stay out there").

These transitions among "lines of talk" within a narrative performance add a further dimension to our analysis of children's ability to produce different varieties of discourse. While a genre provides an overarching social frame for a narrative performance, it is the line of talk that guides the interpretation of utterances within that setting. For example, if a child says "Oh, no, I broke it," the utterance will have radically different interpretations depending on whether it occurs in a line of speech about the real world, or in an ongoing line of character speech in a sequence of make-believe play. In the first case, the utterance refers to an actual, not imagined, event – the agent is the child, not a toy – and the play might stop rather than continue. In the second case, there would be no cause for alarm and the made-up story would simply continue. With the potential for several lines of talk to be active at any point, it is crucial for the speaker to provide some indication of which one should be used as the context for interpreting her speech. A variety of resources can be exploited to accomplish this: eye contact, intonation, choice of words and syntax, and gesture. While the current analysis does not investigate all of these ways of marking shifts between lines of talk, we will examine some of the devices present in children's narratives. Furthermore, the analysis begins to explore issues such as whether genre affects the way contrasts between lines of talk can be made, whether certain narrative contexts seem to allow a greater range of lines of talk, and whether some lines of talk are sustained for relatively long periods of time while others are active only briefly.

10.2.4. Research Questions

The analysis in this chapter addresses four research questions about children's narrative development:

1. *What features, both linguistic and extra-linguistic, help create distinctions among narrative genres in young children's discourse?*

2. *Does the way children form contrasts between genres differ as they get older and thus more experienced at participating in different contexts of narration? If so, what kinds of changes are there?*

3. *Do narrative performances of a particular genre tend to contain a consistent pattern of discourse features all the way through? Or are there shifts in the discourse among different kinds of talk even during the same genre performance? If so, how do these shifts relate to the social dynamics of the ongoing performance?*

4. *How does the context of a particular genre influence the kinds of transitions among lines of talk that take place during a narrative performance? Are some lines of talk more frequent than others, or active for longer periods of time? What strategies are available to young children for creating contrasts between different lines of talk?*

10.3. Methods

10.3.1. Subjects and Data Collection

The data used for the current analysis came from a larger study examining narrative development in 52 children, predominantly European-American, from mostly middle income suburban homes. These children were visited in their homes each year when they were 5, 6, and 7 years old and asked to engage in tasks designed to elicit different genres of narrative and non-narrative talk. The analysis in this chapter utilizes data from three tasks: script (a generalized account of a typical event), personal anecdote (an account of a memorable autobiographical experience), and pretend play (a session where the children were asked to make up a story about animals living in a jungle using small toys and props). Our analyses focus on the 5- and 7-year-old transcripts of one of these children.

10.3.2. Transcription, Coding, and CLAN Procedures

Each of the visits for the child we selected ("Alice") was videotaped and subsequently transcribed in its entirety, according to the minimum CHAT (minCHAT) guidelines (MacWhinney, 1991). In addition to providing a recording of the speech of the child and experimenter during the visit, the transcripts for each task were coded for contextually important actions and gestures, as well as implied referents of words like *it* and *this*. In keeping with other work on narrative discourse (see for example Berman & Slobin, 1986; Labov, 1972; Peterson & McCabe, 1983), we selected the clause as our basic unit of analysis. Therefore, while the transcript already reflected utterance and turn boundaries, we inserted a code **[c]** marking clause boundaries. Clauses are units of meaning that are more or less tied to distinct verbs. For example, the following utterance contains a single clause:

*CHI: he lived by this tree [c] .

Thus, the utterance boundary and the clause boundary are the same. On the other hand, there are three clauses in the next utterance:

*CHI: until Bisse # your teacher # rings the bell [c] and says [c] everyone to come in [c] .

Each verb (*rings*, *says*, *to come in*) is associated with a different clause, even though *rings* and *says* have the same subject ("Bisse").

Finally, an expanded set of speaker codes was used for transcribing the pretend play narratives, because this task often involved the participants adopting the voices of different characters as they enacted a story about animals living in a jungle. For example, *CHL was the speaker code when the child (CH) was speaking as the lion (L) and *EXD (EX) indicated the experimenter speaking as the dragon (D). This coding took place during the initial transcription process when cues from the videotape were available as context.

Our primary goal was to examine the strategies available to young speakers like Alice for creating contrasts among different kinds of narrative discourse. Focusing first on genre distinctions, we selected two discourse features and explored the role they played in producing genre contrasts: (a) the *tense* of each clause and (b) the lexical forms and aspects of performance used for conveying the speaker's *evaluation* of narrative information. We chose tense and evaluation because they represented two distinct dimensions of narrative semantics, with tense relating to time and evaluation to the teller's attitude and feelings. These two features also differ substantially in the way they are embedded in the discourse – tense is tied to verb structure, while evaluation can enter in a number of ways, including paralinguistically in intonation and gesture. By examining both tense and evaluation, we hoped to gain different kinds of information about Alice's acquisition of the skills needed for participating in different contexts of narration.

The two narrative contexts we examined were those where Alice employed the genre of a script and a personal anecdote. We coded each clause in these narratives for tense, indicating whether the verbal element made reference to the *past* ($PAS), *present* – including concurrent, habitual, or generic – ($PRE), or *future* ($FUT). We inserted these codes on a dependent tier (%tns) beneath each utterance. (See Bodin & Snow, this volume, and MacWhinney, this volume, on using the Coder's Editor to enter codes.) The evaluation codes were placed on a second dependent tier (%eva) whenever we identified the presence of a discourse element that functioned evaluatively. The range of such elements is described in more detail below, but the basic distinction we made was between *lexical* items that conveyed attitudes or feelings ($LEX) and *performative* attributes ($PER) that functioned in a similar way. Examples of both tense and evaluation coding are illustrated in (1) through (6):

Tense Coding

    (1) *CHI: and when everything **is all straightened out** [c] we **eat** [c] and **drink** [c].
        %tns: $PRE. $PRE. $PRE

    (2) *CHI: usually **takes** us a half hour [c] before everything **is finished** [c].
        %tns: $PRE. $PRE.

    (3) *CHI: because he **doesn't like** [c] his hair **being washed** [c].
        %tns: $PRE. $PRE

In these three examples, the tense codes for each clause are separated from one another by periods. In (1) and (2), the events referred to by the clauses in bold are habitual and therefore, present tense – not past tense, as the –**ed** in "straightened" and "finished" might suggest (English uses –**ed** for both past tense and participles). In (3), the tense for the second clause is inferred from the first clause, which refers to a generic state of affairs ("he doesn't like").

Evaluation Coding

(4) *CHI: **I liked** it [c]. it was a **really really fancy** place [c].
    %eva: $LEX. $PER $LEX $LEX

(5) *CHI: **I think** [c] **about** sixteen people got sick [c].
    %eva: $LEX. $LEX

(6) *CHI: **but** I **had to** put [c] **because** # I don't know why [=! whispers] [c] I **had to** put a **special** coat on [c] **just** to hold him [c].
    %eva: $LEX $LEX. $LEX $LEX $LEX $PER. $LEX $LEX. $LEX

In (4) through (6), the codes for each clause are again separated by periods, but unlike tense, a clause can contain any number of evaluative devices (or none). These three examples contain a variety of devices that give weight to certain pieces of narrative information, by either heightening or undercutting them. For instance, in (4), several *lexical* devices have the effect of emphasizing and heightening the narrative line: the verb **like** conveys internal feeling, the intensifier **really** adds emphasis, and the adjective **fancy** speaks to the significance of the event for the narrator. In addition, the *performative* tool of repetition (**really really**) further accentuates the importance of this information to the speaker. By contrast, the devices in (5) de-emphasize the narrative information by making it more uncertain and tentative. In (6), there are different kinds of evaluation, including whispering (performative), and lexical devices such as logical connectives (**but, because**) and modal verbs (**had to**). Our coding of performative devices was limited to repetition, gesture, and intonation shifts, and did not include strategies involving eye gaze or more complex prosody.

Once these files were coded, we used the CLAN program FREQ to count the number of clauses in each tense and the number of each kind of evaluative device found in Alice's scripts and personal anecdotes. For example, the following command caused the FREQ program to tabulate the number of occurrences of each tense code in Alice's personal anecdote at age 5:

freq   +t*CHI   +t%tns   +s$*   pa5.cha

+t*CHI	Analyze the child speaker only
+t%tns	Analyze the codes on the **%tns** dependent tier
+s$*	Include any and all strings beginning with **$**
pa5.cha	The child language transcript to be analyzed

Command Box 10.1

If you replicate this command, the following information will appear on the screen:

```
FREQ.EXE +t*CHI +t%tns +s$* pa5.cha
FREQ.EXE (04-MAY-93) is conducting analyses on:
  ONLY speaker main tiers matching: *CHI;
  and those speakers' ONLY dependent tiers matching: %TNS;
****************************************
   17 $pas
    8 $pre
-------------------------------
    2 Total number of different word types used
   25 Total number of words (tokens)
0.080 Type/Token ratio
```

The output indicates that 17 clauses were past tense, and 8 were present tense – making 25 clauses in all. In this case, "Total number of words" means total number of clauses because a code was assigned to each clause. The type-token ratio is unimportant to the present analysis.

To get counts for each tense code in Alice's script at the same age, we issued a similar FREQ command substituting a new file name: **sc5.cha**. Finally, we performed similar operations for the same two genres at age 7 by switching the file name in the command, first to **pa7.cha** and then to **sc7.cha**. This procedure provided the full set of frequencies for the different tenses in each narrative performance, which appears in Table 10.1.

Consistent with our expectations, the results showed that Alice used more past tense in her personal anecdotes and more present tense in her scripts. Future tense only appeared in the 7-year-old script.

Genres and Lines of Talk 301

Table 10.1: The frequency of past, present, and future tense in scripts (SC) and personal anecdotes (PA).

	Age 5		Age 7	
Tense	PA	SC	PA	SC
Past	17 (68%)	0 (0%)	38 (93%)	3 (6%)
Present	8 (32%)	32 (100%)	3 (7%)	42 (88%)
Future	0 (0%)	0 (0%)	0 (0%)	3 (6%)
# Clauses	25	32	41	48

Having obtained counts for each tense, the next step was to count the incidence of evaluative devices in Alice's script and personal anecdote at each age. The FREQ procedure differed only slightly. For example, to examine evaluation in the 5-year-old personal anecdote, we used the command:

freq +t*CHI +t%eva +s$* pa5.cha

+t*CHI	Analyze the child speaker only
+t%eva	Analyze the codes on the **%eva** dependent tier
+s$*	Include any and all strings beginning with $
pa5.cha	The child language transcript to be analyzed

Command Box 10.2

The only difference is that here we are telling FREQ to count the codes found on the evaluation (%eva) dependent tier instead of the tense (%tns) tier. Again, the output indicated the number of times each code was found in the transcript. However, not every clause included an evaluative device, while a number of clauses contained several. Therefore, "Total number of words" in the output indicates the total number of evaluative devices rather than the number of clauses. These counts are listed in Table 10.2.

The results indicate that Alice employed more lexical devices for evaluation, but this may be partially due to the fact that we coded only a limited range of performative devices. The total number of evaluative devices was higher in the

302   Chapter 10

Table 10.2: The frequency of evaluation in scripts (SC) and personal anecdotes (PA).

	Age 5		Age 7	
Evaluative Device	PA	SC	PA	SC
Lexical	24	14	43	18
Performative	0	5	2	10
Total	24	19	45	28
# Clauses	25	32	41	48
Density (# devices per clause)	0.96	0.59	1.1	0.58

personal anecdotes, which is consistent with the general notion that these accounts tend to reveal more about the teller's inner experience than scripts do. To get a sense of how often Alice used evaluation in each performance, we computed the average number of evaluative devices per clause – or the *density* of evaluation in the narrative. Overall, there was approximately one device per clause in the personal anecdotes, and about half that (one device every two clauses, on average) in the scripts.

Having determined the frequency with which Alice employed each tense and type of evaluative device in different genres, our next step was to examine an individual narrative performance more closely in order to learn more about how *lines of talk* operate. We selected one of Alice's pretend play narratives (at age 5) for this analysis because, for most children, this genre induces a longer performance and more lines of talk than other genres.

Our approach to carrying out this part of the analysis began with coding each clause for one of five different modes of speaking, which we derived during preliminary analyses of the videotapes. The codes we used were:

$GEN a line of general, real-world talk
$TSK a line of talk about the here-and-now world of the task, props, and animal figures
$FIG a line of figurative language and negotiation of pretense
$NAR a line of event narration relating to the story world
$CHR a line of character dialogue within the story

We coded the speech of both participants, including utterances like "uh-huh" and "okay" by the experimenter, to which we assigned the same code as the child's preceding clause. We interpreted these utterances as adult scaffolding for the child's ongoing discourse, and anticipated that our coding strategy would offer a useful point of view on ways that certain kinds of talk are co-constructed (Mischler, 1986). Here are examples of the coding:

(7) *CHI: pretend [c] the &dra dragon was bad [c].
    %tlk: $FIG . $FIG

(8) *CHN: so the mother took her little baby <to her> [//] first to her arm-s [c] then she said [c].
    %tlk: $NAR . $NAR

(9) *CHL: if we do not give you to the dragon [c] our jungle shall be destroy-ed [c].
    %tlk: $CHR . $CHR

These examples contain three of the expanded number of speaker codes used in transcribing the pretend play narratives: *CHI, the child speaking in her own voice; *CHN the child speaking as the narrator; and *CHL, the child speaking as the lion. Like the majority of the transcript, the clauses in these examples were assigned a single code for line of talk, but there were also some that received two codes because they were judged to serve more than one communicative function.

Instead of employing the FREQ program as we did for the script and personal anecdote, we used the program CHAINS to generate a diagram of the clause-by-clause progression of the narrative. The CHAINS program creates a graphical display of a coded transcript, representing each utterance (or clause) by a number that indicates the speaker and placing those numbers into different columns according to the code found on a certain coding tier. The program then calculates the length of the "chains" of consecutive utterances (or clauses) in each coding category and produces summary information relating to these chains. The following command generated a diagram of Alice's pretend play narrative, showing the clause-by-clause progression along the five different lines of talk:

chains +t%tlk +t*CH% +t*EX% +c[c] +d1 +w7 +f pp5.cha

+t%tlk	Use lines of talk codes for column headers
+t*CH%	Analyze all child speech regardless of voice
+t*EX%	Analyze all experimenter speech regardless of voice
+c[c]	The unit of analysis is the clause not the utterance
+d1	Suppress all zeros in the output; insert line numbers instead
+w7	The width for each column is 7 spaces
+f	Save the results in a file with the default extension .cns
pp5.cha	The child language transcript to be analyzed

Command Box 10.3

The **+f** option in the command caused the output to be saved in a file (**pp5.cns**), which we then printed. A section of this output appears in Figure 10.1 for illustration (see Appendix A for the full output). The diagram shows the line of talk codes across the top of the page. Down the right side are the line numbers corresponding to the location of the utterances in the file (the missing line numbers are associated with dependent tiers). On each line, the program places a number indicating who produced the clause (1 for experimenter, 2 for child) in the column corresponding to the line of talk code for that clause. In this way, the procedure provide a map of the progression of the pretend play narrative across different categories of talk and different speakers. (See Figure 10.2 for the segment of the transcript corresponding to Figure 10.1.)

By scanning the full diagram, we were able to discern: (a) which line of talk was active at each moment; (b) where shifts to other lines occurred; and (c) whether previously active lines of talk were eventually resumed or remained inactive for long periods of time. The operation also summarized the number of clause sequences ("chains") in each line of talk, their lengths, and the relative involvement of each participant in co-constructing chains of each talk type. Table 10.3 presents a subset of this summary information.

Figure 10.1

Sample CHAINS Diagram

Speaker markers: 1=*EX, 2=*CH

$chr	$fig	$gen	$nar	$tsk	line #
			2		102
			2		106
				2	110
				2	113
				1	117
				2	120
				2	123
				1	127
			2		130
2					134
			2		138

In general, the results show that the longest and most frequent chains of consecutive clauses occurred in the line of event narration (NAR). The longer average length (4.6 clauses) of the co-constructed NAR chains suggests that the

Figure 10.2

Portion of Alice's transcript corresponding to Figure 10.1

(Intervening lines containing additional coding information not shown)

```
line #
102  *CHI:   he lived by this tree [c].
105  %tlk:   $NAR
106  *CHI:   and she [= lioness] lived by that tree [c].
109  %tlk:   $NAR
110  *CHI:   so we-'re change-ing the jungle [c].
112  %tlk:   $TSK
113  *CHI:   so he go-es back over here a little bit [c].
116  %tlk:   $TSK
117  *EXP:   ok [c].
119  %tlk:   $TSK
120  *CHI:   so we-'re change-ing the jungle [c].
122  %tlk:   $TSK
123  *CHI:   so he go-es back here [c].
126  %tlk:   $TSK
127  *EXP:   uhhuh [c].
129  %tlk:   $TSK
130  *CHN:   <the> [//] # the lion father the clos-er [c].
132  %tlk:   $NAR
134  *CHL:   how are we suppose-ed to protect the baby [c]?
137  %tlk:   $CHR
138  *CHN:   the mother said [: say&ed] [c].
140  %tlk:   $NAR
```

(*CHI: child as self; *CHN: child as narrator; *CHL: child as lion)

306   Chapter 10

experimenter played an important role in helping Alice sustain her narration of story events. In comparison, the line of character dialogue (CHR), all of which was created by Alice, tended to have slightly shorter sequences of clauses (approximately 3-clause chains). All three lines of talk dealing with the fictional world of the story (FIG, NAR, CHR) were active for more clauses at a time than the non-storyworld lines of talk (GEN, TSK). The fewest and shortest chains occurred in the line of general, real-world conversation (GEN), suggesting that these were brief asides that never were the locus of sustained joint interest.

To facilitate our analysis of the diagram, we also generated a line-numbered version of the original transcript using the CLAN program LINES:

lines +f pp5.cha

| +f | Save the results in a file with the default extension **.lno** |
| pp5.cha | The child language transcript to be analyzed |

Command Box 10.4

This procedure saves the line-numbered version of the 5-year-old pretend play transcript in a file (**pp5.lno**), which we then printed. A portion of this output is provided in Figure 10.2.

Figure 10.1 provides several examples of shifting across lines of talk in Alice's jungle story. First, we noted that three of the five lines of talk we coded were active in this brief (11-clause) segment of the performance: task-related talk (TSK), event narration (NAR), and character dialogue (CHR). There were four transitions: (a) NAR to TSK (line #111), (b) TSK to NAR (line #131), (c) NAR to CHR (line #135); and (d) CHR to NAR (line #139). The line-numbered segment of the transcript in Figure 10.2 shows that the first shift, from NAR to TSK (line #111), materialized when Alice decided to re-arrange the jungle props. The experimenter supported the new line of talk by responding "OK" (line #118) and "uhhuh" (line #128). The next shift occurred when Alice resumed the line of event narration (line #131). The line of character dialogue was active briefly in the following clause (line #135), then Alice returned to the voice of the narrator (line #139). These results illustrate several different kinds of shifts and reasons for them, and reveal that both the role and the style of the speakers varied with the line of talk.

With the FREQ and CHAINS programs, we generated two views of Alice's narrative skills. The output from the FREQ program addresses her ability to create genre contrasts by means of linguistic and extra-linguistic features. The CHAINS program, on the other hand, provides an internal view of the progression of a single narrative, and thus sheds light on Alice's ability to negotiate and respond to a specific context of narration by shifting in and out of different lines of discourse.

10.4. Discussion

10.4.1. What Features Create Distinctions Among Narrative Genres?

In the 5-year-old data (Table 10.1), the majority of the clauses in the personal anecdote were past tense while all of the script was present tense. There was also a clear contrast in the frequency of evaluative devices, with an average of one device per clause in the personal anecdote (all lexical devices) but half as many in the script. This tendency toward past tense and more evaluation in the personal anecdote, and present tense with less evaluation in the script also held true in the 7-year-old data (Table 10.2).

Thus, we learned that the two features we analyzed helped create genre distinctions in Alice's narrative discourse. These featural contrasts contribute in different ways to making personal anecdotes and scripts two very distinct forms of narrative exchange. By accommodating more evaluation, personal anecdotes permit a greater degree of personal revelation and expand the intensity of emotion carried in the act of narrating. In contrast, scripts tend to restrict the exposure of personal attitudes and feelings, which gives them a more emotionally distanced and neutral nature. But as Riessman (1990) pointed out in her work on narratives of divorce, the very fact that "habitual narratives" lack devices that highlight the particular gives them a "striking lack of emotion" (p. 102). Therefore, a *lack* of emotion in the case of certain kinds of content may not operate neutrally and, in fact, may create increased emphasis via an absence of evaluative discourse devices.

The effect of tense, on the other hand, goes beyond simply establishing time reference. The present tense of scripts, which gives events an habitual and static quality, helps to underscore their generality, while past tense creates a world removed in time, allowing particular meanings and the connections between them to be probed and re-experienced in different ways. Even as early as 5, Alice exhibits a significant degree of control over two of the features that play critical roles in evoking these very different kinds of telling.

10.4.2. Developmental Changes in Creating Genre Contrasts

How did Alice's narrative skills change as she grew older? Perhaps not surprisingly, both her script and her personal anecdote were longer at age 7 with a nearly 40% gain in the number of clauses for each genre. Were these increases in length accompanied by changes in the way she used tense and evaluation to contrast the two narrative forms?

We addressed this question by comparing the featural contrasts between the script and the personal anecdote for the two different ages. Although there may have been age-related differences in the way Alice introduced evaluation into each genre, the average number of devices per clause for her script relative to her personal anecdote was consistent at the two ages. However, the results for tense did vary. At 5, Alice used 68% past tense and 32% present tense in her personal anecdote, and 100% present tense in her script. At 7, these proportions changed. The personal anecdote went up to 93% past tense, while the script became somewhat more heterogeneous with the addition of several past and future tense clauses. Both changes moved the two genres toward a similar mix of dominant (about 90%) and nondominant (about 10%) tenses. By simply observing these patterns, however, we were unable to determine whether they reflected something significant about Alice's developing narrative skills.

The next step we took was to investigate the transcripts themselves to find out where and how the nondominant tenses were entering the narratives. In Alice's 5-year-old personal anecdote, the tense shifted away from past (the dominant tense) in the following passage:

> (narrative is about when her brother was a baby)
> *CHI: and after year-s went by [c] he got old-er and old-er [c] so he did-'nt # sleep so much [c].
> %tns: $PAS . $PAS . $PAS
> *EXP: uhhuh [c].

Genres and Lines of Talk 309

```
*CHI:    and # then he got so old [c] he doesn't sleep # so much [c] <now he
         only has like a couple of nap-s a day> [//] he only has [: have&es] one
         nap a day [c].
%tns:    $PAS . $PRE . $PRE
*CHI:    not always # a day [c].
%tns:    $PRE
*CHI:    like he stay-es awake for the whole day sometimes [c].
%tns:    $PRE
```

As Alice moved from using past to present tense in the boldface clause shown in the middle of this segment, her discourse shifted into a more scriptlike rendition of events which she then retained for all but the last three clauses of the narrative. Along with this change in tense, the frequency of evaluation began to decrease. In effect, Alice changed genres in the middle of the performance. In comparison, the intrusion of present tense into her 7-year-old personal anecdote had a different flavor:

```
         (narrative is about going to a play)
*EXP:    was it good [c]?
*CHI:    yes [c].
*CHI:    we went to [c] +...
%tns:    $PAS
*CHI:    hmm I-'ve forgotten the name of it [c] but it was a really really fancy
         place [c].
%tns:    $PRE . $PAS
```

Here, Alice departed momentarily from the past-tense world of her experience going to the show to interject her reason for leaving out an important piece of information – the name of the theater. This conversational aside suggests that she understands the genre well enough to realize that her audience expects certain details. In fact, she substituted a descriptive clause ("but it was a really really fancy place") to add meaning that the name would have evoked, effectively meeting the expectations given to her listener by the genre. With encouragement, Alice then continued telling about her outing and did not shift away from the genre of personal anecdote in the remainder of the narrative.

At age 7, then, Alice showed signs of understanding the expectations her listener brought to the context of narration better than she had at age 5. Although these two performances provide only a limited basis for this claim, Alice's 7-year-old script lent support to our perception that she had strengthened her skills for participating in different contexts of narration. In this performance, her shifts away from present tense were not departures from the script genre but tended to be relatively brief excursions to other lines of talk. For instance, one of these transitions was to a line of future-tense quoted speech – the waitress saying she'll be back to take your order in a few minutes. Immediately following this quote, Alice resumed present tense. Therefore, while the change in tense at age 5 was a break in the genre that initially governed the interaction (personal anecdote), tense shifts at 7 tended to support the initial genre.

10.4.3. Shifts Within Genres Among Different Lines of Talk

The results so far have indicated that even narrative performances conforming to a particular genre do not do so in a static and reliable way. For example, the analyses showed the presence of future and past at times in the midst of a present-tense script, while the past-tense world of the personal anecdote could move in and out of brief moments of present tense. Evaluation occurred more often in stories of personal experience but was not absent from scripts. What do these departures from the dominant pattern of features in a genre reflect?

We addressed this question by starting with the excerpt from Alice's personal anecdote at age 7, the second example presented in the previous section. In this example, Alice said "hmm I-'ve forgotten the name of it," referring to the name of the theater that figured in her narrative about going to see a play. The verb form is present tense ("have" plus the participle "forgotten"), a deviation from the past tense that predominated the performance. The clause functioned as a conversational aside that allowed Alice to explain the omission of an important piece of information about her experience. Her use of first person ("I"), present tense ("have forgotten"), and perhaps the direction of her eye gaze as well (although we did not code it for this analysis) signalled for this bit of discourse to be interpreted in the here-and-now context of conversation, and not as part of the past experience she was relating (as quoted speech, for example).

We discovered a second example that had to do with the frequency of evaluation in Alice's 5-year-old script, which was about what usually happens when she and her brother take a bath. In the 13 clauses that led up to this excerpt, she employed only three evaluative devices (an average of one for every 4.3 clauses). However, that changed dramatically in the following segment:

*CHI:	<and my brother say-es> [//] my brother call-es me Geckie [c].
*CHI:	**(be)cause** he-'is **only** two [c].
%eva:	$LEX $LEX
*CHI:	so he say-es [c] **Geckie first Geckie first** [c].
%eva:	$LEX. $PER $PER
*CHI:	**because** he does-'**nt like** [c] his hair be-ing wash-ed [c].
%eva:	$LEX $LEX $LEX
*EXP:	uhhuh [c].
*CHI:	so then after my hair-'is [c].
%eva:	$LEX
*CHI:	he keep-es say-ing **Geckie** [c].
%eva:	$PER
*CHI:	<so> [//] and my mother say-es [c] **Geckie already has her hair done** [c] **so it-'s your turn now** [c].
%eva:	. $PER. $LEX $PER

Clearly, the density of evaluation increased substantially as Alice oscillated between explaining why her brother calls her "Geckie" and injecting direct quotation into her description of their bathtub routine. The performative devices of quotation and repetition, as well as the dialogue marker *says*, provide cues that "Geckie first Geckie first" is her brother's utterance in the event world, and not Alice's in the here-and-now realm of conversation with the experimenter. In the next clause, Alice employs a series of lexical devices that mark it as a line of explanation (the connective *because*, negation, the internal state word *like*).

These two examples illustrate transitions away from a pattern of discourse features associated with event narration to quoted speech, to a line of conversation or explanation, or to a line of description and evaluation. Each shift in features signals that a new line of talk is active, which shifts the context for interpreting the speaker's utterances. These moves transform the social qualities of the performance by bringing the participants into a different set of social relations, each accompanied by different expectations for response, content, and meaning. Tense and evaluation are not the only features responsible for creating different lines of talk. Even in the few examples we have examined closely, there are signs that grammatical person, intonational contour, direction of eye gaze, nominal/pronominal reference, and other

312   Chapter 10

discourse attributes also help guide the listener's interpretation during the narrative performance.

10.4.4. Inside a Genre: Mapping and Measuring Chains Within Lines of Talk

The last set of questions we will address concerns how lines of talk operate within an individual narrative performance. Which lines are more frequent? Are some active for longer periods of time than others? Where and why are shifts occurring? How do the roles of the participants change at each transition? The pretend play narrative used for this analysis is a genre that typically gives rise to many lines of talk, several of which may be active at any given moment. For example, a line of event narration might be temporarily suspended while two story characters converse, or a line of pretense might be resumed and re-negotiated during the early stages of setting the scene and structuring the plot. Therefore, this genre affords a unique opportunity to examine the skills involved in negotiating the on-line, participatory process of conversational narration.

The results in Table 10.3 showed that the lines of talk with the most activity were the line of event narration (NAR) and the line of character dialogue (CHR), the two lines of talk constituting the storyworld. Both the number of chains of consecutive clauses as well as their average length were greater in these lines, for Alice as a solo speaker as well as in conjunction with the experimenter. And although figurative/pretense-oriented talk (FIG) was less frequent in comparison (it tended to be concentrated in the earlier stages of the performance), Alice sustained this line of talk almost as long at a time on average (3.0 clauses compared to 3.8 for NAR and 3.1 for CHR). The two lines of here-and-now conversation, about the task (TSK) and about the world outside the task (GEN), were reserved for fairly short asides (1.6-1.7 clauses long), although the TSK line occurred as many times as the FIG line. Finally, in reviewing the chain length results, it was clear that the experimenter adopted a supportive background role most of the time as opposed to an instructional or leading role. This was evidenced by the short (1-2 clause) chains she produced in every line of talk.

The longer chain lengths for the storyworld and pretense lines of talk bring an interesting new dimension to the previous finding that children's narratives are syntactically more complex than their conversational discourse (e.g., Sulzby, 1981). The CHAINS results indicate that the social context for each line of talk varies considerably, leading to more sustained (and perhaps more autonomous) child discourse in particular lines and more mutual, responsive discourse in others. In mapping these differences, the CHAINS analysis extends current research on language development by raising the issue of where particular kinds of complexity occur in everyday discourse, whether it is complexity related to utterance structure (syntactic complexity), to the negotiation of meanings and roles (conversational complexity), or to referential/temporal cohesion and coherence in plot/character (discourse complexity).

As far as how shifts between lines of talk occurred in the pretend play narrative, we did not perform a detailed analysis of how well Alice signalled them, but we did examine the different kinds of transitions evident in the CHAINS diagram. Using the line number references to locate each transition in the transcript, we proceeded to identify the kinds of shifts within different phases of the performance (see Appendix for the full CHAINS output).

Early on in the diagram, the shifts from one line of talk to another tended to be changes in the speaker, as the experimenter initiated the narrative and solicited Alice's participation. Once Alice began to assume responsibility for the plot, we observed two kinds of shifting, each with a contrasting function. The first was a transition from event narration to pretense-oriented talk (line #77: "Pretend the dragon was bad, OK?"), which supplied additional plot structure by suggesting a possible role for a key character. The second type of shifting around this point in the performance was between event narration and task-oriented talk, for example "So we're changing the jungle" (line #110). Like the figurative talk, these utterances added structure to the emerging storyworld, but in terms of its physical setting instead of its character roles. Interestingly, these early transitions brought the experimenter-child dynamic into a more interactive mode, manifested in conversational markers ("OK?" "uh-huh") and question intonation that provided a quality of co-construction and negotiation.

Following these opening phases of configuring and negotiating the storyworld, the next phase of the narrative involved a series of shifts between the lines of event narration and character dialogue (lines #130-211). These transitions dramatized certain elements of the unfolding plot by invoking the voices of key characters, then reinstated the voice of the narrator to move the plot forward. This pattern was broken on line #214 by an abrupt transition to task-related talk. Referring back to the transcript, we saw that Alice had been speaking as the elephant character, holding the toy as she spoke, when its ear suddenly broke off. After exclaiming "Oopsy, this ear came off" (TSK), she explained to the experimenter that the elephant was going to wag its ear (FIG) but it had come off (TSK). Did the experimenter think it could be fixed (TSK)? Alice had some glue, which they could go get (GEN). "Let's finish the story," the experimenter urged instead. The accident thus resolved in the conversational realm, Alice resumed her narrative, but using a line of figurative talk instead of event narration (line #245). Here, the CHAINS diagram shows movement back and forth between the FIG and CHR lines, as Alice proposed new elements of the plot to explain the ear accident and enacted them in the voice of the elephant character (lines #245-281). Having then resolved the broken ear mishap in both the conversational and storyworld realms, she resumed her line of event narration (line #284).

At each of these shifts in the narrative, we detected a change in the social relations between Alice and the experimenter – from teller/audience during the line of event narration, to authorial partners during the negotiation of pretense, to leader/follower in the lines of conversation leading back to the narrative. Different kinds of shifts occurred for different reasons: a tree prop falling down (line #335), the approach of the high point of the plot (line #322), a reminiscence about the task from the previous year's visit (line #361). Along with bringing the pair into a different set of social relations, each line of talk had the effect of suggesting how the utterances within it should be interpreted. This was signalled by linguistic elements of the utterance (grammatical person, tense, and type of verb), as well as its performance aspects (gaze, position, posture, and intonation; see Kendon, 1990).

The analysis of lines of talk within a single-genre pretend play, thus provided a great deal of information about how different modes of speaking operate in a narrative performance. Furthermore, the analysis suggested a new direction of questions concerning the on-line, participatory process of conversational narration. For example, how does practice with adopting and responding to different narrative roles relate to the acquisition of specific discourse skills (e.g., temporal cohesion, tracking reference)? How does the context of a particular genre shape the way lines of talk are signaled and used to guide interpretation? These questions and others await further detailed analyses of different narrative genres and closer examination of young children's control over particular elements of discourse performance.

10.5. Conclusion

The richness of Alice's performances and the analyses of them presented here suggest that a range of approaches is necessary in order to capture the subtlety of even early narrative development. In these samples and their analysis, we have strong evidence that narrative development involves much more than the acquisition of story grammars or the cohesive devices that turn sequential utterances into connected texts. By 5, children already understand that narratives come in genres and that each genre brings with it a particular set of obligations and opportunities. A script may capture the outlines of commonplace experience, but it takes a story, whether fiction or personal anecdote, to sculpt the contours of significant personal experience. Moreover, the analyses conducted here make it clear that narratives are far from sealed and monolithic accounts of what happened when to whom. They are on-line, improvisational performances in which speaker and listener follow one another from one world of meaning-making to the next and back again, following the subtle tracks of different lines of talk.

The two CLAN tools we used to perform these analyses, FREQ and CHAINS, emphasized different aspects of narrative performance. The FREQ program yielded a *featural analysis*, focusing on the patterns of linguistic and performative attributes found within different sorts of performances. CHAINS, on the other hand, provided a useful tool for understanding how lines of talk operate within a narrative performance, thus providing a *progressive analysis* of the narrative.

10.6. Exercises

10.6.1. Analysis of Additional Genre Contrasts

Create an include file named **pronom.inc** containing the following pronominal forms: **I, you, he, she, it, we, they**. These forms roughly capture the grammatical person of the utterances in Alice's narratives. Referring back to Section 10.3.2, where we used the FREQ program to count tense and evaluation codes in Alice's scripts and personal anecdotes, modify the FREQ commands by (a) eliminating the **+t%** option (+t%tns and +t%eva), and (b) substituting **+s@pronom.inc** for **+s$***. Divide the counts you get by the number of clauses in each transcript (see Table 10.1). Is there a contrast between genres in the frequency of each pronominal form at age 5? At age 7?

10.6.2. Evaluation and Lines of Talk

Read the script and personal anecdote transcripts for each age. Identify where evaluative devices occur and determine whether there is a shift to a different line of talk at these points. What is the role of evaluation in signalling transitions to particular lines of talk? How does it change certain dimensions of the performance, thus shifting Alice's "way of worldmaking" at these moments?

10.6.3. The Role of Tense in the Pretend Play Narrative

The pretend play narrative is coded for the tense of each clause. Use an additional option in the CHAINS procedure following +t%tlk by adding +t%tns to the command presented in Command Box 10.3. This will cause the tense of the clause to be printed next to each speaker code on the output. Does tense play a role in differentiating lines of talk and/or signalling shifts between them? In the cases where there is no change in tense or speaker, use the line numbers to locate the shift in the transcript. What other features are responsible for the perception that a new line of talk is underway?

10.7. Suggested Project: Code and Analyze a New Feature

Code a feature of your choice in the four transcripts used for the genre analysis (**sc5.cha, sc7.cha, pa5.cha, pa7.cha**). (See Bodin & Snow, this volume, and MacWhinney, this volume, for instructions in using Coder's Editor to enter codes.) For example, you could code the grammatical person and number of the subject in each clause (first-person singular, third-person plural, etc.), designing your own coding system for doing so and putting the codes on a separate dependent tier. After saving the re-coded transcripts, perform an analysis using the FREQ program that examines genre contrasts in this feature at each age. Compile the results into a table analogous to those presented in Section 10.3.2. What is your hypothesis about the relative frequency of this feature in personal anecdotes as compared to scripts? Is this expectation confirmed by the frequency counts for Alice at age 5? At age 7? Reading through the transcripts, are the shifts away from the dominant pattern in each genre indicative of shifts to other lines of talk?

Now code this feature in the pretend play narrative. Following the instructions in Exercise 10.6.3 for indicating an additional coding tier in the CHAINS command, generate output that addresses the question of whether the newly coded feature plays a role in distinguishing lines of talk and/or marking shifts between them.

Acknowledgments

The preparation of this chapter was supported by grants from the National Institutes of Health (NIH grant HD23388) and the John D. and Catherine T. MacArthur Foundation.

References

Bates, E. (1976). *Language in context: The acquisition of pragmatics*. New York: Academic Press.

Bates, E. (1990). Language about you and me: Pronominal reference and the emerging concept of self. In D. Cicchette and M. Beeghly (Eds.), *The self in transition: Infancy to childhood*. Chicago: University of Chicago Press.

Berman, R., & Slobin, D. (1986). *Coding manual: Temporality in discourse* (Rev. ed.). Cognitive Science Program, University of California, Berkeley.

Bruner, J. (1990). *Acts of meaning*. Cambridge, MA: Harvard University Press.

Cummins, J. (1981). The role of primary language development in promoting school success for language minority students. In *Schooling and language minority students: A theoretical framework*. Edited by the Office of Bilingual and Bicultural Education, California State Department of Education. Los Angeles: California State University.

Feagans, L., & Farran, D.C. (1981). How demonstrated comprehension can get muddled in production. *Developmental Psychology*, *17*, 718-727.

Feagans, L., & Short, E. (1984). Developmental differences in the comprehension and production of narratives by reading-disabled and normally achieving children. *Child Development*, *55*, 1727-1736.

Gee, J. (1989). Two styles of narrative construction and their linguistic and educational implications. *Discourse Processes*, *12*, 287-308.

Goodman, N. (1978). *Ways of worldmaking*. Indianapolis: Hackett Publishing Co.

Goodwin, M. H. (1982). Instigating: Storytelling as social process. *American Ethnologist*, *9*, 799-819.

Heath, S. B. (1983). *Ways with words: Language, life and work in communities and classrooms*. Cambridge: Cambridge University Press.

Hemphill, L., Picardi, N., & Tager-Flusberg, H. (1991). Narrative as an index of communicative competence in mildly mentally retarded children. *Applied Psycholinguistics, 12*, 263-279.

Hemphill, L., Wolf, D., & Camp, L. (1991). *Narrative abilities of children with normal and mildly retarded developmental patterns*. Paper presented at the Gatlinburg Conference on Mental Retardation, Coral Gables, FL.

Holt, T. (1990). *Thinking historically*. New York: The College Board.

Kendon, A. (1990). *Conducting interaction: Patterns of behavior in focused encounters*. Cambridge: Cambridge University Press.

Labov, W. (1972). *Language in the inner city*. Philadelphia, PA: University of Pennsylvania Press.

Linde, C. (1987). Explanatory systems in oral life stories. In D. Holland & N. Quinn (Eds.), *Cultural models in language and thought*. Cambridge: Cambridge University Press.

MacWhinney, B. (1991). *The CHILDES Project: Tools for Analyzing Talk*. Hillsdale NJ: Lawrence Erlbaum Associates.

Michaels, S. (1981). Sharing time: Children's narrative style and differential access to literacy. *Language and Society, 10*, 423-442.

Miller, P. J. (1982). *Wendy, Amy, and Beth: Learning language in South Baltimore*. Austin, TX: University of Texas Press.

Mishler, E. (1986). *Research interviewing: Context and narrative*. Cambridge, MA: Harvard University Press.

Nelson, K. (Ed.). (1988). *Narratives from the crib*. Cambridge, MA: Harvard University Press.

Nelson, K., & Gruendel, J. M. (1986). Children's scripts. In K. Nelson (Ed.), *Event knowledge: Structure and function in development*. Hillsdale, NJ: Lawrence Erlbaum Associates.

Ninio, A., & Wheeler, P. (1984). A manual for classifying verbal communicative acts in mother-infant interaction. In *Working papers in developmetal psychology, No.1*. Jerusalem: The Martin and Vivian Levin Center, Hebrew University.

Ochs, E. (1979). Transcription as theory. In E. Ochs & B. Schieffelin (Eds.), *Developmental pragmatics*. New York: Academic Press.

Ochs, E., & Schieffelin, B. (1984). Language acquisition and socialization: Three developmental stories and their implications. In R. A. Schweder & R. Levine

(Eds.), *Culture theory: Essays on mind, self, and emotion*. Cambridge: Cambridge University Press.

Pan, B., Rollins, P., & Snow, C. (1991). *Pragmatic development and its relationship to morphosyntactic indices of language.* Paper presented at the Society for Research in Child Development biennial meeting, Seattle, WA.

Peterson, C., & McCabe, A. (1983). *Developmental psycholinguistics: Three ways of looking at a child's narrative.* New York: Plenum.

Ricoeur, P. (1981). The narrative function. In P. Ricoeur, *Hermeneutics and the human sciences* (trans.: John B. Thompson). Cambridge: Cambridge University Press.

Riessman, C. (1990). *Divorce talk: Women and men make sense of personal relationships.* New Brunswick, NJ: Rutgers University Press.

Sachs, J. (1983). Talking about there and then: The emergence of displaced reference in parent-child discourse. In K. E. Nelson (Ed.), *Children's language* (Vol. 4) Hillsdale, NJ: Lawrence Erlbaum Associates.

Sulzby, E. (1981). *Kindergartners begin to read their own compositions: Beginning readers' developing knowledge about written language* (Final report to NCTE). Evanston, IL: Northwestern University Press.

Tager-Flusberg, H. (1985). Constraints on the representation of word meaning: Evidence from autistic and mentally retarded children. In S.A. Kuczaj & M. Barrett (Eds.), *The development of word meaning.* New York: Springer-Verlag.

Wolf, D. (in press). "There and then, intangible and internal": Narratives in early childhood. In B. Spodek (Ed.), *Research in early childhood education.* New York: The Free Press.

Appendix: CHAINS Output for Lines of Talk in the Pretend Play Narrative

```
CHAINS.EXE +t%tlk +t*CH% +t*EX% +f +c[c] +d1 +w7 pp5.cha
CHAINS.EXE (04-MAY-93) is conducting analyses on:
  ONLY speaker main tiers matching: *CH; *EX;
    and those speakers' ONLY dependent tiers matching: %TLK;
*****************************************
From file <pp5.cha> to file <pp5.cns>
Speaker markers:  1=*EX, 2=*CH
```

$chr	$fig	$gen	$nar	$tsk	line #
			1		14
			1		17
			1		21
			1		25
			2		28
			1		33
	2				36
				1	39
2					42
2					46
2					50
	1				54
			2		57
		2			61
		1			64
			2		67
			2		70
			2		73
	2				77
	2				77
	2				80
	2				84
	2			2	87
	2				91
	2				91
	2				95
	1				99
			2		102
			2		106
				2	110
				2	113
				1	117
				2	120
				2	123
				1	127
			2		130
2					134
			2		138
2					141

2					144
2					147
2					150
			2		155
			2		159
			2		163
			2		163
2					168
2					168
			2		172
			2		172
2					176
2					176
2					180
			2		183
			2		183
			2		187
2					190
2					193
2					193
2					196
2					199
2					202
2					205
2					208
				2	211
				2	216
	2				219
				2	222
				2	225
				1	229
				1	232
				1	232
		2			236
		2			236
				1	239
	2				242
	2				242
	2				245
	1				249
2					252
2					255
	2				259
	2				259
	2				262
	2				265
	2				268
	1				271
2					274
2					277
			2		280
			2		283

			2		286
			2		286
			2		289
			2		292
			2		295
			2		298
			2		298
			2		303
			2		306
			2		309
			2		312
			2	2	315
			1	1	318
	1				318
	2				322
	2				322
	2				325
	1				328
				2	331
				2	334
	2				337
	1				341
2					344
2					347
2					347
2					350
2					353
		2			357
		2		2	357
2					362
2					362
2					365
			2		369
			2		373
			2		376
			1		379
			2		382
			2		386
			2		386
			2		390
			2		393
			2		396
			2		399
			2		403
			2		406
			2		409
	2				412
	2				416
	1				419
2					422
			2		425

2					428
2					431
2					431
	1				437
			2		441
			2		444
			2		447
			2		450
			2		454
			2		457
			2		460

ALL speakers:
	$chr	$fig	$gen	$nar	$tsk
# chains	12	9	4	13	9
Avg leng	3.08	3.56	1.75	4.62	2.33
Std dev	1.85	2.59	0.43	4.60	1.76
Min leng	1	1	1	1	1
Max leng	8	9	2	15	6

Speakers *EX:
	$chr	$fig	$gen	$nar	$tsk
# chains	0	8	2	4	6
Avg leng	0.00	1.00	1.00	1.75	1.33
Std dev	0.00	0.00	0.00	1.30	0.75
Min leng	0	1	1	1	1
Max leng	0	1	1	4	3
SP Part.	0	7	2	3	5
SP/Total	0.00	0.25	0.29	0.12	0.38

Speakers *CH:
	$chr	$fig	$gen	$nar	$tsk
# chains	12	8	3	14	8
Avg leng	3.08	3.00	1.67	3.79	1.63
Std dev	1.85	2.29	0.47	3.78	0.48
Min leng	1	1	1	1	1
Max leng	8	8	2	14	2
SP Part.	12	8	3	13	7
SP/Total	1.00	0.75	0.71	0.88	0.62

11   Phonological Analysis of Child Speech

Nan Bernstein Ratner
The University of Maryland at College Park

In this chapter, you will learn the following skills:

- To derive the frequency with which different English speech sounds appear in the vocalizations of children at early stages of language development using PHONFREQ.

- To compare this distribution with that seen in parental speech to children by modifying the PHONFREQ alphabet files to perform analyses of non-phonetically coded tiers.

- To compare children's early pronunciation attempts with adult target forms using the MODREP utility.

To replicate the analyses and do the exercises, you will need the data in the **Ratner** and **Adami** directories.

11.1. Introduction

How do children acquire the sound system of a language? Speech sound acquisition is a gradual and complex process, as are other aspects of communicative development. In this chapter, I ask the following questions: Is there continuity between infant babbling and the sounds used in early language efforts? Are sounds that are used more frequently in child-directed speech learned earlier than those that are used less frequently? Do children selectively choose their initial vocabulary on the basis of sounds that they are able to produce? How variable are early speech attempts? I will demonstrate the utility of CLAN programs and computerized language transcripts in answering these questions.

11.1.1. Research Questions

In this chapter, I use samples of young children's prelinguistic verbalizations and early speech to suggest ways in which the child's phonological system matures. First, I ask the following questions:

1. What phonemes are most frequently and least frequently found in the early meaningful speech of children? Stoel-Gammon (1985) and others (e.g., Vihman, Macken, Miller, Simmons, & Miller, 1985; Winitz & Irwin, 1958) suggested that the child's early sound inventory is rather limited, comprised primarily of stops (e.g., [b,p,d,t,g,k]), nasals ([m] and [n], though not [ŋ]), and glides [w,y]. Voiced stops predominate in initial position in early words; voiceless stops predominate in final position. Fricatives appear later, usually in final position before other positions (Farwell, 1977), with voiceless fricatives emerging before voiced ones.

2. Is there continuity in the phonetic repertoire between late babbling and early intentional speech? The majority of research suggests that the sound and syllable shape preferences just described are characteristic of babbling, as well as early word productions. In this sense, there appears to be **continuity** between babbling and speech development. Continuity suggests that acquisition of speech skills may well be constrained by maturation of the motor system.

3. How does the phonetic repertoire expand as the child moves from single-word utterances to early multiword speech? Most prior studies of children's early phonological tendencies have concentrated on a given child's patterns of early word formation, and have not followed the child's transition from babbling to early lexical and later multiword productions.

4. Do children's early phonetic tendencies reflect, in part, the frequency characteristics of the input to which they are exposed? While noting somewhat uniform cross-linguistic patterns of babbling, Locke (1983) has commented that there are also some similarities between early phonetic inventories and general frequency tendencies of adult conversational speech. That is, to some small extent, items that are easily acquired by children are frequent both in adult speech and across the languages of the world, while sounds that emerge later in development are less frequently represented.

In this chapter, I attempt to answer these questions by analyzing both child and input speech for a sample of nine infant girls who range from 13-25 months. A second set of questions about children's phonetic development is investigated later in this chapter, using a different database and additional CLAN programs.

11.1.2. Ways of Studying Phonological Acquisition in Children

Studies of children's speech sound acquisition tend to fall into two major classes: (a) large sample cross-sectional studies to determine the usual ages at which accurate production of individual phonemic segments is mastered (e.g., Bird, Bernthal, Freilinger, Hand, & Bosma-Smit, 1990; Poole, 1934; Prather, Hedrick, & Kern, 1975; Templin, 1957); and (b) smaller investigations of the longitudinal development of the phonological tendencies of individual children or small groups of children (e.g., Ferguson & Farwell, 1975; Smith, 1973; Ingram, 1976; Leonard, Newhoff, & Mesalam, 1980; Menn, 1971; Stoel-Gammon, 1985). Cross-sectional studies provide a picture of the general, normative trends in sound production and word formation strategies which can be used to discriminate normal from delayed or deviant speech development and develop hypotheses about factors that appear to govern universal patterns in phonological development (Locke, 1983). Such studies, however, are limited in their ability to probe the actual evolution of phonological ability in individual children. The processes by which children build their phonological systems and individual variation in the acquisition process are easily masked when the mean performance of large groups is appraised.

It has long been conventional for the two types of study to diverge in their methodology as well. Studies of individuals or small groups are usually observational, taking as their data spontaneous conversation. Conversely, the logistics of sampling the spontaneous speech of large numbers of children have forced many large-scale studies to rely on the elicitation of a small corpus of carefully selected items. For example, the children may be asked to label a series of pictured objects. Many prior studies were often forced to narrowly sample children's spontaneous productions because of the difficulty of manually tabulating patterns of sound usage prior to computerized transcript analysis. Thus, Stoel-Gammon (1985), for example, sampled a maximum of 50 word attempts from each of her study subjects. As we discuss, the development of uniform keyboard transcription systems (such as UNIBET) and of CLAN programs to analyze the phonetic characteristics of child speech allow us to sample larger populations of children engaging in naturalistic conversational interactions over time by greatly facilitating the analysis of their samples.

Finally, the study of children's phonological acquisition, unlike other aspects of their linguistic development, has not traditionally weighed the potential role played by interactive factors. Many of the other chapters in this book demonstrate the ongoing challenge of identifying the possible environmental influences on child language development, such as frequency of particular features in the language addressed to children, and parental responses to children's communicative attempts. CLAN programs have opened up new opportunities in the critical evaluation of bi-directional influences on phonological development by their specific abilities to track multiple conversational participants and examine both frequency and contingency patterns that may be observed in naturalistic interactions between adults and language-learning children.

11.1.3. Concepts Explored in this Chapter

Unlike the other chapters in this book, which have chosen a single major research question and demonstrate the use of CLAN programs in answering it, this chapter illustrates the use of two distinct programs developed specifically for phonological analysis (PHONFREQ and MODREP) and demonstrate their applicability to different types of research questions. Additionally, coding and analytical considerations that arise specifically when examining children's phonological development are addressed.

We first address important CHAT and CLAN conventions applicable to phonetic coding and analysis. Next, the use of PHONFREQ in plotting normal phonological development in a group of nine normally developing young children will be demonstrated, using minimally coded CHAT transcripts. We compare their patterns of sound production with those observed in their mothers' speech to them, and discuss whether or not input frequency appears to play a strong role in determining children's acquisition of phonemic segments. Following this, a more fully coded sample of speech from a child whose phonological development appears delayed are analyzed, and his patterns of production are compared to those seen in the larger sample of normally developing children. The use of the MODREP program to observe variability in children's attempts to meet the adult model is demonstrated. Finally, I conclude by suggesting exercises and projects that you may wish to try using the PHONFREQ and MODREP programs.

11.2. Preliminaries to Phonological Analysis in CLAN

11.2.1. The Need for Phonetic Coding of Transcripts

Students of child language development quickly appreciate the fact that early language differs from the ambient adult model not only in its syntax, vocabulary, and discourse characteristics, but in its phonological accuracy. Many CHILDES transcripts suggest this fact when they periodically note child utterances such as the following:

```
*CHI:   I do-'nt wanna [: want to] look in a badroom [*].
%flo:   I don't wanna look in a badroom.
%err:   a /A/ -> the /DA/; badroom /b&drUm/ -> bathroom /b&TrUm/
```
(adapted from MacWhinney, 1991, p. 57)

The degree to which children's phonological "errors" are coded is to some degree dependent upon the original intended use of the database. For example, Brown's Adam transcripts note when Adam uses what appear to be "empty" syllables to which no word or morpheme can be unambiguously assigned. Cases in which the child's pronunciation complicates interpretation of the structure or meaning of the message are likely to be handled differently from cases in which no listener ambiguity results, as in the case of a child who says "wocket" for *rocket*, or "bwue" for *blue*. In fact, relatively few transcripts currently within the CHILDES archive contain either phonetic tiers or uniform information about children's articulatory realizations of each item in their output.

11.2.2. Deciding How to Code Phonetic Information

In coding a child's productions to "recapture" their pronunciation, a researcher has at least two options. The first is to include the information on the main tier; the second is to establish a separate tier to represent the phonetic characteristics of the child's actual utterance. As Edwards (1989) and Peters, Fahn, Glover, Harley, Sawyer, and Shimura (1991) pointed out, the second option is by far the most desirable in terms of ease of transcript readability and analysis.

Phonological Analyses

In establishing a **%pho** tier for utterances, researchers must be careful to utilize a standard coding system that allows the researcher to unambiguously assign a pronunciation to the child's output. Historically, this task was resolved by the use of mutually agreed-upon systems, such as the International Phonetic Alphabet (or IPA). IPA and other traditional transcription systems, however, contain symbols not found on conventional computer keyboards, such as [ð] and [ʃ] . Thus, in recent years, a keyboard-based phonetic alphabet (UNIBET) has been developed. Table 11.1 displays the UNIBET symbols used to indicate phonetic segments and prosodic information in the CHAT system.

11.3. Using CLAN to Examine Phonetic Characteristics of Infant and Child-Directed Speech

11.3.1. The Transcript Data

For this study, I use a sample of nine infant girls who were observed in free-play conversation with their mothers. These children's data are from Bernstein (1982) and are part of the CHILDES English corpora database (MacWhinney, 1991). Three children ranged from 13 to 18 months at first taping and were considered preverbal by their parents and the investigator. Their parents could not identify any recognizable words in their daughters' vocal attempts (with the exception of *mama* for one child). Three children (who ranged from 13 to 20 months at first taping) communicated using single-word utterances or output that consisted of babble or jargon in which only a single word attempt could be identified. Their expressive vocabularies ranged from approximately 25 to 100 words, according to parental and observer estimate. Finally, a third group of three girls (who were between 17 and 21 months of age at first observation) communicated primarily using two- to three-word utterances.

Each child was observed at play with her mother three times at 6-week intervals. Tapings were conducted in a sound proof playroom in a university setting and were recorded using high fidelity equipment. Transcripts of both the children's and mothers' conversations were typed, then scanned by computer and formatted according to CHAT conventions. Because the data were originally gathered to examine patterns of maternal input to language learners, many of whom had not yet begun to use recognizable English words, the children's data were not transcribed in standard orthography or on multiple tiers. Rather, a decision was made to

Table 11.1: UNIBET transcription symbols (from MacWhinney, 1991).

IPA –> ASCII translations for English

Consonants			
ASCII	IPA Symbol	IPA Name	Example Word(s)
p	p	p	*p*it
b	b	b	*b*it
m	m	m	*m*itt
t	t	t	*t*ip
d	d	d	*d*ip
n	n	n	*n*ip
k	k	k	pi*ck*
g	g	g	pi*g*
N	ŋ	eng	pi*ng*
f	f	f	*f*ew
v	v	v	*v*iew
T	θ	theta	e*th*er
D	ð	eth	ei*th*er
s	s	s	*s*ue
z	z	z	*z*oo
S	ʃ	esh	*sh*oe
Z	ʒ	yogh	plea*s*ure
tS	tʃ	t-esh	ca*tch*
dZ	dʒ	d-yogh	*j*udge
h	h	h	*h*op
w	w	w	*w*itch
W	ʍ	inverted w	*wh*ich
r	r	r	*r*ip
l	l	l	*l*ip
j	j	j	*y*ip

Monophthongs			
ASCII	IPA Symbol	IPA Name	Example Word(s)
i	i	i	h*ee*d, b*ea*t
I	ɪ	iota	h*i*d, b*i*t
e	e	e	h*ay*ed, b*ai*t
E	ɛ	epsilon	h*ea*d, b*e*t
&	æ	ash	h*a*d, b*a*t
u	u	u	wh*o*'d, b*oo*t
U	ʊ	closed omega	h*oo*d, f*oo*t
o	o	o	h*oe*d, b*oa*t (GA)
O	ɔ	open o	h*aw*ed, b*ough*t (GA) h*oar*d (RP)
A	ʌ	inverted v	b*u*d, b*u*t
a	a	a	m*a*, h*o*d, h*o*t(GA) h*ar*d (RP)
3	ɜ	reversed epsilon	h*er*d (RP)
6	ə	schwa	*a*bove
Q	ɑ	ao	h*o*d (RP)

Table 11.1 (*continued*): UNIBET transcription symbols (from MacWhinney, 1991).

Diphthongs		
ASCII	IPA Symbols	Example Word(s)
ai	ai	h*i* de, b*i* te
au	au	h*ow* dy, b*ou* t
oi	oi	ah*oy*, b*oy*
6U	əo	h*o* ed (RP)

R Sounds		
ASCII	IPA Symbols	Example Word(s)
ir	ir	h*ere* (GA)
er	er	h*are* (GA)
ar	ar	h*ar* d (GA)
or	or	h*oar* d (GA)
ur	ur	m*oo* r (GA)
3r	ɜr	h*er* d, h*ur* t (GA)
i6	iə	h*ere* (RP)
e6	eə	h*are* (GA)
u6	uə	m*oo* r (RP)

Suprasegmentals, etc.		
ASCII	IPA Symbols	Meaning
@n		nth alignment point
$		syllable boundary
#		morpheme boundary
##		word boundary
|		rhythmic juncture
IH		hesitation
?	ʔ	glottal stop
"		pitch accent (primary)
'		heavy (secondary)
!		emphatic
.		falling terminal
?		rising terminal
-		continuation terminal
:		long, geminate
_		ligature
/ /		phonemic brackets
[ ]		phonetic brackets
~		comments

332   Chapter 11

represent all of the children's verbalizations in broad UNIBET transcription only, on the main (*CHI) tier. **This is not a typical method of CHAT transcription and would not be recommended for current data transcription.**

The **Ratner** directory contains 3 files for each of the nine children, one for each observation, for a total of 27 files. For example, it contains records for Alice1.cha, Alice2.cha and Alice3.cha. We will use an asterisk to indicate where the session number appears. The other eight children are: Amelia*.cha, Anne*.cha, Cindy*.cha, Dale*.cha, Gail*.cha, Kay*.cha, Lena*.cha, and Marie*.cha.

11.3.2. Using CLAN to Answer the Research Questions

In the following sections I provide an overview of the CLAN programs that can be used to answer our research questions. The use of **include** and **alphabet** files to tailor search procedures is also discussed, along with procedures for grouping data files to permit certain kinds of analyses.

The PHONFREQ program

PHONFREQ is specifically designed to calculate the frequency of UNIBET symbols used on the **%pho** tier. It searches for word-initial phonemes, word-final phonemes, and those phonemes lying between them (medial or "other" phonemes). It uses as its reference point spaces or recognized delimiters between entries on the **%pho** tier. Because UNIBET contains characters that differ only in case, such searches must be case-sensitive (i.e., upper-case *U* represents the vowel in *book*; lower-case *u* represents the vowel in *boot*; additional pairs are *s/S*, *d/D*, *e/E*, *i/I*, *n/N*, *o/O*, and *t/T*.) In PHONFREQ, UNIBET searches are case-sensitive by default.

We recommend that transcripts and output be carefully reviewed to insure that easily made mistakes in case have been avoided during data entry. For example, it is tempting to begin entries on the **%pho** tier with capital letters, in parallel with their glosses on the *CHI tier. An example of incorrect transcription would be:

```
*CHI:   Suzi took me.
%pho:   Suzi tUk  mi
```

Note, however, that placing a capital S on the **%pho** tier here implies that the child pronounced the name as *shoosie*, because a capital S in UNIBET represents the phoneme / ʃ /. In general, it will be valuable to initially examine output from the PHONFREQ program to minimally assure that all of the listed phonemes are indeed UNIBET symbols. If the output provides a frequency for B, Q, or K, for example, there has been an error either in data entry or in the PHONFREQ command sequence, since these capitalized letters are not UNIBET symbols for English.

In coding the **%pho** tier, researchers have the option of using the phonemic brackets / /, phonetic brackets [ ], or no brackets to enclose transcription. While the use of brackets brings the **%pho** tier closer to actual hand transcription conventions, it sometimes complicates PHONFREQ and other CLAN searches. If you decide not to use brackets, you may wish to note this information in an **@Warning** header for future users' information.

Alphabet Files

Although UNIBET contains fewer digraph symbols than IPA, there are still some phonemes that are coded by more than one letter in UNIBET. Examples are all of the vowel diphthongs, and the consonants [tS] (as in *church*), and [dZ] (as in *judge*). PHONFREQ assumes a character-by-character search unless told to treat certain sequences of characters as units. These exceptions should be listed in a file that the user creates, named **alphabet**. Thus, a PHONFREQ search run on UNIBET-coded English will automatically seek to reference an alphabet file that should contain the strings listed in Table 11.2, as well as any other diphthongs representative of the dialect or language under analysis. Alphabet files are created and governed by the same procedures used in constructing include files. They are ASCII files that contain one search string per line followed by a carriage return. The PHONFREQ program assumes that you have constructed such an alphabet file and will warn you if it cannot find one. As I discuss later, the use of alphabet files also allows us to perform somewhat crude grapheme-phoneme correspondences on CHAT files not coded in UNIBET (i.e., lacking a **%pho** tier), as well as to tailor searches to investigate other questions. For example, if we are interested in children's acquisition of consonant clusters, we can develop an alphabet file that contains lists of permissible cluster sequences in English (i.e., *st*, *Tr*, pl*, *ft, etc.), and PHONFREQ will produce frequency counts for these clusters.

334   Chapter 11

Table 11.2: An alphabet file for a PHONFREQ analysis on UNIBET-coded English.

tS
dZ
ai
au
oi
ei

A Final Word About Transcription

Recall that PHONFREQ searches for initial, medial, and final phonemes on a UNIBET-coded tier. This may appear to be rather clean-cut and unambiguous. However, recall that one of our study groups is comprised of preverbal children. Their output consists of strings that, by definition, cannot be related to adult lexical items. Typical output from such children can look like the following:

    *CHI: loyododo

The audiotaped record of this utterance shows it to be pronounced in a single breath, with unified intonation contour, and no apparent silences between syllables. So, we should consider it to be a single vocalization for PHONFREQ purposes. Or should we? An adult (or competent child) utterance, such as "What's the matter?", fits the same criteria. Yet we know that it is comprised of three separate target words.

Because we cannot know what the preverbal child intended as her minimal unit of production, we have chosen to segment such vocalizations syllabically, as shown below, treating each syllable as a "word":

    *CHI: lo yo do do

(An alternative coding option is to use the $ symbol to indicate syllabic boundaries, as in *loyodo$do*.) This decision to tally individual syllabic segments is not without its problems. As the children mature, we are sometimes able to isolate repetitive syllable strings that do seem to "hang together." That is, a child may say, /yo lo do do/, then /mi no do do/, and /sa mi do do/, and so on. In coding the

Ratner corpus, when such a pattern of [do do] could be easily seen, a post-hoc decision was made to recode [do do] as [dodo].

Both accurately identifying and segmenting preverbal phonetic strings is extremely difficult and subject to large interexaminer variability. We strongly suggest that any student who wishes to pursue this aspect of child language development consult the challenging findings of Stockman, Woods, and Tishman (1981) and others who have warned about the inherent transcription difficulties of examining this stage of phonological acquisition.

11.3.3. Running the PHONFREQ Program

Question 1: What is the phoneme distribution in children's early meaningful speech?

Question 2: Is there continuity in the phonetic repertoire between late babbling and early intentional speech?

Question 3: How does the phonetic repertoire expand as the child moves from single word utterances to early multiword speech?

Questions 1 through 3 are closely related and propose to examine phonological growth over the course of the children's development. The children whose files we will use span a particular range of ages; they were also assigned to three discrete linguistic stages (preverbal, one-word, and multiword), based on the characteristics of their verbalizations with their mothers. This information is contained in the **ØØreadme.doc** portion of the Ratner corpus, and in Bernstein (1982) and Bernstein Ratner (1984a, 1984b), but is not specified in the file names themselves, which were historically organized by simple taping order (as in the example with alice1, alice2, and alice3). Using the information in these sources, Table 11.3 groups the files into three discrete age groups: transcripts obtained when the subject child was **preverbal**, those obtained from children at the **one-word** stage of language development, and those obtained from children who were beginning to produce **multiword** speech.

When doing retrospective data analyses of such a longitudinal and cross-sectional data sample (of which there are many in CHILDES), we have found it easiest to develop our hypotheses, and copy files to new subdirectories that capture the variable which interests us. Thus, if we wish to follow the vocalizations of

336   Chapter 11

Table 11.3: The children's files grouped by language age.

Prelinguistic	One-Word	Multiword
Amelia1.cha	Alice1.cha	Anne2.cha
Amelia2.cha	Alice2.cha	Anne3.cha
Dale1.cha	Alice3.cha	Cindy3.cha
Kay1.cha	Amelia3.cha	Dale3.cha
Kay2.cha	Anne1.cha	Gail1.cha
	Cindy1.cha	Gail2.cha
	Cindy2.cha	Gail3.cha
	Dale2.cha	Lena1.cha
	Kay3.cha	Lena2.cha
	Marie1.cha	Lena3.cha
	Marie2.cha	Marie3.cha

prelinguistic infants, we might establish subdirectories called **preverb**, **1word**, and **mword** under the **Ratner** directory and copy all relevant files to them. This procedure enables the following command to group such files and produce group statistics on the phonetic output of preverbal children:

phonfreq   +b*CHI   +u   preverb*.cha

+b*CHI	Analyze the child's speaker tier only
+u	Merge all input files into a combined analysis
preverb*.cha	Analyze all files ending in **.cha** in the **preverb** subdirectory

Command Box 11.1

This command tells PHONFREQ to poll the initial, medial, and final phoneme frequencies for all children whose files reside in the **preverb** directory and combine them to provide a group profile. If we wanted to see the individual profiles of the children within that language directory, we would omit the +u option. PHONFREQ automatically assumes that the dependent tier to search is the **%pho** tier (unless specified differently), and will assume the +k case-sensitivity option, so that neither needs to be included in the PHONFREQ command. In our case, however, we must specify the *CHI tier, using the +b option, because that is where the UNIBET coding is to be found. We must emphasize that this is not a recommended coding scheme for newly collected data. The output of this command is shown in Table 11.4.

Notice that, because PHONFREQ searches each character on the child's main tier, it tallies consonants and vowels, as well as suprasegmental markers indicating juncture, lengthening, and so on (i.e., : | #). It will also tally the Ø symbols, which code lack of verbal response during the child's turn. If we wish to narrow the focus of our research to the development of consonants, we may use the +/-s command to limit the characters which PHONFREQ will tally. To do this, we construct an ASCII file containing the vowels and suprasegmental markers we wish to ignore. The contents of a sample file, called **vowels**, is shown below:

```
ai      Ø       A       a
au      3       E       e
aw      6       I       i
ei      &       O       o
oi      ou      :       U
u       #       |       .
?       !       [       ]
/
```

Note that the actual **vowels** file must be an ASCII file in which each symbol is placed on a single line followed by a carriage return. Finally, we have also taken this opportunity to exclude boundary and punctuation markers (e.g., . ? ! / []).

Only versions of PHONFREQ distributed after September 1992 will accept the +/-s option. It is possible to check the version date of each CLAN program by using the +v option. For example, to determine the recency of the PHONFREQ program that you are using, you would type **phonfreq +v**.

Table 11.4: The distribution of sounds in the output of late preverbal children's speech.

202	&	initial =	48,	final =	103,	other =	51
103	0	initial =	103,	final =	0,	other =	0
2	3	initial =	0,	final =	2,	other =	0
59	6	initial =	19,	final =	35,	other =	5
36	:	initial =	0,	final =	30,	other =	6
374	A	initial =	144,	final =	132,	other =	98
45	E	initial =	9,	final =	26,	other =	10
36	I	initial =	1,	final =	25,	other =	10
7	O	initial =	3,	final =	2,	other =	2
7	S	initial =	4,	final =	2,	other =	1
1	T	initial =	1,	final =	0,	other =	0
14	U	initial =	6,	final =	5,	other =	3
1	W	initial =	1,	final =	0,	other =	0
87	a	initial =	36,	final =	32,	other =	19
24	ai	initial =	13,	final =	6,	other =	5
31	au	initial =	4,	final =	22,	other =	5
41	b	initial =	27,	final =	2,	other =	12
282	d	initial =	231,	final =	17,	other =	34
40	e	initial =	9,	final =	20,	other =	11
8	ei	initial =	3,	final =	2,	other =	3
3	f	initial =	2,	final =	0,	other =	1
32	g	initial =	26,	final =	3,	other =	3
115	h	initial =	105,	final =	2,	other =	8
84	i	initial =	20,	final =	57,	other =	7
140	j	initial =	99,	final =	0,	other =	41
47	k	initial =	7,	final =	34,	other =	6
18	l	initial =	9,	final =	0,	other =	9
30	m	initial =	9,	final =	16,	other =	5
99	n	initial =	14,	final =	75,	other =	10
110	o	initial =	81,	final =	23,	other =	6
3	oi	initial =	1,	final =	1,	other =	1
15	p	initial =	5,	final =	7,	other =	3
1	r	initial =	1,	final =	0,	other =	0
12	s	initial =	4,	final =	6,	other =	2
56	t	initial =	8,	final =	37,	other =	11
25	u	initial =	2,	final =	17,	other =	6
74	w	initial =	54,	final =	0,	other =	20
1	|	initial =	0,	final =	0,	other =	1

The PHONFREQ analysis can then be repeated, using the following command sequence:

phonfreq   +b*CHI   +u   –s@vowels   preverb*.cha   >   kidphons.prv

+b*CHI	Analyze the child's speaker tier only
+u	Merge all input files into a combined analysis
–s@vowels	Exclude all the items from the file **vowels**
preverb*.cha	Analyze all files ending in **.cha** in the **preverb** subdirectory
> kidphons.prv	Redirect the output to the file **kidphons.prv**

Command Box 11.2

The output from this command is shown in Table 11.5. Notice the advantage which is gained when the specific scope of the research question is used to narrow the data analysis. This set of data is much easier to read and analyze.

11.4. Does Adult Input Shape the Early Phonetic Inventory? Adapting PHONFREQ to Nonphonetically Transcribed Data

Question 4: Do children's early phonetic tendencies reflect, in part, the frequency characteristics of the input to which they are exposed?

11.4.1. Problems in Determining Adult Phonetic Inventories From CHAT Transcripts

Unfortunately, no corpora in the CHILDES archive provide UNIBET glosses for the conversation of adult speakers. This is unfortunate for two reasons. The first is that, in English, there is very poor correspondence between a word's spelling and its pronunciation, which makes a PHONFREQ analysis of an adult speaker's main tier virtually useless. The second is that adult conversational speech often deletes sounds or changes their characteristics, though this is rarely represented in written transcripts (Bernstein Ratner, 1984; Cole & Jakimik, 1980). Thus, an utterance such as "What are you doing?" may actually have been pronounced "Whatchya doin'?". Careful listening is required to even remotely code the accuracy of targets in conversational speech and few transcripts offer this degree of precision.

Table 11.5: The results of a PHONFREQ analysis that excludes vowels and suprasegmental markers.

```
  7 S   initial =   4, final =  2, other =  1
  1 T   initial =   1, final =  0, other =  0
  1 W   initial =   1, final =  0, other =  0
 41 b   initial =  27, final =  2, other = 12
282 d   initial = 231, final = 17, other = 34
  3 f   initial =   2, final =  0, other =  1
 32 g   initial =  26, final =  3, other =  3
115 h   initial = 105, final =  2, other =  8
140 j   initial =  99, final =  0, other = 41
 47 k   initial =   7, final = 34, other =  6
 18 l   initial =   9, final =  0, other =  9
 30 m   initial =   9, final = 16, other =  5
 99 n   initial =  14, final = 75, other = 10
 15 p   initial =   5, final =  7, other =  3
  1 r   initial =   1, final =  0, other =  0
 12 s   initial =   4, final =  6, other =  2
 56 t   initial =   8, final = 37, other = 11
 74 w   initial =  54, final =  0, other = 20
```

11.4.2. Using Specially Constructed Alphabet Files to Develop Grapheme-Phoneme Correspondences for Phonetic Searches on Orthographic Strings

In this section, I describe how changing the contents of the alphabet file can permit a crude phonetic analysis of maternal speech on the main tier. To do this, we must first ask ourselves if there are relatively systematic correspondences between certain letter sequences and pronunciation in English. A first approximation of such correspondences is shown in Table 11.6.

In this file, I list doubled consonants, such as the *bb* in *rabbit*, because when consonants are doubled, only one is articulated, and we do not want to over-represent medial *b*, for instance. Likewise, we know that segments such as *th*, *ph*, *sh*, and so on have predictable pronunciations. While this particular alphabet file will bring us closer to an approximation of the frequency with which certain sounds appear in maternal speech, it is not without its problems. Vowels in general present such a dizzying array of spelling potentials that we will not consider them in our analysis. In addition, final *s* is often pronounced as /z/ (e.g., *cries*, *hers*); *–ed* is often pronounced as /t/ (e.g., *kissed*). It is useful to perform a FREQ analysis of words ending in *s* and *d* to determine their actual pronunciation (see Exercise 11.9.2). But what about *laugh* and *high*? Or *listen* and *sister*? Clearly,

Table 11.6: A grapheme-phoneme correspondence file that can be used as an alphabet file to measure sounds distribution in non-phonetically coded text.

this	ca	uge	kn	ff
that	co	age	ng	gg
tho	cu	geo	x	ll
the	chr	gem	qu	mm
th	ce	gen	wh	nn
ff	ci	ger	ck	pp
ph	cy	gia	kk	rr
ough	ch	gira	cc	ss
sh	tch	gin	bb	tt
sure	dg	gn	dd	sion
tio				

this kind of search is subject to a certain degree of error. As I discuss, it is likely that the level of error is not that great and will still permit appraisal of the relative frequency with which certain sounds are used in conversation. As in the earlier analysis, if we choose to exclude vowels, the data are somewhat easier to evaluate. This phoneme-grapheme alphabet file represents an unconventional and creative use of alphabet files, which should be stable lists of diphthongs and digraph phonetic symbols in a given language. After we replace the contents of our conventional alphabet file with the items in Table 11.6, the following command will generate output such as that found in Table 11.7:

phonfreq +b*MOT +u +k –s@vowels preverb*.cha > momphons.prv

+b*CHI	Analyze the child's speaker tier only
+u	Merge all input files into a combined analysis
+k	Treat upper and lower case as the same
–s@vowels	Exclude all the items from the file **vowels**
preverb*.cha	Analyze all files ending in **.cha** in the **preverb** subdirectory
> momphons.prv	Redirect the output to the file **momphons.prv**

Command Box 11.3

Table 11.7: The results of the PHONFREQ analysis of the mothers' speech as listed in Command Box 11.3 (continued on the next page).

```
   4   $     initial =   0,  final =   0,  other =    4
 613   '     initial =   0,  final =  59,  other =  554
 201   +     initial =  93,  final =   0,  other =  108
   4   -     initial =   3,  final =   1,  other =    0
   2   @     initial =   0,  final =   0,  other =    2
 335   b     initial = 243,  final =   3,  other =   89
  31   bl    initial =  30,  final =   0,  other =    1
  26   br    initial =  21,  final =   0,  other =    5
 418   c     initial = 202,  final =   0,  other =  216
 693   d     initial = 375,  final = 183,  other =  135
  15   dr    initial =  15,  final =   0,  other =    0
 233   f     initial = 105,  final =  90,  other =   38
  26   fl    initial =  22,  final =   0,  other =    4
   3   fr    initial =   3,  final =   0,  other =    0
 573   g     initial = 200,  final = 136,  other =  237
   3   gr    initial =   2,  final =   0,  other =    1
2242   h     initial = 502,  final = 349,  other = 1391
  18   j     initial =  17,  final =   0,  other =    1
 680   k     initial = 126,  final = 318,  other =  236
   4   kr    initial =   4,  final =   0,  other =    0
 693   l     initial = 260,  final = 126,  other =  307
 381   m     initial = 126,  final = 100,  other =  155
```

Table 11.7: The results of the PHONFREQ analysis of the mothers' speech as listed in Command Box 11.3 (continued from previous page).

```
1245   n    initial =  127,   final =  323,   other = 795
 325   p    initial =  180,   final =   46,   other =  99
  15   pl   initial =   12,   final =    0,   other =   3
  11   pr   initial =   11,   final =    0,   other =   0
   2   q    initial =    1,   final =    0,   other =   1
 928   r    initial =   71,   final =  265,   other = 592
1304   s    initial =  226,   final =  901,   other = 177
   1   sk   initial =    0,   final =    0,   other =   1
  18   sl   initial =   18,   final =    0,   other =   0
  10   sm   initial =   10,   final =    0,   other =   0
  23   sn   initial =    9,   final =    0,   other =  14
   3   sp   initial =    3,   final =    0,   other =   0
  33   st   initial =   14,   final =   13,   other =   6
   3   sw   initial =    3,   final =    0,   other =   0
2366   t    initial = 1042,   final =  759,   other = 565
   7   tr   initial =    7,   final =    0,   other =   0
  17   tw   initial =   17,   final =    0,   other =   0
  88   v    initial =    7,   final =    0,   other =  81
 675   w    initial =  523,   final =   65,   other =  87
  15   x    initial =    0,   final =   12,   other =   3
 849   y    initial =  395,   final =  332,   other = 122
  13   z    initial =    9,   final =    0,   other =   4
```

Note that, because we are asking PHONFREQ to search non-UNIBET symbols, we inserted the +k option. This option tells the program to *ignore* case when performing its tallies, which is fine for searching standard orthographic transcription, where *s* and *S* mean the same thing. We also use the +b option rather than +t option because we are using PHONFREQ to search a main tier, rather than a dependent %pho tier. Finally, because we are searching an orthographically coded main tier, we will obtain frequencies for certain punctuation and morphemicization markers (e.g., +, −, and @) that are irrelevant to the phonological analysis. These should be ignored.

After re-assigning phonetic identities to the irregular spellings in our alphabet file (for example, tallies of *ph*, *ff* and *gh are added to tallies of [f]), we can then add the phonetic inventory counts from the PHONFREQ analyses to arrive at our estimation of the relative frequency with which certain sounds appear in maternal speech to preverbal children. In this process, it will be useful to remember that tallies of final [w] and [y], for example, are orthographic anomalies that do not represent the use of those sounds in conversation, as they are not pronounced in final position.

344   Chapter 11

In order to answer our original set of questions, it is now necessary to repeat our PHONFREQ searches of the children's output and of the mothers' speech for the **1word** and **mword** groups. Our commands to do these additional analyses would be:

```
phonfreq +b*CHI +u -s@vowels 1word\*.cha > kidphons.1wd
phonfreq +b*CHI +u -s@vowels combo\*.cha > kidphons.mwd
```

For these analyses, we would use our original small alphabet file (from Table 11.2), which assumes a search of phonetically coded tiers. We would follow these with the following commands, using the second, larger alphabet file (from Table 11.6):

```
phonfreq +b*MOT +u +k -s@vowels 1word\*.cha > momphons.1wd
phonfreq +b*MOT +u +k -s@vowels combo\*.cha > momphons.mwd
```

11.5. Results of Our PHONFREQ Analyses

There are a number of ways in which the data may be analyzed. For our discussion, we have calculated the frequency with which consonants appear as a total of all consonants observed in the output of our adult and child speakers. The frequency of vowel usage will not be discussed. To reduce phonetic data, researchers may establish classes of sound distribution for comparative purposes, to appraise general patterns of development (Smith, 1988). Figure 11.1 displays patterns of sound usage by *consonantal place of articulation* for the children, as well as two samples of adult speech. The first is the maternal input to the children in our study, which was analyzed using the grapheme-phoneme correspondence alphabet file and PHONFREQ; the other is a major study of the phonetic tendencies of adults engaged in conversation with other adults (Mines, Hanson, & Shoup, 1978).

As shown in Figure 11.1, bilabials appear to be roughly as frequent in preverbal speech as in adult speech or maternal input; their usage, however, jumps to somewhat disproportionate levels in the speech of children at the one-word stage and the speech of children learning to combine words. Smith (1988) suggested that 1-year-old children prefer to use bilabial sounds more frequently (at roughly a 30% rate) than somewhat older children, whose rate approximates 22%, or adults, whose rate of bilabial articulation is approximately 15%. Our current data suggest that it is the initial stages of language learning that are characterized by a bilabial

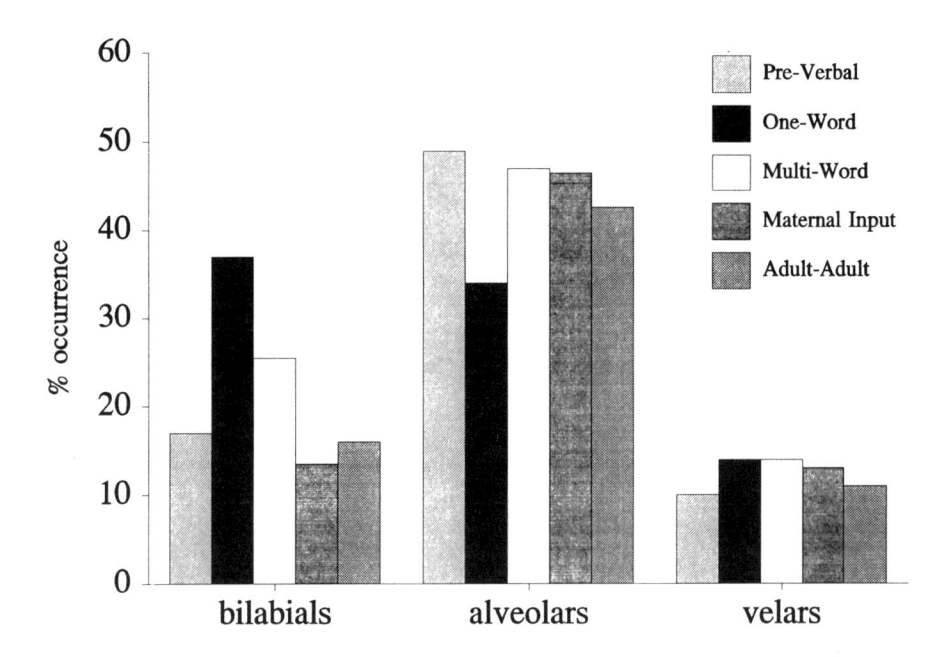

Figure 11.1: Changes in place of articulation across language groups.

preference. In fact, as I discuss in the next section, the children produce bilabial targets in quantities that are disproportionate to the input they hear.

At the one-word stage, this tendency appears to minimize the use of alveolar sounds, which are less frequent in the speech of one-worders than in any other speaker group. That is, there appears to be a labial-alveolar "tradeoff" for children at the one-word stage. The use of velar sounds does not appear to change markedly from the child speech samples to the adult samples we analyzed. Smith (1988) suggests from his data that English-speaking infants must "overcome a phonetic tendency to produce bilabials more frequently than adult speakers of English generally employ them" (p. 88). Although the specific stage of bilabial preference we note here does not exactly confirm Smith's findings, it is clear that young language users display phonemic tendencies that must be modified in order to accommodate more general patterns of sound usage in the English language.

Figure 11.2 displays our information in a different way. When grouped by *manner of articulation*, the transitions from early child speech, to adult input to children, and to adult conversational speech patterns seem more gradual and linear. There is a strong tendency for less mature language users to use stops, nasals, and glides, rather than fricatives, affricates, and liquids. These tendencies gradually become less lopsided as children mature. Such findings are consistent with multiple prior studies of children's phonetic development.

Figures 11.3-11.8 graphically display the results of the PHONFREQ analyses, which tally specific initial, final, and "other" sound occurrences. For our purposes, we will examine only word-, syllable-initial, and syllable-final usage. More than 75% of preverbal children's productions contain initial [d,h,y,w]. Such a pattern does not reflect the nature of the input they hear, which utilizes a much broader

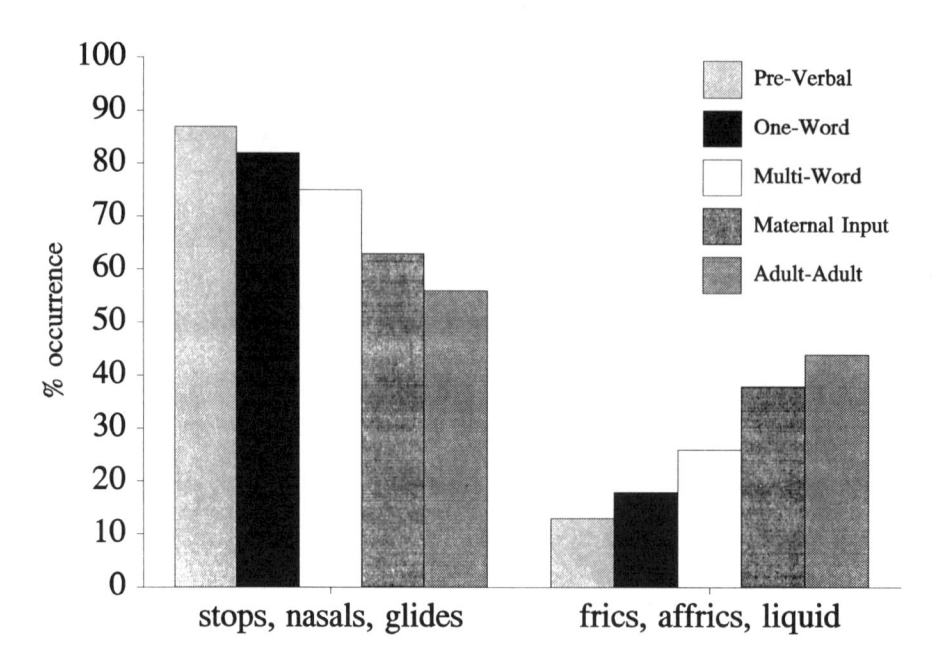

Figure 11.2: Changes in manner of articulation across language groups.

array of initial phonemes, and which tends to under-represent the infants' favored sounds, while more frequently using sounds the infants do not replicate. Such patterns support Locke (1983, 1988) and Smith (1988), who suggest that prelinguistic children's sound patterns represent nonlinguistic, physiologically conditioned preferences in early speech. Our only unusual finding is a very low, insignificant usage of [m], a supposedly frequent target in babbled speech. Infants' final sound preferences are discrepant from the input as well: They tend to close syllables with nasals at rates vastly disproportionate to the input they hear, while avoiding the sibilants [s, z], whose usage is grammatically conditioned and extremely frequent in the speech addressed to them.

Children at the one-word stage of language development show many of the same preferences as do preverbal children; an exception is the emergence of strong preferences for initial [b] and [m]. With the exception of [h], children at the one-word stage initiate words and syllabic vocalizations with voiced sounds; such a pattern is consistent with cross-linguistic and deaf children's patterns of sound preferences early in development (Locke, 1983), and again suggests physiological preferences or constraints on sound production in early speech. Once more, there is little apparent correlation between the children's preferences and those of the adults who converse with them.

Final sound preferences at the one-word stage are generally voiceless (with the exception of [m]), again supporting physiological and maturational constraints on early productions (Locke, 1983). Once more, there is little to suggest that infants choose to, or are able to, replicate the frequency distribution of sounds in the language addressed to them.

As children become more linguistically proficient, their inventories become somewhat more adultlike, as Figures 11.7 and 11.8 show. Their words tend to start with voiced stops, glides, or [m], which was typically found in the vocative, *Mommy*. Such results are consistent with early phonetic tendencies reported in other investigations. While glides are well represented and frequent in maternal input (primarily in words such as *you* and question words), parental usage of initial voiced stops is much less frequent than the children's usage. Words beginning with [ð] are extraordinarily frequent in maternal speech to all groups of language learners, primarily for grammatical reasons, as I discuss further in the next sections.

348   Chapter 11

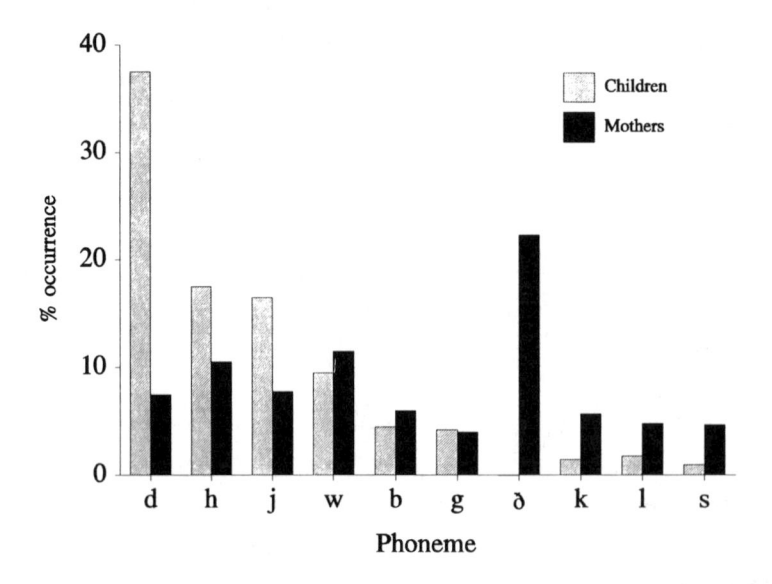

Figure 11.3: Initial phoneme preferences for pre-verbal conversations (Children first 6 morphemes > 90% total; mothers' top 10 = 80% total).

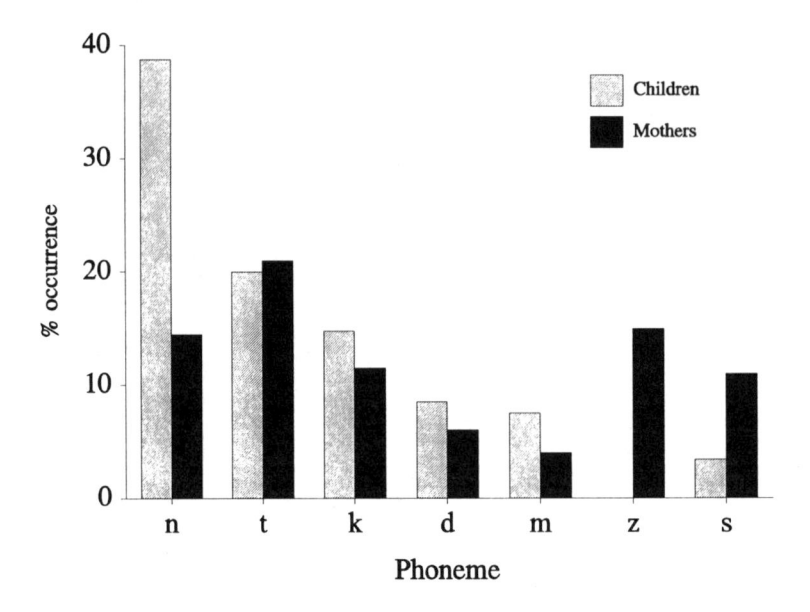

Figure 11.4: Final consonant preferences for preverbal conversations.

Phonological Analyses 349

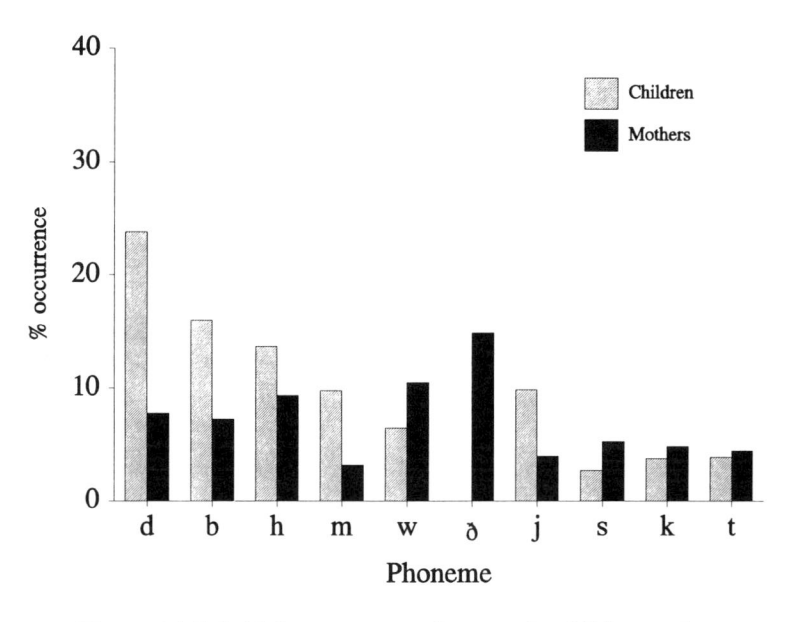

Figure 11.5: Initial consonant preferences for children at the one-word stage (Children's top five = 70% of total usage).

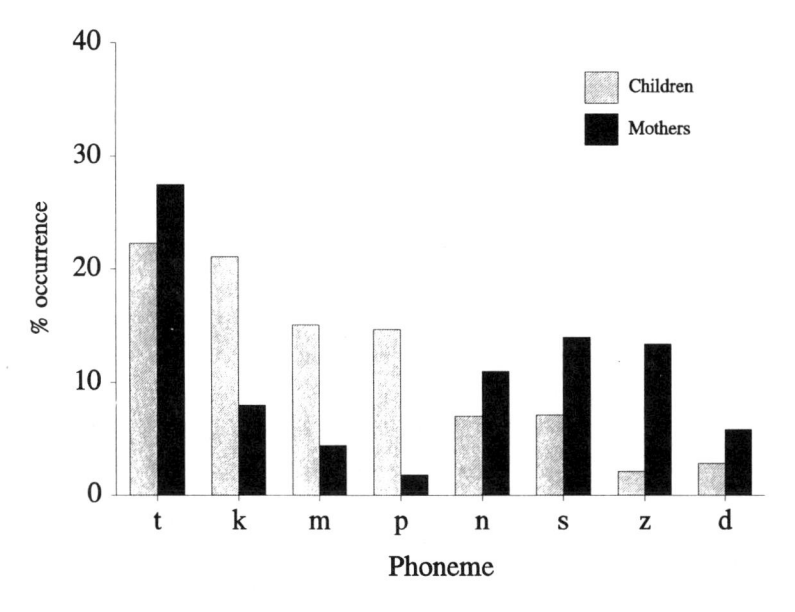

Figure 11.6: Final consonant preferences for children at the one-word stage.

350   Chapter 11

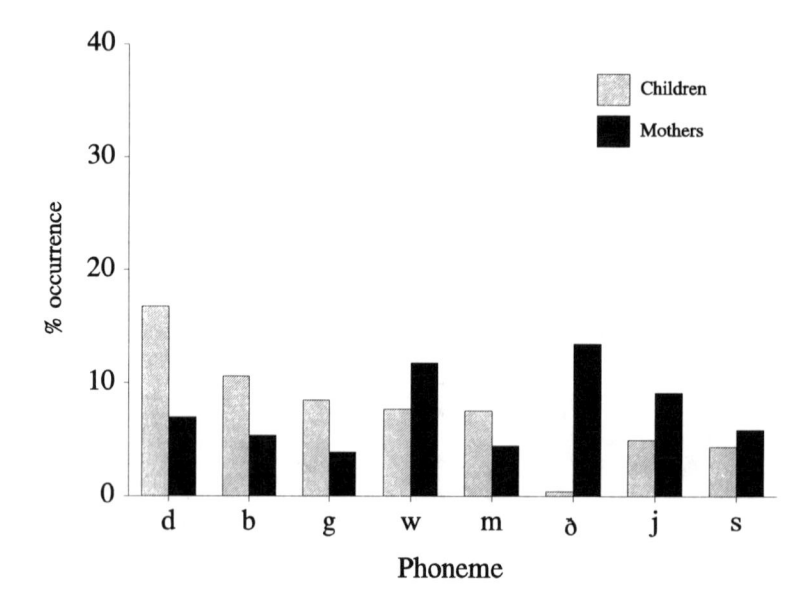

Figure 11.7: Initial consonant preferences for more advanced children.

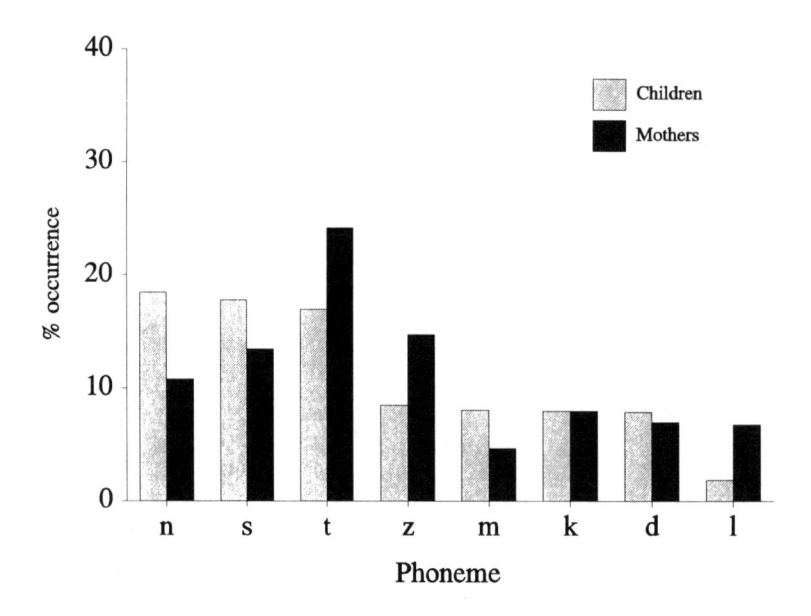

Figure 11.8: Final consonant preferences for more advanced children.

Many of the advanced children's final sound preferences are well-matched to the input patterns they hear. There is clear emergence of final [s] and [z], used primarily in grammatical contexts, and [t] and [d] maintain their strong representation. Final [n], which was under-represented at the one-word stage, is now extremely frequent. Final [k], which was highly utilized in lexical items at the one-word speech, is now less frequently seen in final position, as grammatical inflections move it out of word-final context. In general, the tendency to use voiceless final stops in early speech is mitigated in the more linguistically mature children by the emergence of grammatical affixes, which are **not** formed, with the exception of the past-tense allomorph [t], out of voiceless stops.

11.6. Discussion

As Locke (1983) pointed out, there are a number of issues that could affect the frequency with which sounds appear in conversational speech. For example, languages do demonstrate some striking tendencies to favor certain sounds over other sounds, and certain sounds in particular positions over other positions. Thus, when we examine the lexicon (words) of a language, not all sounds have an equal opportunity to appear in all positions. For example, in English, [b] is much more likely to appear in initial position than final position (by a factor of almost 40 to 1); [z] shows the inverse pattern. It is 145 times more frequent in word-final than in initial position (Mines, Hanson, & Shoup, 1978). In addition, some sounds are clearly more frequently used within a language than others, regardless of position. Use of [n] approximates 12% of all consonant usage in running conversational speech, [g] represents only 2%. Locke has remarked that, to some degree, there is similarity between universal and language-specific patterns of sound use and the acquisition of phonemes by children. These similarities suggest that common considerations may govern both language evolution and language acquisition. But which came first?

Our results suggest that mere frequency of a sound in the input does not lead to its practice or use by children. For example, [D] (IPA:ð) is extremely frequent in maternal speech to our study children. Yet, even at the oldest stages of linguistic development examined here, it is not frequently used by the children themselves. Data from Bird, Bernthal, Freilinger, Hand, and Bosma-Smit (1990) suggest that completely accurate use of this sound does not emerge until children are between 4 and 7 years of age, according to the findings of a number of studies. However,

352   Chapter 11

children can approximate [D] in from 20-32% of instances from 36 months of age. Our data from the preverbal children do not suggest that the sound is "babbled" much, a finding quite consistent with other studies of babbling and early speech. Its absence in the one-word and multi-word corpora is harder to interpret, however.

If we examine the contexts that typically lead to use of [ð], it becomes clear that the high representation of [D] in maternal and general adult conversational speech is conditioned by grammatical considerations. If we remove the previous subdirectory structure, and place all 27 files in one directory (I call it **momtalk**), the following FREQ search will show that the most frequent context for this phoneme is the determiner *the*, followed by deictics, such as *this, that, these, those,* and pronouns, such as *they* and *them*:

freq   +t*MOT   +s"th*"   +u   momtalk*.cha

+t*MOT	Analyze the mother's speaker tier only
+s"th*"	Search for all words beginning with *th*
+u	Merge all input files into a combined analysis
momtalk*.cha	Analyze all files ending in **.cha** in the **momtalk** subdirectory

Command Box 11.4

The results of this analysis are listed below:

2 th'	1 thats	1 they've	41 three
1 th's	1315 the	7 thing	2 three:
1 th:ree:	1 the:re	27 things	1 threes
1 tha's	2 their	104 think	2 threw
1 tha:t's	102 them	1 thinking	1 throat
3 thaaat	10 then	2 thinks	22 through
8 than	370 there	587 this	11 throw
65 thank	2 there'	6 this's	1 thrower
1 thank+ya	4 there're	137 those	3 throwing
812 that	96 there's	1 those:	1 thrown
5 that'	75 these	14 though	1 ths
1 that'll	75 they	6 thought	4 thumb
385 that's	22 they're	1 thread	

Note that some of these words, such as *thank*, *thing(s)*, *think*, and so on, start with the voiceless phoneme [T]. This small set of words constitutes well over 80% of the instances of [D] usage.

We can use the FREQ program to count other sounds of interest to determine their lexical and grammatical environments. For example, the FREQ program is useful in determining how to categorize the actual pronunciation of maternal words ending in *-s*, *-ed*, and so on.

From your study of child language, you can appreciate the fact that very young language learners find it difficult to use free grammatical morphemes such as those in which [D] appears, and often delete them in their early conversational attempts (although competing hypotheses suggest that children merely fail to notice them in the input stream because they are unstressed and of weak intensity, cf. Swanson, Leonard, & Gandour, 1992; Wanner & Gleitman, 1982). Under either view, the result is the same: Children do not tend to use this class of words, and this class of words constitutes the single greatest source of [D] usage in English.

Other discrepancies between maternal use and child use demand other explanations. For example, what can we say about children's tendency to babble and produce words containing final [b] in greater proportion than do their mothers and the language in general? Or to use [g] at rates very much higher than the sound's representation in English? You may wish to use the FREQ program to analyze these classes of sounds in both maternal and child speech to see if any plausible explanations emerge. This question has been left as an exercise for you to do (see Exercise 11.9.5).

In the end, there are no compelling reasons to suspect that the frequency with which children hear sounds in parental speech plays a strong role in determining patterns of sound acquisition and use. Rather, there may be real physiological reasons why children use some sounds early and in particular contexts, while accurate and flexible usage of other sounds must wait until they are more mature (Locke, 1983). Locke lists, among possible patterns of both child and adult conversational speech which may have a physiological explanation, behaviors such as final consonant checking, devoicing and deletion, and voicing of initial stop consonants. The notion that certain classes of sounds and sequences of sounds are physiologically "marked" is also supported by their relative rarity crosslinguistically, as well as errors observed in the speech of motorically impaired individuals. There are also likely perceptual rationales for the lack of certain sounds in the output of children. As Locke notes in his summary of developmental and crosslinguistic data, some phonetic contrasts are clearly more difficult to resolve perceptually than others. Other sounds may lack acoustic salience and literally go unnoticed despite their frequency in the input. The particular contexts that lead to frequency effects for particular sounds in a language (such as initial [ð], and final [s,z,t,d], which are used for marking plurality, agreement, possession, and the past tense in English) can lead to a child profile that lacks substantial representation of these sounds, not for any purely phonological reason, but for grammatical ones (Paul & Shriberg, 1982). Children may have difficulty acquiring sounds embedded in grammatical environments because such environments carry little stress and are more difficult for children to process.

11.7. What are Beginning Talkers *Trying to Say*? An Introduction to MODREP

Mere tallies of the sounds a child produces do not evaluate whether the child was attempting to produce each of these sounds, or produced some in error while attempting other targets. Most of us take for granted the notion that early child speech is characterized by errors of articulation. While PHONFREQ can tabulate the general phonetic characteristics of a speech sample, it cannot make judgements about the **accuracy** of that sample.

Furthermore, it is also commonly agreed that young children's articulation of segments is quite variable. That is, children may articulate a segment correctly in one environment or on a particular occasion, and produce it incorrectly in others. Similarly, their error forms are likely to be variable as well (Menn, 1979; Scollon, 1976; Stoel-Gammon & Cooper, 1981). Such variability cannot be appraised by merely examining the segments produced; the attempted target must be considered.

Finally, recent work suggests that young children actively build their initial lexicon from those words that are composed of sounds the child can produce (Schwartz & Leonard, 1982). That is, children will deliberately seek out those adult words of the language containing segments they are able to say, and avoid using words that call for sounds they cannot produce, and would therefore have to delete or produce incorrectly.

In the next section, I discuss how the MODREP program allows us to appraise the accuracy and consistency of children's speech attempts, and also allows us to consider whether a child appears to select or avoid particular classes of words in early language development.

11.7.1. What Does MODREP Do?

The MODREP program is designed to compare entries across two tiers. The tiers to be compared are designated by the options +b and +c, and can be any two tiers that are identical in length. The +b option represents the "model" tier name, and the +c option determines the nature of the speaker's attempt to replicate the model. It is important to note that this program will only run if the CHAT file to be analyzed contains some "target" coding of the speaker's utterance.

For the purposes of this chapter, I explore the use of MODREP to examine the phonological accuracy and variability of children's early speech. Thus, we will consider our replica tier to be a %pho tier (the UNIBET-coded representation of what the child actually said) and our model tier to be the target well-formed adult pronunciation of the child's word attempts. In the discussions that follow, I call such a tier **%mod** (for "model").

11.7.2. Evaluating the Utility of a Phonetic Model (%mod) Tier

In this section, I examine the phonological development of a young child who demonstrates delays in both speech and language development. The Adami directory contains speech samples from a 2½-year-old child (Adami) with a history of severe chronic otitis media (middle-ear infections). He was being followed by a team of researchers because of this history of transient hearing loss and because of a relatively slow pace of language development. He was diagnosed with Specific Expressive Language Delay (SELD) at age 2;1, using criteria suggested by Rescorla (1990). While children with slow expressive language development are considered most at risk for morphological and syntactic development, there is emerging concern that many such children also have articulation problems and a restricted phonetic inventory (Paul & Jennings, 1992; Rescorla & Schwartz, 1990).

356   Chapter 11

We will first run PHONFREQ on one of Adami's files using the following command:

phonfreq   +t*CHI   –s@vowels   tpjun90.cha

+b*CHI	Analyze the child's speaker tier only
–s@vowels	Exclude all the items from the file **vowels**
tpjun90.cha	Analyze the file **tpjun90.cha**

Command Box 11.5

Remember that the **vowels** file was used earlier to eliminate vowels and delimiters from the PHONFREQ analysis in Command Box 11.2. Be sure your alphabet file is the one shown in Table 11.2. Note that there is no need to specify the **%pho** tier in this exercise, because that is where PHONFREQ assumes the phonetic information is coded, and we do not need to use the **+b** option to override this default assumption as we did with the previous files. The output of this program is listed in Table 11.8. From this table, we can see that Adami does use an array of sounds in his conversational speech. How does this distribution compare to the oldest group of children (the **mword** group) studied in the previous section? These children are at comparable stages of grammatical development, as measured by MLU, although they differ in age by approximately a year.

All consonants are represented in Adami's speech, with the exception of [f]. However, some sounds appear frequently, while others are not seen in numbers in the output. To compare the relative frequency with which sounds appear in his speech and in the speech of the younger, earlier language learners, we can divide the total frequencies for individual sounds by the number of samples that contributed to the group (11). We can then compare their mean use of certain sounds with the observed frequency in Adami's speech. This process provides us with the impression that some early acquired sounds, such as [j] and [b] are not well represented in Adami's sample: [j] is seen only 3 times, while it is seen an average of 21 times in each **mword** sample file. Adami uses [b] 19 times, evenly split between word-initial and word-final position; **mword** group children, as expected in early speech efforts, use [b] an average of 43 times, primarily in initial position. Conversely, Adami used [n] 221 times; average representation in a **mword** sample is one third of that, or 74 instances. Is this because there were multiple

Table 11.8: The results of a PHONFREQ analysis of Adami's file.

```
   12  N    initial =   0,  final =   2,  other =  10
    8  S    initial =   6,  final =   0,  other =   2
   19  b    initial =  10,  final =   0,  other =   9
  129  d    initial =  74,  final =   8,  other =  47
    6  dZ   initial =   4,  final =   0,  other =   2
    1  dr   initial =   1,  final =   0,  other =   0
   32  g    initial =  16,  final =   0,  other =  16
    1  gr   initial =   0,  final =   0,  other =   1
   26  h    initial =   6,  final =   0,  other =  20
    3  j    initial =   1,  final =   0,  other =   2
   36  k    initial =   9,  final =   4,  other =  23
    3  kw   initial =   0,  final =   0,  other =   3
   19  l    initial =   6,  final =   5,  other =   8
  100  m    initial =  13,  final =   7,  other =  80
  219  n    initial =  37,  final =   6,  other = 176
   35  p    initial =   4,  final =  13,  other =  18
   15  r    initial =   0,  final =   5,  other =  10
   86  s    initial =  10,  final =   1,  other =  75
    5  sw   initial =   3,  final =   0,  other =   2
   48  t    initial =   8,  final =  18,  other =  22
    2  tS   initial =   0,  final =   1,  other =   1
    5  tr   initial =   2,  final =   0,  other =   3
    8  tw   initial =   5,  final =   0,  other =   3
    4  v    initial =   0,  final =   0,  other =   4
   50  w    initial =   9,  final =   1,  other =  40
    6  x    initial =   2,  final =   0,  other =   4
   22  z    initial =   3,  final =   5,  other =  14
```

opportunities to use the sound [n], which is Adami's most frequently used sound, but few opportunities to use [j] and [b], which were not used often, or [f], which is absent? Opportunities to use sounds may rely on both conversational context, and the child's avoidance of words containing sounds that he or she cannot yet make accurately (Schwartz & Leonard, 1983).

In order to evaluate whether the sound distribution represents accurate attempts to produce adult sounds in words, we can select the most and least frequently observed sounds in the output and compare them to the well-formed adult pronunciation of his word attempts. To do this, we can use the MODREP utility. MODREP allows us to ascertain what Adami was *trying to say*, as well as *what he said*. This is the utility of a **%mod** (or other target-coded) tier. It allows us to contrast what we perceive to be the child's intention with the child's actual output.

As we shall see, the MODREP program allows us to estimate the range, accuracy, and variability of early speech attempts.

In order for us to specifically know what Adami was trying to say, it is necessary for the original CHAT transcripts to include two different UNIBET-coded tiers. The first, which we have already discussed, is the **%pho** tier. The second, **%mod** tier, takes Adami's output and "corrects" its articulation. Consider the following example from the file:

```
*CHI:       I want (to) play checker-s.
%pho:       ai wan pe tEt6z.
%mod:       ai want ple tSEk3z.
```

In this coding example, the main tier presents what we call a "gloss" of the intended utterance, which is readable, and which contains a minimal amount of grammatical information, such as deletion instances and rudimentary morphemization. The **%pho** tier codes Adami's pronunciation of the utterance. The **%mod** tier "normalizes" the words and morphemes produced by the child back to an acceptable adult pronunciation in UNIBET.

Were there targets containing [j], [b], and [f] in Adami's conversational attempts? To answer this question, we can execute the following command sequences using MODREP to examine Adami's attempts to produce different sounds:

modrep +t*CHI +b%mod +c%pho +k +o"*j*" tpjun90.cha

+t*CHI	Analyze the child's speaker tier only
+b%mod	Use the **%mod** tier as the model against which the +c tier will be compared
+c%pho	Use the **%pho** tier as the comparison for the model tier
+k	Treat upper and lower case as the same
+o"*j*"	Search for target words containing [j]
tpjun90.cha	Analyze the file **tpjun90.cha**

Command Box 11.6

> With older versions of PHONFREQ, you must use the +s instead of the +o option to search for target sounds.

We can then repeat this analysis, and determine whether or not Adami attempted to say words containing [f] and [b] by substituting [f], and then [b], for [j] in the command sequence. Note that we have inserted the +k option into our MODREP command. This is because MODREP does *not* assume searches should be case sensitive, as it can be used to search non-phonetically coded tiers. (I discuss these potential applications later.) In this case, because we know our tiers are coded in UNIBET, we must take care to instruct the search to be case sensitive. If the target was [Su] (*shoe*) and the child says [su], this is an error we want to be able to detect.

To determine why [n] appears so frequently in Adami's output, we can reverse elements in the command sequence to start with the child's productions and relate them back to the presumed adult targets. To do this, we use the following command:

modrep +t*CHI +b%pho +c%mod +k +o"*n*" tpjun90.cha

+t*CHI	Analyze the child's speaker tier only
+b%pho	Use the **%mod** tier as the model against which the +c tier will be compared
+c%mod	Use the **%pho** tier as the comparison for the model tier
+k	Treat upper and lower case as the same
+o"*n*"	Search for target words containing [n]
tpjun90.cha	Analyze the file **tpjun90.cha**

Command Box 11.7

The results for the MODREP analyses for [j], [f], [b], and [n] are displayed in Table 11.9.

11.7.3. Results of Our MODREP Analysis

From Table 11.9, it can be seen that Adami did attempt to say words that contained [f] and [j], although he could not replicate them accurately. Out of 37 targets that contained [j], the child produced only 3 accurately. There were only

Table 11.9: The results for MODREP analyses targeting the child's use of [j], [f], and [b].

The results for [j]:

```
1 /jElo          31 /jEs/.         1 jEs/.
   1 /jEwo       30 /nEs/.            1 dEs/.
1 /jElo/.         1 /nE/.          1 ju/.
   1 /jEwE/.     1 jEs               1 ju/.
1 /jEs            1 dEt
   1 /dEt
```

The results for [f]:

```
2 /dZ3r&fs/.                      1 wUlf
   1 /dZr&ts/.                       1 wUl
   1 /dw&ts/.                     2 wUlf/.
1 fIS/.                              2 wUl/.
   1 watS/.                       1 wUlfs/.
                                     1 wolks/.
```

The results for [b]:

```
1 /b&k            1 /bikOz         3 bUk/.
   1 /d&t            1 /traiz         1 bwak/.
2 /b&k/.          1 /bip           2 bUk/.
   2 /d&t/.          1 /i          1 babar
2 /bAmp/.         1 /blak/.           1 baba
   2 /gAnk/.         1 /bak/.      1 bai/.
1 /bAt            1 /blu/.            1 bwai/.
   1 /bA:            1 /bwu/.      1 bait/.
2 /bOl/.          1 /brekIN/.         1 bait/.
   1 /bOl/.          1 /bwepIN/.   1 bip/.
   1 /ba/.        1 bAmps/.           1 i/.
1 /bai               1 bAmps/.
   1 /bai         1 bOl/.
1 /bikAz/.           1 bOl/.
   1 /bisaiz/.
```

Table 11.9 (*continued*): The results of MODREP analyses targeting the child's use of [n].

1 &n	30 /nEs/.	1 gin
1 &nd	30 /jEs/.	1 grin
1 /In:said/.	1 /na	2 gwinz/.
1 /Insaid/.	1 /mam	2 grinz/.
1 /Inswaid/.	2 /na/.	1 hapEn/
1 /Insaid/.	2 /no/.	1 h&pEn/
1 /daun/.	1 /nani	1 lain/.
1 /daun/.	1 /mami	1 lain/.
1 /daunserz/.	36 /ni	1 n&/.
1 /daunsterz/.	36 /mi	1 wAn/.
2 /gAnk/.	1 /ni/	1 n3rk/.
2 /bAmp/.	1 /mi/	1 w3rk/.
2 /gin/.	13 /ni/.	1 na
2 /grin/.	13 /mi/.	1 nat
1 /grin	1 /nid	1 nak/.
1 /grin	1 /rid	1 w3rk/.
1 /gwin/.	34 /no	2 nami/.
1 /grin/.	34 /no	2 mami/.
1 /lain/.	2 /no/	15 ni
1 /lain/.	2 /no/	14 mi
1 /man	22 /no/.	1 ni
1 /mam	22 /no/.	1 ni/
2 /n&/.	3 /nop/.	1 mi/
1 /no/.	3 /nop/.	9 ni/.
1 /n&/.	2 Insaid/.	9 mi/.
2 /nA	2 Insaid/.	2 nid
2 /no	1 dEn	2 nid
2 /nA/.	1 DEn	2 no
2 /no/.	1 daun	2 no
1 /nA:A/.	1 daun	1 no/.
1 /6h6/.	1 daun/.	1 no/.
1 /nAA/.	1 daun/.	1 nor
1 /nAA/.	1 dont	1 mor
1 /nE/.	1 dont	2 opIn/.
1 /jEs/.		2 opEn/.

seven opportunities to use [f], which is not a very frequent sound in English, but he did not produce the sound in any of these environments. It appears as though the relatively low frequency of [b], however, was lack of opportunity to use it; only 24 of the words that Adami attempted to say should have had [b] in them. He managed to correctly articulate the sound 19 times, and had articulatory errors on 5 additional attempts. Conversely, [n] was substituted for a wide variety of sounds Adami could not accurately reproduce, including [j] ([nEs] for [jEs], as in *yes*) and [m], resulting in the production of [ni] for *me* ([mi]).

11.7.4. Other Applications of MODREP

We have discussed in earlier sections some of the research questions that may be more easily answered if phonetic detail is provided for children's utterances. There are many others. For example, Peters and Menn (1990) tracked the development of grammatical morphemes from total absence, to a diverse array of "filler syllables," such as schwa, to adult form for a number of children across languages. In such an investigation, however, the researcher's target is a small, well-defined group of items whose appropriate pronunciation can be easily determined in advance. It is less easy to track children's attempts at a broader range of lexical targets. However, questions regarding the evolving phonetic characteristics of many grammatical and lexical categories are answerable using properly coded tiers and MODREP. Additionally, phonetic coding of input language may allow us to better appreciate some associations between input and child language learning. For example, Newport, Gleitman, and Gleitman (1977) and Richards (1990) attempted to evaluate the role of parental input in children's acquisition of the auxiliary verb system of English. Frequent use of parental questions appears to correlate positively with children's auxiliary verb growth, possibly because the fronted auxiliary verb in questions (e.g., "Are you ready?", "Can you do that?") is more easily noticed by the child, and thus more rapidly learned. Yet, Bernstein Ratner (1984b, 1987) suggested that parental speech, while often more precisely articulated than adult-adult conversation, is often characterized by concatenated, elided, and deleted segments. Thus, children are exposed to a variety of questions, some of which are well-articulated, and some of which are not ("Whaddaya wan?"; "Whatchya see?"; "ya sure?"; "dya know"; "/zi/ here?" ("Is he here?"), and so on. Careful transcription of both parental and child speech, using both **%mod** and **%pho** tiers, can allow us to better evaluate possible associations between parental use of particular forms and child acquisition.

11.8. Conclusions

In this chapter, we have attempted to obtain answers to a number of questions about children's phonetic development. We have seen that, as children progress from the late preverbal stage through the early stage of multiword speech, their phonetic inventories reflect a pattern of continuous expansion. There does not appear to be any true discontinuity between the sounds used in late babble and those that are used to build early words. It is unlikely that the frequency with which sounds appear in maternal input to children strongly influences which sounds children learn early or late in development. However, some sounds appear primarily in grammatically complex and unstressed environments in mother-child speech. This could have the effect of delaying mastery of these segments.

Children who show delayed language development may have concomitant limitations on their phonetic inventories. The child studied in this chapter appeared to have difficulty using some early acquired speech sounds, while using some later acquired sounds without difficulty. This pattern produces a mismatch between the usual relationships between speech and language development in young children. The use of computerized transcript analysis may facilitate more detailed analysis of phonetic development in larger samples of children than has been possible up to now and allow us to sample the course of phonological development in more naturalistic environments. The ability to appraise children's conversational patterns of articulation makes it possible for future work to assess whether parental feedback or correction appears to play a role in phonetic development, whether children selectively compile vocabularies on the basis of their phonetic abilities, and other related questions about early speech and language development.

11.9. Exercises

11.9.1. A consonant cluster is a sequence of two or more consonants. Examples (in UNIBET notation) are: Tr, tr, fl, st, Sr, and so on. How might one use PHONFREQ to determine the age at which children produce initial consonant clusters in their spontaneous speech attempts? Use the preverbal, one-word, and multiword data from the **Ratner** directory to map developmental change in the use of initial consonant clusters. **Hint**: A modified alphabet file will be helpful.

11.9.2. When final [s] and [z] emerge in the speech of these children, is it more likely to be in lexical contexts (i.e., *bus*, *buzz*) or in grammatical contexts, such as plurals, possessives, and third-person agreement? How might you determine the answer to this question? **Hint**: FREQ using wildcards will be helpful.

11.9.3. Does the phonetic inventory grow at different rates as a child's language ability changes? Each of the children in the sample was taped three times, at 6-week intervals. For Kay, two of these sessions took place when she was not yet using recognizable words, while the third session marked her entry into one-word utterances. For Alice, all three sessions were at the one-word stage of language development. For Anne, all three took place when she used multiword speech. Perform an analysis of the initial inventory and changes in inventory for each of these children over the 18-week study period. Do they differ in any way?

11.9.4. MODREP produces very lengthy output. How could you narrow its focus to examine only a child's rendition of adult target words containing initial stop consonants? A child's use of pronouns? **Hint**: Use include files to focus your analysis.

11.9.5. Some discrepancies between maternal input and child use demand other explanations. For example, what can we say about children's tendency to babble and produce words containing final [b] in greater proportion than their mothers and in greater proportion than in the language in general? Or to use [g] at rates very much higher than the sound's representation in English? You may wish to examine the frequency of these classes of sounds in both maternal and child speech to see if any plausible explanations emerge.

11.10. Suggested Project

Have five children between the ages of 2 and 4 label the pictures provided in the Appendix. Using MODREP, analyze the group's behaviors. Which words were most difficult for the children to produce? Which were most variably produced?

References

Bernstein, N. (1982). *An acoustic study of mothers' speech to language-learning children: An analysis of vowel articulation characteristics.* Unpublished doctoral dissertation, Boston University.

Bernstein Ratner, N. (1984a). Patterns of vowel modification in mother-child speech. *Journal of Child Language, 11,* 557-578.

Bernstein Ratner, N. (1984b). Phonological rule usage in mother-child speech. *Journal of Phonetics, 12,* 245-254.

Bernstein Ratner, N. (1987). The phonology of parent-child speech. In K. Nelson & A. Van Kleeck (Eds.), *Child language (Vol. 6)*. Hillsdale, NJ: Lawrence Erlbaum Associates.

Bird, A., Bernthal, J., Freilinger, J., Hand, L., & Bosma-Smit, A. (1990). The Iowa Articulation Norms project and its Nebraska replication. *Journal of Speech and Hearing Disorders, 55*, 779-798.

Edwards, J. (1989). Computer methods in child language research: Four principles for the use of archived data. *Journal of Child Language*.

Ferguson, C., & Farwell, C. (1975). Words and sounds in early language acquisition: English initial consonants in the first fifty words. *Language, 51*, 419-439.

Goad, H., & Ingram, D. (1987). Individual variation and its relevance to a theory of phonological acquisition. *Journal of Child Language, 14*, 419-432.

Ingram, D. (1974). Phonological analysis of a child. *Glossa, 10*, 3-27.

Leonard, L., Newhoff, M., & Mesalam, L. (1980). Individual differences in early child phonology. *Applied Psycholinguistics, 1*, 7-30.

Locke, J. (1983). *Phonological acquisition and change*. New York: Academic Press.

Locke, J. (1988). The sound shape of early lexical representations. In M. Smith & J. Locke (Eds.), *The emergent lexicon: The child's development of a linguistic vocabulary*. New York: Academic Press.

Menn, L. (1971). Phonotactic rules in beginning speech. *Lingua, 26*, 225-251.

Menn, L. (1979). Towards a psychology of phonology: Child phonology as a first step. *Proceedings of the Conference on Applications of Linguistic Theory in the Human Sciences*. (pp. 138-179). Lansing, MI.

Mines, M., Hanson, B., & Shoup, J. (1978). Frequency of occurrence of phonemes in conversational English. *Language and Speech, 21*, 221-241.

Newport, E., Gleitman, L., & Gleitman, H. (1977). Mother, I'd rather do it myself: Some effects and non-effects of motherese. In C. Snow & C. Ferguson (Eds.), *Talking to children: Language input and acquisition*. Cambridge: Cambridge University Press.

Paul, R., & Jennings, P. (1992). Phonological behaviors in toddlers with slow expressive language development. *Journal of Speech and Hearing Research, 35*, 99-107.

Peters, A., Fahn, R., Glover, G., Harley, H., Sawyer, M., & Shimura, A. (1990). *Keeping close to the data: A two-tier computer-coding schema for the analysis of morphological development*. Unpublished manuscript, University of Hawaii, Linguistics Department.

Peters, A., & Menn, L. (1990). *The microstructure of morphological development: Variation across children and across languages* (Working Paper). Institute for Cognitive Science, University of Colorado.

Poole, I. (1934). Genetic development of articulation of consonant sounds in speech. *Elementary English Review, 11*, 159-161.

Prather, E., Hedrick, D., & Kern, C. (1975). Articulation development in children aged two to four years. *Journal of Speech and Hearing Disorders, 40*, 179-191.

Rescorla, L. (1989). The Language Development Survey: A screening tool for delayed language in toddlers. *Journal of Speech and Hearing Disorders, 54*, 587-599.

Rescorla, L., & Schwartz, E. (1990). Outcome of toddlers with expressive language delay. *Applied Psycholinguistics, 11*, 393-407.

Richards, B. (1990). *Predictors of auxiliary and copula verb growth.* Paper presented at the Fifth International Congress for the Study of Child Language, Budapest, Hungary.

Schwartz, R., & Leonard, L. (1982). Do children pick and choose? An examination of phonological selection and avoidance in early lexical acquisition. *Journal of Child Language, 9*, 319-336.

Scollon, R. (1976). *Conversations with a One Year Old.* Honolulu: The University of Hawaii Press.

Smith, B. (1988). The emergent lexicon from a phonetic perspective. In M. Smith & J. Locke (Eds.), *The emergent lexicon: The child's development of a linguistic vocabulary.* New York: Academic Press.

Smith, N. (1973). *The acquisition of phonology: A case study.* Cambridge: Cambridge University Press.

Stockman, I., Woods, D., & Tishman, A. (1981). Listener agreement on phonetic segments in early infant vocalizations. *Journal of Psycholinguistic Research, 10*, 593-617.

Stoel-Gammon, C. (1985). Phonetic inventories 15-24 months: A longitudinal study. *Journal of Speech and Hearing Research, 28*, 505-512.

Stoel-Gammon, C., & Cooper, J. (1984). Patterns of early phonological and lexical development. *Journal of Child Language, 11*, 247-271.

Swanson, L., Leonard, L., & Gandour, J. (1992). Vowel duration in mothers' speech to young children. *Journal of Speech and Hearing Research, 35*, 617-625.

Templin, M. (1957). Certain language skills in children, their development and interrelationships. *Institute of Child Welfare Monograph Series, No. 26.* Minneapolis: University of Minnesota Press.

Vihman, M., Macken, M., Miller, R., Simmons, H., & Miller, J. (1985). From babbling to speech: A reassessment of the continuity issue. *Language, 61*, 397-445.

Wanner, E., & Gleitman, L. (1982). *Language acquisition: The state of the art.* Cambridge: Cambridge University Press.

368   Chapter 11

Appendix: Pictures and answer sheet for the suggested project
(Selected pictures reprinted by permission from
Pictures Please! An Articulation Supplement, © 1984,
by Communication Skill Builders, Inc., P. O. Box 42050, Tucson, AZ 85733)

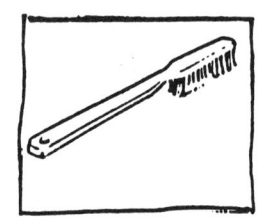

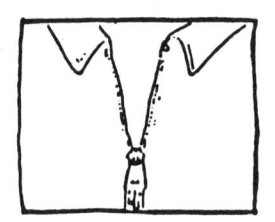

Phonological Analyses 369

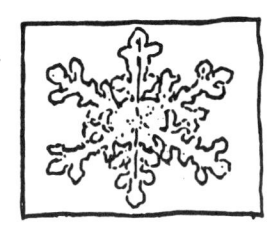

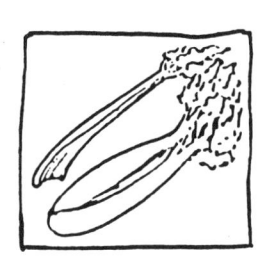

13.
14.
15.
16.
17.
18.
19.
20.
21.
22.
23.
24.

370   Chapter 11

25. 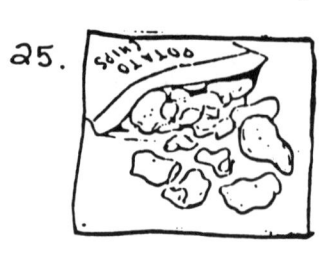
26. 
27. 
28. 
29. 
30. 
31. 
32. 
33. 
34. 
35. 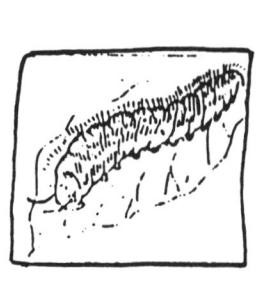
36.

Answer Sheet

1. Airplane [erplen]   10. Jump [dZAmp]

2. Three [Tri]   11. Butterfly [bAt3flai]

3. Rabbit [r&bIt]   12. Telephone [tElEfon]

4. Leaf [lif]   13. Paintbrush [pentbrAS]

5. Popcorn [papkOrn]   14. Giraffe [dZ3&f]

6. Sink [sINk]   15. Bathtub [b&TtAb]

7. Toothbrush [tuTbrAS]   16. Cracker [kr&k3]

8. Zipper [zIp3r]   17. Dragon [dr&gAn]

9. Shovel [SAv6l]   18. Snowflake [snoflek]

Chapter 11

19. Spaghetti [spAgEti]   28. Octopus [aktopUs]
    _____   _____

20. Lunchbox [lAntSbaks]   29. Vacuum [v&kjum]
    _____   _____

21. Raisins [rezInz]   30. Merry go round
    _____   [mEri go raund]

22. Celery [sEl3i]   _____
    _____   31. Kangaroo [k&NgAru]

23. Thirty [T3ti]   _____
    _____   32. Pajamas [p6dZam6z]

24. Elephant [ElEfEnt]   _____
    _____   33. Refrigerator
                                [r6frIdZ3et3r]
25. Potato chips
    [poteto tSIps]   _____
    _____   34. Marshmallows [marSmEloz]

26. Bathroom [b&Trum]   _____
    _____   35. Caterpillar [k&t3pIl3]

27. Pancakes [p&nkeks]   _____
    _____   36. Rhinocerous [rainas36s]

                                _____

12 Language Profiles of Children with Specific Language Impairment

Pamela Rosenthal Rollins
Harvard Graduate School of Education

In this chapter, you will learn the following skills:

- To use post-codes to exclude utterances from analyses using both MLU and FREQ.

- To create an exclude file containing post-codes.

- To perform FREQ analyses on the codes in dependent tiers.

- To use batch files in support of the creation of clinical profiles.

To replicate the analyses you will need the **rickcod.cha** file found in the **conti** directory. To conduct the exercises, you will need the remainder of the files in the **conti** directory.

12.1. Introduction

12.1.1. Background Information

Language is no longer considered a monolithic phenomenon, but rather is comprised of several distinct subsystems. The fundamental subsystems are the morphosyntactic (i.e., grammar, including the modulation of meaning within words), the lexical (i.e., vocabulary); and the pragmatic (i.e., language use for communicative purposes). Tager-Flusberg (1989) likened these subsystems to the strands in a braid. In children developing language normally (NL), the strands are braided together to form the language system whose character comes from the combination of the strands. In disordered populations the braid may be unraveled, and it is this unraveling that differentiates the language of children with language impairments from the language of children developing normally. This metaphor is especially powerful when describing the language production of children with specific language impairment (SLI). For these children, the pattern of development within a single subsystem, although delayed, may by itself appear normal. It is only when the relationships among the subsystems are studied together that qualitative differences in expressive language skills become apparent.

Historically, specific language impairment has been described as "...'specific' because it cannot readily be ascribed to those factors which often provide the general setting in which failure of language development is usually observed; namely deafness, mental deficiency, motor disability, or severe personality disorder" (Benton, 1964).[34] The diagnosis of specific language impairment continues to be defined by exclusion as little is known about the underlying etiology. Contemporary criteria for SLI were developed by Stark and Tallal (1981), whose definition includes what should not be impaired (e.g., normal oral motor functioning and neurological status) as well as the degree of severity of the language impairment.

It is estimated that somewhere between 3%-8% of preschoolers are at significant risk for SLI (Rescorla & Schwartz, 1990; Rice, in press; Stevenson & Richman, 1976). These children exhibit delayed onset of language out of step with social and cognitive skills (Johnston, 1982; 1987; Leonard, 1982; Rice, in press). Unlike children who outgrow their language difficulties by age 3 (Rescorla & Schwartz, 1990), children with SLI exhibit protracted development of all subsystems of language. The general consensus is that the linguistic skills of children with SLI look very much like those of NL children at the same linguistic age.[35] A preponderance of research supports the position that the language development of children with SLI follows the same course as that of typically developing children but at a slower rate (Johnston, 1982, 1987; Leonard, 1982) in all language subsystems, with the possible exception of a more severe deficit in morphology (Leonard, 1987). The majority of this research, however, has focused on a single subsystem of language and has ignored the qualitative differences that may emerge

---

[34] Benton (1964) referred to the disorder as *developmental aphasia*. The terms *aphasoid* (Lowe & Cambell, 1965), *Minimal Brain Dysfunction*, (Aten & Davis, 1968), and *developmental dysphasia* (Wyke, 1978), and others have been used to describe this population of children.

[35] Language age has traditionally been measured by Mean Length of Utterance in morphemes (Morehead & Ingram, 1973).

when the relationships among these subsystems are examined (see Leonard, Camarata et al. 1982a; Johnston & Kamhi, 1984, for exceptions). In other words, the various strands of language may develop at differing rates. The resultant language profile would then show a pattern of strengths and weakness not identical to any age group. The purpose of this study is to shed light on the hypothesized discontinuities described here by examining simultaneously the morphosyntactic, lexical, and pragmatic systems for five children with SLI through the use of language profiles. Before discussing the current study, I will briefly review relevant work on each of the subsystems.

12.1.2. The Morphosyntactic Skills of Children with SLI

Historically, attempts to characterize the language performance of children with SLI have focused on grammatical skill. Studies comparing the syntactic skills of SLI and typically developing, age-matched children have reported qualitative differences (Lee, 1966; Menyuk, 1964). With the introduction of Mean Length of Utterance (MLU) as a language metric in the early 1970s (Brown, 1973), the concept of linguistic age matching was introduced (Morehead & Ingram, 1970). This resulted in children with SLI being matched with NL children on the basis of MLU rather than chronological age. As noted in several of the excellent literature reviews on language disordered children (see Johnston, 1982, 1988; Leonard, 1982), the general impression then emerged that children with SLI look strikingly similar to younger control children of the same linguistic age. In particular, the types of sentence structures used by children with SLI and the sequence of grammatical acquisition appeared to parallel findings from studies with younger NL children. Despite the similarities in the emergence of syntactic components, several investigators found that children with SLI reach the criterion for mastery of grammatical morphemes (e.g., 90% occurrence in obligatory contexts) at higher MLU levels than do typically developing children (Frome-Loeb & Leonard, 1991; Ingram 1972; Johnston & Kamhi, 1984; Johnston & Schery 1976; Khan & James, 1983; Leonard, Sabbadini,

Leonard, & Volterra, 1987; Steckol & Leonard, 1979).[36] These findings suggested a selective impairment in the production of morphology.

Several researchers have attempted to identify the causal mechanism for the morphological impairment. Leonard and his colleagues (Leonard, 1989; Leonard et al., 1987; Leonard et al., 1988; Leonard et al., 1991) propose a "surface account." They found evidence from both English- and Italian-speaking children with SLI to suggest a specific deficit in perceiving and processing morphemes of low phonemic substance (e.g., nonsyllabic consonant segments and unstressed words and syllables of short duration). Counterevidence has been presented by proponents of the "missing feature" account (Gopnik, 1990a, 1990b). In this view, SLI children's problem with morphology is not with the surface form per se but with an absence of underlying grammatical features, such as number or tense (Gopnik, 1991). It should be noted that Rice and her colleagues found evidence that conflicts with both of the above views. Specifically, they found that children with SLI had more difficulty with particles than with prepositions, even though the same unstressed surface structure *on* is needed in both situations (Watkins & Rice, 1991). Furthermore, Rice and Oetting (1991) found children with SLI had more difficulty with the marking of number agreement in the verb phrase (e.g., *they walks*) than they did in the noun phrase (e.g., *two cats*).

In yet another study, Lahey, Liebergott, Chesnick, Menyuk, and Adams (1991) found that for SLI children with an MLU of 3.0 or below, morphological skills fall within the realm of *normal* variation. In their view, the differences in morphological skills found in children with SLI were consistent with the individual variation in which grammatical morphemes are acquired in typically developing children. This suggests that children with SLI may not have extraordinary difficulty with morphemes per se but instead demonstrate individual variation within a normal range.

---

[36] Fourteen early emerging grammatical morphemes were identified by Brown (1973). The grammatical morphemes that occur in the noun phrase are: the regular noun plural -*s*; the possessive noun -*'s*; the articles *a, the*; regular third-person singular present -*s*; and irregular third-person present. Grammatical morphemes that occur in the verb phrase include: progressive inflection -*ing*; regular past tense -*ed*; irregular past tense; the contractible auxiliary *be*; and the uncontractable copula. In addition there are two grammatical morphemes in prepositional phrases: *in* and *on*.

12.1.3. The Lexical Skills of Children with SLI

In contrast to the morphosyntactic subsystem, there has been relatively little empirical investigation into the acquisition of the lexical subsystem by children with SLI. Nevertheless, late emergence of words is considered the first indication of a language impairment (Leonard, 1988). Furthermore, evidence suggests that the rate of lexical acquisition appears to be slower for SLI children than for NL children (Leonard, 1988; Rice, in press; Rice, Buhr, & Nemeth, 1990).

Leonard and his colleagues found marked similarities in the productive vocabularies of SLI as compared to NL children in the one-word stage of language development (Leonard, Camarata et al., 1982a). In a related study, Leonard, Schwartz et al. 1982) provided children with concentrated linguistic stimulation over 10 sessions. They found both SLI and NL children understood more novel object words than novel action words, although children with SLI produced more action words than did the NL children. These authors cautioned against interpreting their results to mean that the rate of acquisition is not slowed since the task did not require the children to extend their word knowledge past the original referent (Leonard, 1988; Leonard, Schwartz et al., 1982).

Schwartz (1988) pointed out that all of the novel action words in Leonard, Schwartz et al., (1982) were intransitive verbs, which are conceptually more difficult than transitive verbs. With this in mind, Schwartz (1988) extended the Leonard, Schwartz et al. (1982) study by examining both transitive and intransitive action word types. He found that unlike the NL children, who had significantly more problems with intransitive verb types, the children with SLI did not exhibit differences across action word types. Schwartz suggested that the SLI children's slight advantage with action words might be attributable to their higher chronological age and hence greater world experience.

The lexical acquisition process has also been studied in slightly older children with SLI. Dollaghan (1987) studied 4;0- to 5;6-year-old SLI and NL children on a fast mapping task (Carey & Bartlett, 1978). Fast mapping, as it is used here, required children to learn a nonsense word for unfamiliar objects on the basis of a single exposure. Dollaghan found that the children with SLI did not differ from the NL children in their ability to learn novel words for unfamiliar objects during comprehension but not production. In contrast, Rice and her colleagues (Rice, in press; Rice, Buhr, & Nemeth, 1990) have found 5-year-old children with SLI to be slower at acquiring novel object words than either language- or age-matched NL children when a more challenging input situation is employed. In Rice's experimental paradigm (see Rice, 1990), children must pick out novel words from an ongoing stream of words during a videotape presentation and match the novel words to the target in an ongoing stream of references and events. Rice and her colleagues contend that their procedure is similar to everyday situations in which the child must pick up novel words within an ongoing stream of talk.

Taken together, the studies on lexical acquisition suggest that children with SLI are at risk for delayed vocabulary development. In other words, they may be better able to acquire vocabulary when directly taught, even though the incidental learning available to NL children (e.g., picking up words they hear in their environment) may be compromised.

12.1.4. The Pragmatic Skills of Children with SLI

In the past decade, there has been considerable evidence to suggest that the assessment of pragmatic skills is crucial to our understanding of the nature of language impairments (e.g., Leonard, 1986; Prutting & Kirchner, 1987; Roth & Spekman, 1984; Wetherby, Yonclas, & Bryan, 1989). Researchers interested in the communicative interactions of children with SLI have, for the most part, focused on one or more component skills of pragmatic functioning. Specifically, they have focused on the speech act level (e.g., statements, requests, or warnings); the conversational level (e.g., speaker initiator or respondent roles); and the interactional level (e.g., the ability to establish attention, maintain a joint focus, or regulate the behaviors of others). Overall, studies that focused on the speech act level found that children with SLI are restricted in the range of speech acts used or produced when compared to chronologically matched controls, but look very much like MLU-matched younger children in terms of their speech act production (Leonard, Camarata et al., 1982; Rom & Bliss, 1981).

Although a majority of research has found parity in the pragmatic skills of children with SLI and language-matched controls, evidence does exist that suggests otherwise. Snyder (1978) found children with SLI to be deficient relative to younger NL children in their use of language to express declarative and imperative intent. Ball, Cross, and Horsborough (1982) found children with SLI used more requests when compared to their linguistically matched pairs. Furthermore, Rollins and her colleagues (Pan, Rollins, & Snow, 1991; Rollins, 1990) found that the pragmatic skills of children with SLI are more advanced than those of NL children of the same syntactic stage. In summary, although several researchers have found similarities in the range and frequency of speech acts used by children with SLI when compared to children of the same language age, other researchers have found differences. So, these questions remain open.

12.1.5. The Goal of This Chapter

Thus far, I have reviewed research on the individual subsystems of language for children with SLI. Johnston (1982, 1987) and Leonard (1982) suggested that comparing several subsystems simultaneously will help to reveal developmental discontinuities across the major language subsystems. The purpose of this study is to construct language profiles for four children with SLI in order to examine these hypothesized developmental discontinuities. Such research has been difficult to perform in the past because of the labor-intensive nature of the language analysis. The advance of computerized technology, such as CHAT and CLAN, within the CHILDES system has made it possible for researchers and clinicians to directly address the labor-intensive questions inherent in cross-subsystem analyses.

12.2. Method

12.2.1. Subjects

The subjects for this study were taken from the Conti-Ramsden corpus (Conti-Ramsden & Dykins, 1990) of the Child Language Data Exchange System (MacWhinney & Snow, 1985, 1989). The Conti-Ramsden corpus consists of specific language impaired children matched during an initial screening with a younger normal-language sibling on the basis of Mean Length of Utterance (MLU).[37] All children functioned within normal limits on the Leiter International Performance Scale (Leiter, 1969), a test of nonverbal intelligence, and on the comprehension subscale of the Preschool Language Scale (PLS-C; Zimmerman,

---

[37] Although matched at the initial screening, one sibling pair did not meet the inclusion criterion when the sample of talk donated to the CHILDES data base was analyzed. This pair was not included in the present study. Further it should be noted that the MLUs from the initial screening sessions were not furnished to me.

Steiner, & Pond, 1979), a composite measure of language comprehension skills (refer to Table 12.1). It should be noted that the children with SLI did less well on specific tests of lexical comprehension.[38] A hearing screening determined that all subjects had normal bilateral hearing, there was no history of chronic otitis media, and all children passed a neurological screening.

An important feature of these data is that the children with SLI were compared with their siblings. By using children from the same family, it was possible to control for all background variables, including language of the home environment. Therefore, this design offers distinct advantages over traditional designs in which children with SLI are matched with NL children from different families. However, the stringent selection criteria did have several ramifications. First, because of the familial aggregation found in SLI (Bishop & Edmundson, 1986; Tallal, Ross & Curtis, 1989), it is not often that one finds an older, cognitively intact child with SLI

Table 12.1: Individual subject characteristics.

Group	Subject	CA	COMP_AGE	MA	IQ
SLI	Sid	4;09	4;10	5;10	110
Sibling	Sue	2;05	2;03	2;03	98
SLI	Clay	5;10	5;04	4;09	85
Sibling	Charles	2;04	2;04	2;00	91
SLI	Kate	4;09	3;10	4;03	95
Sibling	Kyle	2;04	2;01	2;03	101
SLI	Rick	6;09	6;06	6;06	108
Sibling	Rose	3;02	2;09	3;03	101

CA = chronological age; COMP_AGE = comprehension age as measured by the Preschool Language Scale Comprehension Subtest; MA = mental age measured by the Leiter International Performance Scale; IQ = intelligence measured by the Leiter International Performance Scale

---

[38] The children with SLI exhibited mild-to-moderate delays on the Test of Receptive Grammar (TROG; Bishop, 1982) and moderate-to-severe delays on the British Picture Vocabulary Scale (BPVS; Dunn, Whetton, & Pintillie, 1982). The siblings were not administered either the TROG or the BPVS because of their young age.

at the same expressive language stage as a younger, normally developing, sibling. Only 5 out of the 36 potential participating families were included in the final sample. Second, the children with SLI in this study had severe expressive language deficits, reflected in the fact that their mean length of utterance fell far below age expectancies. Consequently, MLU-matched siblings for these children were very young. The severity of the expressive language delay makes this sample of children somewhat unusual for children with SLI.

Videotaped and transcribed spontaneous mother-child interaction provided the basis for the analyses. Each child was videotaped interacting individually with his or her mother in a free-play situation. Each videotape represents 15 minutes of continuous mother-child interaction. Though this study utilized the full 15 minute-videotape, only 10-minute segments were later donated to CHILDES.

12.2.2. Language Measures

Morphosyntactic Measures

Mean length of utterance (MLU) (Brown, 1973) and morphological saturation (Pan & Elkins, 1989; Rollins, Pan, & Snow, 1991) were used to measure morphosyntactic skill. MLU calculations were derived for each child from a corpora of 60 utterances, to control for possible sampling differences across children.[39] Utterances containing imitations, self-repetitions, and routine utterances (e.g., peek-a-boo) were excluded from the MLU analyses. Morphological Saturation scores were derived from all nonimitative utterances in the 10 minute sample. The two measures, MLU and morphological saturation, were chosen for the two reasons discussed in the following paragraphs.

Mean length of utterance was used to measure syntactic complexity. It is considered a general index of syntactic age because of the fairly high correlation with both formal measures of syntactical stage (to an MLU of at least 3 or 4) and chronological age in children developing normally (Brown, 1973; Miller & Chapman, 1981; Rondal, Ghiotto, Bredart, & Bachelet, 1987; Scarborough, 1990; Scarborough, Wyckoff, & Davidson, 1986). Recently, similar relationships have been documented with children with SLI (Klee, Schaffer, May, Membrino, &

---

[39] Sixty utterances were the highest number of utterances used by all of the children in the full 15-minute session.

Mougey, 1989; Scarborough, Rescorla, Tager-Flusberg, Fowler, & Sudhalter, 1992). These authors use somewhat stricter criteria for calculating MLU than are often employed in studies with normally developing children in order to neutralize the effects of utterances that may artificially inflate or deflate MLU calculations (e.g., routines, imitations, or self-repetitions). Furthermore, Rollins (1990) found a close relationship between MLU and the Index of Productive Syntax (Scarborough, 1990), a formal measure of syntactic skill, for the children in this study. Thus, when routines, imitations, and self-repetitions were excluded from the MLU calculations, MLU was found to be a good proxy for syntactic level for the children in this study.

Morphological saturation was used as a developmentally sensitive measure of morphology (Rollins, Pan, & Snow, 1991). Although researchers interested in morphological skills of children with SLI have focused on the occurrence of Brown's (1973) 14 grammatical morphemes in their obligatory contexts, this approach is not practical for the analysis of the morphological skills of children at emergent stages of language development. First, certain morphological categories do not naturally occur at high frequencies, particularly when language samples contain relatively few utterances; and second, considerable interpretation of the child's intended utterance is often required in order to determine which morphological marker is obligatory. Morphological saturation, as it is used here, is not a measure of the child's mastery of particular morphemes, as would be the case in a more traditional Brown-type analysis. Rather, *morphological saturation* refers to the percentage of noun phrases in which the child correctly uses any morphological element when that element is obligatory. For example, in the utterance *I like cat*, the noun phrase *cat* is unsaturated because English requires either an article, a demonstrative pronoun, or a plural marker. Saturated versions of this noun phrase might be *I like the cat*, *I like that cat*, or *I like cats*. Thus, it is not necessary to know which noun phrase a child intended in order to code the noun phrase as unsaturated. Verb phrase saturation was not addressed in this study because the children in this study used too few verb phrases for the measure to be meaningful. Please see the Appendix for a list of morphological saturation codes.

Lexical Measures

The number of different words in 10 minutes (types) and the total number of words in 10 minutes (tokens) were used as measures of lexical skill (see Klee, 1992;

Miller, 1991; Pan, this volume, for a discussion). Although type-token ratio (TTR) has traditionally been used as a measure of lexical diversity, it has been criticized as a language metric when the sample size is below 200 utterances (Richards, 1987). Furthermore, Klee (1992) found that measures of number of different words (types) and total number of words (tokens) were sensitive enough to differentiate the skills of SLI children from NL children where (TTR) was not.

Pragmatic Measures

Pragmatic flexibility is a measure of pragmatic ability and is based on an abridged version of Ninio and Wheeler's (1984) pragmatic coding scheme (see Ninio, Snow, Pan, & Rollins, 1990). In this scheme, each child's communicative acts are coded independently for three different levels of pragmatic intention. The first level, the *interchange level*, describes the child's intention within the social context of an ongoing activity. Coding at the interchange level captures what takes place between the speaker and the hearer. Some examples of interchange levels involving the mother and child include discussion of a joint focus, direction of the hearer's attention to objects or events, or negotiation of the immediate activity. The second level addresses the specific communicative intent expressed by the child's utterance, which motivates his or her act of speaking. This level is called the *speech act level*, and includes such acts as making statements, making requests, or answering questions. The third and final level is the *conversational level,* which includes opening moves, responses to opening moves, and elaborations. Please refer to the CHILDES manual (MacWhinney, 1991; this volume) for a complete list of coding categories. Pragmatic flexibility combines the interchange, speech act, and conversational levels of pragmatic intention into a single measure. This measure is defined as the frequency of the number of different social interchange-speech act types within both openers and responses. For example, if within all interchanges involving negotiate immediate activity (NIA), Rick used 9 different speech acts that were openers and 11 different speech acts that were responses, his pragmatic flexibility score for negotiating the immediate activity would be 20. The overall pragmatic flexibility score is defined as the frequency of the number of different opener and responsive speech act types used within each of the 22 interchange types. Pragmatic flexibility has been found to differentiate SLI children from NL children more accurately than any one of the three levels measured individually (Rollins, 1990; Rollins, Pan, Conti-Ramsden, & Snow, 1990).

12.2.3. CLAN Procedures

This section describes the CLAN procedures used for this study. The file **rickcod.cha** is provided to illustrate the coding conventions and CLAN commands utilized in the analyses performed in this chapter. **Rickcod.cha** is a CHAT-formatted transcript embellished with both morphological saturation and pragmatic flexibility codes on individual dependent tiers (**%mph** and **%spa** respectively). The target child, Rick, is identified by the three-letter speaker code *CHI, and his mother is identified by the three-letter speaker code *MOT.

> The CLAN utility **PAGE** can be used to view the **rickcod.cha** file one page at a time. The command for doing this is: **page rickcod.cha**.

Mean Length of Utterance

The basic MLU program was previously described by Pan (this volume). Going beyond the basics, it is often necessary to exclude certain utterance types from the analysis when calculating MLU for children with SLI. The programs in CLAN can easily accommodate such variations to the MLU calculation if the transcripts to be analyzed contain **post-codes**. Post-codes identify the type of utterance produced by the speaker and are placed after the utterance delimiter (e.g., the punctuation) at the end of speaker tiers. In Example 1, the first child utterance (on the speaker tier *CHI) is coded as an imitation **[+ I]** whereas the second child utterance is coded as a self-repetition **[+ SR]**. The other post-codes found in the Conti-Ramsden corpus are listed in Table 12.2.

```
(1) *MOT:      you want to go out.
    *CHI:      go out. [+ I]
    *CHI:      go out. [+ SR]
```

In the current study, the MLU for each child was calculated on the first 60 utterances that did not contain imitations, self-repetitions, or routines. For example, the following command was used to calculate Rick's MLU using this criterion:

mlu +t*CHI +z1u–60u –s"< + I >" –s"< + SR >" –s"< + R >" rickcod.cha

+t*CHI	Analyze the child speaker tier only
–s"< + I >"	Exclude utterances post-coded as [+ I]
–s"< + SR >"	" " " [+ SR]
–s"< + R >"	" " " [+ R]
+z1u-60u	Analyze the first 60 utterances meeting the criteria
rickcod.cha	The child language transcript to be analyzed

Command Box 12.1

This MLU command utilizes the –s option to specify that those utterances marked with the post-codes [+ I], [+ SR], or [+ R] should be excluded from the analysis. In other words, the three –s options instruct CLAN to analyze all utterances except those ending with the post-codes [+ I], [+ SR], and [+ R].

You will notice that angle brackets (< >) were used in the specification of the individual post-codes rather than square brackets ([ ]). This is an important CLAN feature: In order for CLAN to *manipulate* text preceding square brackets in the transcript file, angle brackets are required in the CLAN command. In this instance, post-codes were placed in angle brackets, allowing for the manipulation of

Table 12.2: The list of post-codes found in the Conti-Ramsden corpus.

Utterance Type	Post-Code
Routines	[+ R]
Book Readings	[+ "]
Interjections/Fillers	[+ F]
Imitations	[+ I]
Self-Repetitions	[+ SR]
Isolated Onomatopoeic Sounds	[+ O]
Partially Unintelligible	[+ PI]
One-Word Answers to Yes/No Questions	[+ Q]

the *entire utterance* preceding the specified code. Notice also that quotations were placed around each of the codes to be excluded. This is necessary whenever the code of interest contains a space, such as the one between the '+' and the 'Q' in the code < + Q>. As a result of the quotation, CLAN treats the space as a part of the string of characters for which the search is being conducted. If there were no quotation marks around the codes in the command, CLAN would note the presence of a space, treat it as a word delimiter, and expect a known CLAN option or input file. Forgetting to place quotations around codes that contain spaces will yield an error message.

The following command illustrates an alternative way to calculate Rick's MLU:

mlu +t*CHI +z1u-60u –s@exmlu rickcod.cha

+t*CHI	Analyze the child speaker tier only
+z1u-60u	Analyze the first 60 utterances meeting the criteria
–s@exmlu	Exclude utterances with the post-codes listed in the file **exmlu**
rickcod.cha	The child language transcript to be analyzed

Command Box 12.2

The –s@exmlu option indicates that the post-codes to be excluded are contained in an exclude file called **exmlu**. This file contains the following post-codes:

    < + I>
    < + SR>
    < + R>

In order for CLAN to recognize and read an **exclude file**, it must contain only ASCII characters. This can be accomplished using any word processor and saving the file as unformatted text. Three other constraints on exclude files are noteworthy: (a) the first physical line of the exclude file must contain a code; (b) only one code (word or string of characters) may be placed on a line; and (c) each line must end with a carriage return. Because of the second and third constraints, it is not necessary to place quotations around post-codes contained in exclude files.

As indicated below, Rick's MLU is identified as the Ratio of morphemes over utterances:

```
MLU.EXE +t*CHI +z1-60U -s@exmlu rickcod.cha
MLU.EXE (04-MAY-93) is conducting analyses on:
  ONLY speaker main tiers matching: *CHI;
*****************************************
From file <rickcod.cha>
MLU for Speaker: *CHI:
   MLU (xxx and yyy are EXCLUDED from the utterance
   and morpheme counts):
      Number of: utterances = 60, morphemes = 123
      Ratio of morphemes over utterances = 2.050
      Standard deviation = 1.477
```

Morphological Saturation

Morphological saturation codes (refer to the Appendix) were entered into the transcript files on the dependent tier labeled **%mph**. For example, the following child utterance was coded as an unsaturated noun phrase ($NP:U) on the %mph tier. This is because English noun phrases require an article, a demonstrative pronoun, or a plural marker to be saturated.

```
*CHI:  car.
%mph:  $NP:U
```

The FREQ program may be used to tabulate the total number of noun-phrase codes that either were saturated ($NP:S) or unsaturated ($NP:U). The following command was used to perform this analysis for the child in the **rickcod.cha** file:

freq +t*CHI +t%mph −t* +s$NP:S +s$NP:U −s@exmlu rickcod.cha

+t*CHI	Analyze the child speaker tier only
+t%mph	Include the **%mph** tier in the analysis
−t*	Ignore material on the speaker tiers
−s@exmlu	Exclude utterances with the post-codes listed in **exmlu**
+s$NP:S, +s$NP:U	Search for all instances of $NP:S and $NP:U
rickcod.cha	The child language transcript to be analyzed

Command Box 12.3

This command contains three **t** options: +t*CHI, +t%mph, and –t*. When used together, they instruct CLAN to analyze only the %mph tiers that are associated with the child's speaker tiers. The +s$NP:S and +s$NP:U options instruct CLAN to search for and tabulate frequency counts for only these two specific codes.

> The use of the **–t*** option is a precautionary measure which insures that CLAN programs will ignore speaker tiers when codes are being analyzed. Another layer of protection may be achieved by always using codes with prefixed dollar signs (e.g., $NP:S). This convention also permits a wildcard search using the string **+s$***. Dollar signs are useful because they do not occur as part of English words and are therefore not likely to appear on speaker tiers as speech.

The following is the output of this FREQ command:

```
FREQ.EXE +t*CHI +t%mph -t* +s$np:s +s$np:u -s@exmlu rickcod.cha
FREQ.EXE (04-MAY-93) is conducting analyses on:
  ONLY dependent tiers matching: %MPH;
*****************************************
From file <rickcod.cha>
  9 $np:s
 11 $np:u
-------------------------------
    2  Total number of different word types used
   20  Total number of words (tokens)
0.100  Type/Token ratio
```

Recall that noun phrase saturation is the percentage of noun phrases in which the child correctly uses a morphological element. To calculate the noun phrase saturation score for Rick in the **rickcod.cha** file, we divided the number of noun phrases that were saturated (9), by the total number of noun phrases (20) which was listed on the line labeled "Total number of words (tokens)." Hence, in this example, the noun-phrase saturation score for Rick was 9 ÷ 20 or 45%.

> You can only use the +s and the –s in the same CLAN command if they contain different types of material. For example, we cannot use a CLAN command that includes one list of words while simultaneously excluding another list of words. Similarly we cannot use a CLAN command that includes one list of post-codes while excluding another list of post-codes.

We can, however, use a CLAN command that searches for a list of words (in this case $NP:S and $NP:U) while excluding a list of post-codes.

Lexical Measures

The CLAN procedure for computing a Type-Token ratio was previously described by Pan (this volume). The procedure for computing the total number of different words (types) and the total number of words (tokens) is exactly the same. What is different is where in the resultant output the answer is found. For example, the following command was used to count the number of types and tokens for the child in **rickcod.cha**:

freq +t*CHI +s*–%% +d4 rickcod.cha

+t*CHI	Analyze the child speaker tier only
+s*–%%	Include everything before the hyphen ignoring everything following it (including the hyphen)
+d4	Output type/token summaries only
rickcod.cha	The child language transcript to be analyzed

Command Box 12.4

The output of this FREQ command is as follows:

```
FREQ.EXE +t*CHI +s*-%% +d4 rickcod.cha
FREQ.EXE (04-MAY-93) is conducting analyses on:
  ONLY speaker main tiers matching: *CHI;
****************************************
From file <rickcod.cha>
-------------------------------
   81  Total number of different word types used
  203  Total number of words (tokens)
0.399  Type/Token ratio
```

Within the output, types are identified as the "Total number of different word types used" (third line from the bottom), whereas tokens are identified as the "Total number of words (tokens)" (second line from the bottom).

Nonlexical items, such as exclamations (*aah, aw, whee*) or interactional markers (*hmm, huh*), often make their way into frequency lists. In addition, frequency lists may have several variants of the same form (*yup, yea, yes, yeah*). The former artificially inflates both the number of different word types and the total number of word tokens, whereas the latter only inflates the number of different word types. There are two ways of handling this situation. One method is to edit the transcript by marking nonlexical words (e.g., *ah*) so that they will be ignored by the FREQ program. For example, you could place a plus sign in front of the word (e.g., *+ah*). An alternative method is to simply subtract the offending words from the total counts by hand.

Pragmatic Flexibility

Codes for pragmatic flexibility were entered into the transcripts on a **%spa** dependent tier. The three-level structure of each code was $INT:SA:C, where INT is a three-letter interchange code, SA is a two letter speech act code and C is a one-letter conversational code. Recall that pragmatic flexibility is the number of different interchange-speech act combinations within both openers and responses. Thus we can use the FREQ program to tabulate Rick's pragmatic flexibility score with the following command:

freq +t*CHI +t%spa −t* +s$*:*:r +s$*:*:o rickcod.cha

+t*CHI	Analyze the child speaker tier only
+t%spa	Include the %spa tier in the analysis
−t*	Ignore material on the speaker tiers
+s$*:*:o	Include all interchange-speech act combinations within openers
+s$*:*:r	Include all interchange-speech act combinations within responses
rickcod.cha	The child language transcript to be analyzed

Command Box 12.5

This FREQ command is similar to the one used to obtain the noun-phrase saturation score. That is, three **t** options (+t*CHI, +t%spa, and –t*) were employed to instruct FREQ to analyze only the %spa tiers that are associated with the child's speaker tiers. As before, the –t* option is a precautionary measure insuring that FREQ analyzes only codes, while ignoring speech. Furthermore, the **+s$*:*:o** and **+s$*:*:r** options were used to instruct FREQ to search for and tabulate the frequency of all the codes on the %spa tier that are openers ($*:*:o) or responses ($*:*:r). Pragmatic Flexibility is identified as the "Total number of different word types used." The results of the pragmatic flexibility analysis are as follows:

```
FREQ.EXE +t*CHI +t%spa -t* +s$*:*:o +s$*:*:r rickcod.cha
FREQ.EXE (04-MAY-93) is conducting analyses on:
  ONLY dependent tiers matching: %SPA;
*****************************************
From file <rickcod.cha>
  1 $dcc:aa:r
  1 $dcc:ad:r
  2 $dcc:an:r
       .
       .
       .
  1 $nma:cl:o
  7 $ooo:oo:o
  1 $ooo:oo:r
  2 $pss:st:o
------------------------------
    53 Total number of different word types used
   115 Total number of words (tokens)
 0.461 Type/Token ratio
```

12.2.4. Repetitive Analyses

To generate the language profiles for all eight children in the sample, the same sequence of commands must be typed over and over again. Such repetitive analyses are easily accomplished using *batch files*. A batch file, in its most basic form, is an ASCII (or unformatted) file that contains a list of system and/or CLAN commands that are to be executed sequentially. Batch files can be created with any word processor by saving the files as unformatted text or by using an ASCII text editor. Though the commands within the file are executed by simply typing the name of the batch file, the exact procedure differs slightly depending on which computer system you are using (e.g., PC, MACINTOSH, or UNIX). If the batch file is intended for

PCs, its filename must end with the extension **.bat** and may be executed by typing the filename without the extension. For example, if the CLAN commands discussed in this chapter were listed in a file named **sli.bat**, the PC user would type the following command from within the **conti** directory:

sli

For MACINTOSH computers, the batch file can take any name (with or without an extension) and is executed by typing **#filename**. Thus, MACINTOSH users would type the following to execute the **sli.bat** file:

#sli.bat

Finally, for UNIX computers, the batch file (called a *shell script*) can also take any name. The catch here is that you must first change the mode of the file to make it executable by typing the UNIX command **chmod +x filename** the first time the file is to be used. Thus, UNIX users would type the following to execute the commands listed in the shell script named **sli.bat** for the first time:

chmod +x sli.bat
sli.bat

For each subsequent usage, they would type:

sli.bat

It should be noted that batch files for the MACINTOSH are a special addition created specifically for the CLAN environment, whereas batch files for PCs and shell scripts for UNIX machines are inherent to their respective operating systems.

PC users should be warned that the % symbol has a special meaning inside batch programs written under the DOS environment. For this reason, PC users will need to insert additional % symbols in CLAN commands placed inside of batch programs. Stated differently, each time the % symbol is used to indicate a dependent tier (e.g., **%spa**) or a metacharactor (e.g.,

+s*–%%), the number of % symbols must be doubled. Thus, %spa would be %%spa, and +s*–%% would be +s*–%%%%.

12.3. Results

The morphosyntactic, lexical, and pragmatic subsystems of each child were examined collectively by generating language profiles.[40] Because each of the language measures was originally in a different metric, each raw score was standardized prior to construction of the profiles.[41] Standardizing the raw scores for each of the different subsystems enforces a single metric and makes it possible to present the scores for each of the different subsystems on a single graph. In this way, it is easy to see how children with SLI compare with their NL siblings.

If a child with SLI is functioning similarly to his or her sibling on all the language subsystems within the graph, then their profiles should resemble one another. If, however, a child with SLI has a profile of relative strengths (e.g., performance that is one standard deviation greater than his or her sibling) or weaknesses (e.g., performance that is one standard deviation less), then that child's language profile will diverge from the NL sibling and be suggestive of a qualitative difference in overall language production skills.

The first pair of language profiles for Clay and Chuck (displayed in Figure 12.1) are very similar across the morphosyntactic, lexical, and pragmatic subsystems. Specifically, the child with SLI in Figure 12.1 functioned remarkably similarly to his younger sibling across all the language subsystems. This pattern of language skills supports previous research that suggests that the language of children with SLI follows the same course of development as that of NL children, only more slowly. However, when the relationships among the subsystems were analyzed for the other three pairs of children such parity was not maintained. Moreover, there was considerable heterogeneity across the four pairs of siblings.

---

[40] These profiles were generated using an earlier version of CLAN and may differ slightly from the results for any current analyses.

[41] Standardization was based on these children only, and refers only to this sample and to no larger population. Each language profile, therefore, signifies only the relative differences in the level of performance between these children with SLI and their NL siblings.

394   Chapter 12

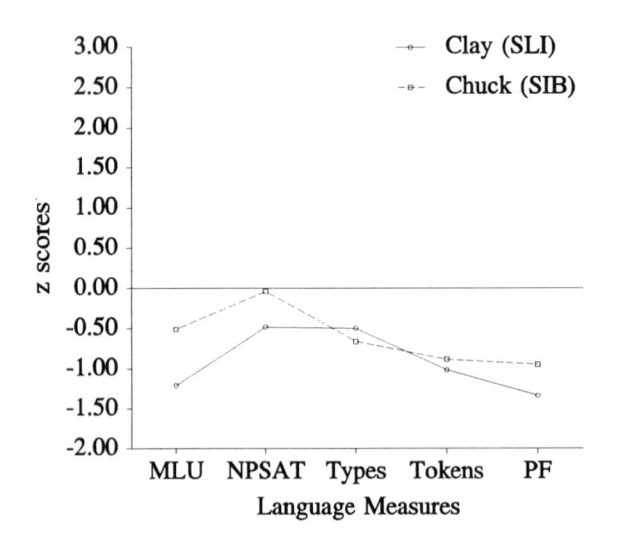

[Graph showing z scores for Clay (SLI) and Chuck (SIB) across Language Measures: MLU, NPSAT, Types, Tokens, PF]

Figure 12.1: The language profile for Clay (MLU = 1.17) and Chuck (MLU = 1.25).

The second and third pairs of language profiles are displayed in Figures 12.2 and 12.3, respectively.[42] The profile for Sid and Rick look quite similar in relation to their siblings. That is, the children with SLI in Figures 12.2 and 12.3 demonstrate relative weakness in morphological development despite similarities in lexical and syntactic skills when compared to their siblings. Moreover, these two children with SLI exhibit relative strength in pragmatic functioning when compared to their siblings. The pattern of language development depicted in these two profiles demonstrates that the language of children with SLI is qualitatively different than that of NL children. The last profile (displayed in Figure 12.4) also supports the hypothesis that the language of children with SLI is qualitatively different from younger NL children functioning at the same syntactic stage. Yet the pattern of relative strengths and weakness for the child with SLI in Figure 12.4 is different

---

[42] A qualitative analysis of saturated noun phrases revealed that Sid, the child with SLI in Figure 12.2, accomplished saturation by using only the demonstrative+noun sentence construction. This is noteworthy because the demonstrative is not one of Brown's (1973) 14 grammatical morphemes. That is, although Sid saturated many of his noun phrases, he did so by using a rather simple morphological marker. For this reason, Figure 12.2 displays the profiles for Sid and his sibling, controlling for the demonstrative+noun sentence construction.

Specific Language Impairment 395

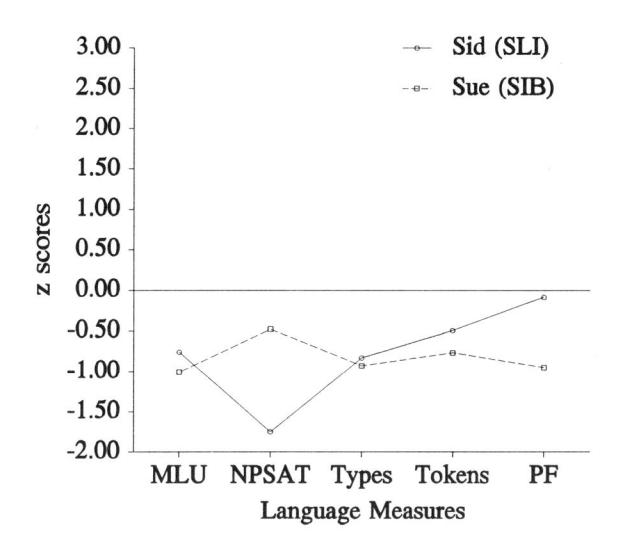

Figure 12.2: The language profile for Sid (MLU = 1.35) and Sue (MLU = 1.25).

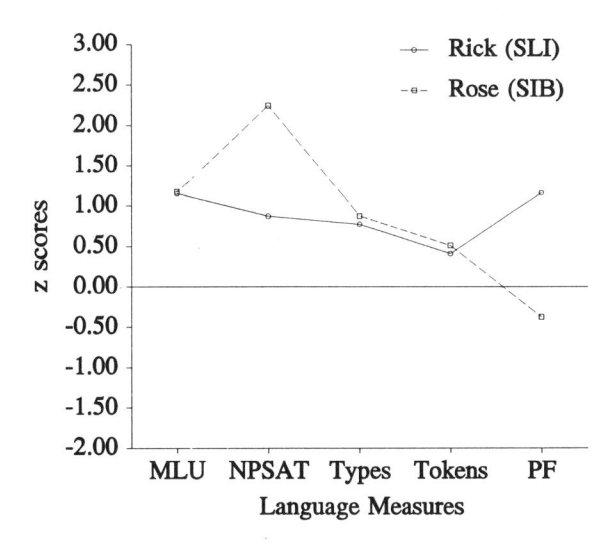

Figure 12.3: The language profile for Rick (MLU = 2.17) and Rose (MLU = 2.13).

396   Chapter 12

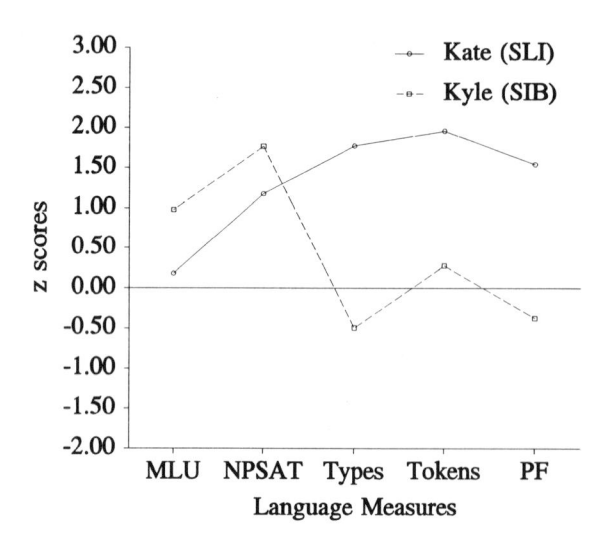

Figure 12.4: The language profile for Kate (MLU = 1.75) and Kyle (MLU = 2.05).

from the other children with SLI in this study. That is, the child with SLI in Figure 12.4 is observed to have relative strengths in both lexical and pragmatic skills. A qualitative analysis confirmed that the child with SLI used many more substantive words (e.g., nouns, verbs, and adjectives) than did the NL sibling.

12.6. Discussion

I began this chapter by suggesting that the simultaneous examination of the major subsystems of language would reveal asynchronous development in children with SLI as compared to NL children of similar linguistic ability. The existence of these developmental discontinuities was demonstrated in three of the four language profiles studied. Of these children, only Clay (Figure 12.1) did not exhibit developmental discontinuities across the language subsystems. However, because Clay's nonverbal IQ (86 on the Leiter International Performance Scale) was at the low end of current diagnostic standards (Tallal & Curtis, 1981), his language development may have been constrained differently than that of the other three children with SLI.

Although the severity of the deficit differed for each child, the other three children with SLI (Figures 12.2, 12.3, and 12.4) all displayed relative weakness in the morphological subsystem. This finding is generally consistent with past research, which indicates that children with SLI have difficulties with the morphological subsystem. The exact nature of the difficulty cannot be identified from this study.[43]

Also consistent with past research was the similarity of the productive vocabularies of three of the children with SLI and their NL siblings. Interestingly, each of these sibling pairs (see Figures 12.1, 12.2, and 12.3) appeared more similar to each other than to the other children in the study. This suggests that environmental influences stemming from family background may have influenced the lexical skills of these children at least during the early levels of language development. It should be remembered, however, that this research focused only on productive vocabularies and cannot say anything about the *process* of vocabulary acquisition.

A new finding of the present study is that three of the children with SLI (Figures 12.2, 12.3, and 12.4) had relative strength in the pragmatic subsystem, although this distinction differed in magnitude across the children. This finding may be related to the higher chronological and mental age of the children with SLI. In other words, differences in cognitive level, social experience, and perhaps verbal interaction may have benefitted the SLI children's use of language within the social context.

The individual children with SLI in this study came to the task of learning language with differences in family background, chronological age, and intellectual functioning. These differences, in turn, may have affected the manner in which the language subsystems of relative strength adapted to compensate for the language subsystems of relative weakness. This process of adaptation may help to explain the variation we see in the language profiles of the four sibling pairs. An example from Sid (Figure 12.2) may help to clarify this point. In one episode, Sid eagerly tried to tell his mother that she was not putting a toy together correctly. He persisted in his attempts over 18 turns until he was finally successful in

---

[43] In order to answer the question concerning the nature of the difficulty, an analysis of obligatory context (Brown, 1973) would be required. As stated earlier, this analysis is problematic.

communicating his message. Sid's communicative attempts were constrained by his limitations in morphosyntactic and lexical skills as compared to his pragmatic abilities. He said things like: "that there," "no!", "Mama," and "that right" while shaking his head to mean "that is not right." Despite these grammatical limitations, Sid's persistence in attempting to communicate his intended message was illustrated by the large variety of different speech acts he used to negotiate the activity: He made statements, criticized the hearer's actions, proposed suggestions, marked the completion of an activity, answered in the affirmative to a yes/no question, and called his mother to gain her attention.

Sid, like the other children with SLI in the study, exhibited relative weakness in one subsystem of language and used his relative strengths in another subsystem to compensate. Thus, to adequately describe the disorder of specific language impairment, we cannot look at only a single-subsystem, but must describe the relationships among various subsystems. As was evident from the review of the literature, the majority of research concerning children with SLI tends to take an in-depth look into only one language subsystem at a time. It is important to point out that this type of research has yielded insights into the nature of the language disorder. The single subsystem approach lays the foundation for understanding the microstructure of the language disorder, but it is only with cross-subsystem research that we can begin to understand the macrostructure of the disorder, and thus the heterogeneity found within the population. Stated differently, the single subsystem approach cannot capture the contributions that each of the language subsystems makes to the overall language product. The manner in which each of the subsystems develops within the language disorder to create the language product may only be understood when both approaches to the study of language disorders are considered together.

12.7. Exercises

The files for the following exercises are in two directories: The transcript for **kid055b.cha**, the normal language child, is in the directory **\NEngland\20mos**; while the transcripts for the language impaired children are in **\conti**.

12.7.1. It is generally accepted that the mean length of utterance of children with language disorders may be particularly sensitive to certain utterance types (e.g.,

Specific Language Impairment   399

routines or imitations). Despite this, there is no clear consensus as to which utterance types should be included or excluded in MLU calculations. Chapman (1981) suggested that the sensitivity of MLU to particular utterance forms be assessed by generating MLU estimates both with and without these forms. In this exercise, you will be asked to estimate the MLU for the child in the **abe.cha** file by systematically excluding each utterance type listed in Table 12.2 and to record the effects of each analysis on the child's MLU. To which utterance type(s) was the child's MLU most sensitive?

12.7.2. Write a batch program to accomplish the analysis in Exercise 12.7.1.

12.7.3. In this exercise you are asked to re-estimate MLU50 for the child in the **kid055b.cha** file by systematically excluding each utterance type listed in Table 12.2 and by recording the effects of each analysis on the child's MLU50. To accomplish this, however, you must first edit the **kid055b.cha** transcript so that it includes these post-codes. Compare the MLU50's obtained in this exercise with the same child's unconstrained MLU50. Does the child's MLU50 change or remain the same with the exclusion of specific utterance types? Why do you think this is true?

12.7.4. Many people interested in the language of children with SLI may want to calculate the total number of words (tokens) and the number of different words (types) only on complete and intelligible child utterances. This may be done if the transcript is post-coded for partially unintelligible utterances [+ PI]. In this exercise, you are asked to perform the following analyses using the FREQ program:

A. Compute the total number of words (tokens) and the number of different words (types) first on all of the child's utterances, and second only on the child's complete and intelligible utterances. Use the data for the child in the **abe.cha** transcript for this analysis.

B. Compare the obtained scores from Part A of this exercise with those from a group of normal children at roughly the same MLU level. To do this, you must generate *z*-scores using the means and standard deviations for the number of types and tokens used by the New England sample at 20 months (refer to Table 12.3). Recall from chapters 2 and 7, that *z*-scores, or standard scores, are computed by subtracting each child's score on a particular measure from the group mean and then dividing the results by the overall standard deviation.

Does excluding partially intelligible utterances from the calculation of these measures influence the answer?

12.8. Suggested Projects

12.8.1. For this project you will be asked to compute the noun-phrase saturation score for the child in the **kid055b.cha** transcript (from the **20mos** subdirectory under the **NEngland** directory). To accomplish this, you must first code the **kid055b.cha** transcript for noun-phrase saturation using the rules in the Appendix. Compare this child's noun-phrase saturation score with his MLU50 by computing z-scores. How does the child's noun-phrase saturation score inform MLU50?

12.8.2. In this chapter, the language of children with SLI was compared to that of their NL siblings by generating language profiles. In this project, you will compare the same group of children with SLI to a group of normally developing children at roughly the same MLU level. To do this, you must compute z-scores using the means and standard deviations for each measure for the whole New England sample at 20 months (refer to Tables 2.4 and 12.3). Then you must plot the language profiles for each of the children with SLI. What consistencies and inconsistencies do you see from the comparison with the NL siblings? Note that to do this project you will have to code Sid's, Clay's, and Kate's transcript files for noun-phrase saturation using the rules in the Appendix. The Pragmatic Flexibility scores for these children are as follows: Sid, 40; Clay, 27; Kate, 57.

Table 12.3: Means, standard deviations, and ranges for Types, Tokens, noun-phrase saturation (NPSAT), and pragmatic flexibility (PF) for the New England sample at 20 months.

Measure	Mean	SD	Range
Types	30.1	20.8	4-107
Tokens	69.5	55.3	11-275
NPSAT	4.3	5.9	0-055
PF	24.8	9.0	3-45

References

Aten, J. L., & Davis, J. (1968). Disturbances in the perception of auditory sequences in children with minimal cerebral dysfunction. *Journal of Speech and Hearing Research, 11*, 236-245.

Ball, J., Cross, T., & Horsborough, K. (1982). A comparative study of the linguistic abilities of autistic, dysphasic and normal children. *Proceedings of the Second International Congress for the Study of Child Language*, Vol. 2.

Benton, A. L. (1964). Developmental aphasia and brain damage. *Cortex, 1*, 40-52.

Bishop, D. V. M. (1982). *The Test of Reception of Grammar*. Medical Research Council. Copies available from: Dr. D. Bishop, Psychology Department, University of Manchester, Manchester M13 9PL, U.K.

Bishop, D. V. M., & Edmundson, A. (1986). Is otitis media a major cause of specific developmental language disorders? *British Journal of Disorders of Communication, 21*, 321-338.

Brown, R. (1973). *A first language: The early stages*. Cambridge, MA: Harvard University Press.

Bryan, T., Donahue, M., & Pearl, R. (1981). Learning disabled children's peer interacting during a small group problem solving task. *Learning Disability Quarterly, 4*, 13-22.

Carey, S., & Bartlett, E. (1978). Acquiring a single new word. In *Papers and reports on child language development* (Vol. 15, pp. 17-29). Stanford, CA: Stanford University, Department of Linguistics.

Chapman, R. S. (1981). Exploring children's communicative intents. In J. Miller (Ed.), *Assessing language production in children: Experimental procedures* (pp. 111-136). Baltimore: University Park Press.

Conti-Ramsden, G. & Dykins, N. (1990). Mother-child interactions with linguistically impaired children and their siblings. Submitted to *British Journal of Disorders of Communication*.

Conti-Ramsden, G., & Friel-Patti, S. (1983). Mothers' discourse adjustments to language-impaired and non-language-impaired children. *Journal of Speech and Hearing Disorders, 48*, 360-367.

Dollaghan, C. A. (1987). Fast mapping in normal and language-impaired children. *Journal of Speech and Hearing Research, 52*, 218-222.

Dunn, L. M., Whetton, C., & Pintillie, D. (1982). *The British Picture Vocabulary Scale*. Windsor: NFER.

Fey, M., Leonard, L., & Wilcox, K. (1981). Speech-style modifications of language-impaired children. *Journal of Speech and Hearing Disorders*, *46*, 91-97.

Frome-Loeb, D., & Leonard, L. B. (1991). Subject case marking and verb morphology in normally developing and specifically language impaired children. *Journal of Speech and Hearing Research*, *34*, 340-346.

Gillman, R., & Johnston, J. (1985). The development of print awareness in language disordered preschoolers. *Journal of Speech and Hearing Research*, *28*, 521-526.

Gopnik, M. (1990a). Feature-blind grammar and dysphasia. *Nature, 344*, 715.

Gopnik, M. (1990b). Feature-blindness: A case study. *Language Acquisition. 2*, 139-164.

Gopnik, M. (1991). *Theoretical implications of inherited dysphasia.* Paper presented at Cross Linguistic and Crosspopulation Contributions to the Theory of Acquisition. Hebrew University, Jerusalem.

Ingram, D. (1972). The acquisition of the English verbal auxiliary and copula in normal and linguistically deviant children. *Papers and Reports on Child Language Development*, *4*, 79-92.

Johnston, J. (1982). The language disordered child. In N. Lass, L. McReynolds, J. Northern, & D. Yoder (Eds.), *Speech, language, and hearing: Vol. II. Pathologies of speech and language* (pp. 780-801). Philadelphia Pa: W.B. Saunders.

Johnston, J. (1988). The language disordered child. In N. Lass, L. McReynolds, J. Northern, & D. Yoder (Eds.), *Handbook of speech-pathology and audiology* (pp. 685-715). Toronto: B.C. Decker.

Johnston, J., & Kamhi, A. (1984). The same can be less: Syntactic and semantic aspects of the utterances of language impaired children. *Merrill-Palmer Quarterly*, *30*, 65-86.

Johnston, J., & Schery, T. (1976). The use of grammatical morphemes by children with communication disorders. In D. Morehead & A. Morehead (Eds.), *Normal and deficient child language* (pp. 239-258). Baltimore: University Park Press.

Kahn, L., & James, S. (1983). Grammatical morpheme development in three language disordered children. *Journal of Childhood Communication Disorders*, *6*, 85-100.

Klee, T. (1992). Developmental and diagnostic characteristics of quantitative measures of children's language production. *Topics in Language Disorders*, *12*, 28-41.

Klee, T., Schaffer, M., May, S., Membrino, I., & Mougey, K. (1989). A comparison of the age-mlu relation in normal and specifically language-impaired preschool children. *Journal of Speech and Hearing Disorders*, *54*, 226-233.

Lahey, M., Liebergott, J., Chesnick, M., Menyuk, P., & Adams, J. (in press). Variability in children's use of grammatical morphemes. *Applied Psycholinguistics, 13*.

Lee, L. (1966). Developmental sentence types: A method of comparing normal and deviant syntactic development. *Journal of Speech and Hearing Disorders, 31*, 331-330.

Leiter, R. G. (1969). *The Leiter International Performance Scale*. Chicago: Stoelting and Company.

Leonard, L. B. (1982). The nature of specific language impairment in children. In S. Rosenberg (Ed.), *Handbook of applied psycholinguistics* (pp. 295-327). Hillsdale, NJ. Lawrence Erlbaum Associates.

Leonard, L. B. (1986). Conversational replies of children with specific language impairment. *Journal of Speech and Hearing Research, 29*, 114-119.

Leonard, L. B. (1987). Is specific language impairment a useful construct? In S. Rosenberg (Ed.), *Advances in applied psycholinguistics: Vol. 1. Disorders of first language development*. New York: Cambridge University Press.

Leonard, L. B. (1988). Lexical development and processing in specific language impaired. In R. L. Schiefelbush & L.L. Lloyde (Eds.), *Language perspectives: Acquisition, retardation and intervention* (pp. 69-87). Austin, TX: Pro-Ed.

Leonard, L. B. (1989). Language learnability and specific language impaired children. *Applied Psycholinguistics, 10*, 179-202.

Leonard, L. B., Camarata, S., Rowan, L., & Chapman, K. (1982). The communicative functions of lexical usage by language impaired children. *Applied Psycholinguistics, 3*, 109-125.

Leonard, L. B., Caselli, M. C., Bortolinin, U., & McGregor, K. (1991). *Some rival accounts of morphological deficits in specific language impairment: A crosslinguistic study*. Paper presented at Boston University Conference on Language.

Leonard, L. B., Sabbadini, L., Volterra, V., & Leonard, J. S. (1988). Some influences on the grammar of English- and Italian-speaking children with specific language impairment. *Applied Psycholinguistics, 9*, 39-57.

Leonard, L. B., Schwartz, R., Chapman, K., Rowan, L., Prelock, P., Terrell, B., Weiss, A., & Messick, C. (1982). Early lexical acquisition in children with specific language impairment. *Journal of Speech and Hearing Research, 25*, 554-564.

Lowe, A. D., & Cambell, R. A. (1965). Temporal discrimination in aphasoid and normal children. *Journal of Speech and Hearing Research, 8*, 313-324.

MacWhinney, B. (1991). *The CHILDES Project: Tools for analyzing talk.* Hillsdale, NJ: Lawrence Erlbaum Associates.

MacWhinney, B., & Snow, C. E. (1985). The child language data exchange system. *Journal of Child Language, 12,* 271-295.

MacWhinney, B., & Snow, C. (1989). The Child Language Data Exchange System: An update. *Journal of Child Language, 17,* 457-472.

Menyuk, P. (1964). Comparison of grammar of children with functionally deviant and normal speech. *Journal of Speech and Hearing Research, 7,* 109-121.

Miller, J. F. (1991). Quantifying productive language disorders. In J. F. Miller (Ed.), *Research on child language disorders* (pp. 211-220). Austin, TX: Pro-Ed.

Miller, J. F., & Chapman, R. (1981). Research note: The relations between age and mean length of utterance in morphemes. *Journal of Speech and Hearing Research, 24,* 154-161.

Morehead, D., & Ingram, D. (1973). The development of base syntax in normal and linguistically deviant children. *Journal of Speech and Hearing Research, 16,* 330-352.

Ninio, A., Snow, C., Pan, A., & Rollins, P. (1990). *Classifying communicative acts in mother-child interaction.* Unpublished manuscript, Harvard Graduate School of Education.

Ninio, A., & Wheeler, P. (1986). A manual for classifying verbal communicative acts in mother-infant interactions. *Transcript Analysis, 3,* 1-81.

Pan, B., & Elkins, K. (1989). *An alternative measure of morphological development in young children's spontaneous speech.* Paper presented to the New England Child Language Association, Northeastern University, Boston, MA.

Pan, B. A., Rollins, P. R., & Snow, C. E. (1991). *Pragmatic and morphosyntactic subsystems in normally developing and SLI children.* Paper presented at the Annual Convention of the American Speech-Language-Hearing Association, Atlanta, GA.

Prutting, C., & Kirchner, D. (1987). A clinical appraisal of the pragmatic aspects of language. *Journal of Speech and Hearing Disorders, 52,* 105-119.

Rescorla, L., & Schwartz, E. (1990). Outcome of toddlers with specific expressive language delay. *Applied Psycholinguistics, 11,* 393-409.

Rice, M. L. (1990). Preschoolers' QUIL: Quick incidental learning of words. In G. Conti-Ramsden & C.E. Snow (Eds.), *Children's language (Vol. 7).* Hillsdale, NJ: Lawrence Erlbaum Associates.

Rice, M. L. (in press). Children with specific language impairment: Towards a model of teachability. In *Biobehavioral foundations of language development.*

Rice, M. L., Buhr, J., & Nemeth, M. (1990). Fast mapping word learning abilities of language delayed preschoolers. *Journal of Speech and Hearing Disorders*, *55*, 33-42.

Rice, M. L., & Oetting, J. (1991). *Grammatical morphemes of SLI preschoolers.* Paper presented at the Annual Convention of the American Speech-Language-Hearing Association, Atlanta, GA.

Richards, B. (1986). Type/Token ratios: What do they really tell us? *Journal of Child Language*, 14, 201-209.

Rollins, P. R. (1990). *An inquiry into the language profiles of specific language impaired children.* Unpublished Qualifying Paper, Harvard Graduate School of Education, Cambridge, MA.

Rollins, P. R., Pan, B. A., Conti-Ramsden, G., & Snow, C. E. (1990). *Communicative skills in specific language impaired children: A comparison with their language-matched siblings.* Unpublished manuscript. Harvard Graduate School of Education.

Rollins, P. R., Pan, B. A., & Snow, C. E. (1991). *Phrase saturation as a measure of morphological skill.* Paper presented at the Annual Convention of the American Speech-Language-Hearing Association, Atlanta, GA.

Rom, A., & Bliss, L. (1981). A comparison of verbal communicative skill of language impaired and normal speaking children. *Journal of Speech and Hearing Disorders*, *14*, 133-140.

Rondal, J. A., Ghiotto, M., Bredart, S., & Bachelet, J. (1987). Age-relation, reliability and grammatical validity of measures of utterance length. *Journal of Child Language,* *14*, 433-446.

Roth, F., & Spekman, N. (1894). Assessing the pragmatic abilities in children: Part I. Organizational framework and assessment parameters. *Journal of Speech and Hearing Disorders*, *49*, 2-11.

Scarborough, H. (1990). Index of productive syntax. *Applied Psycholinguistics*, *11*, 1-22.

Scarborough, H., Rescorla, L., Tager-Flusberg, H., Fowler, A., & Sudhalter, H. (in press). The relation of utterance length to grammatical complexity in normal and language-disordered groups. *Applied Psycholinguistics*.

Scarborough, H., Wyckoff, J., & Davidson, R. (1986). A reconsideration of the relation between age and mean utterance length. *Journal of Speech and Hearing Research*, *29*, 394-399.

Schwartz, R. G. (1988). Early action word acquisition in normal and language-impaired children. *Applied Psycholinguistics*, *9*, 111-122.

Snyder, L. (1978). Communicative and cognitive abilities and disabilities in the sensorimotor period. *Merrill-Palmer Quarterly*, *24*, 161-180.

Stark, R., & Tallal, P. (1981). Selection of children with specific language deficits. *Journal of Speech and Hearing Disorders*, *46*, 114-122.

Steckol, K. F., & Leonard, L. B. (1979). The use of grammatical morphemes by normal and language-impaired children. *Journal of Communication Disorders*, *12*, 291-301.

Stevenson, J., & Richman, N. (1976) The prevalence of language delay in a population of three-year-old children and its association with general retardation. *Developmental Medicine and Child Neurology*, *18*, 431-441.

Tager-Flusberg, H. (1987). On the nature of a language acquisition disorder: The example of autism. In F. Kessel (Ed.), *The development of language and language researchers: Essays presented to Roger Brown*. Hillsdale, NJ: Lawrence Erlbaum Associates.

Tallal, P., Ross, R., & Curtis, S. (1989). Familial aggregation in specific language impairment. *Journal of Speech and Hearing Disorders*, *54*, 167-173.

Watkins, R. V., & Rice, M. L. (1991). Verb particle and preposition acquisition in language-impaired preschoolers. *Journal of Speech and Hearing Research*, *34*, 1136-1141.

Wetherby, A., Yonclas, D., & Bryan, A. (1989). Communicative profiles of preschool children with handicaps: Implications for early identification. *Journal of Speech and Hearing Disorders*, *54*, 148-157.

Wetherby, A., Cain, D., Yonclas, D., & Walker, V. (1988). Analysis of intentional communication of normal children from the prelinguistic to the multi-word stage. *Journal of Speech and Hearing Research*, *31*, 240-252.

Wyke, M. A. (1978). *Developmental dysphasia*. New York: Academic Press.

Zimmerman, I., Steiner, V., & Evatt, R. (1969). *Preschool Language Scale*. Columbus, OH: Charles E. Merrill.

Appendix: Morphological Saturation Rules for Noun-Phrases
(Pan & Elkins, 1989)

NP:S   SATURATED Noun-Phrase – MARKING COMPULSORY
Noun-Phrase which includes whatever article, delimiter, or number marking necessary.

    (A1)   *MOT: what's this?
                *CHI: a bunny rabbit.
                %mph: $NP:S

    (A2)   *MOT: what's this?
                *CHI: bunny rabbit–s.
                %mph: $NP:S

NP:S:P   SATURATED Noun-Phrase – MARKING NOT COMPULSORY
Noun-Phrase consists of either a pronoun or a proper noun.

    (A3)   *CHI: I want that.
                %mph: $NP:S:P $VP:S $NP:S:P

NP:U   UNSATURATED Noun-Phrase
When an unspecified compulsory item is omitted.

    (A4)   *MOT: what's that?
                *CHI: bunny rabbit.
                %mph: $NP:U

NP:E   INCORRECT MARKING PRESENT

    (A5)   *MOT: what's that?
                *CHI: a bunny rabbit–s
                %mph: $NP:E

    (A6)   *MOT: what's that?
                *CHI: my feets.
                %mph: $NP:E

13 New Horizons for CHILDES Research

Brian MacWhinney
Carnegie Mellon University

Conversational interactions between real parents and real children are the empirical bedrock of the study of child language acquisition. It is through these interactions that children are guided through the grammatical and interactional intricacies of their mother tongue. It is in these interactions that children demonstrate most clearly their successful control of the structure and functioning of their language, while also demonstrating gaps in their control of structures, functions, and interactional processes. Any satisfying theory of language acquisition, be it nativist or empiricist, must eventually be able to make contact with the actual shape of these real conversational interactions.

One of the most challenging aspects of the study of language learning is the incredible complexity of real interactional events. Whenever we try to capture this complexity within the confines of some sort of transcription or coding system, the richness of the real world inevitably bubbles out of our test tube. Given this, any overestimation of the veridicality of our transcriptions can lead us to misperceive significant aspects of the language learning situation. These fundamental problems in observational and measurement technique are common to all of the natural and physical sciences. Certainly, there is no reason to give up the study of child language acquisition because of imperfections in measurement. Instead, we should view these imperfections as opportunities for further achievements. Some of the greatest advances in science have involved the construction of tools that address basic issues in measurement and observation. Consider the impact of physical tools such as the microscope, the telescope, the computer, the spectrogram, the polymerase chain reaction, or the linear accelerator. Consider the impact of methodological tools such as the alphabet, the phoneme, the number zero, the calculus, LISP, or Linnaean taxonomy. Much can be said for the importance of physical devices and methodological tools in sustaining the entire edifice of scientific progress.

The CHILDES Project has as its goal the construction of tools that will facilitate both the veridical representation of conversational interactions and the smooth computational analysis of important properties of these interactions. The first major publication of the CHILDES Project was the CHILDES manual (MacWhinney, 1991). The manual presented three major tools for child language analysis: the CHAT transcription system, the CLAN data analysis programs, and the CHILDES database of files transcribed in the CHAT system. The emphasis in the manual was upon specification rather than explanation. Readers were given a set of specific guidelines and detailed descriptions of programs and codes, but the manual gave virtually no examples of the actual use of these tools in real research projects. At the time the manual was written, our plan was to supplement the specifications given in the **manual** with a series of detailed examples and tutorials in a separate **handbook.** This separate handbook – the book which you are now reading – provides hands-on, concrete, detailed examples of real analytic problems and the specific CLAN techniques that can be used to address these problems. The handbook fills the various gaps left in the manual in a way that allows the two books to form a coordinated whole.

At times, the detailed expositions in both the manual and the handbook may have seemed excessive or even tedious. True enough, the learning curve for CHAT and CLAN is unfortunately rather steep. But, once these tools are mastered, they are relatively easy to apply. Moreover, CHAT and CLAN provide a publicly available comprehensive antidote to inaccuracy and inefficiency in data analysis. How inaccurate and inefficient child language data analysis can be is something that many of us would like to forget. The new generation of child language researchers may tend to take precise computational tools for granted, but those of us who have spent years laboring with hand-written transcripts understand how far we have come from the days of diary notebooks, hand-compiled concordances, and blurred mimeographed copies. With the new tools presented in this book, child language researchers no longer need to spend hours poring over transcripts looking for a single use of a word. We no longer need to mark tallies of word occurrences in the margins of our printed transcripts and then turn through our notebooks, page by page, adding up these tallies by hand, only to realize after hours of work that we have been ignoring some crucial dimension and that the whole analysis has to be started again from scratch. Theoreticians no longer have to base major theoretical claims on a few scattered examples from handwritten transcripts photocopied from colleagues. Above all, the entire field now has direct, on-line access to the core set of actual empirical observations upon which our empirical generalizations regarding language learning have been based. This direct access allows us a more direct understanding of both the strengths and the weaknesses of this empirical base.

Yes, we have come a long way, but there is still a long way to go. There is still too much tedium in transcript analysis; our computer programs are still too difficult and clunky; the link between the transcript and the actual visual and auditory events is still far too tenuous and inexact; and there are still many languages and types of children for which child language data are not available. Although there seems to be a broad consensus regarding the basic distinctions that must be captured in transcripts, the actual use of these categories by real transcribers has not yet been fully tested for reliability and consistency. The CHAT system presents a fairly complete framework for the coding of syntax, morphology, phonology, speech acts, and speech errors, but the coding of large amounts of child language data using these systems has only now begun. Until large sets of data have been coded with these specialized systems, we will not be able to fully appreciate the possibilities for computerized analysis of child language corpora. There is still an enormous amount of work to be done before we can say that the computer has reached its full potential as a way of allowing us to better understand language development.

Although we may not yet have arrived in the Promised Land, neither are we wandering adrift in the Desert. The CHILDES tools provide us not only with a solid basis for current work, but also a platform upon which we can stand to reach higher and to see further. Using this platform, we can begin to see what transcript analysis will look like at the beginning of the 21st century. This chapter uses the current CHILDES platform as a way of gaining that broader vision. From where we now stand, there are three horizons across which we can gaze. The first and nearest horizon involves the work of the last two years that has extended, perfected, and enriched the three basic tools outlined in the CHILDES manual. The second, intermediate horizon involves the construction of a blueprint for several new tools that will reshape the way in which we interact with our datasets. The third horizon is the one that extends into the next century. It is the distant horizon with its unclear profile that allows us to dream most wildly about powerful computers, enormously rich datasets, intuitive user interfaces, multimedia exploratory reality, and major new conceptual challenges. Let us begin our quest by making a careful inspection of the recent past. In this chapter, I assume that the reader has now completed an overview of both the manual and the handbook, is basically comfortable with use of the three current CHILDES tools, and is now interested in looking at future directions in the CHILDES Project.

13.1. The Recent Past

The nearest horizon is the one bounded by the publication of the CHILDES manual in 1991 and the present. The publication of the manual in 1991 marked the end of the period which we now refer to as "proto-CHAT." From 1986 to 1990, several versions of the CHAT/CLAN system were circulated in photocopied form. The constant evolution of the system during that period was exciting, but it also often proved frustrating as researchers found they had to continually update both their transcribed files and their understanding of this changing system. In 1991 we decided that the time had come to stabilize the core systems for both CHAT and CLAN. The publication of the manual in 1991 marks the end of the period of proto-CHAT. The stabilized system of CHAT and CLAN published in the manual is the one that is being used by scores of research groups internationally. Since the publication of the manual, the core of both CHAT and CLAN have remained stable, and we intend to continue to maintain the stability of this core. At the same time, we have extended the core of CLAN by adding new programs, new facilities, new options, and new systems for coding.

The next two sections provide an overview of recent changes to CHAT and CLAN. They do not have the tutorial quality of the rest of this handbook. Rather, they are intended to provide an introduction to some new features that will be further documented in the next edition of the manual and in future editions of this handbook. The version of CHAT and CLAN in the first edition of the manual was CHAT 1.0 and CLAN 1.0. The versions I discuss here are CHAT 2.0 and CLAN 2.0.

13.1.1. CHAT 2.0

Since the end of 1990, changes to the CHAT transcription and coding system have been extremely few. The chief changes involved the addition of these coding symbols:

1. +//. In addition to the symbol +/. which codes interruption by another speaker (page 43), CHAT now allows the symbol +//. for self-interruption.

Some researchers want to distinguish incompletions involving a trailing off and then a restart from incompletions involving an abrupt self-interruption. When an incompletion is not followed by further material from the same speaker, the +... symbol should always be selected. However, when the speaker breaks off an utterance and starts up another, the +//. symbol can be used. There is no hard and fast way of distinguishing cases of trailing off from self-interruption. For this reason, some researchers prefer to avoid making the distinction. Researchers who wish to avoid making the distinction, should use only the +... symbol.

2. **+/?** The +/. symbol (page 43) coded only for the interruption of declarative utterances. However, it is important to be able to note that the utterance being interrupted is a question. The symbol +/? is now available for use at the end of an interrupted question.

3. **[/-]** The [//] code is used for coding false starts with retracings (page 52). However, sometimes a speaker makes a false start, but does no retracing. This can be coded with the [/-] symbol. It is important to avoid confusing false starts without retracings from simple self-interruptions. False starts without retracings continue the same basic subject material, whereas self-interruptions involve dropping the current subject and starting up with something entirely new.

4. **$=text(text)** The previous version of CHAT used the form $=text{text} to mark the locus of errors on the **%err** line (page 84). However, the curly braces did not interact correctly with core features of the CLAN programs, so we were forced to change them to parentheses.

5. **[Ø text]** Omitted words can be coded as Øword (page 26). However, some readers tend to miss the initial Ø and think that the word is really being produced. To mark the omission more clearly, transcribers can include the omitted form in square brackets. For the purposes of the CLAN programs, these two forms of coding are equivalent.

For examples of passages in which these codes could be used, please refer to the page citations given.

Other changes to the CHAT documentation include corrections to the IPA consonant table on page 73, correction of "ASCII" to "UNIBET" in the UNIBET tables for English and Italian, addition of UNIBET tables for German and Brazilian Portuguese, and several changes to the tables for Dutch and French. In chapter 14, new tables have been added for English part-of-speech codes, affixes and clitics, and sample morphological codings. The use of the colon within part-of-speech codes has been clarified and the placement of the # sign on prefixes has been moved. Researchers who are doing extensive coding on the **%mor** should obtain a complete copy of the revised version of chapter 14.

The fact that so few changes were made to basic CHAT codes during the years of 1990-1993 is a good sign. It indicates that the core system captures the most important distinctions that researchers typically make in transcribing child language data.

13.1.2. CLAN 2.0

Ideally, changes to the transcription system should be few and far between. Changes to the CLAN programs also need to preserve the core functions that users have learned to rely on. However, it is easy to add new programs and new options without interfering with use of the old programs and old options. In fact, one of the nicest aspects of computerized transcription is that it lays the groundwork for a potentially infinite development of data analysis programs without requiring major changes in the underlying transcription scheme. For central CLAN programs such as FREQ, GEM, and KWAL, CLAN 2.0 only repairs a few bugs and adds a few features here and there. However, the new version of CLAN has greatly expanded analytic capabilities in three major areas: data display, data coding, and morphosyntactic analysis. The major new programs in these areas are LINES, COLUMNS, CED, MOR, DSS, and COOCCUR. Let us take a look at each of these new programs.

13.1.2.1. Data Display – COLUMNS, SLIDE, and LINES.

There is much more to a transcript than a series of codes and symbols. The superficial form of a transcript can also lead us to adopt a particular perspective on an interaction and to entertain particular hypotheses regarding developments in communicative strategies. For example, if we code our data in columns with the child on the left, we come to think of the child as driving or directing the conversation. If we decide instead to place the parent's utterances in the left column, we then tend to view the child as more reactive or scaffolded. Ochs (1979) noted that such apparently simple decisions as the placement of a speaker into a particular column can both reflect and shape the nature of our theories of language development. Because it is important for the analyst to be able to see a single transcript in many different ways, we have written three new CLAN programs that provide alternative views onto the data. The basic principle underlying these data display programs is the motto of "different files for different styles."

The older CLAN programs base their data display modification capabilities on the notion of "limiting." By combined use of the +t, +s, and +z options, programs such as KWAL, COMBO, and FREQ can either include or exclude particular speakers, dependent tiers, headers, regions, or lines matching particular search strings. The files derived from these analyses can either be simply collections of lines or legal CHAT files with certain material excluded. These new files can then either be subjected to further analysis or simply stored as alternative versions of the main data set. The chapters in this book have provided dozens of examples of uses of limiting in the CLAN programs.

Our newer programs attempt to provide more extreme modifications of the basic CHAT format. One fairly minimal modification of the standard CHAT format is achieved by the LINES program, which inserts line numbers in front of each main tier line. When researchers are working on the computer with CLAN, it is easy enough to find line numbers by editor search commands. However, sometimes larger laboratories find it necessary to freeze a transcript into a particular hardcopy form for comparison between researchers and for temporary annotation. For this type of work with hard copy away from the computer, it is often important to have line numbers actually printed on the transcript. Unlike files filtered through COMBO or KWAL, files with line numbers inserted are no longer legal CHAT files and cannot be used with the CLAN programs. For that reason, users should be careful never to do coding or further transcription on files with line numbers added.

The COLUMNS program produces CHAT files in a multicolumn form that is useful for explorations of turn-taking, scaffolding, and sequencing. COLUMNS allows the user to break up the one-column format of standard CHAT into several smaller columns. For example, the standard 80-character column could be broken up into four columns of 20 characters each. One column could be used for the child, one for the parent, one for situational descriptions, and one for coding. The user has control over the assignment of tiers to columns, the placement of the columns, and the width of each separate column. As in the case of files produced by SLIDE, files produced by COLUMNS are useful for exploratory purposes, but are no longer legal CHAT files and cannot be reliably used with the CLAN programs.

Yet another form of CLAN display provides a focus on overlaps and cross-tier correspondences. Using SLIDE, a CHAT file can be displayed as a single unbroken stretch of speech across an "infinite" left-to-right time line. Whereas standard CHAT files use carriage returns to break up files into lines, a file displayed in SLIDE has all carriage returns removed. The SLIDE program converts a CHAT file into a set of single long lines for each speaker. These lines can be scrolled across the computer screen from left to right. At any point in time, only 80 columns are displayed, but the user can rapidly scroll to any other point in this single left-right line by using the cursor keys. When two speakers overlap in a conversation, SLIDE displays the overlapped portions on top of each other. SLIDE can also be used to display accurate placement of material otherwise indicated by <aft> and <bef> and to provide correct display of the match between morphemes on a **%mor** line with corresponding words on the main line, as required in many systems of interlinear morphemicization. This form of display provides far better time-space iconicity than any previous form of display. Of course, this display cannot be captured on the printed page; it is only available on the computer screen because of its capacity to scroll almost limitlessly left to right. An earlier noncomputerized prototype for SLIDE can be found in Ervin-Tripp (1979).

13.1.2.2. CHECK

The CHECK program was available in CLAN 1.0, but it has been extensively revised in CLAN 2.0. CHECK now does a better job of finding errors in tier identifiers and delimiters. In the older version, it was possible to repress overwhelming numbers of CHECK errors by using the **-t%** option. This allowed you to clean up the main line before beginning work on the dependent tiers. However, it is often the case that the main line itself may have the largest number of CHECK problems. To help with this, we have added a **+d1** option, which reduces the output given by CHECK to only one of each error type. For example, if you have been using WordPerfect and have not yet converted spaces to tabs after the speaker identifications, you can use this option and you will only receive one complaint about missing tabs, rather than hundreds. When using the **+d1** option, it is helpful to know that there are 46 different error messages produced by CHECK. What the **+d1** option guarantees is that you will only get one complaint for each of these types of errors: missing line beginnings, missing tabs, missing colons, missing @Begin, missing @End, missing @Participants line, nonstandard participant roles, missing roles, incorrect tier names, duplicate speaker declarations, missing speaker identifications, delimiters in words, unmatched paired delimiters, missing main tiers, undeclared codes, illegal date entries, illegal time entries, multiple utterances per line, undeclared prefixes, undeclared suffixes, duplicate coding tiers, missing terminators, extra terminators, and incorrect pairings of @Bg and @Eg markers.

Ideally, CHECK only needs to rely on the standard **depfile.** CHECK uses the codes in the **depfile** as its guide to understanding which CHAT codes should be permitted on which tiers. The **depfile** we distribute is, in effect, a summary of the CHAT system given in the manual. Sometimes users have good reasons for making exceptions to CHAT conventions. In order to override the definitions given in the **depfile** without having to tinker with that file, we have added the capacity to create a **ØØdepadd** file. This file then also provides an overt record of additions or modifications to CHAT required for particular corpora. For example, if you need to allow for equals signs on the @Comment line and for words with suffixes on the @Bgd line, you could create a **ØØdepadd** file with these two lines:

@Bgd: *-*
@Comment: =

If the **depfile** has a code that is too permissive, such as $*, you will want to remove this before entering the more specific codes in your **ØØdepadd** file. In general, it is still best to focus on using CHECK early in the process of transcription, before you begin to accumulate errors. Whenever possible, it is best to use only the standard **depfile**, but sometimes there will be reasons for extending CHAT by using a **ØØdepadd** file.

CHECK only examines files for their compliance to the syntactic specifications of CHAT. An important second type of checking can be achieved by using FREQ to create a unified frequency count for an entire corpus. This is best done with this command:

freq +u +f *.cha

This command will produce a single file with all the words you used on the main lines of all your files. You can then go over these words to check for spelling errors and other inconsistencies. A useful clue in looking for spelling errors is to search for words with a frequency of 1. If you use FREQ with the +o option, you can immediately find all the words with a frequency of 1 together at the end of the printout. Once your preliminary cleanup is done, you may want to repeat the same analysis using the +t% and –t* options, so you can check for errors in the codes on the dependent tiers. Alternatively, you can provide CHECK with a complete listing of your codes by creating a **ØØdepadd** file.

13.1.2.3. CED – Coder's Editor

The most important CLAN tool for data coding is the CED Coder's Editor, which is a new program in CLAN 2.0. CED can lead to truly remarkable improvements in the accuracy, reliability, and efficiency of transcript coding. If you have ever spent a significant amount of time coding transcripts or if you plan to do such coding in the future, you should definitely consider using CED.

CED provides the user with not only a complete text editor, but also a systematic way of entering user-determined codes into dependent tiers in CHAT files. The program works in two modes: coder mode and editor mode. Initially, you are in editor mode, and you can stay in this mode until you learn the basic editing commands. The basic commands have been configured so that both WordPerfect and EMACS keystroke equivalents are available. If you prefer some other set of keystrokes, the commands can be re-bound.

In the coding mode, CED relies on a codes.lst file created by the user to set up a hierarchical coding menu. It then moves through the file line by line asking the coder to select a set of codes for each utterance. For example, a codes.lst list such as the following:

$MOT
  :POS
     :Que
     :Res
  :NEG
$CHI

would be a shorter way of specifying the following codes:

$MOT:POS:Que
$MOT:POS:Res
$MOT:NEG:Que
$MOT:NEG:Res
$CHI:POS:Que
$CHI:POS:Res
$CHI:NEG:Que
$CHI:NEG:Res

This coding system would require the coder to make three quick cursor movements for each utterance in order to compose a code such as $CHI:NEG:Res.

CED has been successfully used by researchers at Harvard, CMU, and elsewhere to enter codes for speech acts and for narrative structures into CHAT files. Complete documentation of all of the editor commands for CED can be obtained from CMU and will be included in the next edition of the CHILDES manual.

13.1.2.4. MOR – Morphological Analysis

Many of the most important questions in child language require the detailed study of specific morphosyntactic constructions. For example, the debate on the role of connectionist simulations of language learning (MacWhinney & Leinbach, 1991; MacWhinney, Leinbach, Taraban, & McDonald, 1989; Marcus, Ullman, Pinker, Hollander, Rosen, & Xu, 1991; Pinker & Prince, 1988; Plunkett & Sinha, 1992) has focused attention on early uses and overregularizations of the regular and irregular past tense markings in English. The testing of hypotheses about parameter-setting within G-B theory (Hyams, 1986; Wexler, 1986) often depends upon a careful study of pronominal markings, reflexives, and wh-words. Although some of these phenomena can be detected by simple searches for words like "what" or "he," most of them require a more complete characterization in terms of a full part-of-speech coding for entire corpora. This coding could be achieved by hand application of the codes specified in chapter 14 of the CHILDES Manual. However, hand-coding of the entire CHILDES database would require perhaps 20 years of work and would be extremely error-prone and non-correctable. If the standards for morphological coding changed in the middle of this project, the coder would have to start over again from the beginning. It would be difficult to imagine a more tedious and frustrating task – the hand-coder's equivalent of Sisyphus and his stone.

The alternative to hand-coding is automatic coding. Over the last 3 years, we have worked on the construction of an automatic coding program for CHAT files. This program, called MOR, was first developed in LISP by Roland Hausser (1990), modified for C by Carolyn Ellis, and then completely rewritten by Mitzi Morris with assistance from Leonid Spektor. Although the MOR system is designed to be transportable to all languages, it is currently only fully elaborated for English and German. The language-independent part of MOR is the core processing engine. All of the language-specific aspects of the systems are built into files that can be modified by the user. In the remarks that follow, I first focus on ways in which a user can apply the system for English.

How to Run MOR

The MOR program takes a CHAT main line and automatically inserts a **%mor** line together with the appropriate morphological codes for each word on the main line. The basic MOR command is much like the other commands in CLAN. For example, you can run MOR in its default configuration with this type of command:

mor sample.cha

However, MOR is unlike the other CLAN programs in one crucial regard. Although you can easily run it on any CHAT file, for you to get a well-formed **%mor** line, you often need to engage in *extra work*. We have tried to minimize the additional work you need to do when working with MOR, but it would be misleading for us to suggest that no additional work is required. In particular, users of MOR will often need to spend a great deal of time engaging in the processes of (a) lexicon building and (b) ambiguity resolution.

Files Used by MOR

Before I examine ways of dealing with lexicon building and ambiguity resolution, let us take a quick look at the files that support a MOR analysis. For MOR to run successfully, there must be four files present in either the library directory or the current working directory. Although you do not need to have a detailed understanding of the functioning of these files, it will help you to have a view of the shape of these basic building blocks. The default names for these files are **eng.ar**, **eng.cr**, **eng.lex**, and **eng.clo**. These four files and a fifth optional file contain the following information:

1. **Allomorphic rules.** The eng.ar file lists the ways in which morphemes vary in shape. The rules that describe these variations are called "**arules**."

2. **Concatenation rules.** The eng.cr file lists the ways in which morphemes can combine. The rules that describe allowable concatenations are called "**crules**."

3. **Closed class items.** The eng.clo file contains the closed class words and suffixes of English. Because this group forms such a tight closed set, the user will seldom have to modify this file.

4. **Open class items.** The default name of the open class lexicon for English is eng.lex. This file is what we call the "disk lexicon." Words in the disk lexicon are listed in their canonical form, along with category information. The version of eng.lex we distribute contains about 2,000 words. We are also distributing a larger lexicon called big.lex with 24,000 words. However, only machines with very large memories, such as UNIX workstations or high-end Macintoshes, will be able to run this bigger lexicon. We are currently developing tools that will also allow MS-DOS programs access to larger amounts of memory.

5. **Disambiguation rules.** We also distribute a set of local context disambiguations rules or "**drules**" in the eng.dr file. These rules can resolve a large proportion of the part-of-speech ambiguity in English on the basis of local co-occurrence information. In order to use the drules file, you need to use the +b option when you use the MOR command.

MOR uses the eng.ar, eng.lex, and eng.clo files to produce a *run-time lexicon* that is significantly more complete than the eng.lex alone. When analyzing input files, MOR uses the run-time lexicon together with the eng.cr file. As a user, you do not need to concern yourself with the actual shape of the run-time lexicon. And you will usually not have to touch the arules, crules, or drules. Your main concern will be with the process of adding or removing entries from the main open class lexicon file. If all of the words in your files can be located in the eng.lex file, running of MOR is totally trivial. You simply run:

mor filename

But matters are seldom this simple, because most files will have many words that are not found in eng.lex and you will need to refine the eng.lex file until all missing words are inserted. Therefore, the main task involved for most users of MOR is the building of the lexicon file.

Lexicon Building – Finding Missing Words

In order to see whether MOR correctly recognizes all of the words in your transcripts, you can first run MOR on all of your files and then run this KWAL command on the **.mor** files you have produced:

kwal +t%mor +s"?|*" *.mor

If KWAL finds no question marks on the **%mor** line, then you know that all the words have been recognized by MOR. If there are question marks in your *.mor output files, you will probably want to correct this problem by running MOR in the interactive update mode. If you know from the outset that your file includes many words that will not be found in eng.lex, you can directly begin your analysis by running this FREQ command:

freq +d1 +u +k *.cha > output.frq

This produces a simple list of all the words in your transcript in a form useful for interactive MOR lexicon building. The **+d1** option outputs words without frequencies. The **+k** option is needed to distinguish between "Bill" and "bill." The redirection arrow sends the output to a file we have called "output.frq."

Next you can run MOR again using the **+s** option with a filename added, as in this example:

mor +x1 output.frq

MOR will use to use eng.lex to attempt to analyze each word in the output.frq file. If it cannot analyze the word, it will enter it in a output file of lexical entry templates with the name output.ulx. Then you need to look at the words in the output.ulx file, using an editor. Some may be misspellings and will have to be corrected in the original file. Others will be new words for which you will have to enter a part-of-speech. When you are finished, you should rename the output.ulx file to output.lex. Then you can run MOR again in this form:

mor +loutput *.cha

If all has gone smoothly, this time MOR will be able to enter a part-of-speech characterization for every word in the transcript.

The Structure of eng.lex

Users of MOR may want to understand the way in which entries in the disk lexicon (eng.lex) are structured. The disk lexicon contains truly irregular forms of a word, as well as citation forms. For example, the verb "go" is stored in eng.lex, along with the past tense "went", since this form is a suppletive form, and is not subject to regular rules. The disk lexicon contains any number of lexical entries, stored at most one entry per line. A lexical entry may be broken across several lines by placing the continuation character backslash, (\), at the end of the line. The lexicon may be annotated with comments, which will not be processed. A comment begins with the percent sign, %, and ends with a new line.

A lexical entry consists of the surface form of the word, followed by category information about the word expressed as a set of feature-value pairs. Each feature-value pair is enclosed in square brackets, and the full set of feature-value pairs is enclosed in curly braces. All entries must contain a feature-value pair that identifies the syntactic category to which the word belongs, consisting of the feature "scat" with an appropriate value. Words that belong to several categories will be followed by several sets of feature structures, each separated by a backslash. Optionally following the category information is information about the stem. If the surface form of the word is not the citation form of the word, then the citation form, surrounded by quotes, should follow the category information. If the word contains fused morphemes, these should be given as well, using the & symbol as the morpheme separator. The following are examples of lexical entries:

can	{[scat v:aux]} \ {[scat n}
a	{[scat det]}
an	{[scat det]} "a"
go	{[scat v] [ir +]}
went	{[scat v] [tense past]} "go&PAST"

When adding new entries to eng.lex it is usually sufficient to enter the citation form of the word, along with the syntactic category information.

Ambiguity Resolution

MOR automatically generates a **%mor** tier of the type described in chapter 14 of MacWhinney (1991). As stipulated there, retraced material, comments, and excluded words are not coded on the **%mor** line produced by MOR. Words are labeled by their syntactic category, followed by the separator "|", followed by the word itself, broken down into its constituent morphemes.

```
*CHI:      the people are making cakes .
%mor:      det|the  n|people v:aux|be&PRES v|make-ING n|cake-PL .
```

In this particular example, none of the words have ambiguous forms. However, it is often the case that some of the basic words in English have two or more part-of-speech readings. For example, the word "back" can be a noun, a verb, a preposition, an adjective, or an adverb. The "^" character denotes the alternative readings for each word on the main tier:

```
*CHI:      I want to go back .
%mor:      pro|I v|want inf|to^prep|to v|go adv|back^n|back^v|back .
```

The entries in the eng.clo file maintain these ambiguities. However, open class words in the eng.lex file are only coded in their most common part-of-speech form. If you use the +b option, some of these alternatives will be pruned, but some will still remain. The problem of noun-verb ambiguity will eventually be addressed through use of the PARS program, which is currently being developed. A primitive disambiguation facility is currently available in the disambiguation rules in the eng.dr file. Over the next years, we intend to continually improve the abilities of PARS to eliminate ambiguities.

Those ambiguities that remain in a MOR transcript after the drules and the PARS program have operated can be removed by using MOR in its ambiguity resolution mode. The program locates each of the various ambiguous words, one by one, and asks the user to select one of the possible meanings.

MOR for Other Languages

In order to maximize the portability of the MOR system to other languages, we have developed a general scheme for representing arules and crules. This means that a researcher can adapt MOR for a new language without doing any programming at all. However, the researcher/linguist needs to construct: (a) a list of the stems of the language with their parts-of-speech, (b) a set of arules for allomorphic variations in spelling, and (c) a set of crules for possible combinations of stems with affixes. Building these files will require a major one-time dedication of effort from at least one researcher for every language. Once the basic work of constructing the rules files and the core lexicon files is done, then further work with MOR in that language will be no more difficult that it currently is for English. However, construction of new rules files is an extremely complex process. Construction of a closed class and open class lexicon will also take a great deal of time. Although no programming is required, the linguist building these files must have a thorough understanding of the MOR program and the morphology of the language involved. Complete documentation for the construction of the rules files is available from Carnegie Mellon and will also be included in the next edition of the CHILDES manual.

13.1.2.5. DSS – Developmental Sentence Score

Once a **%mor** line has been constructed, either through use of MOR or through hand-coding, a variety of additional morphosyntactic analyses are then available. Some of these analyses were discussed in the CHILDES manual and others were mentioned in other chapters in this book. One particularly elaborate system for morphosyntactic analysis that has been widely used in research on language disorders is the Developmental Sentence Score (DSS; Lee, 1974). Lee's DSS tracks the uses of eight major morphosyntactic types: indefinite pronouns or noun modifiers, personal pronouns, main verbs, secondary verbs, negatives, conjunctions, interrogative reversal in questions, and wh-questions. The CLAN DSS program can automatically compute DSS scores for individual samples. In computing these scores, specific lexical markers and syntactic patterns for each of the eight grammatical categories are broken into developmental stages, and developmental scores are assigned to usages of structures or items at each level. Earlier-occurring constructions receive fewer points, whereas later-occurring constructions receive more points. An additional sentence point is given to each sentence if it meets all adult grammatical standards.

DSS scores are based upon analysis of a corpus of 50 sentences. The DSS program is designed to extract a set of 50 sentences from a language sample using Lee's six inclusion criteria:

1. The corpus should contain 50 complete sentences.
2. The speech sample must be a block of consecutive sentences.
3. All sentences in the language sample must be different.
4. Unintelligible sentences should be excluded from the corpus.
5. Echoed sentences should be excluded from the corpus.
6. Incomplete sentences should be excluded.

DSS can rely on CHAT codes such as xxx for unintelligible sentences and +... for incomplete sentences to compute the 50-sentence corpus automatically. However, there is one additional criterion in the original DSS framework that the DSS program cannot automatically compute. This is the criterion that DSS analysis should be used if and only if at least 50% of the utterances are complete sentences as defined by Lee. If fewer than 50% of the sentences are complete sentences, then the Developmental Sentence Type analysis (DST) is appropriate instead. A warning message will be included on the DSS printout if this criterion has not been met.

Once all 50 sentences have been assigned sentence points, the DSS program automatically generates a table. Each sentence is displayed in the left-hand column of the table with the corresponding point values. The Developmental Sentence Score is calculated by dividing the sum of the total values for each sentence by the number of sentences in the analysis. Here is a sample output file:

Sentence	IP	PP	PV	SV	NG	CNJ	IR	WHQ	S	TOT
I like this.	1	1	1						1	4
I like that.	1	1	1						1	4
I want hot dog.		1	1						0	2
I like it.	1	1	1						1	4
what this say.	1		–					–	0	3

Developmental Sentence Score: 4.2

The table has been specifically designed for users to determine "at a glance" areas of strength and weakness for the individual child for these eight grammatical categories. The low point values for both the indefinite and personal pronoun (IP, PP) categories in the table indicate that this child used earlier developing forms exclusively. In addition, the attempt markers for the primary verb (PV) and interrogative reversal (IR) categories suggest possible difficulties in question formulation.

13.1.2.6. COOCCUR – Co-occurrence Analysis

The COOCCUR program produces a complete list and count of pairs, triplets, or longer strings of words. The analysis of syntactic clusters produced by COOCCUR could be a major building block in an empirical analysis of the child's construction of syntax from lower-order co-occurrences (Braine, 1963, 1976, 1987; Elman, 1991; Ingram, 1972, 1975; MacWhinney, 1974, 1975; Maratsos & Chalkley, 1980). By default, the cluster length is two words, but you can reset this value just by inserting any integer up to 20 immediately after the +n option. The second word of the initial cluster will become the first word of the following cluster, and so on.

cooccur +t*MOT +n3 +f sample.cha

The **+t*MOT** option tells the program to select only the *MOT main speaker tiers. The header and dependent code tiers are excluded by default. The **+n3** option tells the program to combine three words into a word cluster. The program will then go through all of the mother's (*MOT) main speaker tiers in the **sample.cha** file, three words at a time. When COOCCUR reaches the end of an utterance, it marks the end of a cluster, so that no clusters are broken across speakers or across utterances.

Co-ocurrences of codes on the **%mor** line can be searched using commands such as this example:

cooccur +t%mor −t* +s*def sample2.cha

This command would allow one to track the types of morphosyntactic constructions in which particular categories co-occur with definite articles.

13.1.2.7. Modifications to CLAN 1.0 Facilities

In addition to the new programs included in CLAN 2.0, we have made several modifications to the older programs and documentation. One major change involved the dropping of the manuals facility, because it proved difficult to maintain this facility properly across all the computer platforms on which CLAN is being used. A number of program-specific options were added, including the **+d3** and **+d4** options for output formatting in FREQ, the **+o** option for separate control of limiting for the output in KWAL and COMBO, the **+a** option for alphabetization in KWAL, the **+b** option for tier naming in PHONFREQ, and the **+b** option for delimiter control in MLU. Several problems relating to the automatic exclusion of strings such as &*, *-Ø*, or *+Ø* in MLU and FREQ were fixed, and the various MLT documentation errors were fixed. Finally, the BIBFIND, MODREP, and PHONFREQ programs were totally rewritten to work more efficiently and more in accord with the published documentation.

13.1.3. Development of the Database

One of the major goals of the CHILDES Project involved the reformatting of the many different corpora in the database into the single lingua franca of CHAT. Using a wide variety of computational techniques to perform the translation, and relying upon the CHECK program as a filter for syntactic accuracy, we completed this reformatting in August of 1992. There are six corpora that have not been shifted to CHAT format. These are the corpora from: Fawcett; the ESF project; Stern and Stern; Sulzby; Hayes; MacWhinney and Bates. The ESF database and the

Fawcett data are no longer included in the database because reformatting of these data into CHAT would involve too many technical difficulties. The data from the diary notebooks of the Sterns will not be reformatted, because it is of greater historical interest in its present form. The transcripts from the other three projects will eventually be either reformatted or dropped from the database.

In most cases, reformatting required us to take data that was not yet in CHAT format and translate the project-specific codes and formats into CHAT. The fact that these transcripts now all pass CHECK without error means that all of the files now have correct headers, correct listings of participants, and correct matches of coding tiers to main lines. Each main line has only one utterance, and every utterance ends with a legal terminator. There are no incorrect symbols in the middle of words, and all paired delimiters are correctly matched. At this point, we cannot yet guarantee that the files are consistently coded on the level of individual words. However, this level of consistency checking remains a goal for our future work with the database.

13.1.3.1. New Corpora

New corpora that have been added to the database since the publication of the Manual include:

1. **Deuchar**. A case study of bilingual acquisition of Spanish and English by Margaret Deuchar of the University of Cambridge (Deuchar & Clark, 1992).

2. **Hayashi**. A case study of bilingual acquisition of Danish and Japanese, along with some English, by Mariko Hayashi of Århus University.

3. **Peters/Wilson**: A case study of the acquisition of English by a blind child donated by Ann Peters of the University of Hawaii and Bob Wilson of the Foreign Service Institute (Peters, 1987; Wilson & Peters, 1988).

4. **Van Kleeck**: Cross-sectional data from 37 three-year-olds collected in a laboratory setting by Anne Van Kleeck of the University of Texas, Austin.

5. **Rondal**. A case study of French language acquisition by Jean Rondal of the University of Liége (Rondal, 1985).

A variety of additional corpora are currently in preparation in areas such as autism, specific language impairment, focal lesions in childhood, second language acquisition, and the acquisition of Spanish and Swedish. A new edition of the electronic version of the CHILDES/BIB database (Higginson & MacWhinney, 1990) was released in October 1992. This new version includes hundreds of new entries and corrects various errors in the first edition.

13.1.3.2. FTP Access to the Database and Programs

All of the CHILDES materials can be obtained without charge by using anonymous FTP to poppy.psy.cmu.edu. InterNet connections that can reach poppy.psy.cmu.edu are now widely available at universities both in the United States and abroad. The procedure for transferring files varies depending on the type of machine you are using and the type of files you wish to retrieve. However, in all cases, you first need to follow the basic rules for FTP connections:

1. Connect to poppy.psy.cmu.edu (128.2.248.42) using anonymous FTP. If you get an answer from poppy, then you know that you have InterNet access. If you do not get an answer, you may not have access or access may be temporarily broken.

2. When you receive the request for a username, enter "anonymous." Type in your name as a password.

3. If you want to retrieve data files, type "cd childes" to move to the /childes directory. If you want to retrieve the CLAN programs, type "cd clan" to move to the /clan directory.

4. Type "ls" to view the directory structure and use "cd" again as needed. It is easy to confuse directories with files. When in doubt type "cd filename." If that works, it was a directory. If not, it was a file.

5. Type "binary" to set the transfer type. Although some of the files you wish to retrieve may be text files, the binary mode will work across all file types.

6. Use the "get" command to pull files onto your machine.

7. When you are finished, type "bye" or "quit" to close the connection.

Once the files are on your local machine, you must untar them. Tar is always available on UNIX systems. If you are running FTP from a Macintosh or a DOS machine, you can retrieve a copy of the tar program from poppy.psy.cmu.edu. The UNIX or DOS tar command you need to issue is something like:

tar −xvf eng.tar

Untarring the files will recreate the original directory structure. Each corpus has been placed into a separate tar file.

If you are running FTP from a Macintosh, you can retrieve the most recent version of CLAN along with certain Macintosh utilities. You should connect to poppy.psy.cmu.edu and use cd clan/macintosh to move into the directory with Macintosh programs and utilities. These files are all in BinHexed format, as indicated by the **.hqx** extension. The basic CLAN program is **CLAN.hqx**. The file **manual.hqx** has the CHILDES manual in MS-Word format. The Macintosh tar program is in **tar.hqx**. Once the files are on your machine, use any BinHex utility to decode them. When transferring CLAN, also remember to transfer the text files into /clan/lib.

DOS users can also use FTP to retrieve the most recent version of CLAN from poppy.psy.cmu.edu. Get all the files in the /msdos and /lib directories under the /clan directory. Try to maintain the directory structure. The files in the /msdos directory are executable programs that should run immediately on your machine, once you have set the path. Note that the TAR.EXE program will be included along with the other CLAN programs.

13.1.3.3. CD-ROM Access to the Database and Programs

For users without access to the InterNet, as well as for those who want a convenient way of storing the database, we have published (MacWhinney, 1992) a CD-ROM in High Sierra format, which can be read by Macintosh, UNIX, and MS-DOS machines that have a CD-ROM reader. The single disk contains the whole database, the programs, and the CHILDES/BIB system. One directory contains the materials in Macintosh format and the other contains the materials in UNIX/DOS format. If you have been thinking about adding CD-ROM capabilities to your system, the availability of this CD-ROM will provide you with an excellent excuse to make the addition. There is no charge for the CD-ROM, but you will have to spend $500 or so for a CD-ROM reader. This unit fits directly into the SCSI port on the Mac. For the IBM-PC, it requires an adaptor card that will provide a SCSI port. Often these are sold along with the CD-ROM reader. CD-ROM access is relatively slow and you cannot write CLAN output files to the CD-ROM, so you may want to copy over particular CHILDES corpora to your hard drive. However, it is possible to run CLAN programs on files on the CD-ROM and to then direct the output to your hard disk. A major advantage of the CD-ROM is that the entire database can be stored on a single stable disk.

For further information on changes to the database and programs, researchers can subscribe to the info-childes@andrew.cmu.edu electronic bulletin board. To request a subscription to the bulletin board, send your request to info-childes-request@andrew.cmu.edu.

13.2. The Immediate Future

Although we have completed a great deal of work in the past six years, there is still an enormous amount to be done. Our plans for the immediate future focus on these goals:

1. **CHAT**. We hope to keep CHAT relatively stable and free of changes. Whatever changes we anticipate making will probably be mostly in coding systems on dependent tiers, rather than in codings on the main line.

2. **Database**. We expect that new additions to the CHILDES database will no longer require reformatting, since they will be transcribed in CHAT from the start. Already, we are starting to receive most new data files in CHAT format. Soon we expect this to become the norm. Over the next few years, we expect the database to grow beyond the current focus on first language acquisition by normal children. In the future, the database will grow to include large components of second language acquisition data, adult interactional data, and a variety of data from children with language disorders. We have already begun to distinguish between the CHILDES system, the Aphasia Language Data Exchange System (ALDES), the Second Language Acquisition Data Exchange System (SLADES), and the overall Language Data Exchange System (LANDES).

3. **CLAN.** The most exciting prospects for future developments in CHILDES lie in the area of new developments in CLAN. We expect to construct a large variety of new CLAN programs to automate the process of phonological, morphosyntactic, lexical, and discourse analysis. We also plan several new forms of data display. Each of these new initiatives will be discussed separately.

13.2.1. Developmental and Clinical Profiling

Underlying each of these technical initiatives are broader long-term theoretical goals. On the one hand, researchers want to use the CHILDES system to illuminate crosslinguistic regularities in the ways that children learn languages. On the other hand, they want to evaluate individual differences in language development. The search for both differences and commonalities in language development is the fundamental engine that drives developments in our understanding of language acquisition. We can use measures computed from the CHILDES database to fuel and oil this engine. The CHILDES Project cannot supply theoretical interpretations, but it can supply an ongoing stream of data that will motivate the development of these theoretical interpretations.

The CHILDES Project can develop a wide variety of measures that can be subjected to a process of indicator validation. In particular, we need to validate the individual indicators that have been used in previous measurement instruments along three dimensions:

1. **Developmental validity.** Each indicator must accurately predict developmental stage, at least within a given developmental range. For example, during the first stages of language learning, MLU is a good predictor of developmental stage. However, later on, its developmental validity weakens. All indicators have floors and ceilings. For an indicator to display developmental validity, it only needs to correlate with developmental stage for part of the growth curve. MLU is one of the few measures for which developmental validity has been studied (Miller, 1981).

2. **Clinical validity.** Each indicator must also prove useful in allowing us to classify children as belonging to particular groups or populations. For example, we might expect that indicators focusing on the use of personal pronouns or topic maintenance structures would help us identify a child as

autistic. Similarly, retracings, word repetitions, and hesitations would help us to classify a child as having problems with sentence planning (Wijnen, 1990). In some cases, we already have reason to classify a child in a particular clinical group, and we are then interested in the correlation between particular measures and our assignment of children to that group. In other cases, we are using our prior experience with the measure as the basis of the classification.

3. **Processing validity**. Each indicator must be conceptualized in a way that allows us to see how it relates to particular cognitive or social processes. This is a form of content validity.

In order for an indicator to be judged as "useful" it needs to display some combination of these three types of validity along with easy computability. Some indicators may have clinical validity without developmental validity. For example, "initial segment repetition" may be a clear characteristic of children with developmental disfluency, but one that undergoes few changes over time. Because it undergoes few changes over time, it has good clinical validity, but low developmental validity. Although indicators without developmental validity will not tell us much about development, they can be quite useful in making clinical assessments. It is also possible, although somewhat unlikely, that some measures will have developmental validity but no clinical validity.

We want to make sure that the indicators we will construct should be computable from CHAT transcripts. What this means is that there must be programs that can take CHAT files as input and produce tabulations for each indicator as output. There is no one single program that can compute every indicator. Instead, we will need to rely on a variety of programs, including FREQ, STATFREQ, MLU, COMBO, CHIP, MOR, PARS, and CHAINS. These various analyses can be grouped together into "scripts" or "batch files" to further automate the examination of large sets of corpora.

There are three reasons for requiring that all indicators be computable from CHAT files. The first reason is that, when faced with the prospect of tracking hundreds of indicators across as an enormous quantity of transcript data, the use of indicators that require hand calculation becomes simply impossible. The second reason is that the computation of indicators by machine is a fully **reliable** process. Once a program has been given a definition of an indicator, it will always compute this indicator in the same way. Of course, if the original transcript has errors, these will not be corrected. However, errors in transcription would also adversely affect the computation of indicators by human calculation. Moreover, it is often possible to pick up transcription errors by computational filters built into the CLAN programs. Finally, by requiring that each indicator be computable, we are also guaranteeing that the calculation of the indicator be completely operationalized. We then know exactly how the indicator was computed and exactly how it is defined.

Having determined the developmental and clinical validity of our indicators, and having separated out those with low validity, we now have a set of indicators that will be useful for studying developmental profiles in both normally-developing and clinical populations. In the normally-developing child, we expect to find that, for a given part of the developmental curve, many measures will be highly intercorrelated. For example, we would not be surprised to find that increases in the vocabulary for names of plants and animals are highly correlated with increases in the vocabulary for mental states. This **developmental cohesion** in normally-developing children can be explained in a variety of ways. The most basic approach views all developments as driven by a single underlying motor. We can call this motor "experience" or we can call it "maturation." In either case, we are simply recognizing the obvious fact that children gain competence as they get older. Even in normally-developing children, we expect to see points at which developmental cohesion between measures begins to break down. Sometimes this is due to ceiling or floor effects. The **unbraiding** (Tager-Flusberg, 1988) of indicators that occurs in the normally-developing child must be assessed and understood in detail before we can properly understand the more extreme unbraiding that occurs in clinical populations.

Having completed the analysis of developmental cohesion with normally-developing children, we can then begin to characterize the additional patterns of unbraiding that occur in clinical populations. We take our map for normally-developing children and impose upon it our map of the same indicators in a particular clinical population. To do this, we will try to match across age so that the overall fit of the clinical population to the normal map is maximized. Given this, we can then focus on those indicators that are markedly above the normal level and those that are markedly below the normal level. We can speak of these mismatches to the normal profile as **asynchronies**. For example, we might expect to find the control of complex syntax and the more complex mental state verbs to be particularly low in children with Down syndrome across a variety of developmental stages. We might also expect to see the use of particular speech acts depressed in autistic children across a variety of time periods. The exact characterization of the developmental course of these **asynchronies** is one of the major goals that will surely carry us well into the next century.

We cannot realistically assume that the goal of reconstituting the foundations of language assessment will be achieved in the immediate future. However, what we can hope to construct in the immediate future are the computational tools upon which this analysis can be based. Doing this will require new tools for the analysis of lexicon, morphosyntax, phonology, and discourse. Let us now look at each of these groups of new tools.

13.2.2. The Lexical Initiative

What are the most frequent words used by English-speaking children? The most useful account of actual spoken English usage from children is provided by Hall, Nagy, and Linn (1984). That tabulation, while extremely useful for certain comparisons, is based on samples taken from a fairly narrow age range. The other available count is Rinsland (1945). That count was based on a small set of data and is now badly out of date. Construction of a fuller frequency count for English-speaking children would seem to be a simple and important goal.

At first blush, it would seem that one could easily answer this question using the FREQ program and the CHILDES database. It is an easy enough matter to run FREQ on collections of files using the +u option. Using FREQ, one could simply compute the numbers of occurrences for every word in the database. The output would look much like the frequency analysis of the Brown University Corpus developed by Francis and Kucera (1982). However, there are conceptual problems involved in the construction of such a simple summary frequency count. Some of these problems were directly confronted by Hall, Nagy, and Linn. First, one would want to tabulate frequency data for the speech of children separately from the speech of adults. And one would not want to combine data from children of different ages. Moreover, we would not want to merge data from children with language disorders together with data from normally-developing children. Differences in social class, gender, and educational level may lead one to make further separations. And it is important to distinguish language used in different situational contexts. When one finishes looking at all the distinctions that could potentially be made, it becomes clear that one needs to think of the construction of a lexical database in very dynamic terms.

What we plan to do to address this problem is to apply the computational techniques that were developed in building the CHILDES/BIB retrieval system to the lexical analysis of the whole CHILDES database. Each file will be provided with a new header giving a detailed set of codes for the key participants at various age levels. In one large computation-intensive job, we will extract every lexical item in the entire database and attach to each item a set of pointers to the position of the item in every file in which it occurs. Once these pointers are computed, no changes can be made in the database. Storage of the data on CD-ROM in this form would be ideal, since CD-ROM files cannot be altered. Once the pointers from the master wordlist to the individual occurrences of words are computed, the user can then construct specific probes of this database configured both on facts about the child and facts about the words being searched. The program that matches these searches to the pointer file will be called LEX. Using LEX, it will be possible, for example, to track the frequency of a group of "evaluative" words contained in a separate file in 2-year-olds separated into males and females. And the same search can also yield the frequency values for these words in the adult input. Although we may want to publish hard-copy frequency counts based on some searches through this database, the definitive form of the lexical frequency analysis will be contained in the program itself.

Once the LEX tool is completed, the path will be open to the construction of three additional tools. The first of these is a simple extension of the current KWAL program. Currently, researchers who want to track down the exact occurrences of particular words must rely on the use of the +d option in FREQ or must make repeated analyses using KWAL and keep separate track of line numbers. With the new LEX system, instead of running through files sequentially, KWAL will be able to rely on the pointers in the master file to make direct access to items in the database.

A second simple use of the LEX facility will permit automatic analyses of words in particular lexical fields. For example, using this lexical database, we will be able to examine the development of selected lexical fields in the style of the PRISM analysis of Crystal (1982). The goal here is to find particular lexical domains that serve to characterize or classify children by age and clinical subgroup.

Likely candidates for intensive examination include: mental verbs, morality words, temporal adverbs, subordinating conjunctions, and complex verbs.

A third tool that can be developed through use of the LEX facility is the Lexical Rarity Index of LRI. Currently, the major measure of lexical diversity is the type-token ratio (TTR) of Templin (1957). A more interesting measure would focus on the relative dispersion in a transcript of words that are generally rare in some comparison data set. The more that a child uses "rare" words, the higher the Lexical Rarity Index. If most of the words are common and frequent, the LRI will be low. In order to compute various forms of this index, the LRI program would rely on values provided by LEX.

13.2.3. The Morphosyntactic Initiative

The completion of the coding of the **%mor** line for the database will allow us to construct indicators based on: (a) morpheme inventories, (b) semantic relations, (c) phrasal and utterance complexity, and (d) specific syntactic structures.

13.2.3.1. Morpheme Inventories

The study of the acquisition of particular grammatical markers in English has been heavily shaped by Brown's (1973) intensive study of the acquisition of 14 grammatical morphemes in Adam, Eve, and Sarah and the cross-sectional follow-up by de Villiers and de Villiers (1973). The 14 morphemes studied by Brown include the progressive, the plural, the regular past, the irregular past, *in*, *on*, the regular third-person singular, the irregular third-person singular, articles, the uncontracted copula, the contracted copula, the possessive, the contracted auxiliary, and the uncontracted auxiliary. Other markers tracked in LARSP, ASS, IPSYN, and DSS include the superlative, the comparative, the adverbial ending –*ly*, the uncontracted negative, the contracted negative, the regular past participle, the irregular past participle, and various nominalizing suffixes. All of these markers are given discrete categories on the **%mor** line, and it will be easy to use KWAL to search out their occurrence, FREQ to tabulate their frequencies, and COOCCUR and COMBO to study patterns in which they co-occur.

In addition to these basic grammatical markers, researchers have been interested in tracking pronouns, determiners, quantifiers, and modals. As Brown (1973), Lahey (1988), and many others have noted, these high-frequency closed-class items each express important semantic and pragmatic functions that provide us with separate information about the state of the child's language and cognitive functioning. For example, Antinucci and Miller (1976), Cromer (1991), Slobin (1986), and Weist (1984) argued that tense markings and temporal adverbs are not controlled until the child first masters the relevant conceptual categories.

13.2.3.2. Semantic Relations

Many basic semantic relations that have been discussed extensively in the literature (Bloom, 1975; Lahey, 1988; Leonard, 1976; Retherford, Schwartz, & Chapman, 1981) can be tracked by simply studying a few closed-class lexical items. In particular, we can follow these correspondences between semantic relations and lexical expressions:

Relation	Lexical Expressions
Locative	in, on, under, through, by, at
Negation	can't, no, not, won't, none
Demonstrative	this, that
Recurrence	more, again, another
Possession	possessive suffix, of, mine, hers, her, etc.
Adverbial	–ly
Quantifier	one, two, more, some
Recipient	to
Beneficiary	for
Comitative	with
Instrument	with, by

13.2.3.3. Beyond MLU

Beyond the study of individual morphemes, we can construct indicators based on the emergence of syntactic structures. The simplest form of syntactic analysis looks only at the development of sentence length. For example, Templin (1957) used a measure based simply on mean utterance length in words. Brown (1973) refined the analysis of mean length of utterance by treating each morpheme as a separate item. A related measure that can also be computed is MLP or mean length of phrase, which is essentially the measure studied by Loban (1976). The various types of mean length of utterance measures can be automatically computed by the CLAN MLU program. There is a wide variety of options that can be used in the computation of MLU. For example, one may exclude all imitative utterances, all hesitations, all word repetitions, and so on. The MLU program allows the user full control over exactly how these computations should be performed. A good discussion of procedures for computing MLU can be found in Miller (1981), as well as in chapters by Pan (this volume) and Rollins (this volume). Miller and Chapman (1981) report a strong correlation between MLU and age in a sample of 123 children. However, in the higher ranges of the MLU indicator, this correlation begins to decrease.

Miller (1981) emphasized the utility of studying sentence frequency distributions. In these distributions, one simply computes the number of utterances with one word, two words, three words, and so on. This simple computation can be performed by the CLAN MAXWD program.

13.2.3.4. Syntactic Structures

More complex analyses of syntactic development require us to deal with structures defined in terms of traditional syntactic categories such as Subject, Object, and Main Verb. Among the most important syntactic structures examined by LARSP, ASS, IPSYN, and DSS are these:

Structure	Example
Art + N	the dog
Adj + N	good boy
Adj + Adj + N	my new car
Art + Adj + N	the new car
Adj/Art + N + V	my bike fall
V + Adj/Art + N	want more cookie
N + poss + N	John's wallet
Adv + Adj	too hot
Prep + NP	at the school
N + Cop + PredAdj	we are nice
N + Cop + PredN	we are monsters
Aux + V	is coming
Aux + Aux + V	will be coming

Mod + V	can come
Q + V	who ate it?
Q + Aux + V	who is coming?
tag	isn't it?
aux + N	are you going?
S + V	baby fall
V + O	drink coffee
S + V + O	you play this
X + conj + X	boy and girl, red and blue
V + to + V	want to swim
let/help + V	let's play
V + Comp	I know you want it
Sent + Conj + Sent	I'll push and you row.
V + I + O	read me the book
N + SRel	the one you have in the bag
N + ORel	the one that eats corn
S + Rel + V	the one I like best is the monster
passive	he is kicked by the raccoon
Neg + N	no dog
Neg + V	can't come
PP + PP	under the bridge by the river
comparative	better than Bill

Several of these structures also define some of the semantic relations that have been emphasized in previous literature. These include recipient (direct object), agent (subject in actives), verb, and object.

13.2.3.5. Scales

Although it would be possible to track each of these morphological and syntactic structures as separate indicators of language development, there is good reason to expect to find an enormous overlap between these separate indicators in terms of their prediction of developmental stage and clinical subgroup. Given this, it is likely that we will eventually want to merge groups of these structures into composite indicators. However, the exact shape of these composites will have to be inferred statistically.

An alternative way of merging information is to form a scale. In several parts of the grammar, it appears that a smaller set of indicators can possibly be grouped together into a larger scale. For example, DSS, ASS, IPSYN, and LARSP all claim that children move through these stages in the elaboration of the verb phrase:

1. uninflected verb
2. copula or contracted copula
3. is + verb + ing
4. addition of –s or –ed affixes to the verb
5. control of additional forms of the copula
6. modal + verb
7. do + verb
8. past tense modals
9. "get" passive
10. modal + cop + verb + ing
11. have + verb + en
12. modal + have + verb + en

Do these developments really scale in this way? Can one safely say that a child who is using the "get" passive has already controlled the addition of the modal, *do*, and the other suffixes lower in the sequence? If this is true, then we can say that this is a real scale. If there are many reversals of the predicted order, than we will not treat this as a scale.

If we can indeed construct a variety of scales of this type, we can then use the child's level on each scale as a single indicator. For example, a child who controls the "get" passive and nothing higher on the scale would have a score of 9 on the verb phrase expansion scale. Similar scales will be tested for interrogative words, conjunctions, negatives, secondary verbs, and pronouns.

13.2.3.6. Crosslinguistic Applications

The discussion in this section has focused on the construction of indicators for development in English. However, these same tools can also be usefully applied to basic issues in crosslinguistic analysis. Once we have collected a large database of transcripts in other languages and created a full **%mor** tier encoding, we can ask some of the basic questions in crosslinguistic analyses. Are there underlying similarities in the distribution of semantic relations and grammatical markings used by children at the beginning of language learning? Exactly which markings show the greatest language-specific divergences from the general pattern? How are grammatical relations marked as ergative in one language handled in another language? Under what circumstances do children tend to omit subject pronouns, articles, and other grammatical markers?

13.2.4. The Phonological Initiative

Despite all the care that has gone into the formulation of CHAT, transcription of child language data remains a fairly imprecise business. No matter how carefully one tries to capture the child's utterances in a standardized transcription system, something is always missing. The CHAT main line induces the transcriber to view utterances in terms of standard lexical items. This morphemic emphasis on the main line can be counterbalanced by including a rich phonological transcript on the **%pho** line. As Peters, Fahn, Glover, Harley, Sawyer, and Shimura (1990) argued, the inclusion of a complete CHAT **%pho** line is the best way to convey the actual content of the child's utterances, particularly at the youngest ages. Although inclusion of a complete **%pho** line is a powerful tool, even this form of two-tier transcription tends to miss the full dynamics of the actual audio record. If the original audiotapes are still in good condition, one can use them to continue to verify utterances. But there is no way to quickly access a particular point on an audiotape for a particular utterance. Instead, one has to either listen through a whole tape from beginning to end or else try to use tape markings and fast-forward buttons to track down an utterance. The same situation arises when the interaction is on videotape.

Computer technology now provides us with a dramatic new way of creating a direct, immediately accessible link between the audio recording and the CHAT transcription. The system we have developed at Carnegie Mellon, called Talking Transcripts, uses digitized speech, mass storage technology, and the Macintosh operating system to forge these direct links. For each transcript, these steps must be followed:

1. Using the SoundDesigner program and the AudioMedia II digitizer board from Digidesign, a 30-minute audio segment is recorded to computer disk. The recording is done at 22KHz with 16-bit digitization. The audio quality at this sampling rate is excellent. Once the recording is started the tape recorder and

computer can be left unattended. Although the process of digitizing a complete set of tapes will take many hours, there is no need to continually monitor the activity.

2. The resulting size of the digitized file for the 30-minute segment is about 80 megabytes. Because of the large size of these files, we write them directly to optical erasable cartridges. Optical erasable provides limitless, fast, erasable, but stable storage. Currently, the PMO-650 drive from Pinnacle is the fastest of these drives, but standards here are changing rapidly. Prices for this technology are still fairly high, but they are continuing to drop.

3. Once a complete 30-minute segment has been digitized, we can begin to transcribe the data in CHAT within a CED window.

4. Using a special new feature in the CED interface, we can automatically insert a mark in the transcript that corresponds to the next segment of the digitized file.

5. Later, when we want to play back a particular utterance, we simply click on the mark in the transcript in the CED window and the program directly plays the correct segment in the SoundDesigner file.

Although this process requires some additional time setting up the basic digitization and creating the playlist, this investment pays for itself in facilitating transcription. Each utterance can be played back exactly and immediately without having to use a reverse button or foot pedal.

As a user of this new system, I found that having the actual audio record directly available gave me a much enhanced sense of an immediate relation between the transcript and the actual interaction. It is difficult to describe verbally the immediacy of this link, but the impact on the transcriber is quite dramatic. Having the actual sound directly available does not diminish the importance of accurate transcription, because the CLAN programs must still continue to rely on the CHAT transcript. However, the immediate availability of the sound tends to make the transcriber more confident regarding the process of creating full phonological analyses that can be verified for reliability later.

The immediate availability of digitized sound has strong positive consequences for the process of phonological transcription. It will now be possible for us to design an entire Phonologist's Workbench grounded on the immediate availability of actual sound. The new programs for phonological analysis that we now plan to write include:

1. **Inventory Analysis**. We will extend the PHONFREQ program, so that it can compute the numbers of uses of a segment across either types or tokens of strings on the **%pho** line. The program will also be structured so that the inventories can be grouped by distinctive features, such as place or manner of articulation, or by groups, such as consonants versus vowels. The ratio of consonants to vowels will be computed. Summary statistics will include raw frequencies and percentage frequency of occurrence for individual segments. Non-occurrences in a transcript of any of the standard segments of English will be flagged.

2. **Length**. The MLU program will be used to compute mean length of utterance in syllables. This can be done from the **%pho** line, by using syllable boundaries as delimiters.

3. **Variability**. The MODREP program will be made to compute the types and tokens of the various phonetic realizations for a single target word, a single target phoneme, or a single target cluster. For example, for all the target words with the segment /p/, the program will list the corresponding child forms. Conversely, the researcher can look at all the child forms containing a /p/ and find the target forms from which they derive.

4. **Homonymy**. Homonymy refers to a child's use of a single phonetic string to refer to a large number of target words. For example, the child may say "bo" for *bow, boat , boy, bone,* etc. The MODREP program will calculate the degree of homonymy observed by comparing the child's string types coded on the **%pho** tier with the corresponding target forms coded on the **%mod** tier.

5. **Correctness**. In order to determine correctness, the child pronunciation (**%pho** line) must be compared with the target (**%mod** line). The MODREP program will be modified to compute the number of correct

productions of the adult target word, segment, or cluster. For example, the percentage consonants correct (PCC) will be computed in this way.

6. **Phonetic product per utterance**. This index (Bauer, 1988; Nelson & Bauer, 1991) will be computed by a new CLAN program called PHOP. The index computes the phonetic complexity of the utterance as a function of the number of place-of-articulation contrasts realized. This index is low if everything is at one place of articulation; it is high if all points of articulation are used.

7. **Phonological process analysis**. Phonological process analyses search for systematic patterns of sound omission, substitution, and word formation that children make in their simplified productions of adult speech. Thus, such processes refers to classes of sounds rather than to individual sounds. Process analysis must be based upon the comparison of the **%pho** and **%mod** tiers. The Clan Analysis of Phonology, or CAP, will examine rates of consonant deletion, voicing changes, gliding, stopping, cluster simplification, and syllable deletion. In addition, non-developmental errors will be identified and calculated (Shriberg, 1990).

8. **PHONASCII and UNIBET code modifications**. PHONASCII and UNIBET codes will be modified and/or elaborated to enable cross-tier analysis.

9. **Automatic phonetic transcription of high-frequency words**. To facilitate phonetic and phonological transcription of corpora, we will develop an on-line users reference to provide automatic phonological coding of the 2,000 most frequently used words in the English language to facilitate phonetic transcription of naturalistic speech data (e.g., words such as "and" and "the" will not have to be redundantly transcribed each time they occur.

10. **Phonologist's Reference**. To help beginning phonologists and to stabilize reliability for trained phonologists, we will have available a complete set of digitized speech samples for each phonological symbol used in either UNIBET or PHONASCII.

11. **Transcription playback**. The same phonological database used by the Phonologist's Reference can also be used to play back the sounds of candidate transcriptions.

Alongside the development of programs to support these analyses, we will also be working to broaden the CHILDES database of phonological transcripts. There are very few computerized transcripts currently available, so we can reasonably start from scratch in this area. Because we are starting from scratch, we can require that all transcripts in the CHILDES phonological database be accompanied by good quality tape recordings, which will be digitized at CMU and then distributed through CD-ROM.

13.2.5. The Discourse Initiative

Many researchers want to track the ways in which discourse influences ways of expressing topic, anaphora, tense, mood, narrative voice, ellipsis, embedding, and word order (Halliday & Hasan, 1976; MacWhinney, 1985). They want to track shifts in narrative voice, transitions between discourse blocks, and foreground-background relations in discourse. They are also interested in the ways in which particular speech acts from one participant give rise to responsive or nonresponsive speech acts in the other participant.

The complex process of discourse analysis benefits from the use of virtually every aspect of the CLAN programs. The display programs – COLUMNS, LINES, and SLIDE – are designed to facilitate the viewing of turns and overlaps. The CED editor allows discourse analysts to enrich transcripts with a variety of codes in a fully hierarchical scheme. Sequential analysis programs such as CHAINS, CHIP, KEYMAP, and MLT can then analyze sequences, pairs, and links between these codes. Specific types of interactions can be marked with GEM for further analysis.

The time-consuming nature of speech act coding has led us to place particular emphasis on the development and refinement of the CED program (Bodin & Snow, this volume). However, as richly coded transcripts become more available, we will begin to place an emphasis on extensions to programs such as CHAINS or KEYMAP.

The initial uses of the CHIP program focused on superficial lexical matches between consecutive utterances. With the completion of the morphological coding of corpora such as the Brown corpus, it is now possible to use CHIP to study the repetition and expansion of utterances not just in terms of superficial lexical match, but also in terms of underlying grammatical category.

13.3. The Distant Horizon

As we gaze across the immediate horizon into the distant future, we peer into a world where computational power continues to grow and the structure of the database becomes tighter and richer. We can assume that, within the next 20 years, personal computers will have access to virtually limitless amounts of digitized speech and video. These data will be accessible through fiber-optic networks, erasable CD-ROM disks, and powerful memory chips. Formats for data compression and transfer will be standardized across computer systems, further facilitating the transfer of multimedia data.

As these resources become increasingly available, the CHILDES database will shift from its current concentration on ASCII transcripts to a focus on transcripts accompanied by digitized audio and video. Links between events in the audio and video records will be tied to an increasingly rich set of links in the transcript. These "hot" links will be increasingly dynamic, allowing the user to move around through the audio and video records using the transcript as the navigational map. The full digitization of the interaction will allow the observer to enter into the interaction as an explorer. This is not the virtual reality of video adventures. The scientist is not seeking to change reality or to interact with reality. Instead, the goal is to explore reality by viewing an interaction repeatedly from many different perspectives. These new ways of viewing a transcript will be important for phonological and grammatical analyses, but their most important impact will be on the analysis of interactional structure and discourse. Having full video and audio immediately available from the transcript will draw increased attention to codes for marking synchronies between intonational patterns, gestural markings, and lexical expressions in ongoing interactional relations.

Although the core distinctions of CHAT will continue to be important, the underlying computer representation of CHAT may shift to a form more like that of the Standard Generalized Markup Language (SGML; Sperberg-McQueen & Burnard, 1990) or of some successor to SGML. This underlying form will not be displayed to the user; rather, it will be stored in the CHILDES database and transformed when users interact with the database. Movement to this more structured underlying representation will be facilitated by the development of transducers from CHAT to SGML and from SGML to CHAT. Once a full abstract representation of the database has been constructed, additional output filters can be constructed to deal with national orthographies, full IPA markings, and symbols for prosodic contours.

The construction of this new multimedia transcript world will allow us to begin work on the successor to the CHILDES Project. This is the Human Speech Genome Project. One of the first goals of the Speech Genome Project will be the collection, digitization, transcription, parsing, and coding of complete speech records for all the verbal interaction of a set of perhaps a dozen young children from differing language backgrounds. They might include, for example, a child learning ASL, a child with early focal lesions, a child growing up bilingual, and children with varying family situations. The multimedia records will allow us to fully characterize and explore all of the linguistic input to these children during the crucial years for language learning. We will then be in a position to know exactly what happens during the normal course of language acquisition. We can examine exactly how differences in the input to the child lead to differences in the patterns of language development. We will have precise data on the first uses of forms and how those first uses blend into regular control. We will be able to track in total precision curves for overregularizations, item frequencies, and error types.

Alongside this rich new observational database, the increased power of computational simulations will allow us to construct computational models of the language learning process that embody a variety of theoretical ideas. By testing these models against the facts of language learning embodied in the Speech Genome, we can both refine the models and guide the search for new empirical data to be included in the multimedia database of the future.

Acknowledgments

This work was supported from 1984 to 1988 by grants from the John D. and Catherine T. MacArthur Foundation, the National Science Foundation, and the National Institutes of Health. Since 1987, the CHILDES Project has been supported by grants from the National Institutes of Health (NICHHD). For full acknowledgments and thanks to the dozens of researchers who have helped on this project, please consult pages viii and ix of the manual (MacWhinney, 1991). For the recent work reported here, thanks should go to Leonid Spektor for construction of the BIBFIND, CED, COLUMNS, COOCCUR, DATES, LINES, and SLIDE programs and for further elaborations of earlier programs, including CHECK. Mitzi Morris developed the DSS and MOR programs with extensive help from Julia Evans, Leonid Spektor, Roland Hausser, Carolyn Ellis, and Kim Plunkett. Nan Bernstein-Ratner collaborated in the development of guidelines for the creation of a phonological analysis system. Ideas regarding the Talking Transcripts project came from Helmut Feldweg and Sven Strömqvist. Helmut Feldweg also created a prototype version of the COLUMNS program, helped construct the German UNIBET, and supervised the solidification of the transcript database for German. Steven Gillis corrected errors in the Dutch UNIBET table and Christian Champaud corrected errors in the French UNIBET table. Joy Moreton, Catherine Snow, Barbara Pan, and Lowry Hemphill helped test and design the CHAINS and CED programs. Important suggestions for modifications of CHAT coding came from Judi Fenson, Frank Wijnen, Giuseppe Cappelli, Mary MacWhinney, Shanley Allen, and Julia Evans. Roy Higginson was the chief compiler of the CHILDES/BIB system. Thanks also to Julia Evans, Jeff Sokolov, and Catherine Snow for their comments on this chapter.

References

Antinucci, F., & Miller, R. (1976). How children talk about what happened. *Journal of Child Language*, *3*, 167-189.

Bauer, H. (1988). The ethologic model of phonetic development: I. Phonetic contrast estimators. *Clinical Linguistics and Phonetics, 2*, 347-380.

Bloom, L. (1975). Language development. In F. Horowitz (Ed.), *Review of child development research*. Chicago: University of Chicago Press.

Braine, M. D. S. (1963). The ontogeny of English structure: The first phase. *Language, 39*, 1-13.

Braine, M. D. S. (1976). Children's first word combinations. *Monographs of the Society for Research in Child Development, 41* (Whole No. 1).

Braine, M. D. S. (1987). What is learned in acquiring word classes: A step toward an acquisition theory. In B. MacWhinney (Ed.), *Mechanisms of language acquisition*. Hillsdale, NJ: Lawrence Erlbaum Associates.

Brown, R. (1973). *A first language: The early stages*. Cambridge, MA: Harvard.

Cromer, R. (1991). *Language and thought in normal and handicapped children*. Oxford: Blackwell.

Crystal, D. (1982). *Profiling linguistic disability*. London: Edward Arnold.

de Villiers, J., & de Villiers, P. (1973). A cross-sectional study of the acquisition of grammatical morphemes in child speech. *Journal of Psycholinguistic Research, 2*, 267-278.

Deuchar, M., & Clark, A. (1992). *Bilingual acquisition of the voicing contrast in word-initial stop consonants in English and Spanish* (Cognitive Science Research Report No. 213). Unpublished manuscript, University of Sussex.

Elman, J. (1991). *Incremental learning, or the importance of starting small* (TR #9101). Unpublished manuscript, University of California, San Diego.

Ervin-Tripp, S. (1979). Children's verbal turn-taking. In E. Ochs & B. Schieffelin (Eds.), *Developmental pragmatics*. New York: Academic Press.

Francis, W., & Kucera, H. (1982). *Frequency analysis of English usage: Lexicon and grammar*. Boston: Houghton Mifflin.

Hall, W. S., Nagy, W. E., & Linn, R. (1984). *Spoken words: Effects of situation and social group on oral word usage and frequency*. Hillsdale, NJ: Lawrence Erlbaum Associates.

Halliday, M., & Hasan, R. (1976). *Cohesion in English*. London: Longman.

Hausser, R. (1990). Principles of computational morphology. *Computational Linguistics,* 47.

Higginson, R., & MacWhinney, B. (1990). *CHILDES/BIB: An annotated bibliography of child language and language disorders*. Hillsdale, NJ: Lawrence Erlbaum Associates.

Hyams, N. (1986). *Language acquisition and the theory of parameters*. Dordrecht: D. Reidel.

Ingram, D. (1972). The development of phrase structure rules. *Language Learning, 22*, 65-77.

Ingram, D. (1975). If and when transformations are acquired by children. In D. P. Dato (Ed.), *Developmental psycholinguistics: Theory and applications*. Washington, DC: Georgetown University Press.

Lahey, M. (1988). *Language disorders and language development*. New York: Macmillan.

Lee, L. (1974). *Developmental sentence analysis*. Evanston, IL: Northwestern University Press.

Leonard, L. (1976). *Meaning in child language*. New York: Grune & Stratton.

Loban, W. (1976). *Language development*. Champaign, IL: National Council of Teachers of English.

MacWhinney, B. (1974). *How Hungarian children learn to speak.* Unpublished doctoral dissertation, University of California, Berkeley.

MacWhinney, B. (1975). Pragmatic patterns in child syntax. *Stanford Papers and Reports on Child Language Development, 10*, 153-165.

MacWhinney, B. (1985). Grammatical devices for sharing points. In R. Schiefelbusch (Ed.), *Communicative competence: Acquisition and intervention.* Baltimore: University Park Press.

MacWhinney, B. (1991). *The CHILDES project: Tools for analyzing talk.* Hillsdale, NJ: Lawrence Erlbaum Associates.

MacWhinney, B. (1992). *The CHILDES database.* Dublin, OH: Discovery Systems.

MacWhinney, B., & Leinbach, J. (1991). Implementations are not conceptualizations: Revising the verb learning model. *Cognition, 29*, 121-157.

MacWhinney, B., Leinbach, J., Taraban, R., & McDonald, J. (1989). Language learning: Cues or rules? *Journal of Memory and Language, 28*, 255-277.

Maratsos, M. & Chalkley, M. (1980). The internal language of children's syntax: The ontogenesis and representation of syntactic categories. In K. Nelson (Ed.), *Children's language (Vol. 2).* New York: Gardner.

Marcus, G. F., Pinker, S., Ullman, M., Hollander, M., Rosen, T. J., Xu, F. (1992). Overregularization in language acquisition. *Monographs of the Society for Research in Child Development, 57:4.*

Miller, J. (1981). *Assessing language production in children: Experimental procedures.* Baltimore: University Park Press.

Miller, J., & Chapman, R. (1981). Research note: The relation between age and mean length of utterance in morphemes. *Journal of Speech and Hearing Research, 24*, 154-161.

Nelson, L., & Bauer, H. (1991). Speech and language production at age 2: Evidence for tradeoffs between linguistic and phonetic processing. *Journal of Speech and Hearing Research, 34*, 879-892.

Ochs, E. (1979). Transcription as theory. In E. Ochs & B. Schieffelin (Eds.), *Developmental pragmatics.* New York: Academic Press.

Peters, A. (1987). The role of imitation in the developing syntax of a blind child. *Text, 7*, 289-311.

Peters, A., Fahn, R., Glover, G., Harley, H., Sawyer, M., & Shimura, A. (1990). *Keeping close to the data: A two-tier computer-coding schema for the analysis of morphological development.* Unpublished manuscript, University of Hawaii, Honolulu.

Pinker, S., & Prince, A. (1988). On language and connectionism: Analysis of a Parallel Distributed Processing Model of language acquisition. *Cognition, 29*, 73-193.

Plunkett, K., & Sinha, C. (1992). Connectionism and developmental theory. *British Journal of Development Psychology, 10*, 209-254.

Retherford, K., Schwartz, B., & Chapman, R. (1981). Semantic roles and residual grammatical categories in mother and child speech: Who tunes in to whom? *Journal of Child Language, 8*, 583-608.

Rinsland, H. (1945). *A basic vocabulary of elementary school children.* New York: Macmillan.

Rondal, J. A. (1985). *Adult-child interaction and the process of language understanding.* New York: Praeger.

Shriberg, L. (1990). *Programs to examine phonetic and phonologic evaluation records.* Hillsdale, NJ: Lawrence Erlbaum Associates.

Slobin, D. (1986). Crosslinguistic evidence for the language-making capacity. In D. Slobin (Ed.), *The crosslinguistic study of language acquisition: Volume 2. Theoretical issues.* Hillsdale, NJ: Lawrence Erlbaum Associates.

Sperberg-McQueen, C. M., & Burnard, L. (1990). *Guidelines for the encoding and interchange of machine-readable texts.* Chicago: Association for Computational Linguistics.

Tager-Flusberg, H. (1988). On the nature of a language acquisition disorder: The example of autism. In F. S. Kessel (Ed.), *The development of language and language researchers.* Hillsdale, NJ: Lawrence Erlbaum Associates.

Templin, M. (1957). *Certain language skills in children.* Minneapolis, MN: University of Minnesota Press.

Weist, R., Wysocka, H., Witkowska-Stadnik, K., Buczowska, E., & Konieczna, E. (1984). The defective tense hypothesis: On the emergence of tense and aspect in child Polish. *Journal of Child Language, 11*, 347-374.

Wexler, K. (1986). Parameter-setting in language acquisition. In B. MacWhinney (Ed.), *Mechanisms of language acquisition.* Hillsdale, NJ: Lawrence Erlbaum Associates.

Wijnen, F. (1990). The development of sentence planning. *Journal of Child Language, 17*, 550-562.

Wilson, B., & Peters, A. M. (1988). What are you cookin' on a hot?: Movement constraints in the speech of a three-year-old blind child. *Language*, 249-273.

Appendix

Answers to the Exercises

Linda Beaudin and Jeffrey L. Sokolov
University of Nebraska at Omaha

Chapter 2: Basic Measures of Child Language

2.4.1: We used the following command to answer this question:

> maxwd +t*CHI +g1 +c1 +d1 *.cha | mlu
> maxwd +t*CHI +g1 +c5 +d1 *.cha | mlu

A wildcard (*) is used to speed the process by searching through all of the files ending in **.cha**. Note that if we do not include the **+c1** option, the MAXWD program will default to finding the single longest utterance. Thus the following command would have achieved the same result as the first command above:

> maxwd +t*CHI +g1 +d1 *.cha | mlu

2.4.2: We used the following command to answer this question:

> freq +t*CHI +s"*-%%" +z50w *.cha
> freq +t*CHI +s"*-%%" +z51w–100w *.cha

We would continue to compute the TTR for successive 50-word bands by modifying the **+z** option as needed. Notice that the **w** in the **+z** option denotes *words*, in contrast to the **u** in Command Box 2.3, which denotes *utterances*.

2.4.3: This analysis must be performed for all the mothers when their children are 20 months old and again at 30 months. This will require first using the data in the 20mos directory and then changing to the 30mos directory to perform the same analysis. **Hint**: The files for the complete New England corpus are marked with either an **a** (for 14 months), a **b** (for 20 months) or a **c** (for 30 months). Thus, the filename **kid068b.cha** denotes a 20-month-old child. Of course, we are analyzing only the 20- and 30-month-old data. The following command will give us information about the mean length of the mothers' utterances:

mlu   +t*MOT   *.cha

We used the FREQ program to analyze the lexical diversity of the mothers' speech to their children (this command is similar to the one listed in Command Box 2.3):

freq   +t*MOT   +s"*– %%"   *.cha

Chapter 3: The Babytalk Register

3.5.1: You could create an include file. This file would contain only two lines, with the word *bunny* on one line and the word *rabbit** (with the wildcard symbol * to find plurals and possessives) on the other. The FREQ program would find and count every occurrence of *bunny* and every occurrence of *rabbit*. However, you would not know from examining the output of this command whether the two words co-occurred in the form *bunny rabbit*. The advantage of using COMBO is that it will find specified combinations of words, codes, or even lists of words in include files. However, COMBO does not provide summary counts of co-occurrences (see Exercise 3.5.2. for how to obtain summary counts). You could use COMBO to find instances of diminutives and then use FREQ to count them.

3.5.2: The simplest way to search for occurrences of *double diminutives* is to use a wildcard in the command:

combo   +d   +t*MOT   +s"little^*"   kid010b.cha

Using a wildcard would produce a list of all occurrences of *little* and the words that follow each occurrence. This would allow you to check for the presence of diminutives following the word *little*. However, if you have created a file consisting of all of the appropriate diminutives for the sample under consideration (e.g., **real.dim**), then a more elegant command would be the following:

combo   +d   +t*MOT   +s"little^@real.dim"   kid010b.cha

This command asks for all occurrences of the word *little* followed immediately by any of the diminutives present in our include file (**real.dim**).

Review the output of this command to determine if there are any utterances that contain an occurrence of *little* plus a diminutive. If there are none, then we suggest performing the analysis on the second transcript (**kid025b.cha**). Note that you could also have used FREQ (see Exercise 3.5.1) to search for either *little* or diminutives contained in the include file (**real.dim**), but in each case you would not have known whether *little* and the diminutive were in the same phrase.

3.5.3: Use KWAL in the following command:

kwal   +d   +t*MOT   +s@real.dim   +f   kid010b.cha

The output of this command is a file consisting of all the utterances containing any of the diminutives listed in our **real.dim** include file. We did not specify a window because we only want to collect the utterances which actually contain diminutives, not any of the surrounding utterances. Note also the use of the +d option. This causes the output from the KWAL command to be in CHAT format. The second step is to run MLU on the file **kid010b.kwa** to obtain the mother's MLU:

mlu   +t*MOT   kid010b.kwa

This command will output the mother's MLU for those utterances containing diminutives. Of course, this analysis can be performed more easily with a single CLAN command:

kwal   +d   +t*MOT   +s@real.dim   kid010b.cha | mlu

However, we need to know if this MLU is shorter than the MLU of this mother's utterances not containing diminutives. Use the following command to eliminate those utterances that contain diminutives:

kwal   +d   +t*MOT   −s@real.dim   +f   kid010b.cha

The output of this command is a file (in this case, **kid010b.kw0**) that contains all the mother's utterances except those that contain diminutives. Now run MLU on this file and compare it with the MLU run on the file that contained only diminutives:

456 Appendix

> **mlu   +t*MOT   kid010b.kw0**

Once again, this analysis can be performed more simply with a single CLAN command:

> **kwal   +d   +t*MOT   –s@real.dim   kid010b.cha | mlu**

Chapter 4: Learning to Use Superordinates

4.6.1: We start by making an include file, which we will name **super.inc**, that includes the specified superordinates. The file would contain the following items:

> tree%
> dinosaur%
> building%
> dish%
> meat%

To obtain the frequency of occurrence of these superordinates, we used commands similar to the one listed in Command Box 4.2, specifying both Adam's and his mother's speech tiers:

> **freq   +t*ADA   +s@super.inc   +u   adam*.cha**
> **freq   +t*MOT   +s@super.inc   +u   adam*.cha**

To obtain information about the proportion of these terms in Adam's speech, we must divide the number of superordinates in the sample by the total number of word tokens for Adam and his mother. The commands listed above provide the total number of superordinates. In order to determine the total number of word tokens, we would use the following commands:

> **freq   +t*ADA   +d4   +u   adam*.cha**
> **freq   +t*MOT   +d4   +u   adam*.cha**

4.6.2: We first use FREQ to investigate whether there any other kinship terms worth adding to our include file:

freq +d1 +f sarah033.cha

The next step is to create an include file (which we called **kinship.inc**) listing all of the kinship terms in **sarah033.cha**. Then, we use KWAL to collect all of the instances of kinship terms in the file. We also use the **+/−w** options to include a window of context. The final command is similar to the one listed in Command Box 4.4:

kwal +s@kinship.inc +w5 −w5 +d1 +fks sarah033.cha

Now we are ready to code our collection of conversations containing kinship terms. Use the CED program to create your **codes.lst** file and to perform all your coding. Make sure you exercise special care in creating your **codes.lst** file – the format must be exactly like the one listed in the chapter. We highly recommend reading the section on Coder's Editor in the CHILDES manual. Once you have created your **codes.lst** file, you are ready to code the **sarah033.ks** file. Use the following command:

ced sarah033.ks

After coding Sarah's use of kinship terms and her mother's responses to them, we use FREQ to count the number of occurrences of each type of maternal response. Our command for this analysis is similar to the one listed in Command Box 4.6:

freq +t%sup +s$* sarah033.ks

4.6.3: The first step is to create an include file of superordinates (either from the analysis of Adam's data or from your own analysis). Then use the following command to count the number of superordinates in the speech of these children with Down syndrome and their mothers:

freq +t*CHI +s@super.inc *.cha
freq +t*MOT +s@super.inc *.cha

458 Appendix

In order to compare the language sophistication of these children with that of Adam, perform some of the analyses listed in Pan (this volume, chapter 2). Because maternal input was mentioned as a contributing factor to the development of superordinates, we may want to examine the kind of maternal feedback that these children with Down syndrome receive. To do this, we use the KWAL command in the following manner:

$$\text{kwal } +\text{s@super.inc } +\text{w5 } -\text{w5 } +\text{d1 } *.\text{cha}$$

We can then compare the results of this analysis with those from our previous analysis of the Adam sample.

Chapter 5: Common Features of Mothers' Vocabularies

5.5.1:

A. To perform this analysis, use the command listed in Command Box 5.1, but substitute *CHI for *MOT (to specify the child's tier) and +fchi for +fmot (to name the output file):

$$\text{freq } +\text{t*CHI } +\text{d1 } +\text{s"*-\%\%" } +\text{fchi } *.\text{sto}$$

The results from this command will be stored in six separate files, each with a **.chi** extension. In order to determine if these children have a shared vocabulary, we use the command from Command Box 5.2, substituting ***.chi** for ***.mot** and directing the output to **chicore** rather than to **motcore**:

$$\text{freq } +\text{y } +\text{u } +\text{o } *.\text{chi } > \text{ chicore}$$

Alternatively, we could have used the following, more efficient, command:

$$\text{freq } +\text{t*CHI } +\text{d1 } +\text{s"*-\%\%" } *.\text{sto } \mid \text{ freq } +\text{y } +\text{u } +\text{o } > \text{ chicore}$$

B. Use the procedure described in the chapter for answering Question 2 to analyze the data from Exercise 5.5.1A.

C. See the data from Exercise 5.5.1A.

D. The percentage of the children's speech that is composed of core vocabulary is a quotient of the number of core vocabulary tokens divided by the number of all the tokens in the speech sample. To obtain the total number of tokens for the entire sample, we would use the following command:

>   freq +t*CHI +u *.sto

To obtain the total number of core vocabulary tokens, we first need to create an include file containing the core vocabulary. The include file is an edited version of the output of the previous command in Exercise 5.5.1A (the **chicore** file), which we have re-named **chicore.inc**. In creating the include file, be sure to (a) delete all of the header information concerning the command options and (b) add "–%%" string to the end of each noun, verb, and pronoun to include all of the tokens for each type. Next, we used the following command to determine the frequency of occurrence of these tokens (from Command Box 5.5):

>   freq +t*CHI +u +o +s@chicore.inc *.sto

These commands provide all of the information necessary to compute the percentage of children's speech that is composed of their core vocabulary.

E. Analyze the composition of the children's core vocabulary obtained in the previous exercise in terms of content and function words.

5.5.2: In order to determine the core vocabulary for each mother-child dyad, we modified the FREQ command from Command Box 5.1. For example, to analyze the speech of Laurel and her Mom, we used the following commands:

>   freq +t*MOT +d1 +s"*-%%" laurel.sto > laurel.mot
>   freq +t*CHI +d1 +s"*-%%" laurel.sto > laurel.chi

We then used the output of these commands as input to the following command (similar to Command Box 5.2):

freq +y +u +o laurel.mot laurel.chi > laucore

A. All words with a frequency of two constitute the core lexicon for each mother-child pair. We can then create the include file we will need for the remaining questions by editing the file **laucore** to include only core vocabulary items and re-naming it **laurel.inc**.

B. To obtain the answer, we need to know the total number of different words used by the mother and her child and the number of different words shared by the mother and her child. The former is obtained in the TTR summary of the file **laucore**, i.e., the first line of the summary statistics from the FREQ analysis. With respect to the latter, by counting the number of words with a frequency of two in the **laucore** file, we can determine the number of different words shared by a mother and her child. We then divide the shared word-types by the total number of all word-types to determine the extent to which each mother-child dyad shares word-types.

C. Add up the results for each of the six mother-child dyads from 5.5.2B and then divide by 6.

5.5.3: The first step is to create an include file consisting of our basic-level terms. Rather than attempting to create such a list through brainstorming, we can scan the results of a simple FREQ analysis for a list of candidate words. To do this, we used the following command:

freq +d1 +u *.sto > basic.inc

After editing the **basic.inc** include file so that it contains only basic-level terms, we then used FREQ to determine the frequency of these terms in both mother and child speech. To analyze Martin's data, we would use the following commands (which are similar to the one listed in Command Box 5.5):

freq +t*CHI +o +s@basic.inc martin.sto > martin.cb
freq +t*MOT +o +s@basic.inc martin.sto > martin.mb

To determine if all children use the same basic level terms that their mothers use, we review both of the above files for each mother-child dyad. To analyze the linguistic context for each of the basic-level terms employed by mothers, we must collect instances of their use along with the preceding child utterances. Assuming that the preceding child utterance will be included in a window of five utterances prior to the mother's utterance, we can use the following command (similar to the one listed in Command Box 5.6):

kwal   +t*MOT   +s@basic.inc   −w5   *.sto

Chapter 6: Negative Evidence

6.5.1: Use the following commands to find the frequency of the mother's responses to the remaining five types of child utterances:

```
gem  +s$W:SW  +t%res  +d kal7.cha  |  freq  +t%res  +s$*  >  kal7.wsw
gem  +s$I:MW  +t%res  +d kal7.cha  |  freq  +t%res  +s$*  >  kal7.imw
gem  +s$I:SW  +t%res  +d kal7.cha  |  freq  +t%res  +s$*  >  kal7.isw
gem  +s$O:MW  +t%res  +d kal7.cha  |  freq  +t%res  +s$*  >  kal7.omw
gem  +s$O:SW  +t%res  +d kal7.cha  |  freq  +t%res  +s$*  >  kal7.osw
```

6.5.2: Using the instructions in the Appendix for chapter 6 as a guide and Coder's Editor (CED) as a tool, code both the well-formedness of the first 100 of the sibling's utterances and the type of maternal response to these utterances. Note that you will have to create a separate codes file (i.e., a **codes.lst** file) for sibling utterances and maternal responses. As noted in the exercise, you may wish give the codes for the sibling's utterances slightly different names (e.g., $WS for *well-formed sibling*). Code the sibling's utterances first, replace the **codes.lst** file, and then code the mother's responses.

Next, compute the sibling's MLU using the following command:

mlu   +t*SIB   kal7.cha

Finally, use the following command to determine the frequency of well-formed, ill-formed, and other utterances for the sibling:

freq   +t%SIB   +t%cod   +s"$*:%%"   kal7.cha

We can find a percentage by dividing the frequency of each utterance type by the total number of utterances in the sample (which is found in the output of the previous MLU command). In order to analyze the content of maternal responses, we must combine three CLAN commands: We use (a) GEM to examine the content of both adjacent and non-adjacent maternal responses addressed to the sibling; (b) KWAL to collect only maternal responses addressed to the sibling (the "ams" code); and (c) FREQ to count the number of different maternal responses. The following commands perform all of these functions:

```
gem  +s$W:%%  +t%res  +t%add  +d kal7.cha
| kwal  +t*MOT  +t%add  +s"ams"  +o%res  +d
| freq  +t%res  +s$*

gem  +s$I:%%  +t%res  +t%add  +d kal7.cha
| kwal  +t*MOT  +t%add  +s"ams"  +o%res  +d
| freq  +t%res  +s$*

gem  +s$O:%%  +t%res  +t%add  +d kal7.cha
| kwal  +t*MOT  +t%add  +s"ams"  +o%res  +d
| freq  +t%res  +s$*
```

6.5.3: This exercise requires planning an analysis.

Chapter 7: Individual Differences in Linguistic Imitativeness

7.5.1:

A. First, we need to determine the MLU of each child (both non-handicapped and with SLI). To do this, we used the following command (from Command Box 7.1):

```
mlu  +t*CHI  +z100u  *.cha
```

Second, we need to determine the percentage of imitative utterances for each child. Use the following CHIP command to obtain summary statistics for each child (from Command Box 7.2):

chip +bMOT +cCHI −hexchip +d1 +f *.cha

Finally, analyze the percentage of imitative utterances for each child with SLI as compared to the MLU-matched controls.

B. Analyze the data from Exercise 7.5.1A. **Hint:** Make sure to delete all extraneous data files created by MLU and CHIP after finishing this exercise.

C. In order to obtain merged data, we used the following CHIP command, first on the children with SLI and then on their MLU-matched controls:

chip +bMOT +cCHI −hexchip +d1 +u +f abe.cha clay.cha kate.cha rick.cha sid.cha

chip +bMOT +cCHI −hexchip +d1 +u +f ann.cha chuck.cha kyle.cha rose.cha sue.cha

These commands result in two files containing the synthesized data for each group of children, the children with SLI and their MLU-matched controls.

D. Analyze the data from Exercise 7.5.1C.

7.5.2. Analyze the data from Exercise 7.5.1C.

7.5.3. To perform these analyses we simply use the CHIP command from Exercise 7.5.1A. in the appropriate New England directories. We then review the output of these commands and compare the data for adults and children.

7.5.4. In order to create three files for examining the three different imitation types for **carl.cha**, we used the command listed in Command Box 7.3, substituting **eve15a.cha** with the name of the file we wish to analyze:

chip +bMOT +cCHI +d −hexchip carl.cha
  | kwal +t*CHI +t%chi +s$REDUC −w3 +d1 > carl.red

```
chip  +bMOT  +cCHI   +d –hexchip  carl.cha
  | kwal  +t*CHI   +t%chi  +s$EXACT  –w3  +d1  >  carl.exe

chip  +bMOT  +cCHI   +d –hexchip  carl.cha
  | kwal  +t*CHI   +t%chi  +s$EXPAN  –w3  +d1  >  carl.exp
```

We then compared the output of these files with the actual transcript (**carl.cha**) to consider the differences between automatically coded and manually coded imitations.

Chapter 8: Early Morphological Development

8.6.1: The following command collects Morela's five longest utterances at 16 months:

```
maxwd  +t*CHI  +c5  +g2  morela16.cha
```

We can pipe the results of this command to the MLU program to compute the mean length of utterance for Morela's five longest utterances. However, we must include the +**d1** option to insure that the output of MAXWD is in CHAT format. The MLU program cannot analyze data that is not in CHAT format.

```
maxwd  +t*CHI  +c5  +g2  +d1  morela16.cha  |  mlu
```

Morela's MLU can be obtained by executing the CLAN command listed in Command Box 8.1. To answer Questions 1 through 3 in this exercise, compare the results of the MLU of Morela's five longest utterance with her overall MLU.

8.6.2: We see from Table 8.6. that Morela uses three articles: *un*, *una*, and *el*. We can use the KWAL program to search for all of Morela's utterances containing these articles. Since we are interested in determining whether Morela's use of articles is imitative, we must also include a window of context consisting of five preceding utterances:

```
kwal  +t*CHI  +s"un"  +s"una"  +s"el"  –w5  morela.cha
```

We can examine the output of this command to answer Questions 1 through 3.

8.6.3: We must first make an include file (which we name **possess.inc**) consisting of the possessive forms listed in Table 8.8 in Appendix B for chapter 8. Next, we use the FREQ program to count the number of possessive forms while excluding all personal pronouns:

freq +t*CHI +o +s@posses.inc −s"<$PP>" morela16.cha

Since some Spanish possessive forms appear as prepositional phrases, we need to include a command that searches for the string *de*:

freq +t*CHI +o +s"de" morela16.cha

In the second part of this question, we are asked to examine the possessive forms that Morela uses to determine whether they are imitated or spontaneous. We use a command similar to the one listed in Command Box 8.4 for each of the forms discovered in the first part of the exercise:

kwal +t*CHI +s"mio" −w5 morela16.cha
kwal +t*CHI +s"mia" −w5 morela16.cha
kwal +t*CHI +s"de" −w5 morela16.cha

Chapter 9: Young Children's Hypotheses about English Reflexives

9.5.1: Since the question calls for us to search the **adam55.cha** file for instances of reflexives (as listed in Table 9.2) and the syntactic contexts in which they occur, we used the KWAL program with the +s@ and −/+w options. Because we want to include both the adult and child speech tiers, there is no need to specify speaker tiers. The command we used to perform this analysis is similar to the one listed in Command Box 9.3:

kwal +s@reflex −w4 +w4 +frfl adam55.cha

Saving the results in a new file (**adam55.rfl**) allows us to more easily read the information.

9.5.2: All of the information necessary to respond to this exercise is provided in the text.

466   Appendix

9.5.3: To examine children's potential use of non-genitives as genitives, we first need to generate a list of these forms and insert them into an include file (which we will name **genitive.inc**). Then we would use the following command:

    kwal +t*ADA   +s@genitive.inc adam55.cha

You do not have to restrict your analyses to **adam55.cha**. In fact, it is highly recommended that you expand your search to as many subjects and ages as you can.

Chapter 10: Children's Acquisition of Different Kinds of Narrative Discourse

10.6.1: The first step is to create an include file, named **pronom.inc**, as indicated in the question. Next we used this include file in the following FREQ commands to search for pronominals in each of Alice's narrative files:

    freq +t*CHI   +s@pronom.inc +fpro pa5.cha
    freq +t*CHI   +s@pronom.inc +fpro sc5.cha
    freq +t*CHI   +s@pronom.inc +fpro pa7.cha
    freq +t*CHI   +s@pronom.inc +fpro sc7.cha

Note that the **+f** option saves the results of each analysis in a file with the extension **.pro**. So, for example, the results for the **pa5.cha** file would be saved in a file called **pa5.pro**.

10.6.2: Review the personal anecdote transcripts (**pa5.cha** and **pa7.cha**).

10.6.3: In order to evaluate these questions, use the following command (from Command Box 10.3):

    chains +t%tlk +t%tns +t*CH% +t*EX% +c[c] +d1 +w7   pp5.cha

Chapter 11: Phonological Analysis of Child Speech

11.9.1: In order to examine children's use of initial consonant clusters in spontaneous speech, we need to modify our alphabet file as suggested in the exercise. The following is a list of initial consonant clusters in the English language:

tw	kw	sp	st
sk	sm	sn	sw
sl	pl	bl	kl
gl	fl	pr	br
tr	dr	kr	gr
fr	Tr	Sr	skw
spl	spr	str	skr

Now that we have **added** the above items to our existing alphabet file, PHONFREQ will automatically recognize each cluster as one unit and give us frequency information for each one. We used the following command, from Command Box 11.2, to perform this analysis:

phonfreq +b*CHI +u –s@vowels *.cha

Since this question concerns the earliest use of these clusters, you should pay special attention to the age periods being analyzed. There are two ways to approach this question: First, you might analyze first the prelinguistic children (as listed in Table 11.1), then the children in the one-word period, and finally the children who produce multi-word speech. Second, you might follow just a few children but do so longitudinally. For example, you might analyze Alice in the one-word period and later in the multi word period.

11.9.2: In order to examine the use of final [s] and [z] in grammatical and lexical contexts, we use the following commands (which are similar to the one in Command Box 11.4):

freq +t*CHI +s"*s" +u *.cha
freq +t*CHI +s"*z" +u *.cha

Because the output of these commands will be in orthographic form, you are going to have to pronounce each word in order to determine whether the final [s] or [z] is grammatical or lexical. You can approach the developmental aspects of this exercise in the same way as in the previous exercise.

11.9.3: We used the PHONFREQ program to determine the phonetic inventory for Kay, Alice, and Anne. If you have collapsed all of your files into one directory (called **momtalk**), then you can use the following command (from Command Box 11.2) to perform this analysis:

> phonfreq +b*CHI –s@vowels +f momtalk\kay*.cha
> phonfreq +b*CHI –s@vowels +f momtalk\alice*.cha
> phonfreq +b*CHI –s@vowels +f momtalk\anne*.cha

Because we wanted information for each child to be output individually, we did not use the +u option. These analyses will result in the creation of three files for each child – one file for each taping session.

11.9.4: The most efficient way to use MODREP to examine children's production of initial stop consonants or pronouns would be to use include files. For example, to examine the production of initial stop consonants, our include file would contain an exhaustive list of stop consonants (i.e., [p,b,t,d,k,g]). To answer this question, we created two include files, one for initial stop consonants (**stops.inc**) and one for pronouns (**pronom.inc**; e.g., *you, I, we, he,* etc.), which we used in the following MODREP commands (from Command Box 11.6):

> modrep +t*CHI +b%mod +c%pho +k +s@stops.inc *.cha
> modrep +t*CHI +b%mod +c%pho +k +s@pronom.inc *.cha

11.9.5: In order to examine the frequency of these sounds or the classes to which these sounds belong, we used the following commands (from Command Box 11.4). To count the number of lexical contexts for final [b]:

> freq +t*CHI +s"*b" +u *.cha
> freq +t*MOT +s"*b" +u *.cha

To count the number of lexical contexts for [g]:

> freq +t*CHI +s"*g*" +u *.cha
> freq +t*MOT +s"*g*" +u *.cha

You might also want to examine other sounds that are more frequent in child speech than maternal speech, focusing your search around the entire class of early developing phonemes (e.g., [p] or [k]).

Chapter 12: Language Profiles of Children with Specific Language Impairment

12.7.1: To perform this exercise, we must compute eight different MLUs for the child in the **abe.cha** transcript, one for each of the post-codes listed in Table 12.2. Each of the different MLU scores will then represent the exclusion of a different post-code. The commands for performing these analyses are as follows (refer to Command Box 12.1 for an explanation):

```
mlu  +t*CHI  +z1u-60u  -s"<+  R>"   abe.cha
mlu  +t*CHI  +z1u-60u  -s"<+  ">"   abe.cha
mlu  +t*CHI  +z1u-60u  -s"<+  F>"   abe.cha
mlu  +t*CHI  +z1u-60u  -s"<+  I>"   abe.cha
mlu  +t*CHI  +z1u-60u  -s"<+  SR>"  abe.cha
mlu  +t*CHI  +z1u-60u  -s"<+  O>"   abe.cha
mlu  +t*CHI  +z1u-60u  -s"<+  PI>"  abe.cha
mlu  +t*CHI  +z1u-60u  -s"<+  Q>"   abe.cha
```

12.7.2: To create a batch file for the analyses performed in Exercise 12.7.1, we typed each of the commands listed above on a single line (ending with a carriage return). As noted in the chapter, you can do this with any word processor or ASCII text editor. However, you must be sure to save the file as unformatted or ASCII text. See the chapter (Section 12.2.4) for specific file-naming and command execution conventions appropriate to the type of computer system you use.

12.7.3: It is necessary to manually insert the post-codes listed in Table 12.2 into the **kid055b.cha** transcript. Use any word-processor or text editor, but be sure to save the file as unformatted or ASCII text. You might wish to name the coded transcript **kid055b.cod**, while retaining **kid055b.cha** as the name for the original, uncoded, transcript. Once you have coded the first 50 utterances, you are ready to perform the comparative MLU analyses. In order to determine whether this child's MLU changes with the exclusion of specific, post-coded, utterance types, you must: (a) find the MLU50 of the uncoded transcript and (b) find the MLU50 for the coded transcript after excluding each of the different post-codes, one after another. To find the MLU50s for the coded transcript, we used the commands listed in the answer to Exercise 12.7.1, but substituted **+z1u-50u** for **+z1u-60u**. Again, a batch file may prove useful.

12.7.4:

A. We used the following command to obtain the total number of words (tokens) and the total number of different words (types) in the **abe.cha** file:

    freq +t*CHI +s"*-%%" +d4 abe.cha

    To analyze only complete and intelligible child utterances, we must exclude all partially unintelligible ones. The following command performs this analysis:

    freq +t*CHI +s"*-%%" -s"<+ PI>" +d4 abe.cha

B. Use the data obtained in the previous exercise and the information contained in Table 12.3 to answer this question.

Author Index

Adams, J. 212, 248, 376, 403
Adamson, L. 139, 164
Ahrens, M. G. 111, 124, 130
Anglin, J. M. 78, 79, 105
Antinucci, F. 438, 449
Aten, J. L. 374, 401
Bachelet, J. 30, 49, 381, 405
Bakeman, R. 96, 105
Baker, N. D. 161, 164
Ball, J. 30, 95, 170, 172, 187, 198, 378, 401
Barnes, S. 111, 129
Barrett, M. 319
Bartlett, E. 377, 401
Barton, M. E. 128, 129
Bates, E. 30, 48, 53, 75, 77, 106, 132, 163, 175, 177, 178, 180,
. . . . 182, 185, 202, 204, 218, 243, 247, 249, 287, 317, 427
Bauer, H. 445, 449, 451
Beeghley-Smith, M. 105
Beléndez-Soltero, P. 213, 247
Bellugi, U. 2, 79, 175, 202
Benigni, L. 202
Bennett, C. 32, 48
Benton, A. L. 374, 401
Berkowitz, L. 75
Berman, R. 248, 251, 296, 317
Bernstein, N. 324, 329, 335, 339, 362, 364, 365, 449
Bernthal, J. 326, 351, 365
Berwick, R. 283
Bird, A. 326, 351, 365
Bishop, D. V. M. 380, 401
Bliss, L. 378, 405
Bloom, L. 133, 163, 175, 177, 182, 202, 207, 438, 449
Bohannon, J. 136-138, 155, 161, 163
Bonvillian, J. D. 161, 164
Bornstein, M. 165
Bortolinin, U. 403

Bosma-Smit, A. 326, 351, 365
Boyes-Braem, P. 78, 106, 112, 131
Braine, M. D. S. 426, 449
Bredart, S. 30, 49, 381, 405
Bretherton, I. 30, 48, 52, 73, 75, 105, 106, 177-179, 202, 204
Brisk, M. E. 220-226, 238, 242, 247
Broen, P. 138, 165
Brown, R.   2-4, 13, 17, 24, 27-32, 48, 78, 79, 104, 106, 134, 135, 137, 152,
.... 163, 164, 175, 180, 184, 185, 202, 203, 210-215, 221, 222, 224,
.... 226, 233, 236, 237, 242, 243, 244, 247, 249-252, 262, 283, 328,
.... 375, 376, 381, 382, 394, 397, 401, 406, 435, 437, 438, 447, 449
Bruner, J. 132, 163, 165, 179, 204, 288, 317
Bryan, A. 378, 406
Bryan, T. 401
Buczowska, E. 452
Buhr, J. 377, 405
Burnard, L. 447, 452
Bybee, J. 213, 247
Bynon, J. 51, 75
Cain, D. 406
Calkins, S. 182, 185, 204
Callanan, M. A. 89, 106
Camaioni, L. 202
Camarata, S. 375, 377, 378, 403
Cambell, R. A. 374, 403
Camp, L. 286, 318
Carey, S. 377, 401
Carmichael, L. 49
Carroll, J. B. 119, 129
Casagrande, J. 51, 75
Caselli, M. C. 403
Cazden, C. 2, 211, 247
Chalkley, M. 426, 451
Chapman, R. 181, 203, 381, 399, 401, 404, 438, 439, 451, 452
Chapman, K. 403
Chesnick, M. 212, 248, 376, 403
Chiat, S. 263, 276, 281, 283

Author Index 473

Chien, Y. 258-262, 278, 280, 283
Chomksy, N. 202
Chou Hare, V. 258, 285
Cicchette, D. 317
Clark, A. 428, 450
Clark, E. V. . . . 163, 214-216, 218, 219, 237, 238, 245, 252, 262, 247, 284
Clark, R. 181, 202
Clarke-Stewart, A. 133, 164
Cole, P. 165, 279, 284, 339
Collins, W. 163
Conti-Ramsden, G. 185, 200, 202, 379, 383-385, 401, 404, 405
Coon, R. C. 111, 130
Cooper, J. 354, 366
Cowan, P. 30, 48
Crain, S. 258, 284
Crawford, J. 51, 75
Cromer, R. 2, 79, 438, 449
Cross, T. 4, 18, 44, 51, 184, 185, 212, 219, 220, 222, 223, 225, 226,
. . . . 233, 242, 243, 247, 249, 250, 252, 257, 279, 284, 325,326,
. . . . 335, 347, 378, 379, 398, 401, 402, 415, 428, 437, 445, 450
Crystal, D. 30, 32, 48, 214, 247, 250, 251, 436, 450
Cummins, J. 216, 247, 289, 317
Curtis, S. 406
Dale, P. 33, 35, 48, 53, 75, 77, 106, 185, 202, 332
Dato, D. 450
Davidson, R. 32, 49, 381, 405
Davies, P. 129
Davis, J. 374, 401
de Villiers, J. G. 111, 124, 130, 212, 247, 248
de Villiers, P. A. 212, 247, 248
del Río 250
Demetras, M. . . . 135-139, 142, 152, 153, 152, 156, 157, 160, 159, 163, 164
Denninger, M. S. 161, 164
Deuchar, M. 428, 450
Dickinson, D. 185, 204
Dil, A 51, 75
Donahue, M. 401
Dore, J. 178, 202

Dromi, E. ... 248, 251
Dunn, J. ... 52, 73, 75, 105, 106
Dunn, L. M. ... 380, 401
Dykins, N. ... 185, 200, 202, 379, 401
Eckman, F. ... 285
Edmundson, A ... 380, 401
Edwards, J. ... 328, 365
Eisenberg, A ... 214, 248
Elkins, K. ... 30, 49, 381, 404, 407
Ellis, J. ... 51, 76, 419, 449
Elman, J. ... 426, 450
Ervin, S. ... 51, 75, 182, 203, 415, 450
Ervin-Tripp, S ... 51, 75, 203, 415, 450
Esgueva, M. ... 217, 249
Evatt, R. ... 406
Fahn, R. ... 328, 365, 442, 451
Farran, D. ... 289, 317
Farrar, M. ... 131, 164
Farwell, C. ... 325, 326, 365
Feagans, L. ... 289, 317
Ferguson, C. ... 51, 75, 76, 111, 130, 131, 164, 165, 204, 326, 365
Fey, M. ... 402
Fishman, J. ... 76
Fitzgerald, M. ... 30, 48, 248, 250
Fletcher, P. ... 32, 48
Flores d'Arcais ... 284
Folger, J. ... 177, 181, 203
Folger, M. ... 203
Fowler, A. ... 49, 382, 405
Francis, W. ... 435, 450
Franklin, M. ... 205
Freilinger, J. ... 326, 351, 365
Friederici, A. ... 243, 247
Friel-Patti ... 401
Friel-Patti, S. ... 401
Frome-Loeb, D. ... 375, 402
Gallaway, C. ... 129

Gandour, J. 353, 366
García-Pelayo, R. 217, 218, 225, 248, 253
Gardner, H. 180, 205, 451
Garman, M. 32, 48
Garnica, O. 111, 130
Gee, J. 207, 289, 317
Ghiotto, M. 30, 49, 381, 405
Giles, H. 76
Gilligan, C. 52, 76
Gillman, R. 402
Gleason, J. B. 20, 24, 50-53, 61, 64, 65, 68-70, 73, 74,
 .... 76, 114, 129, 130, 132, 133, 164, 203
Gleitman, H. 362, 365
Gleitman, L. 353, 365, 367
Glover, G. 328, 365, 442, 451
Goad, H. 365
Gold, E 134, 164
Goldfield, B. 33, 48, 104, 106, 179, 180, 203
Goldman, L. 51, 76
González, G. 215, 220, 219, 223, 225, 226, 233,
 .... 235, 237, 238, 242, 243, 248
Good Erickson, J. 216, 248-250
Goodman, N. 290, 317
Goodwin, M. 289, 317
Gopnik, M. 376, 402
Gordon, P. 137, 138, 164
Gottman, J. 96, 105
Gray, W. 78, 106, 112, 131
Gruendel, J. 287, 318
Grumet, J. 76
Gutfreund, M. 111, 129
Gutiérrez, M. 217, 249
Hall, W. 435, 450
Halliday, M. 446, 450
Hampsen, J. 126, 130
Hand, L. 326, 333, 351, 365
Hanlon, C. 134, 135, 152, 163, 164
Hanson, B. 344, 351, 365

Hardy-Brown, K. 175, 180, 203
Harley, H. 328, 365, 442, 451
Hasan, R. 446, 450
Hastings, A. 285
Hatch, T. 78, 106
Hausser, R. 419, 449, 450
Hayes, D. 111, 124, 130, 163, 427
Heath, S. 288, 289, 318
Hedrick, D. 326, 366
Hemphill, L. 318, 449
Hermon, G. 279, 284
Hernández-Pina, F. . . . 214, 220, 219, 221-226, 233, 235, 237, 242, 243, 248
Hickey, T. 248, 251, 252
Higginson, R. 10, 24, 185, 203, 429, 449, 450
Hodson, B 248
Hoff-Ginsburg, E. 161, 165
Hollander, M. 418, 451
Holt, T. 204, 292, 318
Hood, L. 177, 202, 207
Hooshyar, N. 5, 22, 24, 77, 104, 128, 130
Horowitz, F. 449
Horsborough, K. 378, 401
Horton, M. 78, 106
Howe, C. 185, 203
Huxley, R. 263, 284
Hyams, N. 136, 164, 280, 284, 418, 450
Hymes, D. 51, 76
Ingram, D. 326, 365, 374, 375, 402, 404, 426, 450
Jakubowicz, C. 258, 259, 284
James, S. 30, 32, 48, 375, 402
Jarvella, W. 284
Jen, M. 111, 130
Jennings, P. 204, 355, 365
Johnson, D. 78, 106, 112, 131
Johnston, J. 248, 250, 374, 375, 379, 402
Jones, C. 138, 164
Kagan, J. 179, 203

Kahn, L. 402
Kamhi, A. 248, 250, 375, 402
Kaplan, B. 161, 164
Karmiloff-Smith, A. 89, 106
Katada, F. 257, 284
Kavanaugh, R. 111, 130
Keenan, E. 181, 203
Keil, F. 79, 106
Kelkar, A. 51, 76
Keller, G. 247, 249
Kempler, D. 179, 180, 203
Kendon, A. 314, 318
Kern, C. 326, 366
Kessel, F. 406, 452
Kirchner, D. 378, 404
Klee, T. 30, 48, 248, 250, 381-383, 402
Klein, J. 30, 48
Konieczna, E. 452
Kramer, C. 30, 48
Kucera, H. 435, 450
Kuczaj, S. 262, 284, 319
Kuno, S. 257, 284
Kurdek, L. 181, 204
Kvaal, J. 213, 215, 220, 219, 224, 243, 248
Labov, W. 292, 296, 318
Lahey, M. 212, 248, 376, 403, 437, 438, 450
Lakoff, R. 52, 76
Lasnik, H. 255, 284
Lass, N. 402
Launer, P. 213, 248
Lebeaux, D. 279, 282, 284
Lebrun, E. 131
Lee, L. 10, 24, 32, 49, 375, 403, 425, 450
Leinbach, J. 418, 451
Leiter, R. 379, 380, 396, 403
Lenneberg, E. 203
Leonard, L. 177, 203, 326, 353, 354, 357, 365,
. . . . . 366, 374-379, 402, 403, 406, 438, 450

Levelt, W. 284
Levine, R. 318
Liebergott, J. 212, 248, 376, 403
Lieven, E. 126, 130, 179, 203
Lightbown, L. 177, 202, 207
Linares, N. 248, 251
Linde, C. 288, 318
Linholm, K. 249
Linn, R. 435, 450
Lipscomb, T. 111, 130
Lloyde, L. 403
Loban, W. 438, 450
Locke, J. 325, 326, 347, 351, 353, 354, 365, 366
López-Ornat, S. 214-216, 219, 221, 225, 238, 248
Low, J. M. 111, 130
Lowe, A. 374, 403
Maciver, D. 161, 165
Macken, M. 325, 367
Macnamara, J. 78, 106
MacWhinney, B. 3-8, 10, 16, 18, 19, 21-25, 37, 40, 53, 57, 76, 93, 113,
.... 114, 128, 130, 137, 139, 143, 163, 164, 174, 183-185,
.... 187, 204, 207, 218, 227, 229, 231, 241, 249, 262, 284,
.... 296, 298, 316, 318, 328, 330, 329, 379, 383, 404,
.... 408, 409, 418, 423, 426, 427, 429, 430, 446, 449-452
Manzini, R. 257, 259, 278-280, 284
Maratsos, M. 221, 225, 244, 249, 426, 451
Marcus, G. 418, 451
Markman, E. 78, 106
Masur, E. 114, 130
May, S. 402
Mazeika, E. 220-223, 225, 226, 238, 242, 249
McCabe, A. 292, 296, 319
McCarthy, D. 27, 49
McDaniel, D. 259-261, 263, 272-274, 278, 284
McDonald, J. 418, 451
McGregor, K. 403
McKee, C. 258, 284

Author Index 479

McNew, S.	202
McReynolds, L.	402
Membrino, I.	381, 402
Menn, L.	76, 326, 354, 362, 365, 366
Menyuk, P.	212, 248, 375, 376, 403, 404
Merino, B.	216, 249
Merrill, S.	24, 203, 216, 248, 250, 402, 406
Mervis, C.	78, 106, 111, 112, 130, 131
Mesalam, L.	326, 365
Messick, C.	403
Meyers, C.	24, 204
Michaels, S.	288, 289, 318
Miller, J.	28, 32, 33, 49, 287, 318, 325, 367, 381, 383, 401, 404, 432, 439, 449, 451
Miller, R.	325, 367, 438, 449
Mines, M.	344, 351, 365
Mishler, E.	318
Mitchell-Kernan, C.	203
Moely, B. E.	111, 130
Moerk, E.	213, 249
Montes-Giraldo, J.	249
Moravcsik, E.	285
Morehead, D.	374, 375, 402, 404
Morisset, C.	33, 35, 48, 53, 75, 77, 106, 185, 202
Mougey, K.	402
Munn, P.	52, 73, 75, 105, 106
Muñoz, C.	245, 249
Nagy, W.	435, 450
Nelson, K.	49, 76, 111, 126, 130, 161, 164, 175-179, 203, 204, 285, 287, 288, 318, 319, 365, 445, 451
Nemeth, M.	377, 405
Nevitt, S.	213, 248
Newhoff, M	177, 203, 326, 365
Newport, E.	362, 365
Ninio, A.	179, 203, 204, 287, 318, 383, 404
Ochs, E.	5, 24, 287, 318, 414, 450, 451
Oetting, J.	376, 405
Omark, D.	216, 248-250

Author Index

Otsu, Y. 258, 259, 284
Padilla, A. 245, 249
Pan, B. 26, 30, 49, 111, 129, 175, 184, 185, 228, 244, 287,
.... 319, 379, 381-384, 389, 404, 405, 407, 439, 449, 458
Paul, R. 109, 255, 256, 282, 354, 355, 365
Pearl, R. 401
Pellegrini, A. 164
Penner, S. 136, 152, 164
Pérez-Pereira, M. 225, 243, 249
Perlmann, R. 50, 52, 73, 76, 129
Peters, A. 179, 204, 328, 362, 365, 366, 428, 442, 451, 452
Peterson, C. 292, 296, 319
Phillips, J. 111, 130, 132, 133, 164
Pica, P. 279, 280, 285
Picardi, N. 318
Pinker, S. 134, 136, 164, 165, 418, 451, 452
Pintillie, D. 380, 401
Plunkett, K. 418, 449, 452
Poole, I. 326, 366
Post, K. 132, 135, 160, 162, 164
Prather, E. 326, 366
Prelock, P. 403
Prince, A. 418, 452
Prosek, R. 32, 48
Prutting, C. 378, 404
Purvis, A. 204
Quilis, A. 217, 218, 249
Quinn, N. 318
Ratner, N. 132, 165, 324, 332, 335, 336, 339, 362-365, 449
Read, C. 285
Réger, Z 51, 76
Remick, H. 111, 131
Repiso-Repiso, S. 249, 252
Rescorla, L. 49, 355, 366, 374, 382, 404, 405
Retherford, K. 438, 452
Reznick, S. 33, 35, 48, 75, 77, 106, 185, 202
Rice, M. 374, 376-378, 404-406

Richards, B.	33, 49, 129, 362, 366, 383, 405
Richman, B.	129
Richman, N.	374, 406
Ricoeur, P.	292, 319
Riessman, C.	307, 319
Rinsland, H.	435, 452
Robinson, W.	76
Rodgon, M.	181, 204
Roeper, T.	136, 165, 285
Rollins, P.	30, 49, 250, 271, 287, 319, 373, 378, 379, 381-383, 404, 405, 439
Rom, A.	378, 405, 430, 431, 436, 446, 447
Rondal, J.	5, 24, 30, 49, 185, 204, 381, 405, 428, 452
Rosch, E.	78, 106, 112, 131
Rosen, T.	418, 451
Rosenberg, S.	403
Ross, R.	7, 262, 263, 267, 272, 275, 380, 406
Roth, F.	161, 165, 378, 405
Rowan, L.	403
Ruiz-Va, P.	217, 249
Rūķe-Drāviņa, V.	51, 76
Ryan Hsu, J.	259, 284
Sabbadini, L.	375, 403
Sachs, J.	262, 285, 288, 319
Satterly, D.	111, 129
Sawyer, M.	328, 365, 442, 451
Saxman, J.	30, 48
Scarborough, H.	10, 25, 30, 32, 49, 381, 382, 405
Schaffer, M.	381, 402
Schaffer, R.	132, 133, 163, 165
Schery, T.	375, 402
Schiefelbusch, R.	403, 451
Schieffelin, B.	24, 287, 318, 450, 451
Schneiderman, M.	134, 164
Schwartz, B.	438, 452
Schwartz, E.	355, 366, 374, 404
Schwartz, R.	124, 129, 131, 177, 203, 354, 357, 366, 377, 403, 405
Schweder, R.	318
Scollon, R.	354, 366

Sebastián, M. 245, 250
Seitz, S. 183, 204
Shatz, M. 161, 165
Shimura, A. 328, 365, 442, 451
Shipstead-Cox, B. 213, 248
Short, E. 312, 317
Shoup, J. 344, 351, 365
Shriberg, L. 354, 445, 452
Siguán, M. 250
Sigurjónsdóttir, S. 280, 284
Simmons, H. 325, 367
Sinclair, H. 284
Sinha, C. 418, 452
Slobin, D. 182, 204, 211, 213, 247, 248, 296, 317, 438, 452
Smith Cairns, H. 259, 284
Smith, B. 344, 347, 366
Smith, M. 365
Smith, N. 205, 326, 366
Smith, P. 76
Snow, C. 1-3, 14, 19, 24, 30, 34, 35, 49, 53, 75-77, 81, 83, 88,
.... 92, 94, 104, 105, 106, 111, 129-133, 135, 137, 143,
.... 163-165, 174, 180, 182, 183, 185, 203, 204, 262, 287,
.... 288, 298, 316, 319, 365, 379, 381-383, 404, 405, 446, 449
Snyder 30, 48, 177, 178, 180, 202, 204, 378, 406
Snyder, I. 48, 202
Snyder, L. 202, 204, 406
Sokolov, J. 1, 5, 10, 25, 129, 163, 174, 183,
.... 184, 187, 199, 201, 204, 207, 449, 453
Solan, L. 258, 285
Soler, M. 217, 220, 219, 224, 225, 233, 237, 242, 244, 250
Spekman, N. 378, 405
Sperberg-McQueen, C. 447, 452
Spodek, B. 319
Stanowicz, L. 136-138, 155, 163
Stark, R. 374, 406
Steckol, K. 376, 406
Stevenson, J. 374, 406

Stewart, C. 133, 164, 183, 204
Stockman, I. 335, 366
Stoel-Gammon, C. 51, 76, 325, 326, 354, 366
Sudhalter, V. 49, 382, 405
Sulzby, E. 312, 319, 427
Suppes, P. 262, 285
Swanson, L. 353, 366
Symons, V. 161, 163
Tager-Flusberg, H. 49, 182, 185, 204, 287, 318, 319,
. . . . 373, 382, 405, 406, 434, 452
Tallal, P. 374, 380, 396, 406
Taraban, R. 418, 451
Templin, M. 33, 34, 49, 326, 366, 437, 438, 452
Terrell, B. 403
Tishman, A. 335, 366
Todd, J. 125, 131
Tolbert, K. 213, 220, 219, 221-224, 223-226, 233, 235-238, 242, 250
Tomasello, M. 125, 126, 128, 129, 131
Toronto, A. 216, 250, 402
Travis, L. 137, 164
Treiman, R. 134, 164
Ullman, M. 418, 451
Ure, E. 51, 76
Uriagereka, J. 255, 284
Uribe Villegas, O. 76
Van Kleeck, A. 365, 428
van Riemsdijk, H. 255, 285
Vasta, R. 181, 204
Viera, S. 247, 249
Vihman, M. 325, 367
Vila, I. 245, 249
Volterra, V. 202, 376, 403
Walker, V. 406
Wanner, E. 353, 367
Waterson, N. 130, 203
Watkins, R. 376, 406
Waxman, S. 78, 106
Weber, J. 30, 48

Weiss, A.	403
Weist, R.	438, 452
Wellen, C.	138, 165
Wells, G.	32, 49, 111, 129
Welsh, C.	182, 204
Wetherby, A.	378, 406
Wexler, K.	134, 137, 165, 257-262, 278-280, 283, 284, 418, 452
Wheeler, P.	287, 318, 383, 404
Whetton, C.	380, 401
Whitehurst, G.	181, 204
Wijnen, F.	433, 449, 452
Wilcox, M.	177, 203, 402
Williams, E.	137, 165, 255, 285
Wilson, B.	428, 452
Wirth, J.	285
Witkowska-Stadnik, K.	452
Wolf, D.	180, 205, 286, 288, 318, 319
Woods, D.	335, 366
Wulfeck, B.	243, 247
Wyckoff, J.	32, 49, 381, 405
Wyke, M.	374, 406
Wyke, M. A.	406
Wysocka, H.	452
Xu, F.	418, 451
Yang, D.	257, 285
Yawkey, T.	164
Yoder, D.	402
Yonclas, D.	378, 406
Zimmerman, I.	379, 406

Subject Index

.cha suffix	145
@ symbol	62
@Warning header	333
addressee codes	142
alphabet file	333-334, 340-341, 343-344, 356, 363, 466-467
angle brackets	36, 385
ASCII	7, 21, 61, 121, 145, 227, 333, 337, 386, 391, 413, 447, 469
autoexec.bat	21
batch file	270-271, 391-392, 469
BIBFIND	10, 427, 449
CHAINS	10, 286, 289, 292, 303-305, 304-307, 312-317, 320, 323, 433, 446, 449, 466
CHAT-formatted	77, 145, 264, 384
CHECK	9, 10, 16, 22, 38, 40, 47, 92, 94, 96, 147, 276, 290, 337, 415-417, 427-428, 449, 454
CHILDES manual	21, 22, 36, 48, 57, 383, 409-411, 418, 424, 430, 457
CHILDES/BIB	10, 24, 429-430, 436, 449-450
CHIP	8, 10, 14, 25, 174, 183, 184, 186-191, 194, 193, 200, 201, 204-207, 433, 446, 447, 463, 464
CHSTRING	10
clause boundaries	258, 297
[c] marking	297
CED, Coder's Editor	10, 21, 77, 93-95, 98, 143, 298, 316, 413, 417-418, 443, 446, 449, 457, 461
codes.lst	93-94, 417, 457, 461
coding system	8, 139, 142-143, 145, 156, 205, 207, 316, 329, 337, 383, 408, 411, 418, 431
coding tier	93, 96, 189, 205, 303, 317, 416, 428
%cod	142, 144, 145
%pho	329, 332, 333, 336, 343, 355, 356, 358, 359, 362, 442, 444, 445
%res	143-145, 148-151, 172, 173
%spa	384, 390-393
COMBO	8, 10, 50, 53, 56, 57, 67, 74, 283, 344, 414, 427, 433, 437, 454

486 Subject Index

Corpora
    Adam corpus 17, 80, 83, 95, 270
    Brown corpus 2, 4, 447
    Conti-Ramsden corpus 200, 379, 384, 385
    Gleason corpus 53, 65, 68-70, 114
    Hooshyar corpus 128
    New England corpus 35, 53-54, 66, 68-69, 74, 453
    Ratner corpus 335
    Spanish corpus 221
default extension 16, 37, 148, 188, 191, 232, 268, 270, 304, 306
delimiters 7, 23, 36, 332, 356, 384, 386, 407, 415-416, 427-428, 444
dependent tier 132, 150, 298, 300-301, 304, 316, 320, 336,
. . . . 373, 384, 387-388, 390-392, 414-415, 417, 431
depfile 416
DOS 20-22, 60, 152, 270, 392, 420, 430
exclude file 373, 386
file extension 16-17, 35, 37, 61, 94, 151, 269
file management 50, 57, 117
FLO 10, 328
FREQ 8, 10, 12-17, 26, 40-41, 47, 50, 53-55, 59,
. . . . 61-67, 74, 77, 82-85, 88, 96-97, 99, 100, 104, 110, 114-118, 120-121,
. . . . . . 132, 141-142, 149-151, 210, 229-231, 245, 254, 263-266, 270, 286,
. . . 299-301, 303, 307, 315-316, 340, 352-353, 363, 373, 387-391, 399, 413,
. . . . 414, 416-417, 421, 427, 433, 435-437, 453-462, 465-468, 470
GEM . . 10, 48, 132, 141-142, 144-145, 147-151, 162, 341, 413, 446, 461-462
    @BG 144-145, 148-149, 416
    @EG 145, 148-149, 416
header 16, 17, 58, 95, 191, 265, 333, 426, 436, 459
include file 13, 54, 61-65, 67, 74, 81, 91, 104, 120, 121, 229-230,
. . . . 263-265, 268, 270, 280-281, 315, 454-457, 459-460, 465-466, 468
input file 12, 23, 38, 82, 95, 266, 386
interactional markers 390
IPA, International Phonetic Alphabet 329, 333, 351, 413, 448
interruption 165, 411-412
intonation 51, 172, 295, 297, 299, 313-314, 334
KEYMAP 10, 141-142, 446
keyword 8, 10, 92, 94-95, 106-109, 122, 189, 208-209, 231-232, 268-270, 281

KWAL 8, 10, 12-14, 16, 74, 77, 89-95, 97-100, 102, 104, 110, 122,
.... 123, 174, 188-189, 201, 210, 231-232, 245-246, 254, 268-271,
.... 281, 413-414, 421, 427, 436-437, 455-458, 461-466
language profile 32, 375, 393-395
longitudinal data 4, 17, 35, 79, 162, 185, 266, 270
Macintosh 20-22, 57, 60, 152, 391-392, 430, 442
macros 145
main tier 231, 328, 337, 339-340, 343, 358, 414, 423
MAXWD 8, 10, 26, 39, 244, 439, 453, 464
MLT, mean length of turn 8, 10, 26, 34-35, 41-44, 46-48, 427, 446
MLU, mean length of utterance 3, 8-10, 12-14, 16, 22-23, 24, 26-30
... 31-32, 34-41, 43-44, 46-48, 50, 53, 55-56, 60, 66, 80, 98-101, 104, 115,
.. 129, 132, 134, 136, 141, 146-147, 153, 162, 174-175, 183, 184-186, 189,
  191-196, 198, 198-201, 204, 212, 220, 224, 228-229, 232-233, 243-244, 248,
. 250-252, 356, 373-376, 378-379, 381-382, 384-387, 394-395, 398, 399-400,
...... 402, 404, 427, 432, 433, 438-439, 444, 451, 453-456, 461-464, 469
merged analysis 83, 95
minCHAT 6-8, 296
model tier 355, 358-359
MODREP 10, 324, 327, 354-355, 357-360, 362, 364, 427, 444, 468
morphemicization 37, 228, 343, 415
nonadjacent utterance 158
omitted words 231, 241, 412
Options
    +b 336, 339, 342-344, 355-356, 358-359, 420, 423, 427, 467-468
    +c 355, 358-359, 468
    −c 283
    +d1 .... 39, 63, 91, 98, 114-115, 117, 188-189, 191, 200,
    .... 304, 320, 415-416, 421, 453, 457-460, 463-464, 466
    +d3 427
    +d4 .... 88, 120-121, 389, 427, 456, 470
    +f 16-17, 36-37, 41, 55, 59-61, 92, 95, 117, 147,
    .... 148, 186, 188-189, 191, 232, 268-270, 304
    .... 306, 320, 416, 426, 455, 457, 463, 466, 468
    −f 23
    +k 23, 336, 342-344, 358-359, 421, 468
    +o 116-117, 121, 230, 358-359, 417, 427, 458-460, 462, 465
    +s 12-17, 41, 57, 62-67, 82-85, 88, 91, 96, 98, 100,

488 Subject Index

	.... 115, 117, 120-121, 123, 148-151, 189,
	.... 230-232, 264-266, 268, 270, 283, 300-301, 315, 352,
	.... 359, 387, 388-391, 393, 414, 421, 427, 453-468, 470
+s$*	.... 96, 149-151, 300-301, 315, 388, 390-391, 457, 461-462
+s*-%%	 389
+s@	.... 62, 465
–s	.... 15, 237, 284, 376-388
+t	.... 9, 12-15, 36-39, 41-42, 54-57, 59-60, 62-67, 82-85,
	.... 88, 91, 96, 98-101, 115, 117, 120-121, 123, 146,
	.... 148-151, 185-186, 189, 228-232, 264-266, 268-270,
	.... 283, 300-301, 304, 315-316, 320, 343, 352, 356,
	.... 358-359, 385-391, 414, 417, 421, 426-427, 453-470
+t*	.... 268, 270, 283
–t	.... 388, 391
+u	.... 17, 23, 60, 62-67, 83-85, 88, 91, 98, 100-101, 116,
	.... 117, 120-121, 123, 200, 265-266, 270, 336, 339, 342,
	.... 344, 352, 416, 421, 435, 456, 458-460, 463, 467-468
+w	.... 13, 91, 98, 465
–w	 285
+y	.... 23, 116-117, 458, 460
+z	.... 26, 36, 38, 47, 414, 453
output file	.... 23, 36-37, 39-40, 59-60, 63-64, 82-83, 92-93, 95, 98-99,
	.... 102, 115, 117, 147, 151, 269, 421-422, 425, 431, 458
PAGE	.... 10, 31, 83, 92, 304, 342, 384, 409, 411-413, 415
part-of-speech codes	 413
PHONASCII	 445
phonetic coding	.... 327-328, 362
PHONFREQ	.... 10, 324, 327, 332-337, 339-340, 342-344,
	.... 346, 354, 356, 357, 359, 363, 427, 444, 467-468
piping	.... 14, 23, 26, 39, 116-117, 150-151, 188-189, 269, 464
post-codes	.... 373, 384-389, 399, 469
redirect symbol	.... 17, 39, 189, 266
replication file	.... 54, 57-58, 64-65, 271
SALTIN	 10
shell script	.... 271, 392
speaker codes	.... 37, 47, 200, 297, 303, 316, 384
speaker identification	.... 12, 270

Subject Index 489

speaker tier 7, 36, 38-39, 42, 54-57, 59-60, 62-64, 82-84, 98, 115, 117,
. . . . 120-121, 123, 145-146, 185, 189, 228-232, 264-265, 336,
. . . . 339, 342, 352, 356, 358, 359, 384-387, 389-390
speech act codes 54
square brackets 385, 412, 422
text editor 263, 391, 417, 469
three-letter code 266
TTR, type-token ratio 3, 26, 33, 40-41, 43-44, 111, 114-115,
. . . . 117, 149, 300, 383, 389, 437, 453, 460
UNIBET 326, 329-330, 332-334, 336, 339,
. . . . 343, 355, 358-359, 363, 413, 445, 449
unintelligible speech 40, 167
UNIX 20-22, 57, 152, 271, 391, 392, 420, 430
wildcards 14-16, 26, 37, 39, 57-58, 60, 62, 67, 82, 92,
. . . . 189, 254, 263, 265, 270, 283, 363, 388, 453-454
word processor 20, 121, 386, 391, 469
word-list, wordlist 55, 114, 117, 436
working directory 94, 191, 266, 270, 419
z-scores 35, 43, 44, 47, 195, 399, 400